GREEN PROSPERITY
Quit Your Job, Live Your Dreams
A Manual for Changing the World
Thomas J. Elpel

Dedicated to my mother,
who taught me that no goal is beyond reach.

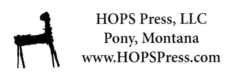

HOPS Press, LLC
Pony, Montana
www.HOPSPress.com

Green Prosperity

Portions of this book were formerly published as
Direct Pointing to Real Wealth: Thomas J. Elpel's Field Guide to Money

Cover design by Thomas J. Elpel
featuring photos from New Zealand, Italy, Mexico, and Montana.
Hot air balloon photos adapted/modified from Flickr Creative Commons:

Anthony Quintano (front, large): "2013 Quick Chek Hot Air Balloon Festival." https://www.flickr.com/photos/quintanomedia/9382386991/in/album-72157634830763864/
Greg Goebel (front, small): "Yabal_4b." https://www.flickr.com/photos/37467370@N08/7428917376/in/album-72157636322252195/
Paul J. Everett (back): "Hot Air Balloon Summer Heat Festival." https://www.flickr.com/photos/paul_everett82/2580087961/in/photolist-QfQX8n-4VZCgc-4VZKrZ-4W4S7s-4VZC1n-4VZJVT-4VZMLB-4W4YUb-4VZJ3H-4VZESt-4VZQ1T-4VZFe4-4W4UGs-4VZNtk-4W55wS-vYZ7H9-vXgLf7-f2zw5N-f2khBp-4VZCQV-4VZKVF-4W55Vd-4W54WN-dZDMQx-6JP4Pb-einsdB-5JbzaV-6JJZzR-v3E59V-4VZLSX-YLNw36-4W51MU-DvB6RD-ojTSi-f2k9uv-shshQo-f2zsc5-yBwzN1-dsz7nG-8KqwyQ-4W54wd-4W4XYW

All interior photos were taken by the author and his family.
Illustrations were done by the author.

Publisher's Cataloging-in-Publication Data
Elpel, Thomas J. 1967-
    Green Prosperity: Quit Your Job, Live Your Dreams / Thomas J. Elpel. —6th ed.

    Includes bibiliographical references and index.
    ISBN: 978-1-892784-41-4 $30.00 Pbk. (alk. paper)
    1. Finance, personal—United States. 2. Economics—United States. 3. Economic Development—Environmental Aspects. 4. Human Ecology. 5. Sustainable Development.
    I. Elpel, Thomas J. II. Title.
    HC 79.E5 E46   333.7   00-102575

HOPS Press, LLC
12 Quartz Street
Pony, MT 59747-0697
www.hopspress.com

Table of Contents

Part V: Turning Dreams into Reality

Part I
The Prosperity Paradox

"The Matrix is everywhere. It is all around us. Even now, in this very room. You can see it when you look out your window or when you turn on your television. You can feel it when you go to work, when you go to church, when you pay your taxes. It is the world that has been pulled over your eyes to blind you from the truth. That you are a slave, Neo. Like everyone else you were born into bondage. Born into a prison that you cannot smell or taste or touch. A prison for your mind."

—Morpheus
The Matrix (1999)[1]

Green Prosperity
Quit your Job, Live your Dreams

Everyone dreams of following their dreams, yet how many people actually do? Most people set aside the big dreams and settle for the best available job options. Be practical and pay the bills. Earn money now in hopes of pursuing dreams later in life.

Tragically, most people work their entire lives away, diligently completing uninspiring tasks for other people without seizing opportunities to live their own dreams. They consume their best years working towards a retirement plan with no guarantee of fruition. Unfortunately, most employment is arguably unnecessary, utterly meaningless, and often harmful to the planet.

As we will see in coming chapters, we are plagued by surplus abundance, and the purpose of most work is to consume wealth, not produce it. The economy is a grand charade that creates the illusion of work to keep people busy. Busy work facilitates social cohesion while providing an excuse to transfer wealth from producers to consumers.

However, consuming precious natural resources for unnecessary work makes us poorer, not richer. True prosperity ultimately requires less work and fewer jobs. The easiest way to escape the rat race and save our world is to seek the nearest exit and engage directly in living one's personal dreams.

Welcome to the Machine

"Listen up first graders. My name is Mrs. Smith."

Good morning Mrs. Smith!

"Welcome to the Machine. In this classroom you will learn to sit quietly and pay attention to me."

Yes, Mrs. Smith.

"Forget your personal interests in life. I will decide what is important to learn. You will be obedient and follow orders."

Yes, Mrs. Smith.

"You will obey your teachers to start with, and when you are an adult you will obey your employers, doing whatever meaningless task they tell you to do."

Yes, Mrs. Smith.

"You will become good consumers and purchase whatever the commercials tell you to buy. You will go to college and pay for a piece of paper that says you are qualified to serve the Machine."

Yes, Mrs. Smith.

"Above all, you will live out the rest of your days enslaved to the Machine, working to make monthly payments on college loans, a mortgage, a car, utility bills, phone bills, and more. Your life is not your own. It belongs to the Machine."

Yes, Mrs. Smith.

The Machine is everywhere and infinitely large. We cannot stop it by yelling at it or throwing rocks. We cannot stop it by marching in protests. We cannot stop it by burning down buildings or engaging in sabotage.

We will lose half of all life on earth to the Machine this century. Below the sea, the coral reefs are dying and fisheries are dwindling. Restaurants are substituting one fish for another on the menus as earlier species disappear from the oceans. The seas will be fished out by the middle of this century.

Above the seas, the world is turning into deserts. For every bushel of corn produced, we lose more than a bushel of soil. We have lost at least half the earth's topsoil already. Soil carbon has been oxidized back into the atmosphere, exacerbating global warming. We have destabilized the global climate and we are losing more species to extinction every day.

The Machine is everything you have ever known and everything you have ever been told. The Machine is the unconscious collective sum of humanity. It assimilates everything in its path, turning meadows and wildlands into subdivisions and shopping malls. The Machine sucks the light and life out of children, making them into automatons that work without meaning and consume without purpose.

The Machine assimilates and grows, assimilates and grows, consuming everything in its path. The Machine is only interested in its own culture of pizza, beer, and celebrity dramas. The real world is irrelevant to the Machine. Automatons live like zombies, oblivious to the loss of soil, habitat, and species around them.

We cannot defeat the Machine, nor can we escape it entirely. We can hide, but the Machine just keeps coming, devouring everything in its path. Hiding places are consumed and assimilated one by one until all are lost.

However, the Machine has one weakness—it is utterly unconscious of its own existence. We can walk and play among the automatons unnoticed. And for those who are interested, we can study the Machine, figure out how it works, and redirect it.

Every human being is born with an inner light. It is a guiding light that can lead you through life, defining a path that is uniquely yours. Learn to listen to your heart and not your head. Allow your inner light to guide you.

The greatest challenge is to stay focused on that inner light, that inner vision, against the pomp and glare of Machine culture. Social conditioning starts at an early age, shaping a child to conform to the expectations of society. Rather than pursuing their own interests and passions, kids are molded to fit the Machine, taught to sit in desks and follow a prescribed routine. Every day they are bombarded by media glamorizing the Machine.

Day by day, year by year, kids become increasingly confused until they lose that inner light. They may emerge as teens or young adults with idealism or optimism, but they lose the ability to steer themselves and crumble under the weight of should's and should-not's. They learn to follow rules and jump through hoops towards imaginary achievements. Between the ages of fifteen and twenty-five, most kids lose the light and become automatons enslaved by the Machine. Some are assimilated into the Machine without regret. Others rebel and try to prove that they control their own destiny. They refuse to be assimilated.

Rebels throw parties, get drunk, and smoke cigarettes and marijuana, thinking they are being wild and free. And yet, they play right into a trap of the Machine. They mimic Machine culture, pretending to have fun until it feels real to them. Ultimately, they are reduced to consumers, dependent upon and addicted to the corporations, money, and jobs that supply the goods.

Those who once knew how to play and have fun in nature as children often find themselves lost as adults. They sit around the campfire, drinking and talking about sports and dumb movies, because they have forgotten how to play and lost sight of their inner light. The only way to "connect with nature" is to pass a joint around and get high. But getting high and thinking one is connected with nature is very different from immersing oneself in nature and truly connecting.

In the end, people are broken by the Machine, plugged into a life without vision. They work meaningless jobs by day, numb themselves in front of the television by night, and get wasted with friends on weekends, each pretending they are free by forgetting they are not.

Unfortunately, those who lose respect for themselves also lose respect for the earth. Automatons are blind to the beauty of nature. A few may profess to love nature, yet many bring the party with them, leaving behind a trail of cigarette butts and beer cans. Once assimilated by the Machine, there are few who wake up again to remember their inner light. All that was human is lost. They may become productive members of society, but merely as instruments of the Machine.

Working 9 to 5

Most of us were mentored by parents who diligently worked 9 to 5 jobs to keep food on the table. We can be grateful for their dedication to do what was necessary to cover rent and utilities, car payments, groceries, and clothing. Sometimes they saved a sufficient surplus to take the family to a movie or an amusement park. These are not easy accomplishments, and it is a wonder that any family can succeed with parents drawing paychecks as office workers or store clerks.

People frequently compete over jobs they don't actually want. From our earliest days we are conditioned to sacrifice our time for future rewards. Finish the chores for the privilege of going out to play. Maintain good grades to participate in sports. Study hard in college to get a good-paying job. Work for other people until you are rich enough to make your dreams come true.

Local help wanted ads and job services proudly post employment options such as: *customer support specialist, store manager, production operator, entry level sales, branch driver, lab technician, electronics assembler, insurance agent, automotive technician, sales associate, laundry attendant, mortgage loan officer, shift production supervisor, maintenance shop clerk.* Do these job opportunities resonate with your soul? Which job best sums up your values and purpose for living? Do you want to be remembered as a customer support specialist or a shift production supervisor when you blip out of existence?

The role models provided by our parents doesn't dictate our own path, yet in practice, it often does. People grow up with deeply embedded assumptions that they will go to school, get a job, start a family, and work their lives away, much like the popular song lyrics:

Tumble outta bed and I stumble to the kitchen
Pour myself a cup of ambition
Yawn and stretch and try to come to life
Jump in the shower and the blood starts pumpin'
Out on the street the traffic starts jumpin'
With folks like me on the job from 9 to 5

Dolly Parton sung *Working 9 to 5* about the absurdity of making somebody else rich while barely getting by, never getting credit, and never getting ahead.[2] The song outlines the trap, yet people fall for it anyway. You may have dreams they can never take away, but if you are working a job while waiting for your ship to come in, then you will wait a very, very long time.

Other people might not have big dreams, and don't mind working a regular job to make a positive contribution to society. That's admirable, except that most jobs consume precious resources without producing anything of lasting value.

Consider the benefits of the golf industry. Golfing is a relaxing pastime that helps people unwind after a stressful day or week in the office. In addition, golf courses provide essential green space in crowded urban landscapes, and one may feel a momentary degree of relaxation just driving by green grass and trees. Golf is otherwise nonessential to our survival, yet we invest heavily to provide it.

We employ two million Americans in the golf industry to water, fertilize, spray, mow, and manicure golf greens, plus caddies and cashiers and people selling golf gear. That number swells considerably if we consider all people employed worldwide to manufacture and distribute golf clubs, golf balls, golf clothes, golf bags, and golf carts, as well as the people employed to produce fertilizer, herbicides, and lawnmowers, plus those employed to pour the concrete and build the associated front office or country club, plus everyone employed to extract, refine, and transport the resources to produce the concrete, metals, lumber, and fossil fuels required to do all of the above, as well as all the accountants, lawyers, and insurance agents associated with each of those enterprises. Golf tournaments are also broadcast on television, employing reporters, producers, editors, video equipment manufacturers, event organizers, and advertising agents.

Golf may be a pleasant pastime, yet the industry is nonessential for survival. Anyone employed in the golf industry is dependent on other workers to provide their housing, energy, water, food, and transportation needs. In effect, the golf industry functions like a voluntary tax on society, employing people to consume wealth rather than produce it, which is true of most occupations in the twenty-first century.

We employ tens of millions of people directly or indirectly to support the sports, recreation, and entertainment industries, everything from Hollywood movies and boxing to gambling casinos, pornography, and motorhomes. We employ people to pave over the planet with parking lots, roads, and office buildings. We add cubicles, computers, and office workers, everyone busy processing orders and accounts, marketing and soliciting new customers, or processing insurance claims and legal disputes. Delivery services bring donuts and pizza to fuel the workers. Custodians clean up after hours.

Some jobs seem essential, like building, plumbing, wiring, and maintenance work, yet much of that essential work goes towards factories that produce nonessential goods and services as well as the associated office buildings where people are employed marketing, litigating, or consulting for those nonessential industries. The economy is an infinite loop of people employed in businesses servicing other businesses, most of which is utterly unnecessary to our survival.

For the vast majority, the work may not be fulfilling, yet the paycheck is needed and appreciated. Employees may stick with a job long enough to develop proficiency as a substitute for satisfaction. Some make the leap to become entrepreneurs themselves, glad to secure lucrative contracts, even if they are not particularly passionate about the work. A few lucky individuals actually pursue their dream careers, though perhaps not as they imagined. A writer may work hard through journalism school to become a reporter, only to be assigned a quota of uninspiring articles that must be submitted by deadline.

Unfortunately, most people are too busy working, consuming resources, and trying to stay ahead of the bills to worry about the fate of the planet. Our coastal cities will soon be flooded by rising seas... would you like a side of fries with that? We will deplete the oceans of fish by the middle of this century... do you want a first class or economy seat? Hurricanes are becoming stronger and more intense... do you want a blue or red tie with that outfit? Some cities may be uninhabitable due to rising summer temperatures... do you prefer regular or synthetic oil, ma'am?

Many scientists argue that we are approaching the proverbial end of times, witnessing the initial stages of global ecosystem collapse, yet our society is principally concerned with the unemployment rate and who won the Super Bowl.

Fortunately, there is a way out of this insanity, and anyone can take the exit ramp. Successfully losing a job to escape the wage economy is the easiest way to build a greener lifestyle while acquiring freedom to pursue your own passions. Break free from the Machine and cease being part of the problem. Rekindle your inner light and vision, and see the world from a whole new perspective.

Survival Priorities

My approach to personal finance grew directly from an interest in wilderness survival living as a teenager and young adult. I enjoyed trekking into the mountains with little gear, attempting to survive principally by my hands and wits. In survival situations, basic needs are prioritized by the rule of threes: a person can survive without air for about 3 minutes, without shelter in extreme weather for about 3 hours, without water for 3 days, and without food for 30 days.

I practiced survival skills in the mountains of Montana, which are cold even in mid-summer. A good shelter with a warm fire is essential to avoid freezing to death. Water is also essential, yet abundant and clean

We have the same basic needs for survival as our ancestors did, just different approaches to meeting those needs.

in the mountains, so that was never a major concern. Food became the next priority, and I learned about edible wild plants and practiced hunting and trapping small game using sticks, rocks, and deadfall traps. After providing these survival needs, I was free to hike, explore, swim, sunbathe, stalk and observe wildlife, or write in a journal. These survival priorities stuck with me and guided my approach towards achieving prosperity in the modern world.

We have the same basic needs for survival now as our ancestors did thousands of years ago, just different approaches to meeting those needs. Reduced to bare essentials, those needs are: shelter (a home), fire (energy and fuel), water, and food. As is true in wilderness survival, a person is free to do anything else once those survival necessities have been met.

A key difference between survival skills and daily living is that wilderness survival is temporary, requiring a short-term investment utilizing sticks and rocks to create a functional shelter, whereas living in society implies a larger investment. Building a permanent shelter requires more manufactured resources for constructing walls and a roof, generating warmth, providing water, and storing food.

Securing these survival basics is the path to financial freedom, or more properly freedom from finances. Most people get stuck on a tread-mill, spending a third or more of every paycheck on rent or a mortgage, often for 20 to 30 years before finally owning their home. Every month of every year is dedicated to survival priorities, paying for shelter, home heating and utilities, water, food, and new essentials, such as a vehicle and Internet. If there is anything left from a paycheck, then it can be dedicated to a family vacation, such as a weekend at the beach.

Figuring out how to eliminate or greatly reduce survival expenses opens up a world of possibilities. Imagine what life might be like if the house was fully paid for, energy was free, water was readily available, and food was available for harvesting. Take the family to the beach during weekdays when everyone else is at work. Return home on weekends when the beach is overcrowded. Or stay for an entire month. Whatever your dreams, whether it is to play the piano or invent an eco-friendly airplane, an essential first step is to wipe out survival expenses as quickly as possible to free up time and money necessary to invest in your most treasured dreams in life.

Imagine receiving a $500 check in the mail every month for life without doing anything. How would you spend it? What about $1,000? $2,500? If you eliminate or greatly reduce monthly expenses then the savings effectively becomes free money in perpetuity. Permanently eliminate a $1,000 per month rent payment and suddenly you have

$12,000 per year surplus cash from a job to spend anyway you want. How would you spend it? Travel the world? Save and pay cash for an electric bicycle or car? Quit your job and start your own business or perhaps a nonprofit organization?

Anyone saddled with monthly bills must necessarily focus on daily survival, which greatly hampers efforts to pursue personal dreams. However, once those survival needs are met, people often apply their prosperity and leisure time towards making a positive contribution to the world. They donate time and/or money to worthy causes or sometimes start a socially conscious green business or nonprofit organization. The more employees liberated from the daily grind, the more people available to make a net positive difference in the world.

Achieving that level of freedom can be accomplished remarkably easily, far easier than building one's own home as I did. It may require some employment, but certainly not a lifetime of employment. For example, an 18-year-old high school graduate with zero job skills—let's call her Robin—might enlist in the military for four years, earning approximately $20,000 per year plus benefits, such as room and board, tax benefits, and free healthcare.

If Robin can resist the temptation to spend tens of thousands of dollars on car payments, barhopping, and other shallow frills, she will quickly accumulate enough money to buy a decent house in a small town, plus a functional used car and all the other basic necessities of life.

Good houses are available for $25,000 to $50,000 in quaint country towns where real estate is cheap because other people left in search of work. Additional funds from Robin's savings can be invested to improve home energy efficiency to lower utility bills. Upon leaving the armed forces, Robin has decent job skills, but more importantly, no house payment, no car payment, low energy bills, and no real need to work. She has the freedom to do anything she wants, to go hunting and fishing, launch a green business and make a million dollars, or raise a family while working just two or three months a year to cover basic expenses.

Sound unrealistic? My friend Kelly spent four years patrolling a fence in Washington for the Navy. Like most jobs, it was utterly meaningless work. But he left the Navy with sufficient savings to buy an 80-acre forest lot with enough extra savings to pay his living expenses for ten years without further employment. In addition, the G.I. Bill provided funds for education, so Kelly enrolled in an accredited yearlong nature program to learn wilderness survival and tracking skills. He later walked a thousand miles on the Pacific Crest Trail. As a twenty-something, he is successfully unemployed and free to explore his own dreams.

Serving four years in the military isn't risk free, nor the only way to break free and achieve virtual retirement, and I wouldn't recommend it unless that is your passion. It wasn't my path, yet it is a convenient example to realistically demonstrate just how easy it is to achieve virtual retirement at a super early age.

There are many other potential pathways to join the ranks of the successfully unemployed, free to pursue your own dreams and goals in life. Some pathways to freedom are faster or slower than others, and each person must choose the most practical path for their unique situation. The effort ultimately increases wealth, facilitates freedom, and nurtures the birth of a greener, more prosperous world.

Envisioning the Green Economy

What might a sustainable economy look like? There are many possibilities. The standard assumption is it would look much like it does now, only greener. Our houses would be the same, only heated and cooled by solar power instead of fossil fuels. We would drive electric cars powered by renewable energy instead of gas or diesel. We would substitute biodegradable materials for single-use plastics. We would have the same products, the same jobs, and the same lifestyles, only greener. These are steps in the right direction, but is that really the world we want to create?

According to various estimates, Americans consume 175 to 500 million plastic straws each day.[3] People are employed drilling, pumping, piping, and refining oil to make plastic pellets, which are heated and shaped to make straws, followed by wrapping, boxing, trucking and delivering them across the country only to end up in the garbage minutes after touching consumers' hands. Most of those straws are trucked to landfills where they will slowly degrade over centuries, persisting long after every human being alive today is dead, decomposed, and forgotten.

Innovative entrepreneurs have created earth-friendly, fully biodegradable, readily compostable straws from organic sources. These straws are an improvement, albeit more expensive. Compostable straws are arguably more sustainable, so we could employ as many or more people in the biodegradable straw industry as in the plastic straw industry. That's a good step in the right direction if one's dream of physical, mental, and spiritual fulfillment is to make disposable straws.

Alternatively, what if we did away with straws altogether? Is our quality of life diminished by not using straws, or by bringing our own reusable straw? Sit-down restaurants need not serve straws with drinks. Fast-food restaurants could eliminate straws by switching from a lid and straw to sippy-lids like coffee cups. Better yet, encourage re-usable cups and add a $1 surcharge for anyone who needs to borrow a restaurant cup. Give a $1 rebate for bringing it back later. Then we eliminate disposable cups, lids, and straws without measurably diminishing our quality of life. Equally important, we eliminate straw-making jobs from natural resource extraction to manufacturing to distribution, freeing those workers to pursue higher achievements than merely making straws.

Politicians fret about the unemployment rate and the health of the economy. Some propose to create jobs programs. Others propose to cut taxes and regulation to remove obstacles to commerce, incentivizing the private sector to create more jobs. Nobody asks why we want more jobs when most jobs are already nonessential. What would happen if we chose to eliminate unnecessary work and share essential jobs to reduce everyone's workload?

Let's assume that only 10% of jobs are strictly essential. However, we want some luxuries, so let's add 15% for a target goal of 25% employment. We could then reduce the workforce by 75%. Rather than have three-fourths of the population unemployed, we could share the remaining 25% workload. Instead of working 40 hours a week, each person works 10 hours. Alternatively, each person works a full-time job, but retires in one-fourth the time, 10 years instead of 40. In effect, the objective is to maintain an equivalent or better standard of living while reducing our economic throughput by 75%. Reducing employment by three-fourths makes our economy vastly greener and more sustainable, even if we don't implement other green measures.

Beyond Jobs

Can we create a futuristic economy where anyone could retire after ten years? Absolutely, and there is no need to wait for government leadership or anyone else to make it happen. In our previous example, Robin walked away from the military with enough money to pay for a house, car, and energy efficiency upgrades after only four years. She has achieved virtual retirement, and if desired, she could work a few more years to secure a full retirement nest egg. Or she could work intermittent jobs, potentially choosing more interesting work until she creates another income stream doing meaningful work true to her inner light.

Bottom line, the easiest way to achieve the most sustainable impact with the least effort is to eliminate unnecessary expenses and drop out of the rat race. Axe the job, and eliminate with it the need to commute back and forth. Eliminate the need for expensive, packaged convenience foods, and eliminate the need for a disposable lifestyle. In the process, become one less person consuming resources for meaningless work. Nurture your talents to offer a positive contribution to the world.

We need to inspire a global movement of people committed to becoming successfully unemployed. My goal in writing this book is to inspire a minimum of one million people to quit their jobs and live their dreams. Will you join the movement? What will you do with your freedom?

In addition to personal freedom and the environmental benefits, leaving the workforce may be critical to economic survival in the coming years. Debt is at an all-time high in America at the government, corporate, and personal levels. From home mortgages to car payments to student loans, people are saddled with debts that are predicted to trigger cascading defaults that will crash our financial system in a repeat of the Great Recession or worse.

Moreover, automation is expected to eliminate millions of jobs in the coming years. Make a plan now and take action to secure your home and basic needs. Secure your home and quit your job before you get fired and lose your home to foreclosure.

Eliminating the need for a job does not preempt one from working, it simply provides the option to work under one's own terms, rather than under duress of overdue bills. When personal profit is not critical it is possible to pursue any dream your heart desires, including potentially world-changing innovations and businesses. Not needing an income is perhaps the single most important step for nurturing a new business into existence, especially a business that requires experimentation and a substantial learning curve. In order to break free and live your dreams, let's step back and take a look at the bigger picture.

"Water purification systems established in an industrial system may produce the same amount of drinking water that would have been available naturally in the hunter-gatherer system. The only reason the industrial system has to purify the water is because it has become contaminated with sewage, agricultural runoff, and industrial wastes. Thus, the water produced by the purification system is not a gain over what would have been available in the hunter-gatherer system. The effort of purification is strictly a cost of the more developed economic system."

— Eileen van Ravenswaay, Ph.D
The Relationship Between the Economy and the Environment (2000)[4]

Wealth Becomes Work
The History of Progress

Technology reduces work and makes life easier. The washing machine, for example, is a great labor saving device. Put dirty laundry in, add detergent, push some buttons, and walk away. That is immensely easier than plunging clothes in soapy water and scrubbing them by hand on a corrugated washboard. Chore for chore, technology wins every time. Life is much easier now than for homesteaders and pioneers who had no electricity. They, too, were far more fortunate than our Stone Age ancestors who struggled every living moment to find enough food to stay alive. That's the story we've been told anyway, and our day-t0-day experience proves it. We know life is easier every time we do laundry. Yet, anthropological studies have revealed a different reality. Our ancestors typically worked significantly less than we do today. They had less work, less stress, and less depression.

Anthropologists have documented that cultural advancements usually result in people working more, not less. Studies of the !Kung people, a hunter-gatherer society in Africa, revealed that they worked half as much as people in industrialized societies. The !Kung worked about twenty hours per week, or three hours per day, for their subsistence. Other chores, such as building shelters, making tools, and cooking, added up to another twenty hours per week for a total of 40 hours per week.

In comparison, those of us in industrial cultures work about 40 hours per week at a job and 40 hours more at home and after work, including commuting, shopping, cooking, washing, cleaning, mowing, and fixing things for a total of about 80 hours per week.[5]

Shoshone Indians, hunter-gatherers from the Great Basin Desert, had a lifestyle that was similar to the !Kung. Observers in the 1800's called the Shoshone lazy because they never seemed to work. More accurately, they had no need to work. They carried all their possessions on their backs, which didn't take long to manufacture. Their lifestyle didn't require them to work full time.[6]

Don't be mistaken thinking that hunting and gathering is an efficient way to earn a living. I've spent a large part of my life learning and teaching Stone Age skills. In timed studies harvesting wild roots and small berries I often found an hour of effort yielded only about a cup of food. Many edible plants were not economical to harvest. An unlimited supply of wild grains, starchy roots, or delicious berries isn't very helpful if they are too small or too labor intensive to harvest. A person could starve to death faster than they could eat amidst crops of great abundance.

However, in other environments, I've gorged myself on big, juicy wild berries that were too abundant to utilize effectively, and I've fattened my belly on spawning runs with fish so numerous that I could grab them with my hands. Through feast and famine, hunter-gatherers typically harvested two or three calories of food for every calorie expended. In comparison, a farmer with an ox and plow can grow and harvest about 33 calories for each calorie expended. A modern American farmer can produce 300+ calories of food for each calorie of physical effort expended.

Imagine calories as plates of food. For every plate of food consumed, the hunter-gatherer harvests 2 or 3 new plates full, the ox and plow farmer harvests 33 plates and the industrial farmer harvests 300 plates of food. Note that the industrial farmer also expends great quantities of fossil fuel energy in the process.[7]

Hunter-gatherers worked less only because they produced less. For perspective, consider wild animals, such as robins and coyotes, which also produce little material culture. There is a flurry of activity in spring when robins build nests to raise their young and coyotes dig dens for a similar purpose. Otherwise, life is pretty casual. Have you ever heard of an animal dying from hypertension, or getting ulcers from stress? Animals forage intensively for a few hours, or nibble the day away, but rarely do they forage frantically to stay alive. Animals spend much of their time wandering, playing, or just hanging around observing and napping. There is inherent efficiency to a lifestyle where the only chore is eating. Life was also pretty casual for our ancestors before they learned to make tools.

The evolution of tools made our species more efficient, yet also meant we had to work more. As animals, all we had to do was eat, but with the arrival of the Stone Age we also had to make tools, shelters, clothing, jewelry, dishes, and gather firewood. Tools enabled us to spend less time foraging, but more time dealing with new chores. Overall, however, work was not too demanding.

The continuing evolution of culture led to more and more work. Farming led to a new kind of prosperity and higher expectations. Living in one place, people constructed fancier, more permanent shelters and

Wealth and Work

Hunter-gatherers work only two or three hours per day for subsistence, yet produce little else. People in more advanced economies spend progressively less time working for basic survival needs, but extra time overall paying for new cultural elements. Houses grow bigger and include many material posessions, such as furniture, entertainment centers, cloests full of clothes, exercise equipment, artwork, and memorabilia.

Advanced economies necessitate additional expenses that most people must pay, including mobile phones, taxes, and transportation.

Increasing Wealth

$

$

$

$

$

wealth spent on new cultural elements

personal wealth

Decreasing Costs

cost of basic goods

| hunter-gatherer economy | agrarian economy | industrial economy | automated economy |

People also pay for goods and services that were formerly provided free by the environment, such as clean water. Hunter-gatherers enjoy drinking directly from streams, while citizens in industrial economies must pay to filter out pollutants and distribute water from source to destination.

furniture. Population growth necessitated spiritual leaders or some form of government to maintain order. Farmers had to contribute a share of each harvest as a tax or tribute to feed non-farming people. Originally, farmers only had to feed themselves, but with cultural advancements they suddenly had to harvest additional calories of food to support other people, from craftsmen to leaders.

Ramping up Production

Imagine being a tailor in a simple economy. You work on the front porch, custom cutting and hand-stitching garments for trade. The sunshine feels lovely. Birds sing, kids play, and neighbors stop by to chat while you work. It takes a week to sew one full set of clothing. In a year you can produce 50 complete outfits, saving a few for family members, while trading the surplus in exchange for other goods and services. Other people in the community are employed at a similar level of productivity, including the butcher, the baker, and the candlestick maker.

Then someone invents a pedal-powered sewing machine to facilitate stitching. The machine is expensive, but it's a worthwhile investment, enabling you to sew a complete outfit every day. Allowing time for other activities, that's 300 sets of clothing per year. It is faster-paced work that demands concentration, so you move indoors and focus on the task. The surplus of additional clothing should make you the wealthiest person in town, except that other tailors have followed suit, ramping up their production as well. Supply swamps demand, dictating that prices must fall. Consumers buy more, benefitting from your productivity, yet you earn less profit per item.

Oversupply and reduced profitability forces some tailors out of the market in search of other work. The industry stabilizes slightly above the level of economic feasibility. Now you have to crank out 300 outfits per year to stay profitable.

Fortunately, the butcher, the baker, and the candlestick maker have all been ramping up production as well, swamping demand and lowering prices per unit. All participants in the economy grow richer from the increased productivity.

Consumers can expand consumption to a degree, buying more clothing, meat, bread, and candlesticks, yet there are limits to how many clothes any one person needs, or how many steaks or loaves of bread can be eaten in a day. Surplus workers must find new work to participate in the economy and trade for the goods and services they need. One starts a laundry service to help clean the extra garments, and one becomes a carpenter to build closets to hold the extra clothes. Another invents and sells oil lamps to facilitate evening activities such as visiting in the parlor or reading a new book—possibly written by someone who used to be a candlestick maker.

The community could not afford such extravagances before, yet now, with increased production and lower prices, everyone has surplus wealth to spend. Soon there is a new standard, so that bigger houses, freshly laundered clothes, reading entertainment, and oil lamps are no longer extravagances, but "necessities" everyone must work for.

Job Displacement

In a developing country, a farmer's entire assets may consist of ten mature cows. The small herd provides milk and meat for the family and an annual surplus of perhaps five or six calves to trade for other goods and services. In contrast, a rancher in our country may raise a thousand cattle and produce an annual surplus of several hundred animals.

At the beginning of the twentieth century America was primarily an agricultural nation, with most families producing enough food for their own consumption, plus a small surplus for trade. However, industrialization has allowed fewer farmers to produce more and more food. At present only about 2% of our population is still employed farming.[8] Many other people are employed processing the food supply or servicing industrial farm equipment, yet the combined total number of people employed in farming and food processing is a fraction of what it was in 1900.

The transition from a nation of farmers to a nation of non-farmers was inherently painful as production efficiency increased wealth for some while driving others off the land. Nearly every decade of the last century brought an exodus of people abandoning family farms for jobs in the city to produce new goods and services.

Increased production efficiency means that a progressively smaller segment of the population provides all the basic survival needs of the culture, including food, water, clothing, and shelter. That makes us all wealthier, except that anyone not employed producing essential goods and services must seek work that is arguably nonessential. For example, rather than taking over the failing family farm, the eldest child might seek employment in the video industry.

Videos did not exist before the 1970s, but soon employed millions of people in the business of manufacturing, distributing, leasing, and selling VCRs, videos, camcorders, and DVDs. Industrial agriculture displaced workers, allowing videos and many other new goods and services to enter the marketplace. It gave us access to nonessential luxuries our ancestors didn't have. Digital download technology later transformed the video industry and eliminated jobs again, forcing workers to invent other new enterprises, such as virtual reality equipment and software.

As productivity escalates, so does our wealth. Americans transitioned from owning one car per family to owning one car for each driver, often with motorcycles, ATVs, RVs, jet skis, or motorboats parked beside the garage. Middle class people own toys once possessed only by the very rich, yet still complain about the bad economy.

Ironically, the more we increase productivity, the more we work. Originally, everyone fed themselves. Now farmers and ranchers are compelled to produce enough food for themselves *and* everyone else. The 98% of the population that doesn't farm must work, or pretend working, to earn their keep.

We could potentially work less, but instead we keep creating new work. Visionaries talk about reducing the workweek from five days to four, yet more Americans are working longer, taking second or third jobs to make ends meet.

Tithing and Taxes

Hunter-gatherers paid no taxes. Every person, even the chief, necessarily participated in harvesting food. However, as technological sophistication and population levels increased, fewer people were needed to gather food, enabling the rise of administrative or priestly classes who lived off the work of others.

Peasant classes provided shelter, clothing, water, and food to their overlords, typically a religious class that conducted ceremonies to ensure bountiful harvests. In early times there was no distinction between religion, government, and banking. In early civilizations, temple priests served as bankers, the law, and the source for divine intervention.

As productivity increased and more people shifted into administrative classes, religion, banks, and government differentiated and specialized, yet retained vestiges of their common ancestry in similar columnar architecture that endured until recent times. Between religion, government, and banking, we now employ millions of people who work as hard as anyone, but don't tangibly produce survival necessities.

For example, think about how many city, county, state, and federal employees there are, including teachers, police officers, firemen, building inspectors, tax assessors, park maintenance personnel, and politicians. Government employees theoretically provide valuable public services, and in return, the public pays their living expenses. That's okay. Increased production efficiency provides more material wealth overall, so we can pay higher taxes to enjoy quality schools, community safety, and beautiful parks. Keep in mind that our hunter-gatherer ancestors had no such expenses.

Greater production efficiency also results in greater demand to share the wealth. Some individuals may earn more income than others, as opposed to primitive economies where nobody owned anything anyway. Contributing money to poor people helps close the gap. Poor people today are wealthy compared to our ancestors, even though they may be poor compared to mainstream society. Through individual donations and programs like welfare and food stamps, we channel money from those who have it to those who don't. We also channel money to important social and environmental causes.

The more we increase our productivity, the more we can afford to donate to worthy causes. With dramatic new increases in production efficiency coming, we may soon see nonprofit social and environmental organizations with multi-billion dollar budgets. Unfortunately, all that money will not be enough to address the social and environmental problems we face.

Escalating Impact

There are advantages and disadvantages to every type of economy, simple or advanced. The hunter-gatherer economy is very simple. People didn't produce much wealth, yet didn't have to work hard either. The land provided food, water, and fuel free for the taking, so there was little work to do. People lived in one place until local food and firewood were depleted then migrated to a new site. There was no need for a garbage dump, because waste was largely organic and readily compostable. The system was sustainable as long as the population remained within the carrying capacity of the land.

An agrarian economy, slightly more advanced, provides more food from the same land base to support a larger population. Production and specialization increases, and anyone not needed for farming is available to provide new goods and services. Some new goods and services are required, such as mining iron ore to forge into plowing implements. There are also luxuries, such as musical instruments or clocks. Overall, the agrarian economy increases material wealth while creating new problems.

Farm production requires additional inputs of resources and energy, leading to more waste and pollution. Environmental disturbance is much greater than in a nomadic hunter-gatherer economy, and people must work to provide some services formerly provided free from the environment. Surface water that was formerly drinkable may become polluted from human and animal waste, necessitating a well. Waste products must be consolidated and hauled away.

An industrial economy leads to similar increases in production and personal wealth, but also demands greater throughput of materials and energy including higher-quality resources and more refined metals. Environmental disturbance greatly increases, and society must take on additional roles that were formerly provided free by nature. For example, large-scale mining and logging disturbs hundreds of acres, necessitating reclamation work and tree planting, which adds work for more people. Waste management, once a matter of dumping garbage in the nearest ravine, becomes more complicated when dealing with toxic industrial substances that could contaminate soil and water.

Since the 1950s plastic production has grown from 2 million tons per year to 440 million tons per year,[9] and plastic trash has become a ubiquitous part of the scenery worldwide. Plastic doesn't readily decompose, but rather breaks down into smaller bits that contaminate the food chain. Studies have found microplastics abundant in bottled water, honey, sugar, sea salt, fish, and shellfish. A person could consume 178 microfibers from eating just one mussel.[10] Yet plastic production is currently projected to double within twenty years and quadruple shortly thereafter. Unless we make major changes to the way we live and work, it is estimated that by 2050 there will be more plastic in the oceans than fish.[11]

Projections

We are rapidly transitioning from an industrial economy to an automated economy. According to a 2013 study by Carl Frey and Michael Osborne of Oxford University, an estimated 47% of American jobs could be replaced by robots and automation in the next twenty years. Truck drivers, cashiers, burger flippers, and all types of manufacturing jobs are at risk of being replaced.[12]

An obvious example is Amazon.com, Inc., which offers customers millions of products. Customers do the work of placing orders via their own computers, while Amazon's computers automatically monitor and order inventory and pay bills. Meanwhile, robots assist human workers with packing orders. Amazon is building automated brick-and-mortar stores that don't need clerks, and the company is developing drone technology for home deliveries. Reducing human labor per transaction means that Amazon can offer greater discounts on products.

Imagine being a garment tailor with a computerized factory where a customer chooses the style they want via the Internet, then submits an image for sizing. Computers custom cut, sew, pack, and mail the garment without human hands. Computers handle all the billing and ordering. Workers maintain the equipment and inspect rolls of fabric, yet even those jobs might one day be automated. Instead of hand-stitching 50 complete outfits in a year, we can produce 50,000 garments in one day. We are already millionaires compared to our ancestors, and we will again be vastly richer compared to where we are now.

If trends continue we might expect the middle class to own one moon shuttle per family. With production costs falling and wealth rising, it should be as affordable as the family sedan—even if it costs a thousand times the price of today's car.

In conclusion, we are far wealthier today than ever before. Life is relatively easy and production is highly efficient. Unfortunately, we work harder than ever before. We work for goods and services that were previously non-existent and unnecessary. We work to provide goods and services to the multitudes who no longer provide for themselves. We work to provide goods and services that were formerly provided free by the environment.

As we will see in the following chapter, we also work just to keep busy. Throughout history, societies have consciously or unconsciously created meaningless work and warfare to engage idle hands and avoid domestic dissent.

"Most men would feel insulted if it were proposed to employ them in throwing stones over a wall, and then in throwing them back, merely that they might earn their wages. But many are no more worthily employed now."

—Henry David Thoreau,
Life Without Principle (1863)[13]

Illusions
Industriously Pretending to Work

Deer don't have jobs, and they don't work. They graze when hungry, rest when tired, and play when frisky. Our ancestors once lived the same way, yet now we have become so indoctrinated to work that people want more jobs and more work, even if it doesn't contribute anything useful. We employ most of the population in jobs as constructive as throwing stones over a wall and throwing them back, yet voters and politicians keep calling for more meaningless work. Ecologically conscientious people advocate for green jobs instead, as though it were ecologically beneficial to shovel organically grown manure over a wall and shovel it back. Either way, the reality is the same: most work is pointless and totally unnecessary. The primary reason people work so much is because idle hands represent a fundamental threat to society.

A function of all societies, large or small, is to maintain relative stability, and the principal threat to stability is restless citizens, especially restless young men. Little actual work is required to provide for basic human needs such as shelter, clothing, warmth, food, and water, and even new necessities, such as smart phones and transportation. People could arguably work two hours a day to make a living, yet all that surplus time represents a genuine threat to societal stability. One solution, subconsciously implemented throughout history, is to keep people busy.

From tribes and chiefdoms to agricultural states and industrial civilizations, societies have maintained stability by channeling surplus labor into one of three tasks: infrastructure, warfare, and meaningless work. However, due to ongoing population growth and technological development, traditional means of maintaining stability now consume our resources at an unsustainable rate, threatening the existence of all life on earth. The solution? Human beings must stop working if we want to stop destroying the planet. The result? Green prosperity for all.

Surplus Wealth, Surplus People

In a world of never-ending work, it is hard to imagine creating a futuristic society without the need for steady jobs. Yet, it is not difficult to create a world of prosperity and leisure. In fact, we succeeded a long time ago, and we've been trying to hide it ever since.

Humanity has struggled to deal with surplus labor since before the dawn of civilization. In hunter-gatherer cultures, people typically worked only two or three hours a day to meet their basic needs. Being nomadic, they couldn't carry much, so they didn't bother to produce much, and therefore had a great deal of leisure time.

In many tribal societies, women did much of the essential work of harvesting and processing wild foods, cooking, dressing hides, and making clothing. Men typically hunted or practiced hunting skills or sat around talking about hunting exploits. They also practiced combat skills and occasionally made war against neighboring tribes. Warfare helped focus restlessness and angst outside their own community.

Testosterone-driven young men represent a fundamental threat to any society. Lacking sufficient distraction, restlessness and arguing can spin out of control into feuds and murder. Tribes channeled that energy into raids against neighboring tribes. For example, the Iroquois, Huron, and Algonkians of the northeastern states once fought fierce battles against each other, although dominion wasn't the goal. They could have killed from a distance with bows and arrows, but instead fought with clubs and tomahawks. One side would be defeated in a battle, and then the other, while no tribe attempted to conquer the other.

According to Peter Farb in *Man's Rise to Civilization*, the social-political structure of a tribe is frail in nature, and they lacked governing institutions to maintain internal order. Similarly, they lacked economic means to wage an all out war, and they lacked the political structure to administer new territory. Living in a continual stalemate of battles with their neighbors gave each tribe an outlet for internal stress, thereby providing a measure of stability to each. Warfare was a sustainable means to hold societies together, and all parties benefited from the arrangement.[14]

Surplus labor becomes increasingly problematic in more productive societies. A chiefdom, for example, may include tens of thousands of citizens across widespread multiple communities. Each area has access to different resources, which are harvested, processed, and brought to the chief. In the Pacific Northwest, some communities specialized in catching and processing salmon, while others harvested berry crops, made lightweight bark canoes, or wove cedar bark clothes and baskets. All these resources went to the chief, who then redistributed wealth back to each community to the benefit of all.[15]

Competing chiefs displayed surplus wealth to visitors as status symbols. However, it is absurd to stockpile immense quantities of excess blankets, containers, and processed foods when nobody actually needs them. To demonstrate how truly wealthy they were, chiefs engaged in lavish displays of disposal. In a highly productive economy, where material wealth is meaningless, what better way to flaunt status than by tearing up blankets, punching holes in canoes, burning down your house, or killing slaves in front of honored guests? Torching surplus goods embellished the chief's vanity, and equally importantly, kept the populace thoroughly occupied working to replace it all.

History shows that our ancestors were inconceivably time-rich. Past civilizations consumed free time through immense public works projects and warfare. For example, the Inca Empire, supported by richly productive horticulture, built and maintained 25,000 miles of roads, wrote Charles C. Mann in his book *1491: New Revelations of the Americas before Columbus*. Inca rulers believed that idle hands led to rebellion, so they engaged the populace in public projects, often for no practical purpose. Spanish traveler Pedro Cieza de León observed three different highways running between the same two Inca towns. Emperor Wayna Qhapaq, who lived from approximately 1464 to 1525, was plagued by surplus labor, so he ordered work brigades to literally move a mountain from one location to another.[16]

Little has changed since the Stone Age, except that societies are plagued by a greater surplus of time and resources, necessitating new ways to focus idle energy towards one task or another, usually something utterly without purpose or meaning.

Working with an ox and plow is roughly ten times as efficient as hunting and gathering for food. Surplus calories allow for a degree of specialization. Rather than farming, part of the population transitioned to specialized cottage industries to make clothing, candles, pottery, jewelry, and so forth, increasing material wealth across society. Some people acquired positions in religion or government, supported entirely by the work of farmers and craftsmen, without producing anything themselves. The rest of the labor surplus was typically channeled into one of two tasks: a) building great monuments, or b) tearing them down.

A certain percentage of any population is implicitly needed to provide basic needs such as housing, clothing, food, and cookware. Surplus labor is superfluous, available for public works projects. For example, well-paid craftsman prepared limestone blocks to build the Great Pyramids of Egypt. These blocks were transported with the aid of lesser-skilled farmers and laborers who were hired during periods of annual flooding along the Nile, when farming was impossible.[17] Egyptians applied their labor surplus toward building pyramids.

In Rome, the Aurelian Walls surrounding the old city were also built with surplus labor, likely initiated as a jobs program under the guise of defense. The walls remain one of the greatest architectural wonders of Rome. Built of brick-faced concrete, the walls were initially 11-feet thick, 26-feet high, and 12 miles long, forming a loop encompassing the ancient city, yet somehow completed in only five years, between 271 and 275 A.D. Additional construction in the fourth century doubled the height of the walls to 52 feet.

Today, the city of Rome remains overshadowed by the Aurelian Wall, the Colosseum, and numerous other structures throughout the city, as

National defense projects are often jobs programs created to maintain social cohesion at home by keeping citizens busy through employment. The Aurelian Walls of Rome, built of brick-faced concrete, form a wall twelve miles long surrounding the old city.

if nothing particularly important has been achieved since the fall of the Roman Empire. Upon seeing the ruins firsthand, it is difficult to fathom the expended effort. How much time, labor, and fuel were required to make and fire the bricks and lime mortar? Having fired pottery in a campfire before, I cannot imagine the scale of deforestation required to fire tens of thousands of bricks.

Officially, the walls were constructed for defense in turbulent times. Barbarians invaded the Roman Empire in the third century, ranging as far south as northern Italy by 270 A.D., prompting Emperor Lucius Domitius Aurelianus to initiate construction of the walls the following year. Rome responded to the Barbarian invasion with the zeal of a people panicked for survival, or so it appears. However, the real threat wasn't outside Rome, but inside.

Mint workers in the capital city revolted against Aurelian in 271, and the battle to suppress the rebellion reportedly cost 7,000 lives. Construction on the wall started immediately afterwards, purportedly to demonstrate Aurelian's commitment to the city and its defense. Yet as noted by Hendrik W. Day in *The Aurelian Wall and the Refashioning of Imperial Rome, AD 271–855*, the project *"was probably to provide regular, paid employment for thousands of potentially idle hands. Just as sailors on ships of war have long been tasked with menial labors — not always strictly necessary ones — to keep their minds and muscles focused away from mutiny, so too might the Wall have served to divert the energies of the masses away from more destructive channels."* [18]

National defense spending is often more about controlling insiders and bolstering politicians rather than fending off outsiders. It isn't strictly a case of government suppression, but rather, the cumulative will of the people to demand employment even if it means doing unnecessary work. Nearly any work is acceptable, as long as the people avoid becoming idle and restless.

Our greatest architectural marvels were built this way. Ancient civilizations channeled surplus energy into building amazing temples and castles, many of which persist into modern times. Laborers worked hard, and farmers worked hard to feed them. The other alternative was war. When people were not engaged in building amazing architectural wonders, they worked to destroy them.

Touring Italy with my son, it was fascinating to learn that most castles had been built, destroyed, rebuilt and expanded, destroyed, and rebuilt again. Constructing these castles was a massive undertaking, requiring immense labor to mortar stones or bricks into permanent walls, often up to 20 feet thick. Destroying fortresses was perhaps more impressive than constructing them. Without bombs or dynamite, and long before gunpowder, armies descended upon and successfully destroyed castles while under a hail of arrows, boulders, and boiling oil.

Forming an army to launch such an attack requires great numbers of men, weapons, livestock, and carriages to move it all, plus massive quantities of food to support the endeavor. Instead of merely growing food for their own families, farmers were taxed to support craftsmen, soldiers, bureaucrats, and priests. And yet, so great was the surplus that ancient civilizations could afford to expend tens of thousands of men in far-flung battles. Warfare is a great way to dispose of surplus wealth and labor—including restless young men who could potentially incite social-political upheaval at home.

Little has changed since the dawn of civilization, except that societies are plagued by escalating levels of production efficiency. The industrial revolution greatly increased production, requiring fewer people than ever to feed society. Surplus labor must be employed in creative new ways to keep busy, or society might rip itself apart.

Cultures are not consciously planned. Through unconscious adaptation, societies wobble along towards a degree of relative stability, or disintegrate in the attempt.

Superfluous Work

Technology reduces the number of workers required to provide everyone with shelter, warmth, water, food, and clothing. Technology also creates new survival requirements. For example, owning a mobile phone or at least a landline has become a survival necessity in our technologically advanced society. The advent of this technology employs many people. In addition, technological advances enable nonessential increases in material wealth and entertainment.

Our immense surpluses of food and shelter enable our culture to support an equally immense entertainment industry. Hundreds of thousands of people produce Hollywood movies, or support the movie industry in every possible way, from providing coffee to manufacturing red carpets.

A city like Las Vegas, as with most of the Nevada economy, is also fabricated around non-essential goods and services. Nevada is a harsh place to produce crops, so the state adapted to consume wealth rather than produce it. Take away gambling and there would be no reason to manufacture all the cement, iron, and glass utilized in the casinos. There would be no need to manufacture gambling equipment, no need for all the lights and electricity, no need for computers, accountants, limousines, wedding chapels, or janitors. Directly or indirectly, nearly every person in Nevada, and countless other workers around the world, expend their life energy enabling people to insert coins in slot machines. From a societal perspective, this is an exceptionally effective way to dispose of surplus wealth and labor, thereby keeping citizens too busy to engage in civil unrest.

Each person earnestly believes they are working, yet it is superfluous work intended merely to occupy people and redistribute goods and services among the population. The more productive our economy becomes, the more people we employ in nonessential consumptive tasks. A "free" toy in a kids meal, for example, employs workers in multiple countries to extract fossil fuels, manufacture raw plastic, mold it into a toy, ship it around the world, distribute it throughout a chain of fast-food restaurants, collect it in garbage bins upon disposal, and bury it in a landfill. By itself, McDonalds is the largest toy distributor in the world.[19]

Step into any big box store, and every isle is stocked with disposable goods with a short shelf life, all destined for the landfill. The sad reality is that the majority of workers are employed not to create wealth, but to destroy it.

Superfluous work isn't a new problem. In the 1800s, Henry David Thoreau wrote about an industrious neighbor who expended much labor to transport a large hewn stone to a customer for no greater purpose than a yard ornament.[20] The worker was undoubtedly thrilled to get paid for his labors, just as the manufacturer or merchant of pink flamingos or lawn chairs would be equally thrilled today, but to what end?

Little actual work is required to support modern civilization, yet we creatively find ways to keep everyone busy. Our income tax collection system, for instance, is an exceptionally inefficient method of raising revenue, yet a great means of occupying people to dispose of surplus wealth. Directly or indirectly, tax preparation employs millions of people to write and update tax preparation software. Others work as accountants, tax preparation consultants, or auditors. Other people build office buildings and computers used by tax consultants, or harvest trees and produce paper to print all the paperwork.

H&R Block, Inc. has 11,000 company-owned and franchised retail locations in the United States, seasonally employing 100,000 people to help American citizens pay—or avoid paying—their taxes.[21] This is one company out of hundreds involved in the tax industry. We might be glad to pay a little money for an accountant or a do-it-yourself software package, however, that expense is effectively a tax. We could easily invest that money towards something useful, such as paying off the federal deficit, investing in education or the environment, or in a better space program. Instead we redistribute the money to pay for office buildings, desks, computers, lamps, cleaning supplies, and employee wages for an army of people who don't actually contribute to the economy.

Most of the work associated with taxes would be unnecessary if we scaled back the IRS, greatly simplified the tax code, and collected "green" taxes against products that are harmful to the planet. Human labor could be largely eliminated if computers calculated and collected taxes from a few fixed points, such as a carbon tax, yet that would leave too many people unemployed. Our convoluted tax system is needed to provide the illusion of work to justify keeping people busy.

The problem of surplus abundance is especially obvious in the growing number of people employed directly and indirectly in virtual reality and online gaming. Fewer workers are needed to grow food or build houses, roads, and infrastructure; instead, we have Second Life or Minecraft and other artificial worlds to work there instead. Virtual reality logically employs people in inventing, manufacturing, and selling VR equipment as well as managing virtual reality worlds. Other people make a living sitting on the couch testing online games or competing in them. A single competition may offer $25 million in prizes for winning "eSports" teams.[22] In addition, video games typically offer digital gold or other treasures which can be earned online and sometimes sold to other players for actual money. In China, an estimated 100,000 "workers" are employed earning game rewards that can be exchanged for cash.[23] Frivolous work consumes resources and keeps people busy without actually producing anything.

The problem of excess abundance may not be evident from inside a culture when so many people struggle with poverty and scarcity. Indeed, poverty and scarcity are arguably tools that help maintain societal stability. Poor people need work, and they will often do meaningless work, walking an endless treadmill without any chance of getting ahead. Some people pilfer what they can, shoplifting to supplement their income, which helps spread jobs to security firms employed to combat such thefts. Products are tagged with security features triggered by gates at the door. Security cameras monitor our every move inside or outside a store. Security officers stand by if needed. Everyone stays busy, and everyone gets a paycheck.

Counter-intuitively, society can sustainably handle a significant level of crime without threatening the stability of the whole. Theft and murder are individually harmful, yet from a societal perspective, these acts keep people occupied either committing crimes or investigating and prosecuting them and managing inmates in prison. The fact that the United States houses an exceptionally large prison population is not testament to having more crime or stiffer laws, but rather, more surplus wealth for disposal than other countries. We dispose of surplus wealth and labor by locking 2.3 million people away in prisons and jails,[24] while condemning countless more workers to build and maintain those prisons, plus 435,000 corrections officers.[25] The U.S. accounts for only 5% of global population, yet is home to 25% of the world's prison population.[26]

Given that most work in the modern world is largely unnecessary, it is unsurprising that we also have massive drug and alcohol problems as people try to cope with a lack of purpose or meaning in their lives. Coincidentally, producing and distributing legal and illegal drugs and alcohol employs a great many people.

Legalizing marijuana is touted as a major boost to the economy in early adopter states like Colorado. Marijuana is grown under lamps in factory buildings, creating thousands of jobs to bulldoze land, pour concrete, and erect insulated steel buildings to grow pot. Marijuana is big business, pumping money into the economy for fertilizers, pesticides, grow lamps, and lots of electricity. Nationwide marijuana cultivation now accounts for 1% of all carbon emissions, the equivalent of adding 3 million cars to the road. Producing just a couple pounds of marijuana exacerbates global warming as much as driving seven times back and forth across the country.[27]

From an economic standpoint however, all this consumption is considered a boon. From accountants to tax collectors, everyone is happy to make a buck. Yet, at the end of the day, marijuana doesn't create wealth, it only consumes it as resources are mined and refined and carbon is spewed into the atmosphere. We take another step closer towards global climatic catastrophe, and for what? How much time, labor, and wealth do we consume on a product that goes up in smoke?

Engaging the populace in meaningless work is essential to maintain societal stability. As we'll see, busy work also provides an excuse to redistribute surplus wealth from those who produce it to those who don't.

"Consumption must rise, and keep rising. Some marketing experts have been announcing that the average citizen will have to step up his buying by nearly 50% in the next dozen years, or the economy will sicken. In a mere decade, advertising men assert, United States citizens will have to improve their level of consumption as much as their forebears had managed to do in the two hundred years from Colonial times to 1939."

—Vance Packard,
The Waste Makers (1960)[28]

Hand-to-Hand
Redistributing Income to Consumers

Successful hunters don't hoard meat. Throughout history it has been customary to share the bounty with friends and neighbors, and sharing was necessary in hunter-gatherer societies. When a hunter made a kill, everybody ate. Sharing served as an insurance policy. The hunter paid a high premium, giving away almost the entire animal, yet he/she was guaranteed a cut of every other big game animal killed by fellow hunters. Sharing also served as a form of welfare, since some hunters were more successful than others. The surplus was consistently shared with those who were less successful at "bringing home the bacon." Think of it as the original entitlement program. Those who made a literal killing shared it with those who were less fortunate.

Entitlement programs are much more complex in the modern world, yet serve the same basic function to redistribute surplus wealth and provide for basic needs such as shelter, food, and medicine. Entitlement programs, as traditionally defined, include government subsidies such as welfare, unemployment compensation, food stamps, agricultural price support programs, Social Security, Medicare, Medicaid, and free colleges. In addition, there is growing support for Universal Basic Income, a proposal to provide a livable stipend to all adults regardless of employment status.

Many people support entitlements as a moral responsibility to take care of our fellow human beings. On the other hand, people often oppose entitlement programs such as welfare or food stamps because the government takes money away from tax-paying workers to subsidize non-workers, penalizing some people for working to reward other people for not working. Both arguments are valid, and both arguments miss the underlying issue.

In a world where little actual work is required to meet the basic needs of society, most employment *is* welfare. Millions of people are employed doing extraneous work that consumes natural resources without producing anything of lasting value. Illusionary employment redistributes wealth from producers to consumers while occupying idle hands to avoid civil unrest.

Maintaining a stable society is essential. Redistributing resources to feed all people is equally essential. However, consuming the planet for unnecessary work is ultimately self-defeating. Being gainfully employed to do meaningless work is worse than contributing nothing and living off welfare. We could arguably eliminate three-fourths of all jobs and pay people not to work, vastly reducing environmental impact while conserving natural resources for the benefit of all.

Wealth Transfer

On its own, private enterprise is highly effective at producing and exchanging wealth. For example, a baker can produce many loaves of bread, pastries, and donuts, exchanging them for other necessities such as light bulbs, shoes, and vegetables.

After paying for the raw ingredients, energy, rent, and labor to run a business, the baker might make a substantial profit. However, taxes take a percentage of production to support other apparent necessities, such as schools, public transportation, police, and national defense. Instead of handing over loaves of bread, the baker pays taxes as money, enabling police officers to buy donuts with the baker's own money. That's fine, because the baker benefits from public services. However, there are limits to how many customers any business can or will subsidize.

The baker may be delighted to see a long line of customers in the form of police officers, teachers, administrators, accountants, lawyers, and welfare mothers or fathers, but what if they all come waving the money he paid in taxes? At what point does it make sense to shut down a business rather than continue chasing one's own proverbial tail?

Conservatives typically favor the ideology that we need to reduce taxes and regulations to stimulate private business. Stop penalizing business owners, they say, and more people will invest in creating jobs and producing wealth, eliminating the need for entitlement programs.

That's true to a degree, except that we already have an overabundance of wealth, and much of our economy is necessarily oriented towards consuming the surplus.

Economics was pretty simple in hunter-gatherer cultures where each person gathered food and there wasn't a substantial surplus. Now, however, only 2% of the population is required to grow enough food for everyone. As a society, we need to invent excuses to spread this food around. Trading for other goods and services is useful to a point, since farmers need houses, clothing, dentists, and barbers. Arguably, farmers should be unimaginably rich, because 98% of the population must cater to their needs to obtain food. However, it would be unsustainable to have all the wealth flowing in one direction, and so we as a society engage in a complex game of illusion to transfer income from producers to all consumers through quasi-work and direct or indirect entitlements.

Musical Chairs

Think of the economy as similar to a game of musical chairs, but with some notable differences. In a game of musical chairs, participants begin on a chair, then stand up and move when the music starts. One chair is removed, the music stops, and everyone attempts to sit down—only now there is one less chair than before, leaving someone out of the game. In the economy version, the goal is to provide enough chairs for everyone at the table, while keeping everyone moving to earn their spot.

Using money as a medium of exchange, the butcher, the baker, and the candlestick-maker produce goods to trade around the table in exchange for other goods and services. As long as the circle keeps moving then everyone has a seat at the table and nobody loses. However, the game can fail due to its own success. A person can consume only so many loaves of bread. When the market is saturated, some laborers must find new work. If they cannot find work, then they lose their seat at the table and drop out of the game, having nothing to trade for food or other necessities.

Equally problematic, the butcher, the baker, and the candlestick-maker lose a customer, leaving them with surplus goods they cannot sell. As a result, they have less income to exchange with other vendors, leading to a domino effect that puts more people out of work, causing a recession where there are plenty of consumers, yet they lack money to buy anything. The solution? Transfer purchasing power from producers to consumers.

Social welfare programs are largely rooted in the Great Depression of the 1930s when unemployment hung at 25%. President Franklin D.

Roosevelt led the country out of the depression with his New Deal programs, including the Works Progress Administration (WPA), Civilian Conservation Corp. (CCC), and the Tennessee Valley Authority (TVA). These programs employed millions of people to construct roads, public buildings, parks, schools, and bridges.

The New Deal rivaled the ambitions of the ancient world, employing three million restless young men over a nine-year period to build public infrastructure, especially in national parks. In Great Smoky Mountain National Park, for example, 4,000 CCC workers from twenty-two camps built hundreds of miles of road through difficult terrain, plus bridges, campgrounds, buildings, and lookout towers.[29] From coast to coast, CCC camps built much of the infrastructure in national and state parks that we still benefit from today. CCC workers were provided with shelter, food, and clothing, plus a wage of $30/month. That works out to approximately $566/month in today's dollars. Of that $30, workers were required to send $25/month home to their families.[30] These public works projects functioned like a circulatory pump to transfer money to consumers to get the economy rolling again.

At the same time, FDR initiated the Social Security Act to take a small cut of each person's wages throughout their working career, which is then given back with interest in retirement. The overt purpose of Social Security was to ensure that our elders have an income when they are no longer working. Equally important, Social Security ensures that our elders can bring money to the table to feed the economy and keep the game of musical chairs in motion. Medicaid and Medicare were signed into law thirty years later to serve a similar purpose.

If America retained FDR's public works programs started in the 1930s then America would arguably have the best infrastructure in the world: the best parks, schools, libraries, highways, bridges, mag-levitation bullet trains, and potentially a space program a hundred times bigger than we have today. However, under pressure from conservative critics, FDR later cut back on government spending, including terminating public works programs to help balance the budget. That led to another recession in 1938. Fortunately, America found a new way to boost the economy: World War II.

Enemies we Need

The war effort opened up government coffers to spend whatever was needed to defeat Nazi Germany and the Japanese. The influx of cash fueled unprecedented investment in factories and production, giving full employment to all. War needs consumed over one-third of industrial output, yet productivity and wages expanded so much as to increase the supply of consumer goods during wartime rationing. The economy grew at a rate of 11 or 12% annually throughout the war. Wages increased by 50% during the war, and war-related innovation led to entirely new technologies, industries, and skills. America prospered by making artillery and blowing it up. Coincidentally, we have been at war almost continuously ever since.

In the wake of WW II, the Cold War (1947-1990) provided economic stimulus and stability to both sides in the conflict, as observed by author Vance Packard in *The Waste Makers* way back in 1960:

> *"Even more massive and crucial in terms of its stimulus to the United States economy has been the defense spending, which has reached fifty billion dollars a year—or a tenth of the nation's entire output of goods and services. Many United States senators find themselves under strong pressure to protect big aircraft and missile contracts, Naval installations, and Army bases in their states. Any cutbacks would throw some constituents out of jobs, and hit some of their local industries. In 1959, when stock-market prices dipped briefly after President Eisenhower announced that he was meeting with Russian Premier Khrushchev, some financial analysts reported the dip was caused by 'peace jitters' among the traders. Financial columnist Sylvia Porter noted that every time there has been a suggestion of a major cut in Pentagon spending 'the stock market has gone into a tail spin.' On the other hand, in May 1960, when the Russian capture of the U-2 plane was followed by the collapse of the summit meeting, Wall Street stock-market prices advanced during seven successive days. The Russians, too, apparently had been having internal trouble because of the 'peace scare.' Various accounts of the turn to greater belligerence on the part of the Soviet Union cited as influential the lobbying of two hundred fifty thousand Soviet officers who were scheduled, under disarmament plants, to be demobilized. They reportedly did not relish the prospects of going into civilian jobs as rank-and-file comrades."*[31]

All told, the Cold War consumed enough wealth to rebuild the entire infrastructure of the world: every house, factory, office building, school, road, and bridge that existed at that time.[32] On both sides of the planet, we employed millions of people to mine and refine resources to build tanks, planes, ship, bombs, and missiles. Millions more were employed training with the equipment or maintaining it, or in various support services. Also consumed was an immense amount of concrete, coal, and oil—enough to rebuild our world.

To maintain stability within, leaders of nations must necessarily focus the surplus energy and angst of their countrymen against the outside world. The events of 9/11 gave our government an excuse to expand government control and spy on American citizens. The Bush administration formed the Department of Homeland Security in 2002, which now employs 230,000 people with a budget of $40 billion/year, including the Transportation Safety Administration (TSA).[33] Homeland Security absorbed several pre-existing agencies, including the Secret Service and Border Patrol, yet also led to the creation of many new jobs. Consider it a reflection of our growing surplus. Fewer people are needed to provide basic goods and services. Creating the Department of Homeland Security gives thousands of people new employment frisking travelers at airports, spying on American citizens, and collecting data from all available electronic sources. In exchange for this "benefit," the rest of us provide food, housing, clothing, cars, and retirement. Funding Homeland Security effectively redistributes income to keep the game of musical chairs in motion.

Likewise, the invasion of Afghanistan and Iraq helped unify the country in support of George W. Bush, ensuring a second term in office. Continuous military action helps consume surplus armaments, justifying keeping factories open and citizens employed. Any external threat, whether terrorism, Russia, China, or Iran also helps focus American attention away from American problems. Rather than deal with our own simmering issues and crumbling infrastructure, we maintain focus on perceived external threats, facilitating a degree of social cohesion at home.

Authentic Fake News

Government spending isn't the only factor that keeps the economy circulating. The private sector has also developed methods to facilitate moving money from person to person. For example, credit cards originated in the 1950s, allowing consumers to continue purchasing goods even without cash on hand. Easy credit also enables businesses to invest and expand, further stimulating the economy. In addition, merchants pay a small percentage of each credit card transaction, almost like a tax, to the bank that issues the credit card.

A fee of 2 to 3% of each purchase is split between credit card associations (Visa, MasterCard, Discover, American Express), as well as the banks that issue them (Bank of America, Wells Fargo, Chase, etc.). Credit card processors that handle transactions also take a cut, as do the merchant account providers who work with individual merchants. As if that weren't enough, a percentage of the fee is often returned to the customer in various rewards programs, such as airline miles. Whether you buy gasoline, groceries, or go to the movies, each swipe of the credit card sends a slice of funds around the table to bankers, accountants, and airlines, providing greater stability to the game of musical chairs.

As material productivity becomes progressively more efficient, fewer people are required to supply the basic needs of society, necessitating increased inefficiencies to spread the wealth. When no real work is needed, we create superfluous work to fill the void. Employees often believe they are doing real work even when they're not. From this perspective, creating and promoting fake news is arguably an honest job, because their work is genuinely fake.

Fake news captured the public's attention with the 2016 Presidential election. Aside from Russian interference, fake news operatives didn't necessarily favor one candidate or the other; rather they discovered through trial and error that fake news stories favoring Donald Trump were highly successful as click-bait, enticing social media users to click through to websites that generated revenues through Google AdSense. In Macedonia, where the average income is $426/month, one twenty-two year-old boasted of earning $2,500/day promoting fake news. He employed fifteen people, including two in the states, to write and distribute fake news stories.[34] Around the world, thousands of people take their jobs seriously, going to work everyday to create fake news. In exchange for their contribution to society, the rest of us provide them with houses, food, clothing, Porches, Mercedes, and BMWs—all accomplished as easily as clicking on fake news stories.

Moving money from those who have it to those who don't is essential to keep the economy circulating and prevent collapse. There is a twisted logic to the system that neatly rationalizes keeping people gainfully employed for life on treadmill to nowhere with fewer and fewer people producing the goods and services that we actually depend on. It would be a sensible way to manage an economy if it wasn't utterly insane.

The economy as we know it is unsustainable. The world is too small to keep bombing or faking our way to prosperity, and we cannot afford to keep mining, milling, and burying mass resources for the purpose of creating quasi-work.

"The United States economy is depending on the willingness of consumers and the government to spend more each year than they have the preceding year. Some economists suggest that whenever United States citizens fail to step up their over-all consumption by at least 4 per cent in any given year they are inviting a 'failure-to-grow' recession. How to live with mounting productivity is each year becoming a more urgent problem for Americans, and soon it will be plaguing Western Europeans."

—Vance Packard
The Waste Makers (1960)[35]

Overshoot
Too Much of a Good Thing

Modern civilization is arguably less than two hundred years old. Prior to that, people achieved little more than a fancy variety of Stone Age living. There were clapboard houses, tables and chairs, silverware and Chinaware, suits and ties, and hoop dresses. Yet, society largely ran on Stone Age technology. People cooked meals over the open hearth, literally an indoor campfire, until the slightly more refined wood-fired kitchen stoves of the 1800s. Refrigeration consisted of harvesting winter ice and insulating a reserve supply to hopefully last through the summer season. People scrubbed clothes on washboards and later hand-cranked washing machines. Fat lamps gave way to oil lamps while households and cities largely remained dimly lit. All that changed in the twentieth century.

Inventions pioneered in the 1800s finally came to market in the 1900s, such as gas and electric stoves, home refrigerators, automatic washing machines, and electric lighting. The automobile, airplane, telephone, radio, television, computer, and the Internet soon followed. Innovation and industrialization changed the world and created markets for new and useful products. On the other hand, twentieth century innovation introduced new and paradoxical problems without obvious solutions. What happens after every household has a working refrigerator, washing machine, and other basic appliances? Factories cannot continue manufacturing appliances if there is insufficient demand. Nor can we shutter factories and stop producing appliances altogether.

By the 1930s people in industry widely recognized the need to artificially stimulate demand for consumer goods. Without sales, factories would go out of business and employees would lose their jobs, thereby aggravating the problem in a domino effect that collapses the economy. Moreover, without mass-production, consumer goods would become more costly and largely unaffordable. To keep the whole shebang going, businesses had to find creative ways to make repeat sales to the same customers. Various solutions to the dilemma include a) designing products to fail efficiently, b) enticing customers to upgrade prior to product failure, c) selling multiple units to the same customers, or d) all of the above.

For example, the auto industry learned to make cars that were less durable and more prone to expensive repairs. Automakers restyled cars from year to year to entice buyers to trade-in early, adding meaningless fins and curves and lights, lengthening cars and shortening them again, all without adding substance to the vehicles. And the auto industry encouraged families to expand from one car per household to two or more, accomplishing an all-of-the-above strategy to maintain and grow sales.

As General Motors CEO Frederic Donner said in 1959, *"If it had not been for the annual model change, the automobile as we know it today would not be produced in volume and would be priced so that relatively few could afford to own one. Our customers would have no incentive or reason to buy a new car until their old one wore out."* [36]

Having owned a number of American-made cars and minivans over the years, every one of them was a disposable pile of junk on wheels. All except for the rugged 1973 Jeep pickup I bought for $800 in 1989. The thing is a beast, and there isn't much that can go wrong with it, so I'm still driving it, though not regularly due to low fuel economy. Based on experience, I've learned to buy many products from as far back as possible to ensure the best quality. For example, twenty-five years ago I bought a secondhand chest freezer from the 1960s, which has thus far worked like a charm without repairs.

In most cases, it is relatively easy to manufacture durable products with a long potential lifespan. For example, heirloom grandfather clocks, pianos, and cherry wood tables and chairs are often handed down from generation to generation. I own a 1946 Army wall tent that is still in remarkably good condition. Even my mother's waffle iron from the 1970s was durable enough to last through my own kids, rendering forty years of use before it finally died. Nowadays, corporations have perfected products that last only a few months or years before they hit the trash heap.

Civilization is drowning in abundance, yet the only way we can maintain prosperity is to mass-produce products intended for disposal.

Breaking the Wheel

Thomas Edison tried thousands of different filaments to make a long-lasting incandescent light bulb. Less commonly known is that early light bulbs lasted too long. One bulb has been in continuous use in a fire department in Livermore, California since 1901.

Long-lived light bulbs were not good for sustained business, and so a cartel of light bulb manufacturers created a pact and set standards to invent more fragile bulbs. The industry standard systematically fell from 2,500 hours to 1,500 hours before the 1,000-hour light bulb was perfected, as detailed in the documentary *The Light Bulb Conspiracy* (also known as *Pyramids of Waste*).

This documentary details economic theory about the need to make short-lived products to maintain consumer demand and keep the economy moving. For instance, Dupont chemists were pretty proud of nylons, first created back in the 1950s. However, chemists were sent back to the lab to rework the formula, because the original stockings were too durable to wear out efficiently. *Light Bulb Conspiracy* takes the viewer into the university classroom to see how engineers are formally trained to satisfy employers by dumbing-down products to ensure failure.[37]

The wheelbarrow, for example, is a highly useful low-tech tool, long ago perfected. It isn't difficult to make a decent wheelbarrow. In my lifetime, however, wheelbarrows have been reverse-engineered to achieve progressively poorer quality. Engineers installed

Light bulb manufacturers progressively reduced bulb longevity from 2,500 hours to 1,500 hours before the 1,000-hour bulb was perfected.

cheaper tires that punctured easily or got bent rims. Buy a wheelbarrow and get a flat, do you take the wheel off and have it repaired, or toss the whole thing in the dumpster and buy another one?

Engineers degraded the tire then the wheel bearings and then turned their attention to the barrow tray itself. Thinner metal makes the wheelbarrow less durable, allowing bolts to pull through the metal. Next, weakening the supporting struts helped insure that wheelbarrows slump to one side if filled to capacity. The latest one I tried was even better. By replacing the triangular wooden wedges between the handle and the barrow with plastic inserts, the wheelbarrow slumped more severely, to the point of being utterly useless.

Walk down the isles of any big box store and imagine how many millions are employed to extract and refine raw materials, design and make molds, build factories, manufacture, ship overseas, and distribute short-lived plastic products that we then hire more people to transport to a landfill and bury underground for eternity.

It's not just plastic junk, either. It is also appliances that break down within a few months or a few years. From freezers to blenders to food processors, the consumer is often better off shopping for secondhand vintage appliances rather than buying new appliances that are likely to fail in short order. There are also disposable tools, including drills, saws, wrenches, and shovels that often break the first or second time we use them, including my all-time favorite, a hammer that bends backwards when driving a nail!

"Reinventing the wheel" is an expression for reinventing something that already works just fine. In this case, however, students pay big bucks to attend schools where they are taught to re-invent the wheel to insure total breakage soon after purchase. This is the American way to achieve prosperity. Millions of people are gainfully employed mindlessly cranking out and distributing useless or inferior products. Money flows around and around the loop, and we work our entire lives to keep ahead of engineered entropy.

Upgrade

Any product that doesn't break efficiently enough can still be discarded if customers are motivated to upgrade. The problem is that most products reach a design climax relatively quickly, making additional upgrades artificial. For example, the common electric pop-up toaster was introduced in 1926 and gradually became a standard household appliance. The basic design hasn't changed since, and any reasonably built toaster will last for decades. To maintain sales, a company must convince the customer to junk a working toaster for something advertised as better. But how do you improve a toaster?

Early designers experimented with everything from new colors to more buttons to aerodynamic design, anything to convince customers their old toaster was boring. By the 1970s, heat-resistant plastics allowed new colors and textures, including popular hues like harvest gold, avocado, or wood-grain finish. Toasters have been embellished with additional slots to cook hot dogs or embedded pans to fry eggs, and even combined with coffee makers. Toasters have been connected to the Internet to "print" the weather forecast with varying levels of heat into the toast. Now you can print any cartoon or your own photo onto a piece of toast. It is still just a toaster.

The same is true for most household appliances from refrigerators to washing machines to vacuum cleaners. Newer models are seldom substantially better, and often worse, all marketed as "upgrades" to convince customers to replace what they already have.

A similar trend is happening with computers and smart phones. The initial technology leaped wildly ahead with dramatic improvements in speed and capability every few years. In the early days of the Internet, for example, I would click on a link, then swivel my chair around to work on some other project while waiting for the page to load. Technological upgrades immensely improved the digital experience. Eventually, however, the technology reached a point where I could write and publish books, edit videos, and surf the Internet without significant inconvenience. Newer models are unquestionably faster and more capable, but why upgrade when my ten-year-old 27" iMac performs adequately and even looks almost identical to newer models, although not as slim?

Similarly, the touchscreen iPhone was lauded as a wonder of the modern world when introduced in 2007. Apple introduced the iPhone fully aware that the new product would kill their best-selling iPod. That was okay. The iPhone quickly became the core of Apple's business, and subsequent upgrades improved speed, performance, and capability. Like any corporation, Apple aims to increase business each year over the previous year. The company sold an impressive 11 million iPhones in 2008 and a mind-boggling 216 million in 2017.[38] Apple has developed infrastructure to create a complex product and instantly (within a year) pump out 200+ million copies. That works out to 1 iPhone every year per every 22 people on the planet between the ages of 15 and 64... not counting smartphones from competitors.

In order to continue expanding sales each year, Apple must encourage people to toss out last year's phone to buy the newest model and/

or increase the cost per phone. While initial improvements to smart-phones significantly improved capabilities, newer innovations are more like adding bells and whistles to a toaster. As sales have begun to level off, Apple has maintained profit by charging more, famously raking in $1,000 for the iPhone X. In addition, Apple introduced software updates for older iPhones that made them run slower, thus encouraging people to upgrade sooner.

So what happens when every person on the planet has a working iPhone and a working toaster? Try selling every person two.

Overkill

One way to increase economic throughput is to convince consumers they need duplicates of every item they purchase. As B. Earl Puckett, chairman of Allied Stores Corporation, proclaimed to a meeting of fashion experts in 1950, *"We must accelerate obsolescence... It is our job to make women unhappy with what they have... We must make them so unhappy that their husbands can find no happiness or peace in their excessive savings."* [39]

Fashion trends were promoted to encourage shoppers to throw out last year's clothes and update their wardrobe. Women were encouraged to purchase multiple colors of lipstick to match their outfits. Deodorant sticks were differentiated into his and her brands. Toasters were embellished with new lines and curves. Cars were gradually restyled with superfluous bells and whistles, becoming more expensive, less reliable, and less fuel-efficient.

Marketers promoted bigger houses and vacation homes, each house and every room needing a plethora of new appliances and furniture. Average house size grew from 983 square feet in 1950 to 2,500 square feet today, even while family size steadily decreased. Construction workers bulldozed and paved roads into scenic landscapes, cutting down forests to erect vacation homes to fill with yet more furniture and appliances.

Similar marketing efforts are the direct cause of gun proliferation in America. Guns were originally manufactured and marketed as hunting tools, which was great until Americans traded rural life for the city. Gun sales declined, and gun corporations needed to establish new markets for their wares. They did so by marketing guns to city dwellers who realistically have little to shoot at other than paper targets or each other. By making guns more sporty and lethal, the gun industry successfully proliferated enough firearms into cities to exacerbate gun violence. That was good for the gun business, because now the industry could also sell guns to people to defend themselves against gun violence. And more recently, the gun industry began targeting women, developing fashionable models and marketing campaigns aimed at increasing gun sales in the name of personal defense against everyone else who owns a gun. As if that weren't enough, now people are calling for armed school teachers in the guise of defense.

From a corporate standpoint, it doesn't matter if every American owns one gun, ten guns or a thousand guns; the function of a business is to sell more products this year than last year. If every street and yard and home were ten feet deep in guns, gun manufacturers must still find a way to sell still more guns the following year. In other words, America's gun problem isn't about Second Amendment rights. It isn't a mental health problem. The problem is rooted in corporate profit and the need to increase sales every year to eternity. If we solve that problem then we solve the problem of gun violence in America.

Excess Surplus Abundance

My grandmother was a teenager during the Great Depression. She learned an ethic of conservation as a matter of necessity, later role-modeling conservation to me. She disposed of very little, and when we did go to the landfill, we always poked around looking for treasures to bring home. Nurtured with that influence, I have maintained a lifelong ethic of conservation. When I remove a staple from a stack of paper, I put the staple in a bucket for scrap metal recycling. I recycle everything I possibly can and largely avoid buying new merchandise unless I have a plan to properly recycle the old.

It is disturbing to see neighbors discard perfectly good recyclables in the community dumpster, including aluminum cans, cardboard, and scrap metal—as if they don't expect to have children or grandchildren who will need those resources.

Worse, people are drowning in abundance, so it isn't uncommon to find $150 boots or other quality merchandise in the dumpster. As a kid, I would have tested pens or markers at the dump to take home only good ones. Now I just assume that every pen and highlighter in the dumpster is basically new. Multiply that by thousands of other products that are thrown away, and we have a problem. I used to find half-used pencils in the garbage. Now I find whole, unopened packs of new pencils. Every year I save a couple thousand dollars on merchandise I don't have to buy because it's free in the garbage. In addition to supplies I use regularly, such as lumber, strawbales, and garden hoses, I also find perfectly good tools and boxes of expensive nails and screws. It's not uncommon to find tools still in their original packaging, never opened.

Thrift stores are also buried in mountains of abundance. As we ratchet up production efficiency, retail stores donate brand new merchandise to thrift stores to clear space for even more new inventory.

We are plagued by surplus abundance, suffering from too much wealth, yet so poverty-stricken that most people are deeply in debt with home mortgages, car payments, medical bills, student loans, and credit card balances spiraling out of control.

Superfluous Excess Surplus Abundance

The problem of excess abundance threatens to annihilate the world in more ways than merely burying the land and seas in trash and debt. During the Cold War, for example, we consumed surplus wealth on nuclear missiles and bunkers to house them. So vast was our surplus that we created more than enough nuclear bombs to assure mutual annihilation—and kept building more.

Call it superfluous excess surplus abundance. Of the 15,000 nuclear bombs in existence today,[40] only about 100 are needed to blast sufficient soot into the atmosphere to blot out sunlight for 25+ years. Anything and anyone that survived the initial bombs, fallout, and nuclear winter would later face an 80% increase in ultraviolet radiation that would destroy ecosystems on land and in the ocean.[41]

Nevertheless, manufacturing more bombs was deemed beneficial to the economy. Being especially close to Russia over the North Pole, my home state of Montana hosts numerous missile silos hidden beneath the prairie, still ready to obliterate life at the touch of a button.

The problem with nuclear weapons is that we really can't use them, so it isn't a sustainable way to consume surplus wealth. Other military hardware is more easily disposable. We just need a place to blow it all up.

It's hard to imagine now, but in the 1960s and 1970s Afghanistan, Iraq, and Iran were fairly progressive, western-leaning countries. Afghanistan had modern cars, roads, factories, schools, and parks. People wore western-style clothes and women could walk freely in skirts with bare faces, arms, and legs. Young men and women at universities freely intermingled with each other. There was a large middle class and many educated professionals.

Summing up forty years of Middle East policy, our own C.I.A. armed and trained thousands of Afghan Islamic insurgents in the arts of bomb-making, assassinations, sabotage, and urban guerrilla warfare to fight Soviet invaders in the 1980s.[42] We effectively created the Taliban and al Qaeda and sowed the seeds for 9/11. We've been allies and enemies of both Iran and Iraq, and we sold arms to both sides to fight each other. We provided battlefield intelligence when Saddam Hussein applied chemical weapons against his enemies and looked away when he turned on his own people.[43] We sent in our own troops when Hussein no longer suited our needs, and we subsequently left behind military hardware, which was less expensive than shipping it home.

ISIS extremism sprouted among militants held in an American military prison.[44] ISIS came to power with the aid of American arms captured from Iraqi forces, including approximately 40 M1A1 battle tanks, 52 M198 howitzer mobile gun systems, 2,300 armored Humvees, and 74,000 machine guns.[45]

ISIS also acquired weapons manufactured in Russia, China, and Eastern Europe, which were procured by Saudi Arabia and the U.S. during the Obama administration and transferred to Syrian rebels to fight Bashar al-Assad's regime.[46] Once again, we became our own worst enemy, necessitating further American support and arms to fight ISIS and overcome the new nemesis we created.

From an economics standpoint, we are totally dependent on sustaining civil unrest in the Middle East to consume surplus armaments. Weapons sales are greatly preferred by the U.S. and all countries that manufacture and distribute arms to sustain their own economies. However, in the absence of paying customers, taxpayer-funded arms deals are nearly as beneficial. We cannot afford to win these wars because that would jeopardize jobs at home. If the wars stop and weapons pile up unused, then the factories must also stop, and our entire economic system begins to falter.

The sprawling wars of the Middle East have become a convenient outlet for all arms-producing nations to dispose of surplus weaponry. Since the initial invasion of Afghanistan, the ongoing conflict has cost American taxpayers an estimated $5.6 trillion dollars, including projected futures costs such as lifetime veteran medical care and benefits.[47] That's theoretically enough to convert America over to 100% renewable solar and wind energy,[48] eliminating household electric bills while vastly reducing our consumption of fossil fuels to make an effective stand against global warming.

Instead of investing in making the world a better place, we've developed a complex means to create wealth and detonate our surplus abundance, while keeping citizens gainfully employed and too busy to complain about it.

"The mass of men lead lives of quiet desperation. What is called resignation is confirmed desperation. From the desperate city you go into the desperate country, and have to console yourself with the bravery of minks and muskrats. A stereotyped but unconscious despair is concealed even under what are called the games and amusements of mankind. There is no play in them, for this comes after work. But it is a characteristic of wisdom not to do desperate things."

—Henry David Thoreau,
Walden (1854)[49]

Fool's Gold
Profiteering to the Poor House

How much time does the average person spend thinking about money? How much life energy is dedicated to getting ahead, working to earn a living, buy a car, pay down debts, or get a better job? From the savannas of Africa to the halls of Wall Street, life revolves around the effort to earn a buck. Unfortunately, the pursuit of profit often has the opposite effect, prolonging poverty with each paycheck.

In principal, the economic activity of millions of people producing and exchanging goods and services should enrich all participants. In practice, however, efforts to maximize profits drive up costs until everyone loses.

We've all heard of egregious government expenses wasting taxpayer dollars, such as $500,000 to build a $50,000 bathroom in a city park. Somebody makes a quick buck at the expense of everyone else. Yet, they too are victims of similar scams every day. We pay excessive costs for everything from government ineptitude to health insurance or hiring a plumber. Even those "free" plastic bags at the grocery store drive up costs and imperil the planet, creating illusionary profits for the bag industry while perpetrating the ruination of the planet.

The Fire Piston and other Taxpayer Expenses
Indigenous peoples of South Pacific long ago developed a method of fire starting based on principals similar to the modern diesel engine.

Slam a tight-fitting rod into a bamboo cylinder. Rapidly compressing air molecules generates enough heat to cause a spark. Attach a little tinder to the end of the rod and it will glow. Simply slam the rod in, pull it back out, and transfer the glowing coal into a nest-like bundle of dry fluffy tinder, then blow it into flame. The fire piston is fascinating and fun to demonstrate, although too finicky to be dependable in a survival situation. It is more of a cool parlor trick than an actual survival tool. So why did the U.S. Army buy them?

As the owner of a niche bookstore, I sold fire pistons and other primitive fire-starting methods, including the bow and drill, hand drill, flint and steel, and fire plow. Wilderness survival gear complemented our selection of wilderness survival books, including my own *Participating in Nature*, giving us a successful bookstore in the age of Barnes & Noble and Amazon. Our supplier for the fire pistons manufactured them from beautiful hardwoods as a side business to his day job. He told me about his sales to the military. Unspent funds at the end of the annual budget cycle would be returned to the general fund, risking a reduced budget the following year. Rather than lose the funds, an officer bought fire pistons as presents for his sergeants. The supplier was pretty thrilled about the military contract, and who wouldn't be? He made a nice profit for the transaction. Who cares anyway? In the overall drama of government waste, it hardly registered as a flyspeck.

When the Chief of Staff for the Army testified before Congress in 2012 that they didn't need or want more tanks, Congress approved $183 million for additional tanks anyway, followed by another unwanted $120 million in 2014[50] and $40 million in 2016 for tank upgrades. We already have 2,000 surplus tanks stored in a supply yard in the California desert.[51] Why such wasteful spending when it isn't wanted by the military? It all comes down to jobs. Members of Congress advocate big military contracts to support jobs for constituents. Similarly, when the Pentagon requested a new $500 million littoral combat ship in 2017, the Trump administration intervened and doubled the order to protect jobs in Alabama shipyards.[52]

Strangely, it doesn't seem to matter to anyone building unwanted tanks or battleships that their work is utterly unnecessary. It is no different than Thoreau's example of men being paid to throw stones over a wall and throw them back again, yet no one seems to care as long as they draw a decent paycheck.

However, every American pays for those tanks, battleships, and fire pistons, impoverishing all to create unnecessary work for the few. The working class shaves off a portion of every paycheck to employ people mining and refining metals and constructing battleships and tanks we don't need.

The problem of artificial employment is not exclusive to military waste. Anyone in pursuit of profit is at risk of advocating meaningless work. For example, the reason we do not presently have universal healthcare isn't because it would cost more, but because it would cost less.

Healthcare for Jobs

Sweden is known as a socialist country with great public benefits, such as universal healthcare, but also high taxes. In comparison, however, Americans actually subsidize healthcare more and receive less. Healthcare spending in Sweden runs about $4,900 per person, paid almost entirely through income taxes.[53] Going to the doctor in Sweden costs an individual about 200 SEK or $25 per visit for a maximum limit of 1,100 SEK ($137) per year. All subsequent appointments are free. For minors in Sweden, healthcare is entirely free.[54] Like most countries with socialized medicine, Swedes like their healthcare system.

Healthcare in America is a more terrifying prospect. We spend $9,267 per person per year, of which $5,960 is government subsidized.[55] Yet, Americans typically avoid doctors and hospitals when possible, and many people suffer debilitating ailments for years or decades because they cannot afford treatment. Visits to the emergency room are avoided except in dire situations. Instead of seeking immediate help, patients must debate the severity of an issue, and when possible, delay treatment long enough to schedule an appointment with a doctor days or weeks later to avoid emergency room or hospital rates.

On vacation in Sweden. If our healthcare system were as fiscally efficient as the Swedes, Americans would save $1.4 trillion per year.

The Affordable Care Act, a.k.a. "Obamacare," was intended to help fix the American system. However, instead of addressing root causes of expensive healthcare, Congress merely passed legislation requiring citizens to purchase costly health insurance or pay a tax penalty. Even with insurance, the deductible and co-pay costs often make healthcare unaffordable for those in need. So why did Congress prop up expensive healthcare with an insurance mandate, rather than switch to less costly universal healthcare? Because inefficiencies in the American system effectively employ powerful constituents doing meaningless work.

As suggested by many economists, the insurance industry greatly inflates healthcare costs in America. The insurance industry makes a profit by collecting premiums while attempting to avoid payments. From 1997 to 2007, employment in healthcare insurance swelled by 52% from 293,000 to 444,000 employees,[56] all paid to crunch numbers and process paperwork without actually producing anything. The rest of us shave off a portion of our paychecks to pay for their office buildings, computers, houses, cars, and vacations. During the same time period, employment among doctors, nurses and other healthcare workers grew only half as fast, 26%, while the economy as a whole grew by only 12%.[57] By 2015, there were 500,000 employees providing healthcare insurance,[58] plus employees in every doctor's office whose primary job is to process insurance related paperwork.

President Obama initially advocated universal healthcare, which would have largely eliminated healthcare insurance. Instead, Congress produced the so-called Affordable Care Act mandating that all Americans prop up the insurance industry.

I was fortunate to come out ahead on the deal when I signed up for Obamacare and obtained health insurance for the first time. I needed surgery and physical therapy to replace a torn ACL, the middle tendon in the knee. With my "bronze" insurance plan, I paid "only" monthly insurance payments, plus the $5,600 deductible, while the insurance company covered the balance due on the $20,300 operation. Paperwork drifted back and forth an entire year between the insurance company and the doctors, hospital, pharmacies, and the physical therapist. Each letter contained columns upon columns of undeterminable numbers and percentages tabulating expenses and cost sharing.

By axing the healthcare insurance industry and switching to universal healthcare we could greatly reduce paperwork, and with it, the per capita cost of medicine. Heath insurance costs are deeply entwined with medical malpractice lawsuits and malpractice insurance and multiple other issues, all of which need to be resolved together. If American healthcare were as fiscally efficient as the Swedish system, American consumers would save a mind-boggling $1.4 trillion per year.

Tragedy of the Consumer

One of the core lessons of economics 101 is the "tragedy of the commons." Resources that are shared by everyone can be exploited by anyone. For example, prior to European colonization, there were an estimated 45 million deer in what later became the United States. However, due to over-hunting, especially for market sales, deer were nearly wiped out by the end of the nineteenth century.[59] Exploiting this common resource diminished the resource for everyone. That's the tragedy of the commons.

Fortunately, the Lacey Act of 1900 outlawed interstate transport of poached wild game, reinforcing emerging state wildlife conservation laws.[60] Hunting regulations, conservation efforts, and other factors allowed deer populations to rebound to 38 million deer by 2000. Thanks to communal oversight in the form of government regulations, hunters can sustainably harvest more than 6 million deer per year.[61] Here in Montana, where the human population is low and the deer population is high, a hunter can draw tags to take multiple animals. When both parents and hunting-age kids all draw tags, it isn't uncommon for one

Managing the Commons
U.S. Deer Population 1450 to 2014

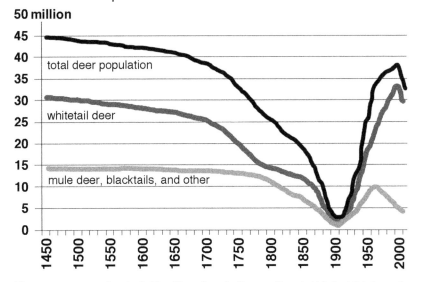

There were an estimated 45 million deer in the continental United States prior to colonization. In a classic case of Tragedy of the Commons, deer were nearly hunted to extinction before hunting regulations and a ban on market hunting allowed deer populations to rebound. Unfortunately, habitat loss to development is again reversing population gains.

family to harvest eight or more deer in a single hunting season. Unfortunately, habitat loss to development and other factors are beginning to erode prior deer population gains.

Through communal management, usually in the form of government regulations, we can avoid the tragedy of the commons, protecting our collective natural resources from exploitation or pollution. Less commonly understood, however, is that we also suffer from a "tragedy of the consumer."

In this case, government meddling often exacerbates the problem, typically prodded by special interest groups seeking to maximize profits. For example, most states have regulations limiting do-it-yourself plumbing and wiring projects. In many states it is illegal to plumb or wire your own home. In some states it is illegal to even repair your plumbing and wiring. On the surface, one would expect such laws to be promoted by safety groups to ensure code-compliant plumbing and wiring. In practice, however, such laws are advocated by associations of plumbers and electricians to guarantee themselves more work. Why allow a homeowner to repair a leaky pipe for the cost of materials when an expert can charge $70+/hour to fix it for them?

Not all such expenses are mandated by government, although government often fails to protect consumers from egregious waste. For example, Americans use 100 billion single-use plastic bags each year, consuming 12 million barrels of oil. The average family brings home 1,500 plastic shopping bags per year, typically used for about 12 minutes apiece, yet only about 1% of all plastic bags are recycled. Those that are buried in landfills take 500-1,000 years to degrade. Worse, bags litter the landscape and imperil wildlife, and 80% of all plastic trash in the ocean comes off the land.[62] Our plastic bag problem is rooted in the illusion that plastic bags are "free."

Plastic bags are not free. The plastic bag industry employs 30,000 people in the U.S.[63] with revenues of $1.5 billion.[64] Where did that money come from? People like you and I, caught in the tragedy of the consumer. Every item in every grocery store includes a built-in fee to cover the cost of "free" plastic bags. As might be expected, banning plastic bags is greatly opposed by industry advocates. Coalitions such as the American Progressive Bag Alliance (APBA), the American Chemistry Council, and the Save the Plastic Bag Coalition spend millions of dollars to fight plastic bag bans in voter referendums and courtrooms.

The tragedy of the consumer is that we are effectively taxed at the store to subsidize fossil fuel consumption, global warming, litter, and pollution. What would happen if we banned single use plastic bags and found more constructive employment for those 30,000 people?

Fortunately, many countries or cities have outright banned plastic grocery bags or imposed taxes such that each bag must be paid for upon checkout. In Kenya, where plastic bags litter roadsides and clog sewers and streams, it is now illegal to use, manufacture or import plastic bags. Plastic waste became such an immense environmental and economic problem that the Kenya legislated fines of up to $38,000 or up to four years in jail for violating the bag ban.[65] Efforts to enact plastic bag bans in the U.S. are advancing, while still being challenged by the political clout of the plastic bag industry.

Marketing Campaigns are Forever

Consumers are also compelled to pay for utterly unnecessary goods whose sole purpose is to extract money from gullible people. For example, wedding bands originated with ancient Egyptians, who exchanged rings of braided reeds. Romans seeded modern traditions, where the groom typically gave the bride a gold ring as a symbol of ownership to wear in public, along with an iron ring to wear at home.[66]

The first known diamond engagement ring dates back to 1477. Diamonds remained rare and expensive until the 1870s when huge diamond deposits were discovered in South Africa, enough to make the precious stones worthless. To maintain product value, De Beers Consolidated Mines, Ltd. secured ownership and control of the world diamond trade, stockpiling diamonds to sell at controlled prices. However, sales remained lackluster, falling off in the 1920s and 1930s until only 10% of American engagement rings contained diamonds.[67]

Unlike precious metals like gold or platinum, diamonds are composed of common carbon, which is infinitely abundant and forms diamond under sufficient heat and pressure. De Beers hired a marketing firm to promote their worthless rocks, initially suggesting that a suitor should spend one month's salary on a diamond engagement ring. This sum increased to two months income after the economy bounced back with World War II. Meanwhile, De Beers continued trickling diamonds onto the market to maintain artificially high prices.

Diamonds finally won over consumers with the 1947 advertising slogan, *"A Diamond is Forever."* Diamond rings now command 80% of the American market, while the average cost of an engagement ring has risen to nearly $6,000.[68] Similar marketing has introduced diamond rings to nonwestern cultures that didn't traditionally have engagement rings. In Japan for example, a gullible consumer is expected to spend three months salary, typically several thousand dollars, on a diamond engagement ring.[69] Instead of spending quality time together, the groom must slave away at a job to buy a carbon crystal. Creating a market where none existed made De Beers' worthless rocks valuable, suckering millions of young people into superfluous work. For this reason, *"A Diamond is Forever"* is recognized as the most successful marketing slogan of the twentieth century.[70]

The tragedy of the consumer is that the global pursuit of profit impoverishes all participants in the economy. We are compelled to pay extra taxes to build tanks and battleships that are unnecessary and unwanted. We are compelled to pay more than double for healthcare compared to other industrialized countries. We are compelled to pay extortive rates for plumbing and wiring projects that could be done by capable do-it-yourselfers. We are compelled to pay for plastic bags at great cost to our common environment. We are compelled to pay for diamond rings to reward a company with a clever marketing campaign. Adding insult to injury, we are compelled to pay artificial expenses just to pay our taxes.

Americans spend $409 billion per year in time and money to comply with tax regulations, enough to fund four missions to Mars every year.

A Tax to Pay Taxes

If we had a simple and objective tax system, such as a carbon tax levied at coalmines and oil wells, tax collection could be largely computerized and automated. Moreover, consumers and businesses would have an incentive to invest in energy efficiency and alternative energy to reduce their tax burden and save money. Instead, we have a complicated tax system designed to maximize work, as noted previously.

To expound on this issue, consider that NASA estimates it would cost about $100 billion to send a manned mission to Mars. This is an enormous sum of money, far exceeding NASA entire annual budget, so the space agency plans to invest in the endeavor through multiple stages spread out over many years.[71]

In comparison, Americans spend an estimated $409 billion per year to comply with tax regulations. This figure includes actual money spent by individuals and corporations on tax services through accounts and lawyers, plus the estimated value of unpaid time spent doing tax-related paperwork. That is the equivalent of 4.3 million full-time workers producing absolutely nothing.[72] Our complicated tax laws benefit many special interests at great detriment to society as a whole. If we eliminated these inefficiencies in the tax system and allocated our collective time and resources differently, we could potentially launch four missions to Mars every year.

Panning for Gold

Growing up around the historic mining town of Virginia City, Montana, I learned how to pan for gold. It's easy and kind of fun. Shovel some promising dirt and gravel in the pan. Add some water and swirl it around. Allow the muddy water and silt to wash over the edge. Swirl the pan a little more and slough off the lighter rocks and debris, while the heavy material settles to the bottom of the pan. Soon all that is left is black sand and shiny gold... or is that fool's gold?

Fool's gold is an iron sulfide with a yellow-brass color and a metallic shine, otherwise known as iron pyrite. It looks similar to gold, and it is common to find a few flecks of real gold and a lot of iron pyrite in the pan.

Panning for gold as a hobby is relatively harmless. Unfortunately, we've created an entire economy based on fool's gold. The indiscriminate pursuit of profit keeps people busy, excited at every fleck of color in the pan, no matter how worthless. Employees earnestly go to work believing they are getting ahead by taking other people's money, yet they too are constantly being scammed. In the final measure, we've consumed resources, mined the earth, polluted our streams, and failed to produce anything more valuable than iron pyrite. The more meaningless work we do, the poorer we inevitably become.

"Adaptation is not a conscious choice, and the people who make up a society do not quite understand what they are doing; they know only that a particular choice works, even though it may appear bizarre to an outsider."
—Peter Farb,
Man's Rise to Civilization (1968)[73]

No Sentient Life on Earth
Automatons at Work

During World War II, western powers set up military bases on remote islands in New Guinea and imported supplies by sea and air. Clothing, canned food, tents, weapons, and other manufactured goods were delivered in great quantity for the soldiers and their native hosts and guides. To the native peoples, these goods seemed to materialize from nothing, appearing like magic from the bowels of ships and planes. After the war, the military posts were abandoned and the soldiers went home, yet the native peoples wanted more western goods.

"Cargo cults" arose from the belief that white men intercepted supplies sent by the ancestors. The natives believed their ancestors would return with more supplies, so they quit working and literally waited for their ship to come in. They abandoned gardens, ate their pigs, and cut down their banana trees, believing that better goods would soon be delivered.[74][75]

To call back the ships and planes, natives mimicked military behaviors. They built communications antennas and wires from branches and vines. People sat at desks and pretended to read and write all day. Men carried sticks that looked like rifles and marched back and forth like soldiers. They painted military insignia and "USA" on their bodies to mimic military uniforms.

Inland, natives cleared flat runways for airplanes to land. They watched the skies from fabricated control towers, wearing headphones carved from wood. They lit signal fires and used torches to light up runways. People stood on the runways waving the landing signals used by the white men. Some even built life-size mock-ups of airplanes from straw. None were successful in calling back the ships and planes.[76][77]

From an outside perspective it ludicrous to imagine exerting so much effort towards such misguided beliefs. Like automatons, these people were mimicking behaviors without a conscious understanding of cause and effect. But who are we to judge? From an outside perspective, most people in our economy are similarly employed, and the results are far more destructive. We design products to fail. We ravage the planet for natural resources to manufacture goods destined for landfills. We are a cargo cult, believing we create wealth by pretending to write or study or calculate numbers at a desk all day. We are as delusional as they were and equally blind to our delusions. Above all, we are blinded by the misconception that our species is self-aware. If we were self-aware then society would be vastly different from the world we know.

This chapter was adapted from material in Roadmap to Reality: Consciousness, Worldviews and the Blossoming of Human Spirit, also by Thomas J. Elpel

Nobody Home

Looking at one's own reflection in the mirror, it is logical to assume that we are self-aware. "That's me. Therefore, I am." The idea that self-recognition is equal to self-awareness is deeply embedded in our culture. Are we truly self-aware, or is it merely something we have mimicked from other people?

English is notably impoverished in words for self-awareness. "Self-aware" consists of two words cobbled together with a hyphen to convey an otherwise foreign concept. The only single word that conveys self-awareness is "sentient." As originally defined, a sentient being is something that is able to sense and feel things—not exactly a demanding standard. However sentient has been expanded through science fiction genre to serve as a synonym for self-awareness.

In *Star Trek*, for example, space-faring humans visit other worlds and recognize the rights of sentient beings they encounter, whether those beings are humanoid in form, self-aware machines, or some kind of highly intelligent space blobs. These television shows presumed that humans were also sentient beings, which hasn't yet been proven.

Human beings learn principally through mimicry. The young brain is highly plastic, mimicking whatever behaviors and beliefs it is exposed to. We don't send infants to school to learn English or Chinese. Language is absorbed and copied from an early age. A child growing up in Mexico is likely to speak Spanish and become Catholic. Growing up in Saudi Arabia, one is likely to speak Arabic and become Sunni-Muslim. A child growing up in a doghouse is likely to bark and become a dog.

A girl named Oxana was raised by dogs in Ukraine. Her home was crowded with older siblings, so three-year-old Oxana crawled into the doghouse and lived there. Her alcoholic, neglectful parents eventually disappeared, so Oxana lived with stray dogs. She ate raw meat and carrion and learned to walk on all fours and bark like a dog. She lapped at her food, bit at fleas, and scratched behind her ear with her foot. She had acute senses for hearing, sight, and smell. Authorities in Ukraine discovered Oxana in 1991 when she was eight years old. With intensive speech therapy she was able to acquire basic language skills. However, at age twenty-two she remained developmentally a six year-old.[78]

Oxana mimicked what she was exposed to as a child and that defined her reality. We also mimicked what we were exposed to, and that defines our reality. Her reality was normal to her. Our reality seems normal to us. She didn't question her reality. We rarely question ours. Yet, her reality was no more bizarre than ours. We are largely a nonsentient species. We seldom reflect on the nature or purpose of employment or the consequences of our actions.

End of the Free Lunch

A cougar doesn't stop to debate the environmental and ethical issues at stake when it chases a jackrabbit. It doesn't wonder how many jackrabbits are left, and how many it can sustainably harvest. When hungry, it kills and eats, even if its prey is the last of its kind. Indeed, 99.9% of everything that ever lived is now extinct. There is no reason to expect that our ancestors acted any differently than other predators.

Aboriginal Australians long ago used fire as a hunting tool upon colonizing the continent, which ultimately changed the vegetation, altered the climate, and helped drive indigenous megafauna to extinction 45,000 years ago.[79] More than 85% of Australia's large reptiles, birds, and mammals were permanently lost, including lizards 25-feet-long, 300-pound marsupial lions, 400-pound flightless birds, car-sized tortoises, 1,000-pound kangaroos, 2-ton wombats, and dozens more.[80]

Like the first Australians, falcons and kites there are known to collect burning sticks from lightning-caused fires and drop them in dry grass to start new fires. The birds then perch in advance of the fire to hunt small game fleeing the flames.[81] Birds and people are equally incapable of perceiving the extended consequences of their actions.

Similarly, there were two-dozen different species of moa birds in New Zealand when the Maori discovered and colonized the remote islands a thousand years ago. In the absence of predators, birds evolved to become flightless and defenseless, with some species growing up to ten feet tall. Meat is often scarce for hunter-gatherer peoples, a literal hit-or-miss challenge. However, moa were the ultimate free lunch. Maori hunters didn't need to construct complex bows and arrows or engage in elaborate hunting strategies or stealth. They merely walked up to the birds and clubbed them to death. Moving down the length of New Zealand over the next five centuries, the Maori wiped out all easy prey in their path. In the 1800s British colonists unearthed hundreds of thousands of bones when plowing the earth. Archaeological evidence has revealed primitive ovens filled with charred bones from countless birds. Several dozen species of birds went extinct with the arrival of the Maori including large geese, ducks, swans, and eagles.[82]

Rather than stewarding available resources and ensuring guaranteed protein and fat for future generations, the Maori slaughtered helpless birds and ballooned their own population. The result? More work. By exterminating easy food, the Maori had to work harder to feed themselves.

Maori history is not unique in this regard. Most of human history is replete with similar stories of people damaging the environment and passing the cost off to future generations. From species extinction and groundwater depletion to extracting easy minerals while leaving behind toxic mining pits, humans have skimmed off the best resources and enjoyed the proverbial free lunch. We leave our children and grandchildren an impoverished and contaminated world.

Megadeath

Paleontologists have documented that every time our ancestors migrated into new territory over the last 50,000 years there was a massive extinction of the large native mammals. For example, 73% of large North American mammals (counting by genus) disappeared with human colonization of this continent. We lost the native camel, two species of llamas, two ox-like animals, three species of horses, four types of ground sloth, five species of deer and moose, a 400-pound beaver, 600-pound armadillo, 2,000 pound glyptodont, the 5-ton mastodon, 6-ton wooly mammoth, and the 9-ton Columbian mammoth. We also lost major predators, including sabertooth cats, scimitar cats, the American lion, and three species of bear, including the world's largest-ever mammalian predator, the 1,800-pound giant short-faced bear. In South America 80% of the large mammals were lost.[83]

Some people argue that mass extinctions coincided with climate change, suggesting that Stone Age peoples were not to blame. While it is true that climate change often contributed to reduced populations, it was the arrival of people and technology that finished them off. In North America for example, many large mammals survived twenty-two previous ice ages, then died out after the twenty-third, coinciding with the arrival of human hunters.[84]

Like the flightless birds of New Zealand, paleontologists have found the remains of recently extinct bird species on every oceanic island they've explored. It is estimated that roughly 10% of all the world's bird species fell victim to prehistoric exterminations.[85] Our ancestors probably never noticed the cumulative impact of hunting. In the case of the Maori, there were initially so few people and so much game that it took five hundred years to exterminate New Zealand's flightless birds. Individuals probably didn't notice much difference during their lifetimes, even while witnessing extinction in progress. All over the world, our ancestors exterminated huntable species left and right without realizing it. Of the remaining 9,000 bird species documented since 1600, an additional 157 have been declared extinct, while many more have not been seen in decades.[86]

By exterminating easy food, our ancestors made life more difficult for future generations. (Photo taken at La Brea Tar Pits.)

What our ancestors started with few people and simple tools, we are finishing at an ever-accelerating rate. The natural background extinction rate is estimated at 0.1 species per million lost per year, more or less equal to the rate organisms diversify into new species. Due to human activity, the extinction rate has risen to 100 species per million per year or 1,000 times the natural rate. Researchers predict that future extinctions will rise 10,000 times above normal rates.[87]

For every species lost, the world becomes more impoverished. From a purely human-centric viewpoint, many species have known or unknown uses that could benefit humankind. Some of our strongest medicines originated from plants, yet we are losing hundreds of species without knowing what medicinal properties they might have.

In addition, many plants and animals offer indirect benefits to the planet that are unknown or poorly studied. For example, elephants transport and deposit seeds in their dung. Their deep footprints can plant seeds in the soil and leave a small crater-like basin to hold water to facilitate seedling establishment. Some people argue that the North American ecosystem has been impaired since the mastodons died out ten thousand years ago, and the only way to restore balance is to introduce elephants in their place.

Many large-fruited trees co-evolved with oversized grazers, becoming dependent on animals for seed dispersal. For example, honey locust trees have oversize, sweet pea pods that were eaten by mammoths and other megafauna. Seeds passed through the digestive tract largely intact, planting new trees with a healthy dose of manure fertilizer. The Kentucky coffee tree, also from the pea family, was similarly distributed, as was the unrelated Osage orange. Megafauna extinction greatly reduced the geographic range of Osage orange, while several closely related species went extinct.[88]

See Nothing, Do Nothing

The world outside the window probably seems completely normal. Except for new roads and houses it is the same world we've always known. Yet the world has changed, and people rarely notice. Iceland, for example, once supported rich forests, as David Montgomery noted in *Dirt: The Erosion of Civilizations*, *"Even though Iceland has lost 60 percent of its vegetative cover and 96 percent of its tree cover, after 1,100 years of inhabitation most Icelanders find it difficult to conceive of their modern desert as having once been forested. Just as at Easter Island, people's conception of what is normal evolves along with the land—if the changes occur slowly enough."*[89]

Few people in the eastern half of our country look up and notice the absence of passenger pigeons. The birds once migrated in flocks of billions, so thick that they would blacken overhead skies. Similarly, the American elm was the dominant tree in eastern woodlands before being killed off by introduced Dutch elm disease. We can still see the forest, but where are the trees? Did anyone notice that nights are more silent than they should be, that frogs don't sing as loudly as they once did?

Here in the West, few people pay attention to bare ground between individual clumps of bunch grass. We've become accustomed to barren, desertified landscapes with rocky ground, exposed soil, and scattered creosote bushes or sagebrush. Not so long ago these same landscapes were lush grasslands supporting vast herds of antelope, elk, and bison. The Salt Lake City area was once described as having grass "belly high to a horse," yet that is not the landscape we know today. The region is gray and brushy because we've altered the landscape.

Across the American West we are creating a desert to rival the Sahara, yet few people can see a difference in their day-to-day lives. Probably less than 1 in 10,000 people are sufficiently knowledgeable to tell the difference between what was, what is, and what will be. To everyone else the world seems perfectly normal and it always will, no matter what we do to it.

We notice when there are bugs splattered on the windshield, but seldom notice the absence of bug activity. Yet, researchers estimate a 45% global drop in invertebrate abundance over the past four decades,[90] with one study showing a 75% decline in flying insect populations over three decades.[91]

The loss of insects threatens countless other plant and animal species. Eighty percent of wild plants depend on insect pollination and 60% of birds depend on insects for food.[92] While many bird species are declining, insect-eaters have suffered much sharper declines than seed-eaters.[93]

Global wildlife populations fell by 58% between 1970 and 2012, predicted to reach 67% by 2020, mostly due to habitat loss to farming and logging.[94] We will permanently lose half of all life on earth to the Machine this century. Plastic trash accumulating in the Pacific Ocean now makes a floating garbage patch twice the size of Texas or three times the size of France.[95] Up to 100,000 sea turtles and marine mammals and sea turtles die each year from eating plastic, along with a million seabirds.[96] Nearly 700,000 tons of fishing nets and gear are lost in the ocean every year. Ghost nets kill countless fish—and all the progressively bigger species that come to eat them.[97] Restaurants are substituting one fish for another on the menus as earlier species disappear from the oceans. Yet, fishing boats routinely discard up to 40% of their fresh, tossing fresh dead fish overboard in the search for higher value species.[98] By the middle of this century there is expected to be more plastic than fish in the oceans.[99] Meanwhile, excess carbon dioxide is acidifying the oceans, dissolving the protective shells of marine organisms and killing coral reefs.[100]

Our planet is dying, and news headlines are primarily concerned with government corruption, celebrities, mass shootings, sex scandals, and sports.

Cultural Evolution

Biologically, our species evolved through millions of years and tens of thousands of mutations. There was never any plan to make us what we are. Our evolutionary journey from amino acids to tool-using primates has been a journey of accidents that worked. Our ancestors did not seek to become *Homo sapiens*, only to survive. Being here is the result of one mutation band-aided over another thousands of times.

Similarly, the evolution of culture and economy occurred without any plan beyond day-to-day survival. As with biology, cultural-economic evolution is a haphazard process of mutations and adaptations, reactions to problems and circumstances along the way. Our

World Populations

People and livestock are replacing wildlife. Global populations of wild animals fell by 58% between 1970 and 2012, predicted to fall by 67% as of 2020. Species are lost to extinction as population levels decline below critical thresholds. We will permanently lose half of all life on earth this century.

- 7.6 billion people
- 1.4 billion cows
- 1 billion pigs
- 112 million deer (estimated total of 47 deer family species, including deer, elk, moose, caribou, reindeer, brocket, etc.)
- 2.4 million combined total of all elephants, rhinoceroses, giraffes, zebras, bison, chimpanzees, and gorillas.

ancestors who shared meat with the tribe did not plan to evolve the New York Stock Exchange any more than their ancestors planned to evolve an opposable thumb or stand up straight. Any mutations that proved to be "economical" or practical were retained as part of our cultural heritage.

Consider differing food habits of cultures around the world. Many ethnic groups eat rats and cockroaches while Americans nearly retch at the idea. Similarly Americans typically disdain the thought of eating dogs, cats, or horses. Meanwhile Hindu people see us as virtual cannibals for eating beef, and Moslems think we sin when we eat pork. According to Marvin Harris, author of *The Sacred Cow and the Abominable Pig*, these beliefs emerge from practical economics.[101]

Americans typically dislike the idea of eating horses, yet horse meat has gone through many surges of popularity and unpopularity in America and Europe according to economic trends. Horsemeat became popular when other meat was more expensive and unpopular when other options were more economical.

Similarly, Hindu people abhor the idea of eating cows, yet that has not always been the case. Indian people regularly consumed beef up until a few centuries BC, when rising population created need for more cropland. Crops produce more calories and protein per acre than livestock. Livestock was needed for plowing fields, producing milk, and producing dung for fuel. Beef consumption dropped over centuries until only wealthy priests consumed it. Disparity between rich and poor created an opportunity for a religion of cow protection among the peasant masses. Hinduism and cow protection became the dominant religion because it reflected the economic reality of the area.

In America we could eat dogs, cats, mice, and cockroaches. However, we have good economical alternatives, so we scorn uneconomical choices as bad or filthy, even while other cultures consider the same foods edible and delicious.

Throughout history, cultural practices were not determined through effectiveness strategies, plans, or goals, but through the need to maintain stability within the social group. The collective group reacts to problems at hand, adopting beliefs that reflect economic realities.

Jewish and Moslem peoples preach against eating pork, yet pigs were indigenous to the rich cedar forests of the Middle East. People domesticated and consumed pork until deforestation, desertification, and competition with human crops made it impractical to raise pigs. Pork subsequently became "bad to eat" among local religions.

Adapting to change over centuries, the collective culture adopts beliefs that reflect economic realities. However, the underlying reality is that we are a nonsentient species that caused the deforestation and desertification that ultimately made pork uneconomical.

Biological and cultural evolution is an unconscious process. Our survival is testament to luck, not foresight. Biologically, 99.9% of everything that ever lived is now extinct.[102] Similarly, history is littered with the ruins of collapsed civilizations, typically caused by poor resource management and subsequent ecosystem degradation.

Within this cloud of doom there is one bright spot: a growing number of people are aware of the destruction we are causing.

Glimmers of Consciousness

From moas to mammoths, nature provided a free lunch for our ancestors, and they wasted it. We've continued the tradition ever since, depleting nature's abundance and making life progressively more difficult for future generations. We live in a greatly impoverished world, still indulging in an orgy of consumption to use up our remaining resources before our grandchildren get their hands on it. However, there are glimmers of hope, glimmers of consciousness that could lead to a leap forward in the conscious evolution of our culture. As natural resources become increasingly scarce and we are haunted by the mistakes of our past, we are forced to look ahead at the future as never before.

Consider ozone depletion. Chlorofluorocarbons or CFCs were used as coolant in refrigerators and as a foaming agent for some types of insulation, until it was discovered CFCs were destroying stratospheric ozone that protects our planet from harmful ultraviolet radiation. Scientists observed ozone depletion starting in the 1970s with a visible ozone hole by the mid-1980s. Conscious exploration of the problem led to the collaborative effort and international treaties to end production of CFCs. The problem worsened for some time, as my son and I experienced firsthand upon arrival in New Zealand without hats or sunscreen. My son quickly burned and blistered under the southern sun and depleted ozone layer. Fortunately, halting production of CFCs enabled surprisingly quick recovery, with scientists noting measurable reduction in the ozone hole by 2016.[103] Unfortunately, nitrous oxide from excess fertilizer use is also linked to ozone depletion reducing UV protection worldwide.[104]

Around the world, people are starting to wake up and question the status quo. In regards to species extinction, researchers are searching jungles for new medicines that could benefit our species. People are recognizing that other species have value that may lay beyond our ability to comprehend, that we ought to protect them not merely for our own benefit, but because they have the right to exist.

If humanity becomes increasingly aware, society will evolve vastly different from the reality we now know. Imagine a world where resources were used wisely. Houses would be durable, low-maintenance, and energy independent, producing as much electricity as they consume. Appliances, such as refrigerators, freezers, and washing machines, would be lifetime purchases. A blender would last for decades. Any appliance that fails could be repaired or recycled, rather than junked. Clothes would also be durable, and a pair of socks lasts years, rather than weeks. Cars would be fully electrified and readily repairable. Rather than employing millions of people to mine, refine, and dispose of natural resources, we would make a conscious effort to produce only what is needed and strive to make only high quality products that don't need constant repairs or replacement.

If human beings were self-aware, then climate change could have been avoided before it became a problem. We wouldn't kill off the coral reefs or fill the oceans with trash. We wouldn't turn the world's grass-lands to deserts, deplete our groundwater reserves, or contaminate the world with radiation. We wouldn't be mining precious resources to make weapons and warfare to bomb each other to oblivion.

Instead, we would discover a world of nearly unfathomable abundance where little actual work is required to meet every person's basic needs. Hunger and poverty would be reduced or eliminated, and people would be free to explore and pursue their dreams.

Collectively we could decide to direct a percentage of our leisure time to develop our infrastructure with well-maintained national parks and monuments, quality roads and high-speed trains, and a vastly more advanced space program.

A bright and abundant future is possible, and it's an easier path than the way we live now. Getting from here to there begins with acknowledging and breaking free of meaningless work and expenses. Individually, we may not have much say in the broader picture of society and decision-making, yet we can take control of our own lives and take concrete steps to detach from the treadmill of meaningless work and endless bills. We can achieve green prosperity for ourselves and provide an alternative model for others. Once successfully unemployed or reasonably detached from senseless work, we have the option of investing time and resources in a better world for all.

"The modern capitalist state has manoeuvred to manage surplus labor in a number of disparate and mostly ad-hoc ways. The inexorable rise in the rate of the prison population has been one consequence... However, perhaps the most prominent policy to contain and manage surplus labour and sustain control over 'free time' has been to expand training and education."

—*Peter Kennedy,*
"The Knowledge Economy" (2012)[105]

Break Free From the Machine
Path of the Successfully Unemployed

My youngest son hated wearing shoes as a child. Hiking a trail together in Glacier National Park, I remember how people marveled as he ran along the stony path barefoot. *How does he do that? Doesn't it hurt?* Walking or running barefoot is almost inconceivable to many people, yet our ancestors lived that way for 99% of human history.

Imagine trying to hunt barefoot over rugged terrain, stalking up on your quarry, *Ouch! Damn! Ow!* If walking were that painful then our species would have gone extinct long ago. However, many people have rediscovered barefoot walking and running and now live barefoot much of the year. As for my son, he hated wearing shoes, yet shoes were required for school, so he hated going to school. One of my biggest regrets as a parent is having taken his freedom away. He learned to wear shoes and eventually forgot how to go barefoot.

Freedom is a foreign idea to most people, especially to anyone who grew up with parents who worked every day and expected nothing more from life than two weeks vacation per year. That is what we teach our children. They learn they will transition from grade school to high school to college to a cubicle where they will sit until retirement. Then they will be free to pursue their dreams and follow their heart's desires.

A Brief History of Education

Living as a hunter-gatherer requires vast knowledge about plants, animals, and the landscape through the seasons. It also requires highly developed skills to craft tools, clothing, and shelter from the natural materials at hand. Our ancestors did not study animal behavior in biology books or learn to make stone tools in shop class. They learned to be hunter-gatherers through experience and play, as noted by Peter Gray, PhD in *Psychology Today*.[106] A child, for example, would be given a toy bow at an early age. He grew up with bows and arrows, gradually making better, stronger bows while simultaneously increasing accuracy. There was no distinction between play, education, and work. It was all simply life. Hunter-gatherers were typically nomadic so life was often a never-ending adventure from season to season and place to place.

Agriculture enabled people to produce more food and more children, out-populating hunter-gatherer societies, yet farming was labor intensive and highly repetitive. People lived in one place and endlessly worked the same plot of land. Formal education was hardly necessary. Raising livestock and growing crops required long hours of mostly unskilled, monotonous labor, much of it done by children. Education emphasized suppressing children's natural willfulness and playfulness, cultivating an ethic of obedience, hard work, and dedication. Nevertheless, people had fresh air, sunshine, and at least some opportunities for play to balance out the monotony.[107]

The Industrial Revolution brought deteriorating conditions, especially for poor families. Children and adults often worked 12 to 14 hours per day seven days a week just to earn enough to survive. They did hazardous work in dark, crowded factories without dust masks or other basic safety equipment. Injuries and fatalities were common. Thousands died from diseases, starvation, and exhaustion every year. Child labor laws were slow to come, but gradually reduced horrific working conditions. For example, England's Factory Act of 1883 forbade textile manufacturers from employing children younger than 9 years old and limited the maximum workweek to 48 hours for 10 to 12 year-olds and 69 hours for 12 to 17 year-olds.[108]

Eventually, the need for child labor fell as factories achieved greater automation and industrialized nations became wealthier. Progressively tighter labor laws moved surplus labor from factories to classrooms, facilitating the spread of compulsory education.

It was all part of the same system. In school, children were conditioned to follow directions, be punctual, and learn to tolerate hours upon hours of tedium. As U.S. Commissioner of Education William Torrey Harris wrote in his 1889 book *The Philosophy of Education*, "*Ninety-nine [students] out of a hundred are automata, careful to walk in prescribed paths, careful to follow the prescribed custom. This is not an accident but the result of substantial education, which, scientifically defined, is the subsumption of the individual."[109]*

Graduates were adequately educated to be diligent farm and factory workers. Schooling inculcated students with a sense of patriotism and nationalism, binding citizens together in a homogenous culture. Workers engaged in largely unskilled, monotonous, repetitive work that required discipline more than education.

Further development of the industrial economy led to more wealth and more surplus labor. Between 1910 and 1940, secondary schools, a.k.a. "high schools" sprouted across America[110] absorbing the labor surplus and delaying the age at which people entered the workforce. Additional education polished students' reading, writing, and mathematic skills, preparing them for office work with similar requirements to factory work: be punctual, follow directions, and learn to tolerate hours of tedium.

College has since filled a similar role. We reduce the labor surplus by encouraging young adults to stay in school to earn a bachelor's degree, or better yet, a master's degree or doctorate. College degrees initially enabled workers to earn higher wages while serving a similar function to provide well-disciplined employees to serve other people. However, as the problem of surplus labor continues to grow, new graduates are less likely to find work in their chosen field and more likely to be saddled with student loan debts for decades to come. Statistically, 60% percent of people with student loans expect to pay them off in their forties.[111] The challenge of paying down those debts is obvious in this Facebook post and all the associated comments. Fortunately, there are better options.

It is possible to break free from the machine of civilization and walk one's own path in life. Indeed, I know many people who are successfully

Molly Mason
9 hrs ·

A little more than 20 years later, I have finally paid off my last student loan.

👍 Like   💬 Comment

😊💙😮 You, Marci Brown, Jack Smith and 94 others

View 14 more comments

Lorie Winton Holden I dream of that day! Congratulations!!!
Like · Reply · 1 hr

Molly Mason Also, I didn't actually complete a degree program!
Like · Reply · 😊 3 · 1 hr · Edited

Jen Wils I hope I POST THIS SOMEDAY! 😄
Like · Reply · 1 hr

Bonny Mets Congratulations!
Like · Reply · 1 min

Heather Smith Not me! Still plugging away....
Like · Reply · 8 hrs

John James I'll probably never pay mine off...
Like · Reply · 8 hrs

Sally Bergman Congratulations! It took me 20 years too.
Like · Reply · 7 hrs

Colleen Paris Ramsay That's amazing!
Like · Reply · 7 hrs

All names and profile pics have been altered to obscure identities.

unemployed, living free and doing whatever they want, typically augmented by intermittent work. Whatever your dreams in life, now is the time to pursue them.

Successfully Unemployed

In the 1980s I met a middle-aged musician who said, *"If you are interested in the arts, or music, or any creative field then you need to fight not to get a job."* He bought a house for $4,000 in Butte, Montana as part of his strategy to stay unemployed. There are many similar success stories.

My friend Kris started adulthood with a modest nest egg his parents originally intended for college. However, Kris wasn't any ordinary kid, and college wasn't a good fit. He attended Green University® LLC as an alternative to college and later stayed on as a part-time instructor and even co-authored *Foraging the Mountain West*. Needing very little money to get by, Kris and his partner Bartle spend most of their time camping and adventuring around the American West. As though working two or three months per year was too much, they took a yearlong sabbatical to redouble their focus on camping and wilderness survival skills.

Similarly, my friend Tamra shared her experiences,

> *"I have been nomadic (homeless) for a year. Didn't mean to go quite this long, but it's hard to want to get a job and pay rent when all I really miss is occasionally a kitchen. In 12 months I have worked about 10 weeks and made about $8600. I traveled Europe for 3 months, backpacked Copper Canyon Mexico, went to Fiji, attended gatherings, conferences, retreats, and reunions, valued beautiful people and saw magical places throughout much of the US. I have no debt, get good gas mileage, am on my brother's company phone plan, have affordable auto insurance, I don't buy stuff, and I know how to sleep anywhere and eat cheap ... we are programed to see wants as needs, to have these false dependencies. We are taught discontent. It's all fabricated and contrived. We need so very little to be fulfilled—thermoregulation, food, water, and each other. This is not to say that the bonus stuff isn't great, but how liberating to recognize that is truly is only bonus. We can own it without having IT own US."*

As the founder and director of Green University® LLC, I feel that I am doing my best work when students discover that employment is optional, that they are free to pursue their dreams in life. Most people are not aware that employment is optional until they have been immersed in the lifestyle with like-minded people. Neal arrived here as a student, later worked two months as an instructor, then bought a one-way ticket to vacation and adventure in Hawaii for six months. I consider that a success story!

In contrast, I remember paying a parking ticket at the local university. There was a sizeable building constructed for the sole purpose of parking enforcement. It was filled with computers, desks, and office workers. A middle-aged woman mentored a wide-eyed young student in processing the ticket via computer, and the student attentively absorbed the details as if she were learning to perform an important job. After years and years of sitting at a desk at school learning to follow orders she could now become proficient at doing meaningless work.

Likewise, I remember one young man visibly bored to death with his job charging parking fees at the University of Utah. Life is too short, too magical, too wonderful, too mysterious to spend a single afternoon sitting in a tollbooth. What a crime to condition our young people to accept such jobs either temporarily or for life! It is no wonder that so many young people turn to drugs and alcohol to numb the disenchantment and endure another day.

Most young people I know are interested in travel, exploration, and adventure. Fortunately, they've learned that it's not difficult to save up enough money to buy an old house or to build their own from scratch whenever they choose to settle down. Through temporary jobs they know it is possible to save enough money to walk away from the Machine and essentially retire at an early age. Anyone can be free to follow his or her dreams. Moreover, any person who doesn't need a paycheck is well positioned to launch his or her own green business.

Escaping the Job Trap

As someone who has successfully built a resource-efficient home and a green business, people often ask me what they can do to make their own life situations more sustainable. That is a challenging question to answer since sustainability issues are interconnected. It may be difficult to make substantial change without changing everything. Creating a sustainable lifestyle often requires a whole new approach to living and working. The key to success is in being able to escape the job trap.

I meet a lot of people with great Dreams. For many it is a Dream to own their own home without a mortgage. For others it is a Dream to start their own business and be free from an unsatisfying job. Some people simply want to travel the world or be free to sit under a tree and play the fiddle. Some people have a million-dollar idea they would love to bring to fruition, but neither the time nor resources to make it happen. Other people have described their frustration of being trapped in a lifestyle they do not believe in and how they Dream of living greener and more sustainably. Nearly everyone I meet is too busy treading water, trying to stay afloat among the bills and debt to even think about their Dreams anymore. Like a mantra, I hear people say it over and over again: "I know I could break free if I could just make a little more money." That idea is one of the grand illusions of the universe.

It is unfortunate to see wave after wave of kids graduate from school and fall into the same trap, subject to the powerful allure of money. Junior is delighted to get his first job flipping hamburgers, making minimum wage. It's new, it's different, and the paycheck seems liberating. So he spends it. Stereos, CDs, clothes, movies, dates, Saturday night outings. It doesn't take long until that paycheck is no longer enough. He discovers credit cards and payment plans and pretty soon he has a nice car and quite a bit of debt, and oh what a thrill it is to have his own apartment too!

Realizing that this flipping hamburger thing won't do, Junior goes off to college, accumulates more debt from student loans and works part-time after school to keep the cash flowing. All that studying and working makes him kind of crazy and reckless by the weekends, so he spends more than he should to "loosen up and have a good time."

He goes back to the weekly grindstone, only to discover a few months later that he on his way to becoming a daddy. Suddenly there's another person and a baby in the picture and a whole lot more bills. He successfully gradates from college, finds a better paying job, and rents a bigger house to have some "elbow room" for the family, and still struggles to pay bills. He feels trapped, disillusioned and ultimately desensitized to his childhood Dreams. He doesn't work out of inspiration, but desperation.

A Matter of Time

Ask anyone what stops them from pursuing a dream to write a book, start a business, or spend a month watching polar bears in the arctic, and it all comes down to the same mantra, "I know I could break free if I could just make a little more money..." However, it isn't money that most people need. It's time.

You've probably heard people say, "I know I could make a million dollars, if I just had $250K to invest in my ideas." They may be joking, but it is also true. I bet you could invest $250,000 and make a million. So, where do you come up with initial funds? If you had $50K and a few years of free time to pursue your ideas, you might make that $250,000. Simple enough. We can play this game backwards until you only need a thousand dollars and some free time to make the $10K needed to make the $50K to make the $250K you'll need to make a million.

From that standpoint, you could make a million with the money you have, but not right now because it's time go to work and pay bills before the landlord bumps your family out on the street, or worse, the cable company disconnects your Show Time channels. Most people are so busy treading water that they never have time to make a million dollars or pursue other dreams.

The key to success is simply Time, having the freedom to pursue your dreams without worry of being dragged under in a sea of bills. Granted, more money would help eliminate bills, so here's a suggestion: Ask the boss to quadruple your hourly wage. If you don't think that will work, then keep reading and let's consider alternative means.

I am frequently asked for financial advice, usually from people who earn far more than I do. Together we review their life and work situation. However, it isn't a matter of punching numbers into a calculator and spinning it around to come up with additional money to solve their worldly problems. Real results require real change. It's not about working harder. The key is in conserving materials, energy, money and time to get more out of what you have. Since all things are connected, one savings leads to another in a positive feedback loop that gets better and better.

Conserving energy conserves money, which in turn conserves time since you can work less. And if you have time to spare then you can achieve your greatest dreams. The opposite is also true: wasting resources encourages a negative feedback cycle, encouraging more and more waste.

Consider the light bulb. Incandescent bulbs were cheap up front, but cost more to operate and burned out quickly. Compact fluorescent bulbs were initially more costly, but lasted longer and used about one-third as much electricity. Each bulb saved about $40 in electricity over its lifetime. However, people who were strapped for cash struggled to justify spending $120 on a dozen new fangled light bulbs, especially when there were a dozen incandescent bulbs on the same shelf for only $12. So they bought cheap bulbs and paid more for electricity, virtually guaranteeing they would be broke when those bulbs burned out too. Poor choices lead to further poor choices. Wasted energy translates to wasted money, which translates to wasted time. When short on time, one may not get around to weather-stripping a leaky door, wasting more energy, money, and time. Following this line of reasoning, it appears that a person could get stuck in a meaningless job paying endless bills simply because they bought the wrong bulb! Sound far-fetched? Maybe not by the time we get through examining cycles of waste.

Let's take a look at a home mortgage, because that is typically the biggest investment, as well as the biggest loss a person will ever make.

Normally we buy the largest house we can afford payments on without starving the family for more than a few days each month. Let's say the purchase price is $150,000 with payments of $805 a month at 5% interest for thirty years. In the beginning, most of the payment is lost towards interest. Only $180 actually goes towards the principle the first month. We might as well take a match and burn the other $625 spent on interest. It's gone! Fifteen and a half years later, we've paid the bank $150,000 for the house, yet only $51,000 towards principle. At the end of the mortgage, we've paid $290,000 for a $150,000 house. Is that a bad deal or what?

Regardless of income level, most people earn enough money to pay off a house in a few years, yet waste nearly 100% of that income on expenses such as interest payments, unnecessarily high energy bills, and really bizarre things such as garbage bags which are purchased for the purpose of throwing them away.

Here is one alternative: Buy a house that costs half as much ($75,000), and pay the same $805 a month as for a $150,000 house. The house will be paid off in less than ten years, and you will own $75,000 equity, which can then be applied towards a bigger house if desired.

Some people feel forced into a situation where they pay a premium for rent to live close to work. They have a high wage job, but pay such high rent that they remain trapped, having nothing to show for it. A $64,000 income and they barely scrape by from paycheck to paycheck. What if they bought an inexpensive house for the family in a small country town? Keep the fancy-schmancy high paying job in the city and pay off the house in less than a year while living in a camper parked alongside truckers at a travel station. Sound a little extreme? Not at all! A year of discomfort versus a lifetime of slave labor? I'll take the shortcut any time.

I had one marketable skill when I graduated from high school: I could start a fire with a bow and drill—basically rubbing two sticks together. At the age of twenty I was hired as an instructor to take troubled teens on backcountry expeditions. I earned $1,100 for each three-week outing, hiking around the desert with kids. Food was included free, even if it was only rice and lentils. The rent was free, since we each carried a wool blanket and poncho and slept on the ground. Soon my partner was leading these trips too, and our incomes grew with experience. We quit for summer, bought land, moved into a tent, and started building our dream home. That was in 1989.

With a combined income averaging $10,000 to $12,000 a year we lived simply and invested in building materials. Building the house more than doubled the value of our income. Avoiding interest on a home loan doubled our money again. Construction proceeded slowly throughout the process, due to a chronic lack of money. We moved into the house after the second summer with no doors, few windows, and no insulation in the roof. Winter stopped about three feet from the stove. That might sound extreme, but we saved at least $150,000 in interest payments by eliminating the need for a loan.

By camping out, investing in building materials, and avoiding mortgage interest, we squeezed $50,000 per year in benefits from our poverty level income. At the same time, we paid very little taxes because our wage income was so low. Utility bills were also low, since we designed the house for energy efficiency, aided by passive solar and wood heating. Not having a mortgage or other significant bills enabled us to later invest in solar panels to generate electricity and run the utility meter backwards, zeroing out our electrical consumption. We could afford this extravagance only because we had few other bills to pay.

Financial Freedom

Nearly everyone dreams of achieving financial freedom to do whatever they want. Most people run the treadmill without getting any closer. Many people scheme, innovate, and sacrifice decades towards the goal. Some people succeed financially. Few people achieve actual freedom.

Most great dreams require freedom, which is most reliably obtained by eliminating expenses. For example, many people dream of traveling

Building our home more than doubled the value of our income. Avoiding interest on a home loan doubled our money again.

the world, yet don't have the necessary time or money. Work only allows two or three weeks vacation per year, and travel is expensive. Paying monthly bills consumes most of the paycheck, requiring several years of savings to pay for one international vacation.

On the other hand, there is a subculture of people who don't have regular jobs, and they travel all over the world. These are mostly young people who are not ready to settle down. They work a few months, save money, buy a ticket, and travel. They camp or stay in inexpensive hostels. They do work trade or seek temporary employment at their destination, spending months instead of weeks in a foreign country. Many of my friends, even older people, don't want a career. They prefer to take part-time jobs and enjoy months of vacation every year.

My approach was different, yet ultimately enabled a similar level of freedom. My partner and I worked intermittently and invested everything in building the house. I racked up a lifetime total of eleven months of employment as measured by W-2 forms, supplemented by occasional jobs helping family members. My partner was employed longer, earning money to purchase building materials, while I stayed home to do actual construction. However, these were not full-time endeavors. We enjoyed a great deal of vacation, hiking, camping, adventuring, or hanging out with family. We traveled, mostly via backpacking into nearby mountains. I also invested time in writing articles and books. Not needing an income proved to be the most essential asset in launching a successful writing career and publishing business.

Starting a business is challenging, and 80% of all new companies fail within eighteen months. Successful businesses typically lose money for three years before turning a profit. A significant threat to any new business is the living expenses of the entrepreneur. Extracting $1,000 a month from the business to pay a home mortgage can quickly kill an otherwise promising business.

As an aspiring author, I earned about $1/hour for my time writing wilderness survival articles for newspapers and magazines. My writing career took many years to mature into a legitimate income. I would not have succeeded as an author and publisher if we had to pay rent. Nor could we have afforded to start a family or buy a nice canoe for our extended scenic paddling adventures.

If we paid rent or a mortgage, we would have been dependent on a regular income instead of our own resourcefulness. We would have been forced to take lower paying local jobs, forgoing opportunities for irregular short-term high-paying jobs. We would have spent time commuting to and from work each day, and we may have frittered away more funds just because we were in town and tired of working.

When you successfully eliminate mortgage payments, high-energy bills, and other similar limiting factors, then you will find that the world is a new and exciting place full of grand opportunities. You can be idealistic and optimistic because you have a unique freedom to pursue your dreams, whatever they might be. If you want to spend a season photographing polar bears in the arctic, then get a job for a few months to save the money and go. It doesn't take long to save up a pile of money when you have few other expenses. This is true financial freedom—or should we call it freedom from finances?

Admittedly, the path we took was not always easy, nor is it the solution to everyone's problems. For years, while struggling to launch my writing career, we often felt both immensely wealthy and desperately poor. Our house is the sort that people look at and exclaim, "Those people must be loaded!" Yet we rarely had enough spare change to go to the movies.

The point is simply to look for different solutions. Making more money is helpful, but not always something one can control. If you find yourself chanting the mantra, "I know I could break free if I could just make a little more money," then maybe it is time to look for other answers.

Transitions

How do you change your life situation from where you are? My partner and I had a pretty idyllic situation when we started out. No debts, no payments, no kids. Just the two of us and an old, yet reliable car. Other people I've talked to have big credit card debts, student loans, and dependents. These factors make it more challenging to pay down a mortgage and quit a job, yet also more worthwhile to really go for it.

The reward for the effort is directly proportional to the amount of change you make. Switching light bulbs, riding a bicycle to work, or eating weeds from the garden will make small, yet positive differences in your financial situation while also helping to make the world a slightly better place. However, if you want to make real change—to be out of debt and successfully unemployed—then you need to stack up multiple changes. Step outside the cycles of waste and create a whole new lifestyle, conserving energy, resources, money, and time wherever you possibly can. It is almost like creating a new identity—you as a person who is free from the treadmill of waste, free to do whatever you want for the rest of your life.

For example, a schoolteacher named John read an early edition of this book. He wrote to say how he was deeply in debt, but very inspired.

He moved out of his apartment into an old chicken house he renovated on a neighbor's property. That seemed a bit extreme, but it worked. Through three or four years of correspondence John went from being deeply in debt to having enough money in the bank to live for the next two years without working. More importantly, he had Time on his hands to pursue all of his Dreams. He was ultimately fired from his job, apparently because he left work without permission to audition for the reality TV show *Survivor*. He wasn't selected for the program, but didn't mind losing his job. Adventuring became a career. John traveled extensively, taught English in Korea, and accidentally developed a business selling desert-adapted worms in Las Vegas. Being free to do whatever he wanted, he reconnected after twenty years and joined me on a two-week adventure paddling the Tongue River in southeastern Montana. I hope to inspire many more people to get fired from their jobs!

I met another success story while on a business trip to sell books in Saint George, Utah. Being a thrifty guy, I drove around looking for a safe, quiet place where my son and I could sleep beside the car. We found a good spot early in the day and returned after dark. I was surprised to find several other campers there. Our neighbors were not in sleeping bags, but landless families living in motorhomes who drove out to park on state land each night after work. The family I camped near actually owned land farther away and were preparing to build their own home. For now they were minimizing expenses where they could and raising kids in a motorhome. They had a small commuter car, but basically they drove their house to work each day, successfully avoiding rent payments to save up for their own home.

I also met a couple in Texas who were living in an RV and volunteering at a state park through the southern winter. The woman was a musician needing quiet space and time to produce a new album. Her husband was a photographer. In exchange for rent, electricity, water, and Internet access, they did manual labor for the park. Manual labor and desert hiking provided a nice counterbalance to their creative endeavors. Having few expenses provided the essential freedom to follow their dreams and launch successful careers.

Where there is a will, there is always a way. The key to success is in being able to escape the job trap. Having large debts or being straddled with dependents makes the path to freedom more challenging, yet there is always a way if you commit to finding and achieving it. When you successfully eliminate expenses and the need for a regular income, then you will find clear sailing ahead and a freedom that you probably have not experienced in a long, long time.

"I too had woven a kind of basket of delicate texture... and instead of studying how to make it worth men's while to buy my baskets, I studied rather how to avoid the necessity of selling them."
—Henry David Thoreau,
Walden (1854)[112]

Prosperity through Conservation
Negadollars and Opportunity Cost

"A penny saved is a penny earned," mused Benjamin Franklin (1706–1790). Two centuries later, energy guru Amory Lovins brought similar thinking to electric utilities. Rising demand for energy in the 1970s seemed to necessitate more power plants, more coal extraction, more pollution, and more transmission lines. Energy experts foresaw energy trends escalating off the charts in the coming decades. Lovins, however, demonstrated in his book *Soft Energy Paths* that the economy could continue to expand without new electrical capacity simply through conservation. Improving building insulation, installing energy-efficient windows, and fine-tuning weather-stripping would conserve energy at less expense than the cost of producing it.[113] Think of it as an alternative means to increase the energy supply. Energy saved through conservation is effectively new energy that can be applied elsewhere without expanding production capacity.

Amory Lovins founded Rocky Mountain Institute in 1982 to advise utilities and governments in innovative ways to profit through conservation. By calculating and demonstrating that conservation is a viable and cost-effective means to increase the energy supply, Rocky Mountain Institute inspired enough energy savings to power several countries. *Soft Energy Paths* was a proposal more than a prediction, yet twenty years later the American economy had grown vastly larger while energy consumption barely changed. Lovins later coined the term "negawatt" to refer to energy produced through conservation.

Lovins applied similar thinking to water management. Cities with tight water supplies sought different options for expanding supplies, such as wells, pipelines, or dam construction projects. Lovins, however, demonstrated that it was more economical for cities to promote water conservation than to expand supply. Switching to low-flush toilets, for example, could conserve enough water to eliminate the need to build a new dam.

Gleaning inspiration from Lovins, I applied a similar conservation philosophy towards money management. Every dollar conserved was a dollar I need not earn, which could be called a "negadollar." For example, by doing my own basic car repairs, such as replacing the alternator, I conserved money and reduced my need for employment. Instead of working a 9 to 5 job, I was self-employed in my own "negajob," creatively finding ways to avoid the necessity of earning money.

Imagine being in charge of a dam, assigned to keep the reservoir full. What would you do if there were a leak? Would you plug the leak or find a new source of water to replace the loss? Most people would rather cure the problem than mask the symptoms. Yet, everyone does manage a reservoir of sorts, often bleakly empty as wealth gushes out numerous cracks in the dam. Like water, money can be invested to grow crops and nurture prosperity, but not if the supply is flooding away for rent, energy, food, and other expenses. Unfortunately, people respond by working harder to bring home more resources to throw behind the leaking dam.

A home is like a business, and the same basic rules apply to both. We have a gross income from work and a net income after all expenses are paid. Whether we earn $10,000 or $100,000 a year, most people find that their income and expenses are nearly identical, leaving little net profit to invest in hopes and dreams.

It is often assumed that there is one ladder to financial success and the only way to climb upwards is to make more income tomorrow than today. Rich or poor, everyone wants a higher raise or greater sales, as if a slightly higher income will solve all financial problems. Meanwhile, people neglect to ask what is at the top of the ladder or if there is a top. They strive to climb to the next rung on the ladder without asking how that rung is different or better than the present one. This conventional model of success is misleading.

In reality, there are many ladders of success. We can be financially successful with a little wealth or a lot. A person with little wealth may be at the top of a short ladder, while a person with vast wealth may be at the top of a taller ladder. Reaching the top has little to do with income. That is, more income does not necessarily bring us up a ladder, rather it brings us across to ladders that can be climbed higher. Net income is what's leftover after all necessary expenses are paid from one's gross income.

A person with high income may have a big house and many toys, yet that does not guarantee they are wealthy or secure. What would happen if they lost their job? What would happen if they failed to show up for work? Would the bank repossess everything and leave them on the street? A big income carry us to a tall ladder, yet it does not necessarily put us at the top.

On the other hand, a person with a modest income, even $10,000 to $20,000/year, can be at the top of their ladder if they have few expenses. I raised a family without much income, and I didn't have to live by the

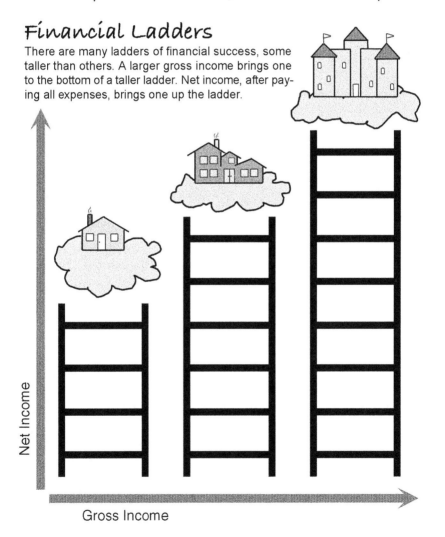

Financial Ladders

There are many ladders of financial success, some taller than others. A larger gross income brings one to the bottom of a taller ladder. Net income, after paying all expenses, brings one up the ladder.

Net Income

Gross Income

clock. I've been fortunate to choose how I spend my time. I've enjoyed a certain level of financial freedom, or freedom from finances, that allowed me to do what I want. I can enjoy being home or disappear on a camping adventure. I have enjoyed extended vacations from work without fear that my home will be repossessed or the power or phone will be shut off.

Eliminating expenses is simple logic, like insulating a house, yet we sometimes miss it in everyday life. Most people turn up the thermostat when the house is cold, but isn't it more sensible to plug leaks to keep available heat inside? Either option requires an expenditure of wealth and makes the house warm, yet one option eliminates the problem while the other only prolongs it.

Hunter-Gatherer Lottery

Farming is far more efficient than hunting and gathering, yet farmers work more. A farmer must grow a surplus to trade for farm equipment, housing, a car, movie subscriptions, and so many things that hunter-gatherer peoples had no use for and no means of producing. Consider then, what might happen if a person maintained an industrial level of production, yet only a hunter-gatherer level of consumption?

My strategy for financial success was to live cheaply and invest in buying land and building a home. Constructing an energy efficient house helped reduce energy bills. Eliminating expenses helped me secure a comfortable lifestyle at the level of an industrial culture with bills not much higher than those of a hunter-gatherer.

Thoreau applied a similar equation when he spent two years and two months conducting experiments into the "economy of living" at Walden Pond in the 1840s. Agriculture was based on farming with oxen and plows, with an efficiency of about 33 calories obtained for each calorie expended. Through intermittent employment, Thoreau earned wages equitable to the production capabilities of his culture, yet he maintained a hunter-gatherer level of consumption.

Conventional houses cost about $800 (a fifteen-year mortgage in the 1800s), yet Thoreau built a simple cabin for twenty-eight dollars, twelve and one half cents. He earned wages at a similar rate as his neighbors, yet had a more primitive lifestyle. With his little cabin, a simple diet, and almost no possessions, Thoreau could work six weeks per year to earn a living, plus additional time tending to home chores. That left him with forty-six weeks vacation each year "free and clear for study."[114]

Imagine our work year if we adopted a lifestyle similar to Thoreau's, yet maintained an industrial level of production (more than ten times as productive than in Thoreau's time). We would hardly have to work at all.

Granted, few people want to give up houses, telephones, electricity, and plumbing, among other things, to live a Spartan life as Thoreau did. Even he went back to a conventional life when he finished his living experiment. Nevertheless, this concept of relativity between economies can be very useful.

Consider a typical married couple saving money to buy a house or land. They might rent an apartment and pay the usual expenses for power, water, telephone, food, and so forth. They could spend 95% of their income on living expenses, sacrificing a dinner date and movie night to save the remaining 5% or less to eventually realize their dreams. Our approach was just the opposite, living on 5% while investing 95% in our dreams.

Similarly, Thoreau could have lived cheaply and worked all year to accumulate an investment surplus. He chose to work part time because that suited his goals. However, today's Mennonite and Hutterite colonies are highly successful because they maintain a minimalist level of consumption while working hard. They reinvest income in production, buying tools and accumulating land, occasionally splitting off to form new colonies. Their modest lifestyle enables them to thrive and expand while neighboring farms and ranches sell out or succumb to bankruptcy.

My partner and I also minimized consumption and allocated most income towards buying land and building a house. We lived on the trail while working, or with our parents when home. About 5% of our income went towards expenses, while the other 95% went into savings. We saved up almost $10,000 in one winter. Later, when we bought land, we moved into a tent while building our home.

Living in a tent or camper trailer is not for everyone, especially not for indefinite time periods. It is adventurous for a while, yet it is also nice to have insulation, heating, and plumbing. However, living as "hunter-gatherers" can be a temporary measure to rapidly store up capital in an advanced economy to achieve big dreams.

Anyone can get a jackrabbit-fast start by maintaining an industrial level of production while temporarily adopting a hunter-gatherer level of consumption. Looking back, it was very worthwhile to live simply. By the age of twenty-six, we built and paid for a very nice home on our five-acre homestead, gaining freedom to do whatever we wanted. At the age of 27, we adopted three kids and started our family, later having a fourth child. Raising a family increased our expenses, yet we still had freedom. Few people could survive on our income, yet we were able to cover music lessons for the kids and go on extended family vacations. With our house and land paid for and low power bills, we lived comfortably. Only a fraction of our income went towards required bills. The rest was available to spend as we chose. It was like winning the lottery every year!

Anyone can win the lottery and climb the ladders of financial success. It is a matter of plugging leaks that drain those winnings away. Net caloric income is the path to climb the ladder towards financial freedom.

A higher gross income is certainly helpful because there is more income for a potentially higher net profit. It is possible to live comfortably on very little, yet it is also nice to have the option of spending money. I like books, movies, and nice computers. A new fuel efficient car might be nice, as would an arboretum and an observatory! I especially enjoy traveling and not having to worry about money along the way. These dreams can be achieved via modest means, although admittedly easier with a greater income. With a gross annual income of $30,000 a family could spend $20,000 on living expenses and still net $10,000 a year as profit to spend on hopes and dreams.

Each of us has tremendous resources even if we earn very little. What would you do if I gave you ten or fifteen thousand dollars to spend? Would you go on a shopping spree? Chances are, you already have that much to spend every year. That is an amazing amount of money, especially considering that half the world's population lives on less than $2.50 per day.[115]

Opportunity Cost

Spending $15 on a movie takes away the opportunity to spend it on food, a smart phone, or real estate. Also lost is the opportunity to avoid working in the first place. Thus the true cost of every purchase is not measured in money, but in terms of opportunities forgone by making the purchase. In economic lingo this is called opportunity cost.

There are three types of opportunities: disposable, depreciable, and appreciable. Every consumer choice is an investment into one of the three categories. Each investment towards a specific gain costs the opportunity to invest in alternatives. In a nutshell the three opportunities can be described as follows:

1) Disposable. Spend a dollar and it is gone.
2) Depreciable. Keep a dollar when you spend it, yet it loses value.
3) Appreciable. Keep a dollar when you spend it, and it maintains or gains value.

Disposables: People spend most income on disposable purchases. Disposables are the black hole of finances where money goes in and never comes out. Included here are survival expenses such as rent, energy, food, telephone, and interest payments, as well as entertainment expenses, including movies, recreation, and travel vacations.

There is nothing wrong with spending money. However, most people don't understand and prioritize how they utilize their hard-earned dollars. For instance, a person drinking two 50¢ cans of pop each day spends $365 in one year. It is easy to fritter away hundreds of dollars here and there, yet most people would make different spending choices if they had the whole wad at once.

What would you do with $365? Would you buy 730 cans of pop? Or would you buy something more lasting? Presented this way, few people would choose to invest in soda pop. Yet, at the rate of a few dollars here and there, people make major investments in minor things every day.

Similarly, imagine spending $1,000 a month renting a nice apartment. Most people work hard to earn money every month. An apartment with half the rental cost may not be as luxurious, yet it would free up $500 a month, or $6,000/year to invest elsewhere. The savings could be spent on another disposable investment, such as a ritzy vacation, or perhaps a depreciable or appreciable investment, something that will bring benefits for years to come.

Surprisingly few people recognize that they are free to choose, and even fewer realize they can choose freedom. Starting at an early age, people are conditioned to believe they will seek a job and work until retirement. In this context, people fritter away income because they envision endless work. Money is spent to dispose of it, consumed before the next paycheck. People work without questioning why they do it, but work is optional. We are free to choose.

Depreciables: Depreciable investments include gadgets such as cars, smart phones, entertainment centers, recreational equipment, appliances, clothes, and furniture. They depreciate dramatically at the moment of purchase and continue depreciating all the way to the landfill or recycling center. People spend most of their remaining surplus money on depreciables after covering disposable purchases.

However, investments in things or gadgets, if truly desired, are best acquired secondhand, after initial depreciation. A new car can cost $25,000 or more. Monthly payments with interest may raise the cost by half again. By the time a new car is completely paid for, it might be scratched, dented, worn, and in dire need of major repairs, potentially no better than the jalopy you are driving now. Many people continuously upgrade, making car payments for decades.

Personally, I really like new cars. Whenever I'm in the market for a new vehicle, I browse the latest offerings for fuel efficiency or electric range and maneuverability on rural roads. I can see myself in a new car. On the other hand, for the cost of a new car, I could travel the world, spending an entire year on vacation. Or I could invest in real estate, buying land for Green University® LLC and Outdoor Wilderness Living School, LLC (OWLS). $25K wouldn't buy a whole property, but a good portion of a small acreage. There are many possibilities for a large sum of cash that would otherwise be lost if the money were merely spent on a new car.

In addition, taxes and insurance cost more on a new vehicle. And living in a rural area, I would probably load dumpster treasures, firewood, strawbales, and rocks in the car within a month or two. For that, I'm glad to drive a car that isn't excessively nice. My current car is a recently purchased, very nice twelve-year-old Subaru. It is a great adventure car. I put a lot of miles on it. I can load two canoes on top and five more on the trailer, plus gear and passengers. It is old enough to be permanently licensed in Montana, so that I don't have to pay vehicle registration ever again. Insurance costs are low. I'll invest the savings in more adventures.

Imagine what your existing car might look and run like if you invested even a quarter of the money saved into repairs instead of buying a new car. Fixing an existing car can be the best option of all, provided it is not a gas-guzzler or a lemon. If you really want a new car, consider saving money until you can pay cash and avoid interest payments.

With a steady job, one can budget a continuous, albeit non-growing money supply to support these buying choices. However, disposable and depreciable investments are inherently money-losers, so it makes sense to minimize such expenses in favor of long-term investments.

Appreciables: Appreciable investments are true investments that bring continued future dividends. Invest in growing assets to have more income to purchase depreciables and disposables later. Investment opportunities could include a new business, interest bearing accounts such as stocks or bonds, investments in eliminating expenses or a higher education.

Unfortunately, college education is oriented towards teaching one how to get a job, as opposed to learning how to not need a job. Moreover, people often graduate with expensive degrees, yet cannot find employment in their chosen field. A higher education is most valuable if self-driven and focused on your dream endeavors.

Alternately, investing in stocks, bonds, or other interest accounts often yield steady growth. Unfortunately, many investment opportunities yield profits only slightly greater than the rate at which inflation devalues the investment. Some people invest heavily in the stock market then lose everything when the market temporarily crashes. Riding through lean times is better than cashing out at the bottom. Yet, anyone with money in the stock market and a mortgage on the home is not very secure. A faltering economy can impact employment income and market investments, potentially leading to home foreclosure. The investor may be forced to withdraw funds from the market when stocks are lowest in order to cover mortgage payments and other survival expenses until new employment can be found.

It is far safer to invest in eliminating expenses, so that it doesn't matter what happens to the stock market and economy. Owning a home mortgage free is the greatest financial security. Not having a utility bill or other significant monthly expenses is also liberating. Eliminating monthly bills is the true do-nothing approach to real wealth. Eliminate your expenses and gain freedom to do whatever you want.

One couple I know bought "literally the cheapest house" they could find in a college town. Travis worked full time as an artist, while Linda went to school. Renovating the house was an intermittent hobby. Nine years later they sold the house, paid off all debts, and had enough money to buy a 7-acre farmstead. This time, the house was so run down that the seller planned to bulldoze it before selling the property. He offered a $10,000 discount for accepting the house intact. That was perfect for Travis and Linda. They moved into the house debt-free to enjoy country life with their children.

Having few bills enabled Travis to reduce his work hours, gaining more time to enjoy fatherhood and farming. They grow a big garden, produce their own dairy products, and raise their own meat and eggs. Their primary ambition is to spend quality time with their children and to live a good, happy life while learning to be more self-sufficient. They are gradually renovating the old house with mostly free, salvaged building materials.

Financial Planning

Although this book is about personal finance, we haven't discussed stringent savings plans, accounting, or budgeting. As I see it, we eventually spend every dollar we earn. Being financially successful isn't necessarily about saving money; it is about spending it effectively. By itself, money has no value; it only becomes valuable when we spend it. The key to financial success isn't to save a mattress full of money, but to spend it on investments that achieve personal goals.

Knowing what you want is thus the most vital step on the path to success. Budgeting is hardly required when intensely focused on a particular goal or vision.

You will automatically find resources to make your dream into reality. The strategies listed here are more like icing on the cake to facilitate getting from here to there. I speak from experience. I don't have a master in business administration (MBA), and I've never written a budget. Even when building a house, I didn't need to estimate and price every board and nail. Instead, I work to keep costs as low as possible, which is doable without a budget. Taking time to do the math only adds more work.

The first year with my partner was the only time we accumulated savings. We saved money until we married and bought land. After that, we invested our income directly into building materials. We spent money on our dream before we could spend it anywhere else. You may discover a similar experience, where the only time it is necessary to save money is for a short period to build up financial capital to initiate a larger investment. There are many ways to do that.

For example, as a two-soda-per-day person, you decide to gain $365 additional capital this year for a special investment. You substitute tap water for soda pop, saving $1 per day. Unfortunately, that dollar quickly disappears if it isn't consistently set aside. Put the dollar in a jar and write your dream on the label. The jar might fill up faster than expected. This savings strategy is helpful to gain the financial leverage needed for smaller dreams, such as a new canoe.

There are many different savings schemes to accumulate a modest nest egg. For Marie C. Franklin, it was the impulse to start saving $5 bills. She and her husband were financially stressed supporting two daughters in private colleges, and it seemed like they could never get ahead. However, Marie had the inspiration to put $5 away into savings without causing undo stress, whenever she received $5 bills as change. She spent cash for groceries and other common expenses and saved every $5 bill. After accumulating $100, the money went into a special account. After accumulating $1,000 in the account, she invested it in a Certificate of Deposit. Playing into the game, she preferred paying cash, thus accumulating more $5 bills. In twelve years she diverted $36,000 into savings and now shares her financial techniques on her 'savemoneyfastwithfives' blog.[116]

Big dreams, such as a house, business, or new car, requires more aggressive savings strategies to accumulate sufficient financial capital. Consider placing a finite limit on overall spending. In *Holistic Management* Allan Savory outlined an interesting budgeting procedure, which is equally applicable to a home or a business. Determine how much you expect to earn this year; that is your gross income. Now divide that amount in half. The leftover amount is your ceiling, so plan a budget to meet all expenses on that amount of money. This discipline insures 50% profitability, ensuring leftover profit at the end of the year.[117] Whether you are managing a home or business, 50% profitability is really huge!

Attempting to survive on half the accustomed income may seem entirely impossible and dire. Yet, with pencil and paper, plus a strong desire to achieve a Dream, you may be surprised at how quickly a household or business can generate a sizeable nest egg.

For those who are heavily indebt, half of all income may not be enough to cover required expenses, such as a mortgage, car payment, school loans, and extensive credit card balances, not to mention groceries or anything fun. In this case, try subtracting required payments from the anticipated income then divide the remainder in half to cover all other expenses. This will not yield 50% profitability, but in any case, planning for some profitability, even 10%, is better than none.

These strategies can work well, especially if one enjoys budgeting. However, if you are adverse to accounting, then consider trying the opposite approach. Try putting a percentage away into a special dreams account *before* paying other expenses. The budget struggle no longer requires pencil and paper work, but day-to-day resourcefulness through self-imposed necessity. It works.

It is important to earmark your newfound profitability for an intended purpose, such as separating it into its own account, or doubling the amount paid on a mortgage each month. For example, I ratcheted up the mortgage payments on our brick and mortar bookstore as high as possible every month, draining the bank account before we could fritter money away elsewhere. Setting money aside ensures that your financial capital is there when you need it, and not just a figment of your imagination and calculator. Use the money to help realize all of your dreams.

"I was more independent than any farmer in Concord, for I was not anchored to a house or farm, but could follow the bent of my genius, which is a very crooked one, every moment. Beside being better off than they already, if my house had burned or my crops had failed, I should have been nearly as well off as before."

—Henry David Thoreau,
Walden (1854)[118]

Make it Happen
Exit Ramp Ahead

Our ancestors were allowed to exist free of charge. Travel back in time far enough in any culture, and there was a time when people could freely sit, stand, camp, or build a shelter pretty much anywhere and call it home. One of the grim realities of the modern world is that we must lease or purchase a place to exist. Rent an apartment, and it is yours only as long as you pay monthly rent and the landlord doesn't sell the property or raise rates beyond your means. Buy a house on loan, and it belongs to you only if you follow through with monthly payments to the bank for the next twenty or thirty years.

Alternatively, forgo a house or apartment and live in a recreational vehicle instead, and drive around looking for a place to park. Nightly fees in RV campgrounds cost almost as much as a night in a hotel. State and federal campgrounds cost less, but are far from free, and one is required to move every fourteen days or so. Ditto for tent camping. There are millions of acres of public land available for free camping, but nowhere that you can legally stay for more than a couple weeks. Living on the run is okay for a time, maybe for years, but at some point, it is nice to stake a claim, have a roof overhead, and own the right to hang your hat for as long as you please.

We can complain that life is unfair or we can work with the situation we have. Anyone is capable of staking a claim and securing a permanent, legal place to exist, and there is no need to mortgage one's soul to the banker to achieve it.

Escaping the Mortgage Trap

Mortgage payments are the biggest monthly and yearly expense for most people and businesses, typically consuming one-third of a person's income. It is a major expense that returns month after month, year after year, sometimes all the way to the grave. Permanently reduce or eliminate this expense and you have really accomplished something, gaining a 30% budget surplus every month thereafter.

Eliminating mortgage payments is a rewarding challenge, and there are many routes towards that end. The most important requirement is to buy rather than rent. Renting pays someone else's mortgage, and your money is lost forever. To keep your income it is essential to buy your own place.

Unfortunately, buying doesn't always seem like a great bargain either. People are often shocked to discover after many years of mortgage payments that they have very little equity. To reiterate, consider a $100,000 loan at 5% interest over 30 years. The monthly payments would be $537, yet only $120 from the first payment goes towards principal. The other $417 is lost to interest. This ratio changes slowly over time so that more money goes towards principal and less towards interest. Ten years of mortgage payments adds up to $64,440, yet only $18,856 goes towards principal, leaving $81,144 due on the loan. The black hole of interest payments consumes $45,584, lost and gone forever. After thirty years, the $100,000 loan is completely paid off, along with $93,256 in interest payments, nearly doubling the cost of the home. That isn't much of a deal!

There are many pathways to avoid a home mortgage altogether. As discussed earlier, one can live ultra-cheaply while saving 95% of every paycheck to pay cash for a home. I've met many people who live this way already. They go to Alaska to work on a fishing boat, or they get a temporary high-paying job in the city and live in a shared apartment. One young couple was hired as a team to drive semi-trucks. They expected to rake in $30,000 each in a single year. Living on the road and sleeping in the truck, they would have only modest living expenses. Their plan was to save money for a couple years and then "retire." Their dream was to build a cabin in the country and enjoy hunting and fishing.

It helps to buy a low-cost home where real estate prices are artificially low. I would choose a rural area, yet there are also many cities with ultra-low housing prices. In Detroit, Michigan, for example, housing prices crashed after automobile factory jobs relocated outside the country and residents abandoned the city looking for work. Homes were foreclosed upon and offered for sale for a pittance, often $1,000 or less. Granted, many homes needed $30,000+ in renovations to make them habitable, but that is still a grand bargain. Many artists moved into Detroit, renovating old homes on the cheap. Other homes were bulldozed away, leaving whole city blocks open for community gardening.

Most states or regions have at least some towns or cities with low-cost real estate. There are even towns in Italy with historic stone houses for sale for $1 for anyone willing to "homestead" there. Invest $25,000 to fix up a house, and you have a bargain deal in a quaint Italian town. Don't expect to find a job locally anywhere real estate is cheap, but you can travel elsewhere to earn the cash. Purchase the house, put a little money aside, and take time out to enjoy life. In addition to homes, many commercial businesses have apartments in back or upstairs, getting a two-for-one deal as a house and potential income.

For those unwilling to move away in search of cheap real estate, or unwilling to live homeless while saving money, there are other options to expedite paying down a mortgage. As mentioned earlier, one approach is to trade down for a smaller house, then make larger monthly payments to rapidly build equity while minimizing losses on interest payments. Pay off a small home first. Then sell it and reinvest the equity in a larger home if still desired. Even better, pay off the small home, then accumulate enough savings to pay cash on a larger home.

For anyone unwilling or unable to sell out from their current house and mortgage, there are good alternatives to accelerate payments and finish the mortgage sooner, saving tens of thousands in interest payments in the process:

Bi-Weekly Payments: Rather than making 12 monthly mortgage payments, arrange to make bi-weekly payments, paying half the monthly amount every other week. This system works well if you receive a paycheck every other week. There are 52 weeks or 26 biweekly periods in a year, resulting in the equivalent of 13 monthly payments. That extra payment each year saves $17,767 in interest over the life of a $100,000 loan, paying off the balance five years early.

Double Principal Payments: Making two principal payments each month can cut mortgage time in half and save oodles in avoided interest payments. Using our hypothetical loan, the first $537 payment is mostly eaten by interest, with only $120 going towards principal. The second month's principal payment is slightly better at $121. Add that to the first payment, paying $241 towards principal out of a total of $658 for the month. Use an amortization calculator online to determine the principal payments and combine two months principal every month to pay off the mortgage in half the time.

Making double principal payments pays off a 30-year loan in 15 years, and in this example, you would save tens of thousands of dollars in interest. Extra payments are initially fairly low, but steadily grow over time, presumably as you earn more money, thus making it easier to make larger payments. More importantly, the schedule is non-binding. The $537 payment is required each month, while the rest is voluntary, so funds can be utilized elsewhere in an emergency.

Flat-Rate Extra Payments: Make an extra principal payment of any amount for the life of the loan. Pay an extra $100 per month in our loan example, and save eight years, eight months, and $30,581 in avoided interest. Higher payments equal greater savings.

Shorten the Loan: Instead of a 30-year loan, apply for a 20-year or even a 15-year loan. Converting our sample loan to 20 years increases the monthly payment from $537 to $660, saving ten years and $34,867 in avoided interest payments. Converting it to a 15-year loan increases the monthly payment to $791 and saves $50,913 in avoided interest. Shorter loan terms demand a rigorous payment schedule, which is beneficial for ensuring fiscal discipline, yet also more risky if an emergency or job disruption impacts the ability to maintain high payments.

Any accelerated payment strategy will shorten a mortgage and save money on interest payments. After building our own home without a mortgage, we bought an old-fashioned general store and contract post office in a nearby town for our growing book business. We were previously selling books exclusively online out of our home.

Not having a home mortgage or rent payment gave us the financial stability we needed to purchase the business, yet by doing so, we essentially bought a mortgage and a job. We were unaccustomed to working full time jobs, yet created a situation where work was necessary to make monthly payments.

We purchased the business for $180,000 with $30,000 down, making mortgage payments on the balance. We started with the minimum due then slowly increased payments to the best of our ability. I added $25 to our monthly payments, then ratcheted that up to $50, $75, $100, increasing by $25 each month until we were paying an extra $1,000/month on the mortgage. We could afford to channel that much income towards the business loan because we owned our home mortgage free and had already installed solar panels to generate electricity. We had few expenses of our own, so we channeled our resources into quickly paying down the business mortgage.

The property was large enough that we built a passive solar stone house beside the store, working with recycled materials and paying cash as we went. The home was originally envisioned as a teaching facility and student housing. However, my partner and I split up after twenty years of marriage, so she kept the bookstore and moved into the new stone house. I kept my publishing business and our original home. We were very fortunate that we owned two houses and two businesses, since neither of us had the means to buy out the other.

The best strategy to escape the mortgage trap is whichever method works for your circumstances. A system as simple as making a once-a-year extra payment from your tax refund can seriously whittle down a mortgage. Some people will take the shortest route, saving money, buying cheap, and avoiding interest payments altogether. Others will take a longer route, making additional payments where possible. Either path leads to the same end goal. With the mortgage paid off, you can pay yourself each month thereafter, instead of the bank. Own your home without a mortgage and you own a place to exist, giving you unparalleled freedom to decide what to do with the rest of your life.

Likewise for other monthly expenses. Imagine having no electrical bill, no car payment, no student loans, and no carryover balance on a credit card. Achieving freedom from these expenses provides a unique level of prosperity, the freedom to invest time and money anyway you choose.

Zeroing Out the Power Bill

Household energy costs are typically vastly smaller than rent or mortgage payments, yet they add up over time. Electricity, natural gas, propane, firewood; whatever combination warms, cools, and powers your home, the bills keep coming in. I'm always astonished when I hear what other people pay for energy, $100 a month, $200 a month, sometimes much more, especially in the frigid depths of winter. Having paid nominal utility bills from the start, I cannot imagine how anyone could afford the disposable outlay each month. A little creativity goes a long way toward shaving off high utility bills, leaving cash for higher pursuits.

Household heating typically accounts for the biggest portion of the energy bill. Electric radiant heat is especially expensive because two-thirds of the energy value is lost when coal or gas is burned to produce electricity, and more is lost in transmission over the grid. Switching to a ground source heat pump, which functions much like a refrigerator, is a more efficient use of electricity, but also expensive to install, so the payback period for the investment may take many years. Switching from electric to gas heat can also be a good way to reduce energy costs, or better yet, install a wood stove and cut your own firewood to become your own energy provider. Even in urban environments there is a great deal of dead wood from tree trimmings and scrap lumber from construction projects that can be readily acquired at little or no cost.

My community disposes of enough wood waste to potentially heat every home in town. Strangely, many people fell cottonwood trees and cut the wood into firewood lengths, so it is manageable to load it in a truck and unload it at the dump. They use more gas and time and labor to drive up in the mountains to cut Douglas fir or pine. Granted, cottonwood has less fuel value than the other woods and produces lots of ash, but it burns great in a fireplace and easily holds a fire through the night. I obtain the majority of my heater wood for free, pre-cut to size, all for the mere labor of loading it in my truck and hauling it home.

I also have a wood cookstove, which isn't a particularly fuel-efficient way to cook, though I like it anyway. My grandmother cooked on a wood stove, and I grew up around it. The wood cookstove is a handy waste-to-energy incineration system, converting any unrecycled scrap of paper, cardboard, or wood into useful energy for cooking food and heating the house.

Collecting free firewood.

Whatever fuel source you use, even self-cut firewood, it is sensible to continually upgrade and fine-tune household energy efficiency. Many improvements can be made at little or no cost. For example, beside the bookstore we bought, we dismantled and recycled a mobile home to make way for building the stone house. Mobile homes don't have much insulation, yet all the clean fiberglass insulation from the walls, roof, and floor added up to quite a pile. The bookstore only had about four inches of loose vermiculate insulation in the attic, so we added eight inches of fiberglass insulation for a total of twelve inches, a vast improvement at zero cost.

My original house, insulated with 10-inch fiberglass batts in the ceiling, was inexpensive to build, yet not as warm as I'd hoped for, so I am re-insulating the roof in sections. Friends and I unscrewed the steel roof over one-third of the house, and removed the fiberglass batts, which I traded to a neighbor for bales of hay for my horse. Having more money at this time in my life, I hired an insulation contractor to spray high density foam insulation in the roof. Six inches is considered good and seven inches top notch, but we filled the entire 10-inch cavity, partly to eliminate any potential mouse or rat habitat. My retirement goal is to make the house so energy efficient that I won't have to light a fire every morning when I'm an old man.

One woman I met asked some advice about her home. It was built with structural insulation panels (SIPs), making it very well-insulated—except for a 2-inch gap at the top of the walls that didn't match up with the roof. She and her husband spent $600/month to heat the house, and they were still cold, plus they had a horrible mouse problem. The contractor-built house had some major oversights, which is shockingly common in house construction. The solution was easy enough. Spend a couple hundred dollars on a bulk can of expanding foam sealant to fill the gap, instantly eliminating the mouse problem as well as drastically reducing the home-heating bill.

There are many other ways to improve energy efficiency in a house, such as installing better windows or adding quilted window curtains or applying a plastic film during winter months. Caulking and weather-stripping to seal leaks around windows and doors is also essential. Collect passive solar heat to the greatest extent possible, such as by adding a hot air collector or an attached greenhouse. See my book *Living Homes* for a complete discussion on the principles of energy efficiency and how to economically build or retrofit a home. No matter how efficient a home, there is always something that can be done to improve it.

The water heater is typically the next big expense in the home energy bill. Adding an extra layer of insulation to the tank is one of the easiest, cheapest steps to save energy. Adding a solar water preheating system is a bigger investment, but definitely pays for itself. I don't need a gas or electric water heater, since my water is heated entirely via solar and wood. The two systems compliment each other beautifully. The solar water heater provides free scalding hot water in summer. Pipes in the cookstove thermosiphon to a tank, producing free scalding hot water in winter.

Installing efficient light bulbs and appliances also helps trim the utility bill. Light emitting diode (LED) lights use about one-fourth as much energy as incandescent bulbs. Seek the most energy efficient appliances when replacing or upgrading refrigerators, washing machines, dishwashers, etc. Also carefully consider where to place the appliances. A spare freezer is great for storing surplus food, but consider putting it in a cold garage, rather than in a warm house, and make sure it isn't in a place where the sun will shine directly on it.

The primary reasons I was able to afford to install solar panels to generate electricity and run the meter backwards were a) we had no home mortgage to pay, and b) I trimmed the electric bill so low that it wasn't excessively expensive to install enough capacity to generate the rest. My solar panels slowly but steadily run the meter backwards when the sun shines, yet the system is grid-tied so I can draw as much juice as needed without the hassle of dealing with batteries.

I don't pay for electricity unless I use more than I produce in a year. I pay a $5 monthly meter fee for the privilege of being connected to the grid. It's a great deal. Opening the monthly power bill never gets old. It is still a thrill to get a bill that says I've used zero electricity. Trimming a large utility bill saves money every month for life. Conserving energy is also great for the environment.

Water is Life

Water is often treated like air, something we take for granted because it is usually available there and often free, or nearly so. However, water is increasingly scarce relative to the number of people in the world. Many cities already dictate water conservation policies, often through restrictive landscaping guidelines and high water bills to incentivize miserly water consumption.

My grandmother taught me the basics of resource conservation every time she made mashed potatoes. She boiled the potatoes in water then poured the water off into a pitcher while she mashed the potatoes. After the potato water cooled, she watered her houseplants with the nutrient-rich solution. Waste nothing. Recycle everything. It's that simple.

My house is somewhat unique in that I have a natural spring and gravity-fed water, with plastic pipe carrying the water downhill to my home without need for a well, pump, or electricity. The supply is adequate, but low pressure and limited to about 1,000 gallons per day, which must run my house and my entire five-acre homestead. I rely on some greywater, plus rainwater collection off the roof, and extensive use of automatic timers, hoses, and drip hoses to water hundreds of trees and shrubs. My lawn is seasonal, because there isn't enough water to keep it alive in mid-summer. I only need to mow the grass two or three times per year.

Water is especially scarce in hot, arid regions, and I'm always shocked to drive by mile after mile of half-insulated mobile or modular homes plopped down in the open desert with no shade whatsoever to protect either the house or the yard from the blistering summer sun. It's not so hard to plant a tree, and every house has options for landscaping water.

During a drought in California, my father replumbed the shower so that the bathwater came out a hose into the yard, rather than going down the drain. That wastewater effectively watered several trees along one side of the house. This lightly-used water, known as greywater, includes any secondhand water from a house except toilet water. Any house can be replumbed to optimize the use of the greywater or to capture rainwater from the roof to extend the watering supply. Read the book *Create an Oasis with Greywater* to turn any yard into a veritable garden of fruit trees, vegetables, and energy-conserving shade for the house.[119]

Equally important, water conservation can also conserve energy. Installing a low-flow showerhead reduces water consumption with every shower, but most importantly conserves hot water, greatly reducing energy demands for the water heater. Similarly, front-loading washing machines use less hot water than top-loading machines. Optionally, try washing laundry with cold water. My solar and wood heated water system produces plenty of hot water for showers and dishes, but not quite enough for laundry too, so I do most laundry with cold water, and it works just fine.

Learning to conserve water may or may not save a lot of money, but it teaches a person to think differently about resources, to conserve and re-use everything. Any money saved on water will likely be matched many times over by applying resource conservation to all aspects of life.

Free Food

A typical couple spends $7,500 per year on groceries.[120] How long does it take to earn that money at a job? How much vacation time could you take if you reduced food expenses by $5,000 a year? Alternately, how much faster could you pay off a mortgage by diverting $5,000 from the kitchen to the bank? Reducing food expenses can be surprisingly easy and profitable for the time invested, and often healthier too. Less food from the grocery store also translates to less agrichemical impact on the planet, less waste, and less packaging trash.

Mountains of Meat: I'm always shocked at how expensive meat is at the grocery store and incredulous that other people somehow pay for it week after week. Although I'm not a hunter myself, I grew up around hunters, and in Montana it isn't uncommon for each member of a family to draw multiple deer and elk tags, accumulating sufficient meat during the fall hunting season to last through the year, plus extra to share. Hunting is a viable means to fill the freezer, and many states allow hunting of some species all year long. In Hawaii, for example, pigs and goats are invasive, and hunting is encouraged to help control their numbers. Imagine being able to fill the freezer with free wild pork!

Hunting is not always free, however, since travel expenses, a gun, and a hunting license are necessary. Many hunters extend "necessary" to include specialized hunting clothes, a new pickup truck, an ATV, a new freezer, and sometimes a private-land access fee that can range into the hundreds or thousands of dollars. Anyone who spends that kind of cash for the hunt is unlikely to do the butchering themselves, so they drop their animal off at a wild game processor and pay a hefty fee to have the meat cut and wrapped. The end product is healthy, organic, wild meat, but the cost may be $100 per pound when factoring in payments on a new truck and gear.

Alternatively, I pick up fresh wild meat free on the side of the highway. Montana and many other states legalized use of roadkill game. Having processed many such deer, I can gut, skin, butcher, and bag a deer in less than three hours without careless waste. Big meaty chunks are cut into steaks. Bones are separated at the joints. Meaty bones are saved as roasts. Bones with scraps of meat or sinewy meat are saved as soup and stew bones. Ribs are cut into sections for spare ribs. Everything is packaged in secondhand plastic bags, such as bread bags, labeled with a permanent marker, and put in the freezer. Read *Participating in Nature* or *Foraging the Mountain West* for complete step-by-step butchering instructions.

Another potential source of free meat is the wild game processors themselves. Green University® LLC students skin deer for game processors in exchange for the hides for tanning and also bring back loads of

In many states it is legal to pick up roadkill game, saving hundreds of dollars per year on meat purchases.

scrap meat. Game processors often have whole rows of garbage cans or a construction dumpster for waste. Our crew brings back carloads of meaty ribs and bones then trim off the bits and pieces. Lacking freezer space, my friends Kris and Bartle canned 400 quarts of venison one autumn, potentially a two-year meat supply, all for free without buying a hunting license or firing a shot.

My brother established a separate trade with the game processor, gifting honey from his hives in exchange for buckets of meat trimmings, bits and pieces that were perfect for grinding into hamburger.

After all the effort to hunt and butcher deer and elk, it is shocking to see hunters toss out all of last year's meat at the start of each new hunting season. It is not uncommon to find an entire box of frozen packaged venison, elk stakes, moose, sausage, and trout set beside the community dumpster free for the taking.

Free wild meat accounts for most of my protein, although I do buy meat from the store for variation. One local grocery store started offering half price meat that reached its sell-by date, which makes it reasonably affordable. As I see it, buying the meat saves it from going into the dumpster, which is a win for the planet, as opposed to buying the same meat at full retail before the sell-by date, when the purchase directly supports industrial agriculture. I've also salvaged hundreds of pounds of meat from numerous grocery store dumpsters. It's normal for red beef to turn brownish, as happens in the home fridge. It is obscene just how much perfectly good food gets thrown away.

Dumpster Diving: Digging food out of dumpsters sounds desper-ate, not something anyone would choose to do if they had other means. Yet, resourceful people are increasingly turning to dumpster diving as a legitimate way to fill the larder while saving big money and reducing their impact on the planet.

Food doesn't magically spoil on the sell-by date printed on the label. Most grocery stores dispose of hundreds or thousands of dollars of perfectly good food every week. If it is too ripe to eat, it probably turned that way in the dumpster itself. Undated foods like vegetables are disposed of for minor blemishes. For example, if there is one bad orange in a bag, the store will throw away the entire bag.

Unfortunately, many grocery stores heave the goods into oversize trash compactors or locked dumpsters, but look around and you will learn to find rich dumpsters, as detailed in *Foraging the Mountain West*.

The biggest challenge to dumpster diving is getting over that fear of being seen and recognized. I don't know why that should bother me personally, since I write about dumpster diving and post photos online, but still, I prefer dumpster diving outside of the normal zone where people are likely to recognize me. I especially enjoy dumpster diving as a shared experience—something to do with friends, or as an alternative date—let's go to town for a movie and dumpster diving. My favorite time to dumpster dive is when traveling, doing it for sport to contribute to the adventure, while reducing travel expenses to enable longer vacations at lower cost.

Dumpster diving is hit-and-miss, sometimes yielding nothing, sometimes hundreds of dollars of free food from a single dumpster: cheese, yogurt, avocados, hamburger, milk, eggs, juice, sausage, cheese-cakes, pies, cookies, you name it. I've also rescued loads of fresh salmon, halibut, swordfish, and tilapia that were tossed simply because they didn't sell that day. On the other hand, it is also easy to bring home a trunk full of cakes and cookies and binge on sweets, making dumpster diving less than optimal for healthy living. As with shopping, some restraint is required.

Dumpstering behind some restaurants can also be worthwhile. For example, my impression is that some national pizza chains seem to hire one employee who's full-time job is to cook pizzas, box them, and throw them in the dumpster. It is not uncommon to find dozens of whole boxed pizzas. I often enjoy a slice or two and feed the rest to my chickens.

If you can build up courage to try dumpster diving, you will quickly see how obscene the food waste is in our country. We employ thousands of people to grow, package, and transport food to ultimately dispose of it in a landfill. Every grocery store seems to employ someone whose sole job is to bake cakes and donuts, frost them, and dump them in the garbage. Dumpster diving helps reduce personal impact on the planet while saving money to potentially facilitate quitting a job.

Gleaning: If there are farm fields in the region, there is likely free or nearly free food that can be obtained for gleaning. For example, there are potato fields near my home where potatoes can be gathered for free after the farm equipment is done mechanically harvesting and processing the mass crop. It doesn't hurt to ask. Likewise, any place shipping open-topped trucks of vegetables is likely leaving a trail of food for some distance along the highway. I've picked up potatoes and sugar beets off the side of the road in season. My favorite is the Walla Walla sweet onions that sometimes litter the side of the roads for hundreds of miles from farm fields in Washington.

Look for smaller crops too, such as an unpicked fruit tree in a yard down the street. Sadly, many people prefer to buy apples pre-bagged in the store than to pick the fresher, tastier, unwaxed apples growing in their own yard. They'll pay money to buy apples, then pay a neighborhood kid for the chore of raking up nuisance apples rotting into the lawn.

Harvesting free fruit is another of my favorite vacation adventures. We regularly pick gallons of blackberries, apricots, and plums in Idaho, Oregon, or Washington, plus oranges, lemons, and grapefruit in Arizona, dates in California, and most recently, pecans in Texas. Fruit can be processed and canned along the way with a propane stove and pressure canner, or hurried home to freeze or distribute among friends and neighbors.

Gardening and Foraging: Growing a garden is another great way to obtain healthy produce while saving big dollars. Any small patch of ground or even a flowerpot has potential to be converted into a vegetable garden to grow salad greens, tomatoes, herbs, and vegetables. I plant a garden every year although I travel so much that gardening turns into foraging. Most garden weeds are as edible and as tasty as garden greens, so I eat a few vegetables and a lot of weeds. A greenhouse attached to my home also provides a source of greens all winter long. If I'm home for the winter then I'll grow sprouts in jars for supplementary greens. Every little step towards trimming the food bill frees up more funds to pay down a mortgage, invest in solar panels, take a vacation, or quit work and live off the saved surplus.

<u>Food Stamps and the Food Bank</u>: As a successful author and publisher, it would be unethical for me to seek hand-outs from the food bank or to apply for food stamps to spend at a grocery store. However, unemployed students at Green University® LLC and other colleges often utilize these programs.

Some people would argue that our young people should work hard and contribute to society, rather than expect handouts. However, as we've seen, most jobs are totally unnecessary, functioning merely to dispose of wealth rather than create wealth. Instead of being tied to a dead-end job working as a bouncer at a night club or a clerk at a convenience store, I would rather see our young people supported by food stamps while studying and learning essential life skills to follow their dreams and find a greener path that keeps them successfully unemployed and ultimately self-sufficient for life.

Although I've never been to the food bank myself, a local senior used to drive to town and bring back food bank items to distribute locally, unloading milk, bread, and pastries throughout the community. The food was appreciated when we had small children and little money.

Nowadays, my students make regular trips to the food bank. As is true throughout society, some food bank locations suffer from excessive abundance. There is demand for canned goods, and I've donated to the food bank myself. However, perishable items provided by farms and grocery stores sometimes overwhelm the local food bank, so much that the students sometimes have to tie the car trunk closed to avoid losing it on the highway. They bring back a carload of fruits and vegetables and spend days eating, canning, and/or drying the goods to prevent loss to spoilage.

Ironically, one of the best dumpsters to check is the food bank itself, where excess abundance must be disposed of because there is not enough demand to take it all. Keep in mind that the supply and demand may vary significantly from one food bank to another. Avoid taking food that may be genuinely needed by other people.

In addition to the food bank, some grocery stores donate bread to various thrift stores. At one local store, for example, customers are allowed to take two loaves of free bread. Even that trims a few dollars off the food bill. Unfortunately, free is not free enough, and sometimes they are plagued by excessive abundance. I've brought home an entire carload of bread for my chickens because the racks were full and more bread was on the way. I use what I need and give the rest to my chickens, saving the plastic bags for meat processing, thereby avoiding the need to buy bags or wrapping paper.

What can you do to trim your food bill this year? A penny saved is a penny earned. $100 saved will fatten your wallet and allow new freedoms and luxuries. $5,000 saved will help pay off a mortgage, accelerate plans for early retirement, or cover a luxurious vacation. How you apply the savings is entirely up to you.

Everything Else

In addition to shelter, fire, water, and food, our ancestors needed clothing, dishes, gear and tools. Nowadays, we arguably need all the same and more. A phone number is a virtual necessity as is a postal address and email. Transportation is also a necessity, easily accomplished via bicycle and/or public transportation in cities, while life in smaller towns or rural areas virtually requires an automobile. However, such expenses need not shackle one to a permanent job.

For example, I prefer $90 Merrill shoes, although I cannot imagine forking out that much cash for a disposable item. I buy them at thrift stores for $10 a pair, typically as nice as if I'd bought them new a month ago. I collect them whenever I find the right size. I have a pile of Merrill shoes, and I wear them until they fall off my feet. Granted, I am dependent on someone else buying those shoes at full price so that I can buy them cheap at the thrift store. I would rather that fewer shoes were manufactured in the first place, but I simply do my best to absorb the surplus abundance without negatively impacting the planet.

We have such excess surplus now, that thrift stores increasingly sell new clothes donated by retail outlets. Checking the dumpster behind the dollar store one day, we found an entire garbage bag full of brand new flip flops, discarded because it was the end of the summer season and the inventory was not deemed valuable enough to hold over winter. I put the bag in my garage and brought it to a thrift store in the spring, taking a tax deduction for donating fifty pairs of new flip flops.

Almost any item can be acquired secondhand at a substantial discount without settling for second best. For example, I bought a pricey new Old Town canoe for $800 way back in 1999 without checking the classified ads. I've since accumulated a fleet of canoes for adventures with friends, family, and students, typically paying only about $200 per canoe, saving many hundreds of dollars per boat. In addition, I always wanted a beautiful cedar strip canoe, but wasn't willing to pay $3,000+ to purchase one. However, I found one on Craigslist for $300, which was lacking seats and had a third of the fiberglass sanded off. I spent a week refinishing the canoe and transplanted seats and gunnels in from a salvaged canoe. I have since enjoyed this cedar strip canoe as the proverbial Cadillac of the fleet.

Similarly, I've always driven secondhand vehicles. I've never made monthly payments or interest payments on a car, buying only what I could afford in cash. My newest car ever was a three-year old Volkswagen Jetta, which my ex-wife kept when we split up. I kept a 1982 Toyota pickup, which could only be driven in summer. With my finances devastated from the divorce, I bought an old Subaru for $1,200. I drove it into the ground, then traded up when my finances allowed. Most recently, with a successful business and few bills to pay, I could have bought a new car, but instead bought a twelve-year-old car in excellent condition. Then I helped my son purchase a ten-year-old car also in good condition.

If being thrifty isn't your idea of being successful and prosperous, think again. It all comes down to priorities. Anyone who can afford to buy a latte en route to work can afford to spend two weeks in France instead. Anyone who can afford to smoke cigarettes or go to the bar has the necessary resources to pay off all outstanding debts. Anyone who can afford to pay $1,000+ for a smart phone could just as easily apply those funds towards a systematic plan to quit work and join the ranks of the successfully unemployed.

Then What?

Growing up in western culture, our lives are largely dictated by other people. We get dressed and go to school, we sit at a desk and follow orders. We move from class to class and grade to grade. After many years we are told we know enough to graduate from one school and go to another. Ultimately, we get a job and people continue giving assignments. If that's the only reality we've ever known, how can we do anything else?

This can be a major problem for retirees at any age. Imagine what it's like to work a job Monday through Friday for 40 to 45 years, then suddenly quit and go home. Sometimes people cannot adapt to a new routine. Working not only defines the week, it also defines the weekend, since personal activities must be scheduled into these two-day slots. Taking away the work routine leaves a person with 365 days/year of free time with little or nothing scheduled. Stories abound of people who quit work and lost all meaning and purpose in their lives, often dropping dead within a year of retiring.

Younger people retiring early can also struggle with a lack of routine. Ironically, a primary reason people are constantly broke is because they need a job to get out of bed every morning. As long as there are bills to pay, it seems reasonable to show up at a job and throw stones back and forth over a wall. Take away the need for a job, and one is faced with unavoidable existential questions. What do I do now? What is my purpose in life? What should I do for the next ten, twenty, thirty, forty years? These are difficult questions for the successfully unemployed.

However, many people become even busier after retiring and sometimes earn more money than they did through employment. After dutifully showing up for work year after year, they are finally free to follow their inner light and pursue their personal passions. For some that might be hiking and biking or playing the violin. For others, travel and photography. For some, volunteer work in the community, or all of the above. Some individuals will turn a passionate hobby into a partial or full income, either intentionally or accidentally.

For anyone striving to eliminate monthly expenses, the reward is likely virtual retirement, not full retirement. It is relatively easy to own a home and escape the job trap within a few years, yet supplementary income may remain a part-time necessity. That's probably a good thing for most people. A part-time or seasonal job provides a degree of structure and social interaction. Fight wildfires for the summer, then come home for the other three-quarters of the year. With work on the schedule, you may accomplish more at home immediately before and after the job than in the entire rest of the year.

Part-time or seasonal work can also facilitate transitioning to self employment in line with your personal vision. If you work a job three months a year that leaves plenty of time to explore hobbies, interests, or green business endeavors that may become profitable over time. As noted earlier, I initially earned only about $1 per hour for my time as a writer. Yet, by having ample free time to write, I eventually turned my passion into a successful writing career and publishing business. The pages ahead will guide you along the path towards owning your own career and hopefully making a tangible, positive difference in the world.

Part II
The Nature of Wealth

"Since the Kapauku have a conception of balance in life, only every other day is supposed to be a working day. Such a day is followed by a day of rest... However, many individuals do not rigidly conform to this ideal. The more conscientious cultivators often work intensively for several days in order to complete clearing a plot, making a fence, or digging a ditch. After such a task is accomplished, they relax for a period of several days, thus compensating for their "missed" days of rest."

—Leopold Pospisil,
Organization of Labor Among the Kapauku,
from *Work in Non-Market and Transitional Societies* (1984)[1]

Real Wealth
Taking Stock of our Capital

Wealth is something that nearly everyone seems to want, yet what is it? People get caught up in the illusion of money and think money is wealth. But what if money were all we had? We might stuff paper dollars in our clothes for insulation from the cold, crawl into a heap of money for shelter, use it for toilet paper, or burn it for warmth, yet we would not call this "wealth." It is only when we exchange money for things we want that we have wealth—or at least material wealth. Material wealth is the physical stuff we have in our lives—our homes, furniture, cars, clothes, books, music, and computers.

Other forms of wealth include the health and happiness of our families and the quality of our community and environment. After all, money for material wealth doesn't mean much if our loved ones are ailing, unhappy, constantly fighting, or afraid to drink the water, breathe the air, or walk down the street alone. If we can create happy, healthy, secure, and physically comfortable lives, then we have truly achieved real wealth.

Unfortunately, in the quest for material success people often end up trading one form of wealth for another and sometimes lose it all. Many people have made millions only to lose their health or families along the way. Success can be eclipsed by divorce, depression, bankruptcy, and even suicide.

Neither you nor I would be foolish enough to seek such an unbalanced approach to prosperity. Yet collectively, our species is trading the natural wealth and health of the planet for material wealth to be bought and sold at the Mall of America.

Priceless or Worthless?

In traditional economics material wealth is thought of as "capital." Capital is the net assets of an individual or business, such as money, real estate, and equipment. With the aid of human labor and knowledge, capital assets may be utilized to produce an income. For example, a bow and arrow would be the capital of a hunter-gatherer, useful to produce an income of venison for the family.

The problem with the traditional view of economics is that the bow and arrow has value, yet the deer does not, at least not until dead and removed from the ecosystem for human consumption. The same is true for all natural resources, from trees to gold ore to oil. Resources are free for the cost of extracting them from the ecosystem. Nature has little value until it is plundered for human use. From Wall Street to the gross

According to traditional economics, a bow and arrow has value, while a deer does not until it is dead and removed from the ecosystem for consumption.

national product, consumption of natural resources registers as a gain in our economic indicators rather than a loss. A hunter is doing really well if he takes a thousand deer in one year, even if he leaves none to replenish the population. The industrial economy is consuming worthwhile resources today while saving little for tomorrow.

In order to correct this economic blind spot, environmental economists attempt to calculate the value of natural resources and services. For example, tropical mangrove swamps were traditionally perceived as having no real value. Mangrove trees thrive in brackish estuaries where freshwater mixes with salty seawater. Lacking measurable value, mangrove swamps were uprooted to make room for shrimp production ponds. Unfortunately, coastal areas without a protective belt of mangrove trees are more vulnerable to damage from tsunamis, typhoons, and hurricanes, such as the 2004 Indian Ocean earthquake and tsunami that claimed 227,000 lives. Mangroves provided an unrecognized service, and many coastal communities from Indonesia to Thailand have since replanted mangroves as essential shelterbelts.[2]

In addition to coastal protection, mangrove swamps provide many other valuable services. Mangrove wood is highly resistant to insects and rot, making it useful for construction in local communities. Mangrove swamps provide habitat for many species of fish, crab, shrimp and mollusks, plus they serve as nurseries for many other fish species.

According to a study conducted in Thailand, converting a mangrove swamp to a shrimp farm produces an economic benefit of $1,220 per hectare per year—at the expense of losing extensive services provided free by the mangroves. Researchers calculated the value of an intact mangrove swamp at $10,821 per hectare per year for coastal protection, plus $987 as a fish nursery, and $584 per year as a source of wood. Economists conservatively estimated that global mangrove swamps contribute $186 million per year in goods and services to the economy.[3]

Assigning value to natural services provided by the ecosystem enables planners and participants in the economy to view natural resources as having inherent wealth in the form of "natural capital."

Natural Capital

Goods and services provided by nature are considered natural capital. Nature provides an abundance of natural capital, which humans tend to squander and deplete. Assigning value to natural resources enables people to perceive the true costs of exploiting those resources. Consumption of any resource then registers as a loss against potential economic gains. For example, an individual tree in the forest provides numerous services, such as protecting the soil against erosion, producing oxygen, and providing wildlife habitat. Calculating the value these services enables decision-makers to evaluate tradeoffs between different types of available economic capital. In this case, does the tree provide more value dead as lumber, or alive as a contributing member of the ecosystem?

Putting a price tag on nature is ethically controversial, much like putting a price tag on your mother or father. How much are they worth? How much is one species of frog worth or the swamp that it lives in? What is the value of a coral reef or a tropical forest? What is the value of natural beauty and recreational pleasure? Environmental economists contend that assigning value to the natural world is better than allowing resources to be exploited as if they have no value.

Assigning value to natural capital is inherently humancentric. How much would it cost in labor and materials to replace services freely provided by nature? For example, nature regulates gases in the

atmosphere, recycles wastes, and purifies and stores water, all to our benefit. To replace just seventeen basic services provided by nature would cost approximately $125 trillion per year. For comparison, Gross World Product (GWP) is about $75 trillion.[4] That's the total market value of all the goods and services produced by all people everywhere in one year.

Even if we could raise the additional $125 trillion there is considerable doubt as to whether or not the effort to replace nature's services would be successful. Environmental economists point to the Biosphere 2 project as an example. Researchers spent $200 million (1991) to develop the fully enclosed 3.15-acre artificial ecosystem, yet they were unable to maintain the necessary balance

How much is a living tree worth? Assigning value to nature is inherently humancentric.

of oxygen in the atmosphere for the eight people living inside. Fresh air provided free from "Biosphere 1" (Earth) had to be introduced to the structure to sustain the occupants.[5]

By recognizing the inherent value of natural capital we can make better resource management decisions. We can achieve material wealth while maintaining a healthy, wealthy environment.

Investing in Sustainable Development

Environmental organizations traditionally focused solely on the task of protecting nature from economic development, seeking to prevent natural capital from being liquidated and converted to material wealth. Environmentalists often met great resistance from people who felt that their livelihoods were threatened. When forced to choose between material wealth and natural wealth, people typically choose the former. However, some environmental organizations have embraced green economics, working to save nature by encouraging sustainable economic development. Instead of protesting clear-cut logging in developing countries, for example, some organizations work with local citizens to establish renewable forestry practices and healthy communities, which may include contributing environmental funds towards building schools and hospitals.

Similarly, many humanitarian organizations are embracing environmental and economic solutions as means to improve quality of life. For example, Scott Bernstein, director of the Center for Neighborhood Technology in Chicago, does not consider himself an environmentalist in the conventional sense, yet he often employs environmental solutions to help rectify social and economic problems in the city. When sky rocketing energy costs drove renters out of inner city neighborhoods, Bernstein helped form a coalition to retrofit more than 10,000 apartments, saving more than $1.5 million per year in energy bills. His goal was to make the inner city livable, yet it also helped conserve energy.[6]

Businesses are also starting to embrace environmental thought, using resources and energy more efficiently to make a greater profit with fewer materials. For instance, in the highly competitive market of producing silicon chips for computers, one Singapore manufacturer cut its energy use per chip by 60% in six years, saving $5.8 million every year from just $70,000 in retrofitting costs.[7]

Investors are starting to recognize the economic benefits of stable returns from sustainable forestry, agriculture, and fisheries. In just two years, conservation investments rose by 62% from $5.1 billion to $8.2 billion, with Wall Street betting on projects with solid conservation objectives that also produce a financial return.[8]

These kinds of projects demonstrate that it is possible to increase material prosperity while helping conserve or enhance community and natural wealth. Any individual, nonprofit organization, or business that strives to honor all forms of wealth will inevitably find innovative solutions to make the world a happier, greener, and wealthier place.

"I went to the woods because I wished to live deliberately, to front only the essential facts of life, and see if I could not learn what it had to teach, and not, when I came to die, discover that I had not lived. I did not wish to live what was not life, living is so dear; nor did I wish to practice resignation, unless it was quite necessary. I wanted to live deep and suck out all the marrow of life, to live so sturdily and Spartan-like as to put to rout all that was not life, to cut a broad swath and shave close, to drive life into a corner, and reduce it to its lowest terms."

—Henry David Thoreau,
Walden (1854)[9]

Calories
The Currency of All Economies

Most financial planners and businessmen rely on computer printouts of numerical data for strategic planning. By comparing one series of digits with another they can identify immediate trends in the economy and act on those trends. To most people that seems normal, but not to me. Throughout my life I've sought means to make a positive difference in the world, and I realized early on that knowledge of the economy could be a powerful tool for affecting change. However, I was looking for something bigger than mere numbers. I searched for universal truths. I sought knowledge about the economy that remained constant from year to year, from culture to culture. I wanted knowledge that would be useful to a poor person or a rich person, in our culture, or in any culture. The truths that I found were not in the New York Stock Exchange, but in anthropology and nature.

Some things haven't changed since the Stone Age. We still have the same basic needs as in millennia past for such things as physical and mental well-being, shelter, fire, water, and food. It is only the ways we meet those basic needs that has changed. As hunter-gatherers we met our needs mostly individually. Each of us produced every aspect of our culture, from shelter to clothing to entertainment. Today we have the same needs, yet we meet those needs through the network of society, trade, and money. Nevertheless, if we look beyond the illusion of money, we discover that our economy, like the economies of all past cultures, is based not on dollars, euros, or yen, but on calories of energy.

A calorie is a unit for measuring energy. A calorie is the amount of heat required to raise the temperature of one gram of water one degree Celsius. The caloric value of food is measured by igniting it to find out how much heat is released. As human beings, we require approximately 2,500 calories of energy to fuel us each day. Those calories originate from the sun. Plants convert sunlight into food that we and other animals can eat. Petroleum and coal also contain calories of solar energy, energy that was captured by plants millions of years ago. Calories from these and other sources form the basis of all economies.

The economies of our ancestors lacked our institutions of finance, yet there were similarities even before the invention of money, even before the first trade or barter took place. Our ancestors didn't have money, yet they had to make decisions that were economical. For example, many plants and animals are edible, yet not economical to harvest. An economical food resource had to provide sufficient calories to replace those expending harvesting, plus additional calories to expend on other chores and activities such as making tools and shelter, sleeping, singing, and dancing. People initially harvested only food calories. Later they started harvesting additional calories in the form of fuel, such as firewood, coal, and oil.

Money is a token we use to represent calories of energy, expressed through human productivity. I expend energy to write books, which I exchange for money. I use that money to purchase goods and services from workers who have invested their energy. For example, I could hire help digging a hole, where the laborer expends sweat and calories moving earth with a shovel. I exchange my energy for theirs, and money is the medium of exchange. For simplicity, we can say that money is a token that represents calories of human energy or labor.

Money also represents fuel calories, but not directly. In industry, a person can spend a day harvesting tens of thousands, potentially millions of fuel calories. That fuel can be firewood, petroleum, uranium, or any other type of fuel. A small amount of human labor is expended to acquire a tremendous number of fuel calories. One person can only consume a few thousand calories per day and is therefore limited in the amount of work they can do. However, a person can use fuel calories to run machinery, thereby increasing output. For example, I could hire my neighbor to dig holes or move earth with his backhoe, and he accomplishes more in minutes than a person can do in a full day with a shovel.

Products are shaped by food and fuel calories. For example, a drinking glass is made from resources mined from the earth and shaped with the calories of human endeavor. Fuel calories are like cheap labor. On average, we benefit from the calorie equivalent of having between 100 and 300 laborers working for us 24 hours per day.[10] [11] We apply a combination of food and fuel calories to produce goods and services. Fuel calories account for 3 or 4% of the cost of producing most goods and services.

People who produce food and fuel calories provide the basis for our entire economy. Directly or indirectly, we produce goods and services for people who produce the energy that fuels us through our tasks. We earn calories at our jobs, paid in dollars, which we pass along to others in exchange for their goods and services. We could carry around bags of food, batteries, and gas cans, but instead we carry money. Money represents calories of food and fuel energy and serves as a medium of exchange to make life a lot more convenient.

Calorie Conscious

All aspects of the economy are tied to calories, including inflation, taxes, insurance, stocks and bonds, and interest. For example, insurance in a primitive economy meant having neighbors who would share their calories with you if you were incapacitated, and you would do the same for them. Insurance is similar today. We pay calories into a common fund, and any person or family in need draws from the fund. If a person's house is destroyed then that person withdraws enough calories from the fund to rebuild the house. Having built three houses, I know that building requires a lot of calories. The person whose home is destroyed withdraws calories from the common fund to fuel carpenters as they rebuild the house, plus enough extra for the carpenters to exchange for the goods they need.

In simple economies every member produced calories and contributed to the insurance pool. In our more complex economy, insurance agents oversee the pool, and we sustain them with an additional share of our calories.

Similarly, banks are places to store surplus calories, or to borrow calories when needed. Banking is a simple as a family borrowing calories from a neighbor's surplus while building their home. This year they build the house. The following year they will raise crops and repay the loan, giving back additional calories as interest to pay for the loan service.

Banking institutions are usually safe places to store surplus calories until needed. Bankers sustain themselves without planting crops and producing their own calories. They loan calories out with the stipulation that the borrower must eventually pay back more than they borrowed. If enough people store calories at the bank then it is unlikely everyone will withdraw their funds at the same time. Therefore, the bank can loan out most of calories deposited there.

Inflation can also be discussed in terms of calories. Inflation is a word we use to describe the changing relationship between calories and the tokens that represent them. Inflation occurs when a given amount of tokens cannot be exchanged for as many calories as in the past. Inflation is usually caused by expanding the number of tokens in circulation, typically by the government and connected banking institutions, as detailed in the following chapter.

Stocks and bonds are also related to calories. Investing in stocks makes you a banker and gambler. Stock investments are basically loans, providing calories to sustain a company's managers and employees as they bring products and services to market. If the business is successful, then you gain extra calories back as profit. If the business fails to profit, then the calories you invested were expended as sweat and tears without gain.

All in all, little has changed since the Stone Age. Throughout the ages the calorie has remained the universal measure of economic wealth. We seek to harvest more calories than we expend. Money conveniently represents those calories.

Money is a token that represents calories of energy. Increasing the number of tokens in circulation devalues them all, causing inflation.

The problem with money is that people get caught up in the illusion that it is real wealth. People manipulate numbers in an effort to make money while failing to create real wealth. We hear it every day in advertising, get-rich schemes, and political speeches. Get-rich proposals often seem plausible according to the math, yet lack commonsense when considered in terms of calories.

Money Logic versus Calorie Logic

Whether you are an individual, business, or policy maker, it is important to evaluate proposals and work in caloric terms. Consider a cashier in a grocery store. At first it seems like he provides a valuable service, scanning bar codes to calculate the total cost. In caloric terms, however, the only benefit is that groceries are bagged and moved a few feet closer to the door. The cashier contributes no real caloric value to the products, except when considered in context of the efficiency of the entire system. For this service, we pay the cashier calories of energy to provide for shelter, food, clothing, and all other needs. Many stores have adopted self-checkout systems to reduce or eliminate cashiers. Businesses have been testing scanners that allow customers to scan and bag items in their cart while shopping.[12] In stores with RFID tags attached to products, it is possible to instantly scan all items in a shopping cart upon checkout.[13] Meanwhile, Amazon is deploying computer vision, sensors, and machine learning in a prototype Go store to allow customers to take whatever they want off the shelves and walk out the door. The goods are automatically billed to a customer credit card on file.[14] These innovations reduce the labor or calorie cost of providing goods and services, which ultimately lowers prices for all.

Other people earn a living while contributing absolutely nothing to society, such as buying and selling money for profit. The value of the dollar, euro, ruble, and all other types of money is constantly changing in relationship to one another. Money traders buy and sell different currencies, hoping to buy money from one country when it is cheap and sell when its relative value goes back up. They may make a million dollars one day and lose it the next, but apparently win often enough to continue gambling.

At first glance, this game seems harmless enough. People can earn a living without bulldozing the rainforest, drilling in the Arctic, or conning people out of their hard-earned tokens. Trading money offers the illusion of free wealth. Nobody gives up anything; nobody suffers. In that sense it may seem like an ideal way to make a living. We may even be delighted if a money trader spent several thousand dollars in our business. However, in terms of calories, we provide goods and services to a person who produces nothing in return. Money is a token for calories, and all calories come from somewhere, even if it is impossible to trace the original source. They are inevitably spending money taken from our own pockets.

"Competitive potlatching went wild, particularly so among the Kwakiutl, where an intricate system of credits to finance the feasts developed.... (with interest rates of 20 to 200% or more).... In one Kwakiutl village, the population of somewhat more than a hundred people possessed only about four hundred actual blankets. Yet, so pyramided had the system of debts, credits, and paper profits become that the total indebtedness of everyone in the village approached 75,000 blankets."

—Peter Farb,
Man's Rise to Civilization (1968)[15]

Abstractification
The Invention of Money

Social animals look out for each other. Wolves hunt together and share a kill. Bison herds share security, providing many eyes to watch for predators. Crows group together in winter, sometimes assigning one individual to watch for threats while the rest of the flock feeds. My rooster cackles to call the hens when he discovers a tasty morsel. This "mutualism" is highly developed among humans. A brother may watch your dog while you are away on vacation. A neighbor may plow your snow-covered driveway without being asked. A stranger might jump-start the car when your battery is dead.

Mutualism isn't barter or trade. There is no tit-for-tat accounting to reconcile accounts. Rather the opposite, exchanges are necessarily unequal. If, for example, we borrow two eggs from a neighbor to bake a cake, it would be exceptionally rude to return two eggs the following day. It is better to bring a slice of cake or a jar of jelly. Returning exactly two eggs would effectively change mutualism to commerce, in which the accounts are reconciled and we have no further business together. Unequal exchanges keep the flow open, ensuring favors go back and forth or are passed along to others.[16]

Mutualistic societies historically functioned like tight-knit families. Survival depended on cooperation, so there could be no hoarding of food or supplies. When a member of a tribe comes up and says, "That's a really nice knife..." there is a social obligation to gift it to the admirer. The new owner may enjoy the knife for a week or two, until the next person comes along and praises it. Given enough time—and assuming nobody breaks or loses it—everybody takes a turn owning knife.

Mutualistic societies are necessarily egalitarian, so no individual can be allowed to accumulate noticeably more than anyone else. This custom works great in tribal societies, yet becomes a problem when adapting to market economies. If one person becomes semi-successful on a Native American reservation, other people may expect or pressure them to share their newfound wealth. Everybody rises together or nobody does.

People have cooperated as mutualists throughout human history. Commerce and money were relatively unimportant until recent millennia. Now, money has come to define so much of our reality that it is difficult to imagine a world without it. Early money was relatively tangible, while newer forms are becoming increasingly abstract. As we move towards a world of automation, we must necessarily consider Universal Basic Income to provide people with money to buy goods and services from machines. But what if machines have no use for money?

Have Surplus, Will Barter

Fish reproduce externally when females release unfertilized eggs in the water and males concurrently release sperm that find and fertilize the eggs. To increase the chance of successful fertilization, most fish species group together in mass-spawning runs, typically triggered by changing water temperatures or other seasonal fluctuations. During the spawning run, congregating fish are so numerous that it is easy to catch them in abundance by net, spear, bow and arrow, or even by hand. The result? A surplus.

Fish are best consumed fresh, yet spawning runs are short-lived, so it is necessary to smoke, dry, freeze, or otherwise preserve the surplus to live upon until next year's spawning run. A well-organized fisherman, family, or village can quickly accumulate a large surplus for consumption and for barter with others. If 365 days of fish dinners doesn't sound appealing then bartering with an upland village for their surplus rabbits or venison is desirable. Both sides expend calories of energy to harvest and preserve food, and both benefit from trade to diversify the diet. Barter wasn't traditionally part of the internal life of mutualistic societies, but rather a function of the external economy of exchange with outside groups or individuals.

While mutualism is based on trust, barter and commerce are rooted in distrust, with both parties angling for the better deal. Even in modern bartering or dickering there is a degree of tension since neither party wants to be swindled. Distrust was often a major issue between alien societies, and trading parties were frequently armed to the teeth to fight. Money existed in pre-market societies, but not usually for the purpose of buying goods or services.

Jewelry to Flaunt

Money or wealth was greatly valued in many pre-market societies, just not very useful for daily living. Any item that is sufficiently scarce, such as shells, beads, livestock, or precious metals, could be used as currency, and was often worn as ornamentation to display wealth. As pointed out by David Graeber, author of *Debt: The First 5,000 Years,* "*Money almost always arises first from objects that are used primarily as adornment of the person. Beads, shells, feathers, dog or whale teeth, gold, and silver are all well-known cases in point. All are useless for any purpose other than making people look more interesting, and hence more beautiful.*"[17]

However, money wasn't used for day-to-day shopping in mutualistic societies. Wealth was used for status and could be traded for social transactions, such as bridewealth. In other words, just as a peacock fans its tail to attract a mate, people displayed wealth to demonstrate worthiness and traded wealth to take a mate. Anything valuable enough to trade for a mate was also valuable enough to potentially pay a major debt, such as a blood debt for murder. A life lost cannot be compensated at any price, but the victim's family might gain a bride and have more children.

Mutualistic societies didn't need money because nearly everyone produced and shared tangible goods and services. However, as production efficiency and population size increased, mutualism became more complicated.

A chiefdom, for example, is something like a conglomerate tribe, numbering tens of thousands of citizens spread out over multiple eco-regions. As previously described, different groups specialized in local skills, such as fishing, berry harvesting, boat-building, or weaving clothes. Think of it as a communist society. All goods flowed to the chief, who then redistributed goods among all communities within the chiefdom. A chiefdom is arguably the largest social-political unit capable of functioning as a mutualistic society.

More technologically advanced societies produce a greater surplus and support a larger population within city-states or nation-states. Some form of money is necessary, not merely to facilitate commerce, but more critically, to transfer goods and services from producers to non-producers.

Commodity Currency

Early farming cultures in Mesopotamia coalesced into chiefdoms, then gradually evolved into city-states with market economies.

Archaeologists have unearthed thousands of small clay tokens of many different shapes and sizes, dating back to 7,500 B.C. Each type of token had a specific shape and markings to symbolize a specific quantity of a specific commodity for accounting and trade. A cone represented a quantity of grain. An ovoid symbolized a jar of oil. A cylinder stood for a sheep or goat. A tetrahedron represented a person-day worth of work. These tokens could be traded, each one's value understood by its size and form.

The risk of using clay tokens is that they could easily be counterfeited. To remedy this problem, Mesopotamians developed a tamper-proof ceramic ball called a "bulla" to contain tokens in debt transactions. Tokens were enclosed inside the ceramic ball and symbolized on the outside to indicate the contents. The bulla provided an official account of the debt, which was certified by an official seal. Anyone holding a bulla owned the debt demarked on the surface and inside the bulla. The value of that debt could be traded as currency, passing the bulla along to someone else. The bulla would be destroyed when the original borrower repaid the debt. Mesopotamian cultures gradually transitioned from three-dimensional tokens to two-dimensional cuneiform writing and math.[18]

The clay tokens of Mesopotamia symbolized commodities and functioned as money, which is different from trading actual commodities. Wherever market economies formed, people traded commodities when money was absent or insufficient.[19]

Commodities are basic goods and raw materials, such as salt, wheat, sugar, cotton, or tobacco. To serve as currency, a commodity should be somewhat scarce, portable, easily recognizable, divisible into smaller portions, and interchangeable with other units of itself. For example, tobacco can be used as a currency. One can trade fish for tobacco then trade the tobacco for a ceramic pot, and the potter can trade the tobacco for venison from a hunter. Any party can consume some tobacco and trade the rest.

When tobacco is recognized as currency, participants in the economy can produce goods to trade for tobacco, or plant tobacco themselves, growing a literal cash crop. As long as tobacco is scarce, then it has value. However, a bumper crop can devalue tobacco as a token of exchange, and conversely, a poor crop causes scarcity, increasing the value of tobacco. The value all other goods and services must be recalculated according to the relative scarcity of tobacco, leading to potential instability and uncertainty in trade circles.

Conversion from commodities to precious metals began with rings of silver that could be cut and weighed to make financial transactions. It is unknown how often people attempted breaking off specific weights of silver versus simply trading IOUs that could be redeemed for silver. The "shekel" started out as a unit of weight, later evolving into standardized coins.

From Coinage to Carnage

Mining and refining gold and silver is hard work that requires a great expenditure of calories. Coins therefore represented densely packed calories. A small number of coins could be traded for a large quantity of calorie-rich food.

Coins first arose in the kingdom of Lydia in today's Turkey about 600 B.C., imprinted on one side with the Lydian lion. The coins were minted from a naturally occurring alloy of silver and gold called electrum. The production and use of money soon spread to the Greeks and beyond.[20]

Coins expedited transactions and facilitated long-distance trade. Minting a steady and consistent supply of standardized coins allowed

A king could pay soldiers and staff with coins to buy basic goods without needing to produce tangible goods in exchange. In effect, money facilitated the transfer of goods and services from producers to non-producers.

economic growth and stability. The Roman gold solidus was produced with remarkable consistency for 700 years starting in AD 301.[21] Highly durable, coins have outlasted the civilizations that minted them.

Coins consolidated wealth and power among those who minted them, typically priests, merchants, goldsmiths, kings, and emperors.

Coins facilitated taxation, either directly by demanding tribute paid in coins, or indirectly through debasement, diluting coins with inferior alloys, reduced weights, or impure metals. These lower-value coins were issued as though they had full value, enabling the source to purchase goods and pay debts. Prices eventually inflated to reconcile with the lower-value coins.

Money and warfare are inextricably linked. By minting money, a king could pay soldiers and staff with coins to buy basic goods without needing to produce tangible goods in exchange. In effect, money facilitated the transfer of goods and services from producers to non-producers. Minting coins and collecting taxes enabled rulers to accumulate wealth, build armies, and rain carnage upon other kingdoms in hopes of accumulating ever-greater wealth and power. In rare cases, they succeeded to their own detriment. The Spanish conquest and mining in South America in the 1500s flooded European markets with silver and gold, devaluing existing coins and destabilizing the economy.[22]

The American dollar was originally based on the silver Spanish Peso, also known as the "Spanish milled dollar," which was prevalent in U.S. colonies when our country was founded. The American dollar was minted to similar specifications so that both dollars could be used interchangeably.[23]

Congress established a bimetallic standard utilizing interchangeable silver and gold coins based on a 15:1 ratio in value between the two metals. However, world markets valued them at a 15½:1 ratio, making gold coins slightly more valuable than an equal denomination of silver coins. Other countries paid silver for American gold, taking gold out of the country. In 1834, Congress adjusted the ratio to 16:1 for new coins, which reversed the flow, bringing gold back into the country in exchange for silver. The California Gold Rush of 1849 then flooded the markets with gold again, further reducing its value relative to silver. The U.S. finally abandoned the bi-metallic system and adopted the gold standard in 1900.[24]

Gold and silver coins were especially useful to facilitate international transactions, providing real and tangible value for commercial transactions or debt payments. However, it was also very risky to transport shiploads of precious metals back and forth across open seas. Ships carrying gold or silver were often attacked by pirates or sometimes sank from severe storms or unseen hazards. Similarly, gold stored at home could be stolen and encouraged robbery. People long ago discovered that it was safer and less costly to exchange symbolic money rather than precious coins.

Paper Gold

Instead of hoarding and trading gold or silver coins, precious metals could be deposited in a bank vault for security. The customer walked away with a deposit receipt as proof of ownership. The value of the gold was now stored on paper. One could then write a claim "check," transferring a specified amount of gold to another person. The check was purely symbolic, having no value in itself. The person accepting the check trusted that the piece of paper was legitimate and that one had sufficient gold at the bank to cover the check. Rather than withdrawing gold, however, the recipient simply deposited the claim check and took home a deposit receipt. The banker subtracted numbers from one account and added them to another without touching the gold in the vault.

Similarly, paper dollars originally functioned like a claim check. Gold coins were deposited in the bank in exchange for paper dollars. The value of the gold was transferred to the paper. Anyone possessing paper dollars could exchange them straight across for gold coins at the bank. Paper currencies were variously issued by banks, goldsmiths, and governments. The system was stable as long as people trusted the source of currency. The U.S. fixed the price of gold at $20.67 per ounce in 1834, guaranteeing the price by which paper dollars were exchanged for gold. The paper to gold ratio remained locked at that value until 1933.[25]

The Federal Reserve Bank was established in 1913, issuing a single nationwide currency backed by gold in government vaults. The Federal Reserve bought gold and issued paper dollars.

The stock market crash of 1929 triggered the Great Depression and brought the economy to a halt. To stimulate purchasing, the Roosevelt administration developed policies to inflate the number of paper dollars in circulation. The government outlawed private ownership of gold coin, gold bullion, and gold certificates, purchasing it from the public at the inflated price of $35 per ounce. Gold flowed into the treasury from throughout the world, and U.S. paper dollars flooded out,[26] establishing the dollar as an international currency. At one time, the U.S. government owned half of the world's gold supply.

Many people feel that we should return to the gold-backed dollar. From a calorie standpoint, however, it is ludicrous to mine and refine gold for the sole purpose of burying it in a vault. Tying the dollar to gold greatly increases demand for gold and artificially stimulates gold mining. Living in Montana gold country, I've witnessed mining companies materialize from thin air whenever gold rises in value. They haul in equipment, build roads, dig holes, and leave behind an ecological mess. Ore-bearing rocks are pulverized and mixed with cyanide to separate the gold. In our watershed, mining operations have left behind toxic tailings, spilled cyanide and sulfuric acid, eroded hillsides, impaired water quality, invasive weeds, and dangerous mine shafts. Reverting to the gold-backed dollar would cause further environmental devastation on an unprecedented scale.

The other problem with the gold-backed dollar is that it limits economic growth. Money supply is constrained by the amount of gold stored in a vault, yet population and productivity continue to grow, thus creating more competition for limited dollars. President Nixon severed the U.S. dollar from gold in 1971, meaning that the value of paper money was no longer pegged to gold.[27] A paper dollar is worth a paper dollar. Its value is based solely on the perceived scarcity of dollars and trust that the government will not excessively inflate or deflate the money supply. It was not, however, the first time people put full faith and credit in mere paper. Indeed, America's founding fathers bought our freedom by printing money.

Faith in Paper

Paper can be a powerful tool. America came into existence on paper via the Declaration of Independence in 1776. The founding fathers conjured the Continental Army into existence on paper. They also paid for the Revolutionary War with paper.

There was no federal government until after the war, so there wasn't a treasury to fund an army, nor any system of taxation to raise money. The Continental Congress paid for the new army by printing currency known as Continentals. To the degree that people accepted the new money, it was used to pay wages and purchase supplies. Continentals were also sold to supporters of the war based on the hope and promise that the currency could be redeemed for Spanish silver dollars upon victory. However, the war dragged on longer than expected, and the presses kept printing Continentals, creating $241,552,780 from nothing. The more money they printed, the less valuable it became. In addition, the British printed counterfeit Continentals, putting even more money into circulation.

People traded Continentals as currency, yet the bills quickly dropped in value. By 1780, Continentals were worth only 1/40 their designated face value. People stopped accepting payments in Continentals the following year, and the currency was abandoned.[28] By paying for real goods and services with worthless paper, the Continental Congress effectively taxed Americans, extracting goods and services without compensation.

Money represents calories of energy, serving as a convenient medium of exchange to trade one person's work and sweat for another's. However, there is no set ratio between money and calories, for establishing that one dollar equals x amount of calories. The ratio between calories and money constantly fluctuates according to management of the money supply, typically leading to a slow, steady rate of inflation.

Many people have lost their life savings to a quick spurt of inflation. They held onto money itself, stuffing a mattress or bank account with cash for twenty years. Then, in a moment of crises, their government increased the amount of money in circulation tenfold, so that twenty years of savings were reduced to 10% of their original value. This problem would not happen if we exchanged actual calories, and had "pocket calories," instead of pocket change. Money is not fixed like calories, and it is constantly changing value, even now inside your pocket.

Big Bang Theory

Governments still print money to pay bills without collecting taxes. It is kind of like the Big Bang, creating a lot of something out of nothing. If you own the printing presses then you can print as much money as you want. Printing additional money does not increase the number of calories in circulation; it merely changes the ratio of tokens to calories. Suppose one calorie is equal to one token. Double the number of tokens in circulation, and each token is worth half as much. Then you need to exchange two tokens for one calorie. The universe keeps expanding bigger and bigger, and so does the money supply. However, printing too much money leads to hyperinflation.

After World War I Germany canceled its internal debts by printing lots of money. The government printed tons of paper money and instantly paid off all internal debts. The money supply grew to 4 quintillion (4,000,000,000,000,000,000) Reichsmarks, diluting the caloric value of currency in the years 1922-1923 so much that wheelbarrow loads were required to purchase basic goods.[29] Hyperinflation has its benefits, but at the cost of crashing the economy.

Imagine a $30,000 annual income and a home mortgage of $100,000. Let's say bread costs $1.00 a loaf. Suddenly, the government prints gobs of extra money to pay overdue bills. Printing new money dilutes the value of money already in circulation. When adjusted for hyperinflation, a loaf of bread now costs $1,000. The bread isn't more valuable; rather, money is less valuable. Wages eventually adjust to hyperinflation as well. Like the cost of a loaf of bread, personal income gradually increases a thousand fold, from $30,000 a year to $30,000,000 per year. Thanks to hyperinflation you can pay off the entire home loan in about a day!

On the other hand, maybe you worked hard and saved $10,000 for retirement before inflation kicked in. That was once a third of your annual income. Now, however, your retirement fund is worth only ten loaves of bread.

Hyperinflation and debt cancellation benefit debtors at the expense of creditors. Paying off a mortgage in a couple days is great if you are a homeowner, and not so great if you are the creditor being paid in worthless dollars. Likewise, it is good for a landlord who can pay off an apartment complex all at once, and not so good for renters who ante up rent each month, now at the inflated prices. It is impossible to implement a strategy for debt cancellation fairly and equitably to all citizens. Printing money for debt cancellation is a drastic measure applicable only to drastic times, such as for restructuring a collapsed economy.

Germany's method of debt reduction worked only with internal debts. To pay external debts the country had to trade virtually worthless Reichsmarks for foreign currencies. To effectively erase foreign debts, all countries have to agree to the arrangement, which helps debtor nations at the expense of creditor nations. Russia succeeded in erasing foreign debts using another approach. Following the Bolshevik Revolution of 1917, the new government simply refused to assume and pay for debts of the old government. Legal wrangling over the debt has persisted ever since, and some parties have collected a fraction of the original debt. [30] [31]

We have not dealt with hyperinflation in this country, yet we experience similar results with steady inflation of the money supply. Everyone will eventually become millionaires because inflation is gradually devaluing the worth of a million dollars.

Debt as an Asset

The more abstract money becomes, the more creatively financiers can manipulate it towards perceived benefits. For example, in an economy without credit, an aspiring merchant must first earn and save money to invest in growing a business. Lack of credit remains a major obstacle for millions of people in impoverished countries, as well as for many people struggling to make ends meet in industrial societies. Income is consumed for day-to-day expenses, making it impossible to save and invest in a better future. One surprising solution to the problem is to trade debt.

Instead of paying for groceries with a $50 bill, imagine paying with a $50 IOU. Fortunately, the grocer knows you personally and trusts you will sell many hot dogs as a new vendor on the street corner. He accepts the IOU with confidence you can repay the debt later.

The next customer wishes to break a $100 bill, but the grocer is short on cash. However, he has a $50 IOU in the drawer, which the customer accepts in change with confidence that it is redeemable for $50 cash from you, the hot dog vendor. The paper debt can be traded as if it were actual money, circulating through the economy.[32]

The Medici family in Florence, Italy rose to prominence as middlemen in promissory transactions in the fifteenth century, forming the largest bank in Europe.[33] A French merchant, for example, could order Italian olives and promise to pay 100 gold coins through Medici Bank. Having the gold on hand wasn't necessary as long as the bank trusted that the merchant would have it later. The promissory note thus had a value of 100 gold coins, which could be traded to purchase leather from England and might return to France to purchase wine. Eventually, the debt might be returned to source as payment for goods or services, effectively balancing the books. The system worked even if no one owned any actual gold.

Medici Bank managed transactions utilizing a double-entry bookkeeping system,[34] also known as credit clearing,[35] where any debit in one account was matched by an equal credit in another account. As long as debts and credits were properly accounted for, no one needed to pay with coins. Medici Bank evaluated merchants' credit-worthiness, effectively vouching that all debts would be paid. Managing such transactions made the Medici family very wealthy and influential.

Credit clearing is still used as an alternative credit and payment system today, and it can be transacted between individuals or merchants without going through an intermediary bank. A community of farmers, for example, can trade IOUs back and forth to rent equipment, buy hay, fix a tire, or hire help to paint a house. If neighbors extend credit to neighbors in a circular system with double-entry bookkeeping, then there is no need for anyone to borrow money from the bank and get saddled with origination fees and interest payments.[36]

Unfortunately, credit clearing is not as common as it should be, and most people and businesses depend on bank loans to some degree or another. As of 2017, the average American household carried debts totaling $134,643. Every person paying debt is channeling money and resources to the banking industry through the great magic money machine of interest payments.

Magic Money Tricks

Loans and interest payments are as old as commerce. Loan wheat to a neighbor to help them through hard times. They plant the wheat, grow a crop, and expand the supply, producing enough to repay the loan plus interest. However, the system doesn't work unless the economy keeps expanding.

For example, suppose Anne loans $1,000 worth of gold to Bob at 5% interest. To repay the debt, Bob must return $1,000 in gold, plus $50 more. If he isn't a gold miner then he will have to exchange his services with somebody who is. Thus, the loan cannot be repaid without expanding the economy.

Expanding the economy becomes more problematic with banks. Suppose Anne deposits $1,000 in gold in the bank and takes home a paper receipt. Anne doesn't need the gold at present, yet she can return to the bank to claim it at anytime. Meanwhile, the gold in the vault is gathering dust, so the banker loans it out to earn a living off the interest. Being cautious, he reserves 10% or $100 in the vault and loans the remaining $900 at 5% interest to Bob. Bob takes the gold out of the bank, strolls down to the used car lot and buys a heavy-duty truck from Charlie. Charlie then deposits the gold in the bank, pleased to have a paper receipt proving he owns $900 in gold. The bank vault once again holds $1,000 in gold. Anne can withdraw her gold at anytime, except that would leave the vault empty, and Charlie has a receipt proving that $900 of the gold belongs to him.

No worries. The books will be square when Bob repays the loan. The problem is that Bob must dig up new gold from outside the system to pay back the $900 loan, plus $45 for interest. Meanwhile, the banker has $900 in gold that Charlie deposited, so he sets aside 10% or $90 on reserve, and loans out the remaining $810 in gold to Dave. Dave buys a secondhand mini-excavator from Earl for $810, and Earl deposits the gold in the bank. The bank once again has $1,000 in gold coins in the vault, only now Anne, Charlie, and Earl have total receipts claiming $2,710 against that gold. In order to balance the books, Earl must use his excavator to load fresh gold ore into Bob's truck, which will be hauled to town, refined, and milled into new gold coins. Just like planting wheat, the economy must grow every time a loan is issued.

Detaching the dollar from gold simplifies the process, so that the economy grows by printing more money instead of mining more gold. Using the same example, Anne deposits $1,000 into her account. The bank sets aside 10% on reserve and loans $900 to Bob. According to the books, Anne still has $1,000 in her account, which is accessible at any time, and now Bob has $900 in his, which he can use to pay to Charlie. The bank added $900 to one account without subtracting it elsewhere. This is new money, created out of thin air. If 10% of each deposit is set aside, then the original deposit of $1,000 can theoretically inflate to $9,000 through ninety-three progressively smaller loans. Anne still owns $1,000, yet it is worth less than before.[37]

Some money leaks out of the system to pay taxes, or is held as cash, so the actual number of loans is less than this theoretical example. The cycle stops, stabilizing the money supply until new money enters the system.

Priming the Pump

The Federal Reserve is the specific part of our government responsible for managing the country's money supply. The Federal Reserve tries to stimulate the economy without causing excessive inflation, using various tools to seek a balance between tightening or loosening the money supply.

One management tool is to adjust fractional reserve requirements for the banking system. The Federal Reserve can require banks to keep more money on hand. The money is still there, just not in circulation. This tightens the money supply. Conversely, the Federal Reserve can lower fractional reserve requirements, so banks can loan out more funds and pump more money into the economy. Raising or lowering reserve requirements has a temporary effect on the economy; in the long run it does not change the total amount of currency in circulation.

Another way to affect the money supply is to adjust the prime interest rate. The prime interest rate is the rate at which the Federal Reserve loans money to the banking system. Banks borrow money from the Federal Reserve and loan it out to businesses and individuals. Where does the Federal Reserve get that money to begin with? Is it tax dollars? No. It is printed as needed by the U.S. Treasury. That is why news media often reports that the Federal Reserve is considering raising interest rates to prevent inflation. Raising interest rates immediately reduces the number of people borrowing money, and thus reduces the amount of new money being created.

A third way the Federal Reserve manages the money supply is by buying and selling U.S. Government bonds. When the Federal Reserve sells a bond for money, that money ceases to exist. The money is removed from circulation, and the Federal Reserve can shred the money or save it for future circulation. It has no value. However, the government can print more money at any time to buy back bonds. This increases the amount of money in circulation and again leads to inflation. The Federal Reserve can only buy back as many bonds as it has sold, so in the long run there is no increase or decrease of the total money supply, except that the Federal Reserve pays interest on those bonds, which does increase the money supply.

None of these tools enable the Federal Reserve to permanently remove money from the economy. From that standpoint, it seems that deflation is impossible over the long run. However, there are some ways deflation can occur. One is to collect taxes and shred the money. That decreases the amount of money in circulation. Instead of having ten dollars floating around for every loaf of bread, there is only one dollar available. Money becomes scarce and prices go down.

Deflation can also occur as the money supply is increased. If businesses borrow money and invest in increased production, then growth can match the pace of inflation. Rather than decreasing the number of dollars, we increase the number of loaves of bread. Caloric production surpasses the increased number of tokens. The same thing happens due to an expanding population. If more people share the money supply, then money becomes scarce, and prices fall.

Paradox in the Time-Money Continuum

Suppose you own a nice home. You borrowed money, bought a house, and now make payments on the loan. Now consider the person who built the house. They are probably living in a similar home. They may have borrowed money, bought their home, and now they are making payments. Now think about the banker who holds the loans on both houses. The banker probably has a house and mortgage of her own.

Like many Americans, you may be making monthly installment payments on a car. How about the company that made it? They could be making payments on a billion dollar loan for the factory that built your car.

Then there is the national debt. It's unimaginably immense, numerically too large for the brain to comprehend. Counting 1-2-3, it would take 31,000 years to count to one trillion, yet how many trillions of debt do we have now? The debt grows so fast that any recorded number quickly becomes inaccurate.

Many developing nations are also heavily in debt. Countries that borrow money from the International Monetary Fund (IMF) for infrastructure projects are often pressured to exploit and export natural resources to repay the loans. Researchers have documented a systematic increase in annual deforestation among countries that participate in IMF programs.[38] Some environmental organizations hope to pay down those debts to save the rain forests.

So what would happen if we picked up a pencil and erased all debts and set account books back to $0.00?

Perhaps you have heard of the paradox in the space-time continuum. You travel back in time and meet yourself. Because of this encounter, the other you makes different choices and changes your history until you don't travel back in time to meet yourself, creating a paradox. Now consider a paradox in the time-money continuum.

Think back to the purchase of your house and car. Maybe it started after drawing your paycheck of $1,000. "Whoa." you said, "This isn't enough." So you went to the bank, and the banker escorted you in a time capsule to the future, scooping up your future paychecks. You return home loaded with cash and bought a $150,000 house and a $25,000 car. Cute trick.

Then you begin to encounter the future. Deposit your paycheck in the bank and "Whoosh!" Most of it suddenly vanishes into the time vortex, flowing back to your past. There is little left in the account to pay for new expenses.

That's frustrating, but you have an idea. You decide to cash the paycheck without depositing it in the bank. Then you can spend the same money again, confident that the banker cannot travel the altered time stream again to stop you from borrowing money for the house and car. Great plan.

Unfortunately, the banker shows up in your present.

"You think you own this house and car?" the banker says.
"Sure." you say, "This is my house and car."
"No." She says," You only think it is your house and car"
Drats! You rush to the bank to deposit the money.

But what if the banker (along with the rest of the world) were in cahoots with you? What would happen if we erased all debts and started from scratch?

The work is already done. The houses are built. Cars have been manufactured. Highways and bridges are built. We built it all in the past, so what's the harm? We borrowed money from the so-called future and used it to build the wealth we have today. In caloric terms, however, loans don't come from the future; they come from the present.

Building a bridge or house requires calories of food and fuel energy. We cannot build anything without calories or people die and machines quit. In effect, we never actually borrowed anything from the future. We created material wealth with calories we had.

Our species created the economy. Yet it is the economy that controls us. The economy exists as a series of numbers darting back and forth over electronic circuitry. If the numbers are positive then we are happy. If the numbers are negative then we have a national problem. People lose their jobs when there is a recession, and without a paycheck, they lose their houses. The houses don't disappear. The houses sit there empty, while families are forced out onto the street. Numbers in a computer determine whether or not people are allowed to go inside the houses.

The economy is an imaginary entity we created. If we created it once, then we can create it again. We live at a time when debts threaten the fabric of society. Many people are stressed to the breaking point to pay bills. Is it worth putting ourselves through hard times just to protect an imaginary entity? Is it worth sacrificing our rain forests? Is it worth permanently losing thousands of species of plants and animals for mere numerical convenience?

What would happen if we mutually agreed to stop channeling money to the past? We know the houses, cars, and infrastructure would not disappear into a time vortex. The work is done, and we would still have the fruits of our labors. The unknown is what would happen to money. Money would have no value until we regained trust in the system and mutually agreed that money was scarce and therefore valuable.

Law of Jubilee

Debt cancellation acts are as old as the market economy. Issuing coins created a mechanism for goods and services to flow from producers to non-producers, such as from farmers to soldiers. In the process, money inherently accumulated among the priests-kings-bankers who actually issued the money and wrote the laws. Over time, the rich got richer and the poor got poorer.

In times of hardship, such as a drought, commoners were often forced to borrow money against their holdings to feed the family. Landowners lost title to their lands, effectively becoming renters. Unable to keep up with accumulating debts, the losses escalated. Throughout the history of "civilization," peasants were forced to give up their sons and daughters or wives to bondage, meaning slavery and sexual slavery, to settle debts. When all other assets were lost, men or their sons were drafted into armies and sent off to war.[39]

Uprisings against inequality were often violently suppressed. However, people tolerate only so much oppression before banding together and risking death over debt. Hence, the biblical Law of Jubilee stipulated that all debts must be cancelled on the Sabbath year—that is every seven years—to rebalance the system and free those who were held in bondage.

Debt cancellation events are recurrent throughout history whenever disparity between the rich and poor grows too extreme and debts spiral out of control. According to investment advisor Porter Stansberry, author of *The American Jubilee*, we are due for a debt correction. Our combined federal, state, local, corporate, and consumer debts add up to $808,000 per family, far more than can realistically be repaid.[40]

In regards to the consumer portion, including home mortgages, car payments, student loans, and credit card debts, Stansberry writes, *"This debt will create a depression that will be worse than it was in 2008. This time, the government has allowed massive amounts of debt to be piled on the weakest in our society. The poor — and especially the young and poor in our country — have no hope of being able to afford the American dream anymore... Debts of this magnitude cannot be financed normally. Debts that can't be paid won't be paid. In other words, it's not just the size of American's debts that's the problem. It's who owes the money that's the bigger concern."*

In hard times, citizens resort to populism from left and right to overthrow the norms. In 2016, President Trump was elected as a self-serving populist. The Trump tax cut baited supporters with a small, temporary break for the middle class in order to pass a larger, permanent tax cut for the wealthiest people like himself—all while further exacerbating the national deficit. In other words, it brought us even closer to a debt cancellation event, which as Stansberry fears, could turn bloody before the accounts are balanced. Stansberry is not in favor of debt cancellation. He simply believes reconciliation is inevitable, and he advises people how to secure their assets against losses.

Cryptocurrencies

The next step in the ongoing abstractification of money is the production of digital cryptocurrencies like Bitcoin. Cryptocurrencies are promoted as an alternative money and a secure way to conduct transactions in the digital world free from government intervention, such that the value cannot be diluted or co-opted by lowering interest rates or printing new money. In the case of Bitcoin, the system is locked to prevent the total currency in circulation from ever exceeding 21 million Bitcoins. Although imaginary, scarcity made Bitcoins increasingly valuable, and the built-in security features makes it a suitable medium for exchange. However, instead of releasing all 21 million Bitcoins at once, the system releases a few at a time, ensuring value even when there were only a few Bitcoins in circulation. The rest are "mined" to release them.

In this case, mining requires complex mathematical computations for no apparent purpose other than releasing Bitcoins. For a given number of computations, a new Bitcoin is released, and the miner earns a coin or some fraction thereof. To manage the release of Bitcoins over time, computations automatically become more difficult as more people start mining, bringing a lower return for the investment. In addition, the reward for mining Bitcoins drops by half approximately every four years.

Bitcoins have no actual value beyond the perceived scarcity among those who buy and sell or exchange them. Yet, mining for Bitcoins is lucrative enough that speculators have invested in buildings full of computers dedicated to mining computations for Bitcoins. Here is Montana, investors are establishing Bitcoin mining operations because our northern climate helps cool computers processors, saving energy and therefore money. An expense of $251 million in land, buildings, and computers is perceived as a worthwhile investment for a significantly greater return in Bitcoin.[41] As of this writing, it is estimated that the worldwide energy consumption to mine Bitcoins is approximately equivalent to that used by the entire country of Denmark...[42] all without actually producing anything!

The End of Money?

Money arose with market economies to funnel goods and services from producers to non-producers such as priests, kings, and soldiers. Most economic activity was calorie intensive, including the effort to mine and refine precious metals to make coins. As economic production has increased over the millennia, the number of non-producers has steadily grown, leading to increasingly creative strategies to employ people consuming resources rather than producing.

In the case of "mining" cryptocurrencies, no actual human labor is involved in the computational work. Instead, we employ armies of people to mine natural resources from the earth to construct buildings, transmission lines, power plants, and computers that burn up fuel energy, exacerbating global warming while producing nothing.

Will growing demand necessitate covering the earth with nuclear power plants to double world energy supply to produce nothing on a global scale? What happens as automation increasingly displaces workers, until there is nothing left but robots consuming resources and running the economy? At what point do we start taxing robots to provide the unemployed masses with Universal Basic Income to purchase goods and services from robots?

"The final dream of civilization is that everything will be controlled, organized, categorized; all wildness and spontaneity will be eradicated. Fish will live in fish farms. Trees will grow in tree farms. Animals for our food will live in feedlots. Humans will live in cities completely isolated from any other creatures (except cute pets), isolated from anything that might remind them of true wild nature. 'Inferior races' will wither in poverty until they vanish. The Earth will be remodeled in the name of production. Any spontaneous, uncontrolled expression of life will be crushed."

—Miles Olson,
Unlearn, Rewild (2012) [43]

Frack This Planet
Whatever Happened to Peak Oil?

It's one thing when environmentalists predict the end of civilization. It is quite another when bankers, geologists, oil drillers, and the military agree with them, as was the case with "peak oil" as recently as 2011. The best information available indicated that world oil production would climax by about 2015 and start declining every year thereafter.[44] Meanwhile, demand would keep climbing, leading to spiking oil prices that would drastically impact our economy and our way of life. On the positive side, it was believed that high oil prices would necessitate a rapid transition to more sustainable living. We would be forced to wean ourselves off of fossil fuels, thus halting climate change and saving the planet from global warming.

However, a completely different picture emerged by 2012. Oil production surged, prices fell, the economy picked up, and life continued on as usual. Few people seemed to care that climate change symptoms progressed faster than worst-case scenarios predicted. That is a staggering discrepancy between forecasts from one year to the next. How were the experts so wrong?

Malthusians vs. Cornucopians

The Peak Oil saga was another round in a two hundred-year-old debate between Malthusians and Cornucopian beliefs. The overly pessimistic Malthusian perspective perceives natural resources as similar to a pie. There is only so much to go around. The overly optimistic Cornucopian belief, on the other hand, perceives that humans are creative, and we shouldn't worry about things like overpopulation and resource consumption, because new technologies will produce more pies, increasing prosperity for all. Neither viewpoint accurately models reality.

The Malthusian perspective originated with Thomas Malthus (1766–1834), a British economist and philosopher. Being a citizen of an island nation, Malthus naturally predicted that the burgeoning population would expand exponentially, while resource production, especially food, would eventually plateau, leading to mass die-offs to balance population with available resources.[45] The Brits have successfully dodged fate thus far, along with the rest of the industrial world, largely by expanding the resource pie beyond national boundaries to efficiently exploit natural resources from pole to pole around the globe.

On the surface, the Cornucopian perspective seems blindly dependent on faith that technology will save us from ourselves. To Cornucopians, however, it isn't blind faith, but proven faith in the dynamic interplay of supply and demand. Rising demand raises prices, which triggers more investment in production and alternative substitutes, which ultimately expands supply, lowers prices, and leads to increased prosperity.

For example, the cost of gasoline rose from $1.45 to $4.12 per gallon during the Bush administration from 2001 to 2008,[46] just before the economy faltered. The shocking rise in fuel costs seemed to presage vastly higher prices that were predicted when worldwide production peaked and started declining. However, the relationship between supply and demand is more complicated.

In the short term, high fuel prices contributed to the financial crises of 2008 and the Great Recession, which slowed the economy and reduced global oil consumption. That alone helped stabilize oil prices. In addition, rising fuel prices impacted everyone. Job or no job, people reacted to higher prices one way or another. Many people re-evaluated every potential trip and drove less than before. Gasoline consumption dropped by 3.2% in 2008, stayed about the same in 2009 and 2010 then dropped another 2.9% as fuel prices rose again in 2011.[47] Less driving further helped reduce demand and stabilize prices. Consumers also bought more fuel-efficient vehicles, driving more miles on less fuel.

People embraced new technologies, such as hybrid and electric vehicles, or unconventional alternatives. My brother built a biodiesel processing unit and started making fuel from used vegetable oil (French fry grease) obtained free from restaurants. Another brother experimented with wood gas, driving his truck around on firewood for a while, before switching to a diesel truck with a straight vegetable oil (SVO) system. Across America, people experimented with crazy new innovations, looking for ways to squeeze a few more miles per gallon. Millions of people adapted to higher prices, each in their own way. The result is that fuel consumption dropped to 2000 levels, even though the U.S. population grew by an additional 31 million people in need of transportation.[48]

Peak oil and the anticipated end of civilization fizzled with a new oil glut.

Higher oil prices also make the oil business more lucrative, rewarding those who can increase supply by conventional or innovative new means. Setting aside the issue of fracking for the moment, there are tremendous reserves of oil shale and coal buried underneath this country, enough to fuel the economy for several hundred years, as noted in earlier editions of this book. Converting oil shale or coal to gasoline is more expensive than pumping oil out of the ground, and higher prices make these alternatives more feasible, thereby increasing supply to further stabilize oil prices. Higher fuel costs result in lower consumption and greater production, stabilizing prices over the long haul.

Texas banking executive Matthew R. Simmons wagered $10,000 against New York Times columnist John Tierney in 2005 that, according to Malthusian thought, the average daily price of crude oil would exceed $200 per barrel in 2010. Oil rose from $65/barrel in 2005 to $145/barrel in 2008, then dropped to $50/barrel in the aftermath of the global financial crises, and back up to $80/barrel in 2010 (or $71/barrel when adjusted for inflation). Simmons died before the wager ended on January 1, 2011, but his estate dutifully paid up on the bet.[49] Even then, lay persons and analysts alike were forecasting peak oil and the decline of civilization in just a few short years.

The biggest factor stabilizing oil prices was "fracking," which is short for hydraulic fracturing. Oil companies pump a witches' brew of toxic chemicals into the ground under intense pressure, typically 5,000 to 9,000 psi, to fracture rock and force residual oil or natural gas back to the wellhead for extraction. Fracking is a comically appropriate term, given that "frack" and "fracking" has been used as a television-friendly expletive in the show *Battlestar Galactica* since 1978. We are indeed fracking the planet.

Fracking chemicals include friction-reducing additives referred to as "slickwater" to facilitate the flow of facking fluid underground, along with biocides to prevent microbial growth and oxygen scavengers to prevent corrosion of metal pipes. Fracking chemicals include hydrochloric acid, polyacrylamide, ethylene glycol, sodium chloride, borate salts, sodium and potassium carbonates, glutaraldehyde, isopropanol, and methanol.[50] Fracking companies claimed that the toxic chemicals would not contaminate the groundwater and the hydraulic pressure would not cause earthquakes. Not surprisingly, they were wrong.

The incentive to live in denial is huge. Fracking allows us to increase oil production, stabilize or lower prices, expand the American economy, and avoid dealing with realty for another day. And the reality is that our economy effectively places zero value on the future.

Fracking Ourselves

In terms of resources, anything that can be extracted and profited from today has value. Anything left behind for future generations has no value. For example, oil wells produce a great deal of natural gas, yet it is often too far away from pipelines to bring it to market. The problem is easily remedied by venting natural gas into the atmosphere and setting it on fire, called flaring. OPEC countries previously burned off enough natural gas to supply world needs for several hundred years, because it had zero value to them at the time. The same thing is happening on a smaller scale in the oil fields in North Dakota[51] and Texas.[52] As a fuel, natural gas is relatively clean and low in carbon content. It can also be combined with air under high pressure to make nitrogen fertilizer in the form of ammonia. Instead, we are burning gas off as a waste product, globally adding as much carbon to the atmosphere as 70 million cars with nothing to show for it.[53]

In another famous bet, Paul Ehrlich, author of *The Population Bomb* (1968) and Malthusian in his perspective, wagered against economist Julian Simon of the University of Maryland that resource scarcity would lead to a rise in the cost of copper, chromium, nickel, tin, and tungsten from 1980 to 1990. On paper, they invested an imaginary

$1,000 ($200 in each metal) and waited ten years to see what happened. If prices went up (adjusted for inflation), Simon would pay Ehrlich the value in excess of the original $1,000, and vice versa.

Ehrlich lost the bet as metal prices fell during the ten-year time period, reducing the value of their hypothetical investment. Ehrlich paid Simon $576.07 for the difference between the imaginary investment and the final, lower value.[54] This story has become part of the Cornucopian mythology in spite of the fact that four out of the five metals have since increased in inflation-adjusted prices.

Resource extraction used to be much like it was for Jed Clampett of the Beverly Hill Billies:

"Come and listen to a story about a man named Jed. A poor mountaineer, barely kept his family fed, then one day he was shootin' at some food, and up through the ground came a bubblin' crude. Oil that is, black gold, Texas tea."[55]

Our descendants will never have it so easy. Speculators are only interested in the easiest, most accessible resources to extract. Past investors hopped all over the globe, skimming the cream off the top. There are still plenty of resources to be extracted, yet deposits are of lesser and lesser quality or more costly to extract, and often highly damaging to the environment.

At the peak of fracking, investors were drilling more than 15,000 wells per year in the states.[56] Unlike oil fields in the Middle East, however, these are mostly small volume, short-lived wells. In the Bakken shales of North Dakota, production can decline by 80% within the first two years, necessitating additional drilling.

I wonder what would have happened if we long ago raised the price of fossil fuels with green taxes. Instead of income tax, what if a green tax was added to the cost of oil, gas, and coal? We could have a tax system where citizens could reduce their tax burden by investing in energy efficiency, rather than wasting time searching for income and deduction loopholes on paper. We would seek to minimize our use of expensive oil, gas, and coal by driving 100-mpg cars and living in much more efficient houses. Energy taxes would have conserved supplies, greatly reduced our carbon emissions, and potentially avoided trillions of dollars in future expenses associated with global warming. Unfortunately, we didn't adopt green taxes. Instead, we consumed the easy oil in an orgy of inefficiency. Rather than making conservation profitable, we facilitated yet more resource exploitation.

The next generation is unable to bid against us for the resources we consume. Investors and speculators comb the planet for every

The more damage we do to the environment the more dependent we become on additional resource extraction and energy consumption.

marketable resource, trying to make a quick buck. As a society, we leave nothing behind for future generations, except toxic mining sites, toxic fracking sites, and a destabilized global climate.

Ironically, the more damage we do to the environment, the more dependent we become on additional resource extraction and energy consumption. When the climate is too hot we turn on the air conditioner and burn more fossil fuels. When crops suffer from hot temperatures or lack of rain, we build pipelines, pumps, and even desalinization facilities for irrigation water. When superstorms damage our cities and infrastructure we consume more energy and resources to repair the damage and build levees for protection. Our children and our grandchildren face not only the challenge of depleted resources, but also the challenge of living on a fracked planet with a fracked climate and a fracked government with trillions of dollars in federal debts to pay off.

The Malthusians were wrong about Peak Oil because they failed to grasp the complex system of checks and balances that work to stabilize supply and demand. Cornucopians were also wrong, because we have not expanded the resource pie. We merely increased our efficiency at exploiting whatever worthwhile resources remain. We are fracking the planet in a misguided attempt to maintain the status quo.

The tragedy is that we could have invested in energy efficiency decades ago. We could have built more fuel-efficient vehicles and better insulated houses to reduce our dependency on fossil fuels at a profit, increasing our prosperity and keeping prices lower in the short-term, while ensuring a supply of resources for the future. Instead, history will likely remember ours as the most environmentally irresponsible generation in all of human history.

Montana has especially high oil consumption, the sixth highest in the country measured on a per capita basis.[57] Coincidentally, we are thirty-seventh in the nation for median household income.[58] Between those two factors, Montanans spend more income on oil than most Americans. As a matter of necessity, Montanans drive big, heavy-duty trucks for pulling horse trailers, hauling supplies, or driving into the mountains to cut firewood. Being a rural state, a trip to the grocery store often exceeds 100 miles of driving. Just getting a 40-pound kindergartener to school can entail a thirty-mile drive twice a day, often accomplished with a full-size, 19 mpg pickup truck, capable of hauling a one-ton payload!

Personally, I appreciate fossil fuels. I appreciate being able to drive to town and back (120 miles) every week or two for groceries. I appreciate that my neighbor plows my very long driveway for me. I appreciate the fact that a small amount of gasoline in my truck and chainsaw enables me to bring home a much larger supply of firewood to stay warm through the winter. I would abhor all that work if it were with handsaws and a team of horses.

I value fossil fuels enough to want to conserve them for future generations. It is for this reason that I built an energy-efficient passive solar home and installed solar panels to generate electricity. I value our natural resources enough to do whatever I reasonably can to make a positive difference for our planet and climate for the next generation.

In the short term, we have enough oil to keep the economy rolling. In the long term, we need to wean ourselves off fossil fuels before we run out. Solar power and other alternative energy technologies are increasing in efficiency and dropping in price, just as computers did. We can look forward to the day when virtually every human-made object becomes a source of energy, from solar panels blanketing every roof to windows that generate electricity. Even the paint on our houses and electric cars will one day generate electricity. Cornucopians will prevail, and we will inevitably build a sustainable economy, but not before we destabilize the climate, toxify the planet, and wipe out half of all life on earth. Sadly, we may ultimately succeed in building a green economy on a dead planet.

"Increasing efficiency in work means more goods. In order to keep the economic system going, more consumption must occur to buy back the increase in goods. Thus, free time is converted into consumption time. Time spent neither at work nor in consuming is increasingly viewed as wasted time."

—Herbert Applebaum,
Work in Non-market & Transitional Societies (1984)[59]

Too Many Jobs?
Prosperity with Less Work

Nearly every politician campaigns on the promise to strengthen the economy, create jobs, and put people back to work. Jobs are a big issue in the best of times and in the worst of times. In fact, jobs are often the only issue in the news. But what if job creation actually makes us poorer instead of richer? And what if the path to prosperity called for less work and fewer jobs?

Consider the "Recovery and Reinvestment" signs that sprouted up in every community as part of the stimulus package President Obama promoted to create jobs and get the economy rolling in 2009. While there was no specific cost accounting, realistic estimates range from $5 million to $20 million spent on producing and installing signs.[60] People were employed to mine and refine metals for the steel posts and aluminum signs. More people were employed to print and distribute the signs and to mix concrete and install the signs. If these signs were so beneficial to our economy, why don't we install a million times as many and grow the economy that much faster?

A few million dollars wasn't a huge expense in comparison to the overall size of the stimulus package, yet those millions could have been invested more productively, such as for energy efficiency upgrades in government buildings.

Recovery and Reinvestment signs contributed nothing towards our standard of living, our quality of life, or the health of our environment. On the contrary, essential natural resources were mined, processed, and used for no net benefit. At the end of the day we were left with fewer natural resources, potentially higher prices, and thousands of signs that will degrade until it becomes necessary to hire workers to remove them.

Similarly, consider something as ubiquitous as junk mail. How many tens of thousands of people are employed to cut down trees, mill them into paper, produce ink, design graphic artwork for catalogs and political campaign brochures, address them, mail them, ship them across the country and sort them into boxes, only to have most junk mail recycled or landfilled without even being looked at?

Everyone along the way, from the graphic artist to accountants and janitors, are glad to have the work, a chance to earn money and keep food on the table, without anyone seeming to notice that they are functionally employed to do nothing more than consume and dispose of our natural resources.

Taxpayers invested between $5 million and $20 million hiring people to manufacture and install "Recovery and Reinvestment" signs.

In the 1850s, Thoreau observed that many people were employed doing meaningless work, the equivalent of throwing stones over a wall only to throw them back. Our situation is far worse today, because throwing stones over a wall is harmless compared to consuming resources without purpose.

Burning billions of barrels of oil permanently depletes the resource, devastates the landscape with drilling sites, contributes to global warming, and results in higher prices at the pump. We employ millions of people directly or indirectly to extract and process our remaining natural resources for no other purpose than to dispose of them. If we have nothing tangible to show for the investment, then we literally make ourselves poorer by working too much, leaving less wealth for the next generation.

Disposable Jobs

Sadly, any company that builds quality products risks saturating the market and putting itself out of business. If products were designed to endure, then people wouldn't need to buy anything, factories would shut down, employees would be laid off, and no one would have money to buy anything. Products that are designed to fail are believed to be good for business, a means of keeping the economy rolling. It is an effective way to keep people busy running on a treadmill to nowhere.

This inverted logic might have made economic sense when markets were finite and natural resources seemed infinite, yet we are faced with the opposite problem now. Resources are limited, and anything tossed in the trash raises the price of our remaining natural resources. For example, copper is becoming increasingly expensive, and every time we discard an electrical cord in the trash instead of recycling it, we effectively raise the cost of copper products everywhere.

We've not only created a disposable economy, we've created a disposable country. Even the houses that shelter us are little more than temporary shanties, dressed up on the surface. Most houses are designed so poorly that they require a constant influx of fossil fuel energy for summer cooling and winter heating. Most houses are so flimsy that you could punch a hole in the wall. From leaky water heaters to failing asphalt shingles to carpets that must be replaced and bathrooms that rot, houses require an army of maintenance workers to keep the structures habitable long enough to pay off the mortgage. We've built millions upon millions of houses, and yet almost none were engineered to last more than a few decades without major repairs. All that work, which is supposedly good for the economy, keeps people gainfully employed converting raw wealth into more garbage for the landfills.

By the same reasoning, earthquakes, tornadoes, and other natural disasters are often considered good for the economy because people find work cleaning up the mess, rebuilding infrastructure, and replacing everything from building materials to merchandise.[61] Every major oil spill is recorded as a positive economic entry in our national accounts due to the jobs and income created to clean up the mess while completely ignoring resource loss and damage.[62] According to this kind of logic, America would be richer than ever if we torched every house, office, and factory and demolished all our possessions.

Never mind that carbon emissions are spiking upward when they should be tapering off. Never mind that global warming is happening faster than predicted, or that cumulative factors could potentially lead to a runaway greenhouse effect. When the economy is in the doldrums and unemployment levels up, all other concerns are secondary. It is imperative that we put everyone back to work making plastic toys to go with every Happy Meal®.

We are arguably victims of our own success. The industrial economy is so productive that a few percent of the population can supply all our needs, and everyone else must be employed doing meaningless work to pretend they are contributing to society.

Dead-End Jobs

Consider the funeral industry. There was a time when funeral services were handled directly by family members. Wash and dress the body, nail some boards together for a casket, call friends and family members over for a nice service and burial.

Now we have turned death into an enterprise that employs millions of workers. We hire specialists to not only clean and dress the corpse, but to embalm them with toxic chemicals, pumping our loved ones full of formaldehyde, glutaraldehyde, methanol, and other solvents. In the U.S. alone, we produce and bury about 5.3 million gallons of embalming fluids annually, threatening groundwater supplies with toxic corpses.[63] Morticians orchestrate elaborate ceremonies, and we entomb the dead in expensive caskets and plant marble headstones to mark their passing for eternity. Not surprisingly, the typical cost of a funeral in North America runs between $7,000 and $10,000.[64] We employ countless people to literally mine the earth for resources to bury in the ground.

The irony is that job creation is intended to sustain the economy, yet there is nothing remotely sustainable about employing people to decimate life on earth. There have been five past mass extinctions in the history of life on Earth. From asteroid impacts to massive volcanic eruptions that smothered the planet, each event permanently wiped out half or more of all species. Nature required tens of millions of years for surviving species to diversify and fill ecological voids. Now we are in the midst of the sixth mass extinction, the result of the collective human effort to exploit all remaining marketable resources before our grandchildren reach adulthood.

We have destabilized the climate, with the forecast calling for more job-building natural disasters, ranging from floods to droughts, heat waves, tornadoes, hurricanes, and rising sea levels. Meanwhile, grasslands are turning to deserts, tropical forests are being logged to oblivion, Arctic ice is rapidly melting away, coral reefs are dying, and the oceans are predicted to be fished out by 2048.[65] We are expected to wipe out half of all life on earth this century,[66] and politicians everywhere are worried about the unemployment rate.

Committing labor and natural resources towards work that doesn't produce anything ultimately results in a net drag on the economy. It raises costs by diminishing resource supply and makes us poorer. That is the sad reality of our present economic situation: the faster the economy grows, the more impoverished we ultimately become.

Conversely, the path to building a sustainable and prosperous economy is to eliminate extraneous work and dedicate our resources towards investments that make a tangible, positive difference. Call it the path to green prosperity. The more we invest in conservation and eliminating waste, the wealthier we become.

Positive Profit

If other companies market products that are engineered to fail, what happens if a business manufactures a quality product? For example, the first portable circular saw was created by Edmond Michele in 1924, which was later refined to become the worm-drive Model 77 Skilsaw in 1937. Eighty years later, the Model 77 remains in production with only minor variations from the original design. It is known as "the saw that built America."[67] It was also the workhorse in building my own home. The Model 77 is built to last and readily repairable. Unlike other tools, a Skilsaw doesn't break and get tossed in the trash. It is a successful product because of its durability, and it has been a positive strategy for the company. Consequently, the Skil Corporation historically spent less money on advertising than its competitors, allowing the quality of their products to advertise themselves.[68]

While Skilsaws are almost infinitely repairable, contractors use them hard and periodically buy shiny new replacements, often saving old saws for parts. Between new and returning customers, the company maintains steady sales. Moreover, the sheer size of the global marketplace is hard to fathom. It might be possible to saturate one market, yet there are always other markets to expand into. Any company that produces quality, essential products and services has billions of potential customers around the world. There is no need to manufacture disposable junk.

Under the reign of Steve Jobs, Apple focused on making premium products that commanded a premium price. That strategy propelled exponential growth, with Apple temporarily gaining recognition as the world's most valuable company. Apple and its competitors were so successful that they largely achieved global market saturation with combined annual sales of 1.5 billion smart phones.[69] That's okay since we all benefit from equal access to quality technology. If the product works, let's not degrade it with software or hardware designed to make it run more slowly with age. Let's saturate the market with quality products and call it a success, producing only as many new phones as necessary to replace those that are broken beyond repair.

Surplus labor can be applied towards other worthy goals. We do not need to destroy the world for employment. From quality products to conservation efforts, there is ample opportunity to profit while making a positive difference.

Profit through Conservation

Prosperity in the twenty-first century will be created by those who seek profit by making the world a better place. Ecopreneurs will out-compete inefficient, abusive industries by starting green businesses that close the loop on wasted materials, energy, time, money and labor. They will heal wasted ecosystems and restore biodiversity at a profit while delivering useful goods and services to the public. Homeowners too, will profit by seeking ways to eliminate everything from high energy bills to mortgage payments, even eliminating the need for a regular job.

Fortunately, there is no need to wait, for the revolution has already started. The door is wide open, and anyone can walk the path to green prosperity, changing the world every step along the way.

One small step is to install a solar water heater or hire a contractor to do the installation. A solar water heater reduces a household's dependence on fossil fuels, lowers the utility bill, and brings a timely return for the investment. By making similar investments and upgrades in a house, a person can greatly reduce their utility bill. Then add photovoltaic panels to run the utility meter backwards, zeroing out electric consumption entirely. It is far easier to avoid expenses and debt in the first place than to work a job and attempt to spend one's way out of debt.

As a young adult, I abhorred the idea of spending my entire life working to pay a mortgage, rent, utilities, car payments, school loans, and other bills. I didn't mind working, but I wanted it to count for something. I have succeeded in life by avoiding extraneous work, rather than creating it. I successfully avoided paying rent or a home mortgage, college loans, car payments, big utility bills, or any other substantial recurring expenses. Indeed, there is no greater feeling of security than having a durable and efficient home with no mortgage and no utility bill. The greatest job security is not needing a job at all, and it was that freedom that allowed me to indulge in writing until I turned it into a successful career.

There are many pathways to eliminating expenses, debt, and the need for jobs, yet the reality is that most people won't seize the opportunity to break free. For instance, shockingly few people install solar water heaters or properly insulate their homes, even though the economics are really good, and tax incentives often make it better. Installing a solar water heater or competently hiring a contractor requires an investment of time, knowledge, and money. As a result, disappointingly few solar water heaters have been installed.

A simple solution is for utilities to install and maintain solar water heaters for their customers. By installing solar water heaters on thousands of homes, the utility can benefit from volume discount pricing, repetitive installation experience, and easy maintenance when installing mostly identical units. The utility can pay the installation costs upfront, collecting a portion of the savings each month to recoup the investment. The customer could benefit from a slightly lower utility bill in the beginning, growing larger after the solar water heater is fully paid for. The utility would benefit from saved energy, which could then be sold to other customers without having to invest in expensive new power plants.

With the right incentives to spur investment in conservation and alternative energies, we could create real jobs and put millions of people to work weaning our civilization off of fossil fuels once and for all. In fact, with appropriate incentives for companies to manufacture long-lasting products and recycle everything, it wouldn't take long to create a futuristic world where everyone has everything they need, and nobody has to work much.

I know from experience that it is possible to break free from the rat race, to live in prosperity with minimal bills, and to choose whether or not to work. This freedom allows one to pursue their own Dreams and ultimately makes the world a better place. We can build a green economy, end poverty, and conserve resources for future generations. First, we need to stop creating meaningless work and consider what kind of world we really want to bring into existence. Indeed, re-envisioning the meaning of work is the only chance we have of saving the planet from ourselves and leaving something for the next generation.

"The economics of the future is somewhat different. You see, money doesn't exist in the 24th century... The acquisition of wealth is no longer the driving force in our lives. We work to better ourselves and the rest of humanity."

—Captain Jean-Luc Picard,
Star Trek: First Contact (1996)[70]

Everything is Free
The Past and Future of Abundance

Stone Age life was relatively easy much of the time. Real estate was free, and a functional shelter could typically be constructed in a day from local materials with the aid of friends and family members. The utility bill entailed collecting sticks for firewood. Clean running water was available from nearby streams and springs. Clothing and tools were labor intensive to make, but lasted for years. There were no taxes to pay, no gardens to plant, and no weeds to pull. Hunter-gatherers practiced ecosystem management, such as burning the understory of a forest to favor some plants and shrubs while discouraging others; otherwise, work largely entailed harvesting and eating. How did life become so miserable that a couple must work full time for twenty to thirty years merely to buy a place where they can legally sleep without trespassing? Is it still possible to enjoy the freedom our ancestors knew?

We often assume civilized life is easier and better than the brutish ways of our ancestors who struggled each day to find food and shelter. Yet, the transition from hunting and gathering to farming typically led to more work, less dietary diversity, poorer nutrition, and widespread health problems. Imagine growing grain and eating grits or bread for breakfast, lunch, and dinner every day. It was neither interesting nor nutritional. Farming cultures out-competed hunter-gather cultures, not because the lifestyle was better, but because farming produced more calories per acre, leading to denser populations that eventually displaced hunter-gatherers.

Surplus calories logically should have enabled greater prosperity and leisure, yet actually had the opposite effect. On the positive side, surplus calories enabled specialization, spawning cottage industries in textiles, ceramics, and metalworking to provide a plethora of new products. On the negative side, surplus calories and larger populations led to the rise of an administrative class of priests, rulers, and armies who demanded payment of tributes or taxes from the working class.

Subsequent increases in production efficiency exacerbated the problem. In order to redistribute wealth from producers to consumers, societies invented creative new jobs to keep people busy. As discussed earlier, common folk were employed building monuments, conscripted into armies, or hired to produce disposable products and provide quasi-services. In addition, people learned to sell goods and services that were formerly free, creating work from nothing.

The Price of Freedom

Land was originally free. It wasn't manufactured. Nobody slaved to create it. It was just there. People didn't buy land or sell it. Throughout the ages, different cultures owned or defended territories, yet the land within the territory was often free to all members of the society. There was no mortgage and no interest payments. Land was free to whoever came along and remained free thereafter. Now we expect to expend tens of thousands of dollars and potentially years of our lives working to pay for something that was originally free.

In many cultures the idea of buying or selling land was as sacrilegious or bizarre as buying or selling one's own mother. Many tribal societies had a concept of property rights, such as the right to hunt or farm an area without including ownership of the land itself or the right to block other people from being there. Larger societies with higher population densities logically had more complex ideas about property rights and land ownership, and for those of us acculturated to the modern world, it is difficult to imagine *not* having to buy land.

Additionally, houses were originally constructed for free out of locally abundant materials. It doesn't take long to construct a wickiup, for example, which looks much like a tipi, but is constructed of sticks and slabs of bark and grass and debris. A wickiup allows for a comfortable fire inside, making a cozy home in the middle of winter, with smoke filtering up and out through the roof. More elaborate homes could be made with walls of mud and straw, and still cost only a few days labor to construct.

Houses today are vastly larger and unfathomably more expensive. The average American home increased in size from 1,660 square feet in 1973 to 2,687 square feet by 2015, while average household size dropped from 3.01 to 2.54 people per household.[71] The average cost to build the average home is nearly $300,000.[72] Add that to the cost of the land, and the average homeowner will have to work for a very long time to fully own their home. Mortgage interest rates often double the lifetime cost of a home loan. Unfortunately, most houses are constructed so poorly that they don't last the duration of a mortgage without extensive repairs and maintenance.

Sadly, the greater the population density, the higher the cost of land and housing. In some parts of California, for example, building permits and impact fees alone can cost $40,000 to $60,000,[73] which is more than I spent on my entire house in Montana. In Tokyo, where housing is really expensive, one man famously bought a building lot the size of a parking space and built a compact three-story home for $500,000. That was considered a bargain in Tokyo.[74]

Food has also become expensive, particularly meat. Wild game was once free to anyone who could harvest it. There was a labor cost in making a weapon, stalking close enough to kill, and butchering the animal to haul the meat home. Yet meat was often greatly abundant.

From 1804 to 1806 the Lewis and Clark Expedition hunted with muzzle loading rifles as they explored up the Missouri River, crossed

Land was originally free, and houses were constructed free from locally abundant materials.

over the Rocky Mountains, and descended the Columbia River to the Pacific Ocean, then journeyed all the way back. The thirty-three-member expedition worked hard and ate heartily, each person consuming up to nine pounds of red meat per day, the equivalent of thirty-six quarter-pound hamburgers. The expedition often described "immense" numbers of wild game, from bison to beavers to waterfowl. Expedition members killed and ate 1,001 deer, 375 elk, 227 bison, 62 antelope, 43 grizzly bears, 23 black bears, 113 beaver, 16 otters, 104 geese and Brant, 46 grouse, 9 turkeys, 48 plovers, and a long list of miscellaneous small game.[75] Not far from my home, the expedition wove willows together to make a crude drag net, catching 528 trout in about two hours time.[76]

Bison were especially numerous, roaming the Great Plains in untold millions until hide hunters wiped them out and settlers replaced them with cattle.

The "problem" with bison was that they were self-sufficient. They fed themselves. They continuously rotated pastures without the need for fences or cowboys to herd them or semi trucks to move them. They built new soil by moving in massive herds, trampling carbon-rich grass, forbs, seeds, and brush into the ground, fertilizing it with manure and urine, then leaving the land alone to recover. They didn't even require hay. With their big heads, the animals pushed the snow aside to access rich grasses beneath.

By comparison, raising cattle is a labor-intensive job that successfully employs many people. Building fences is a Herculean effort that never ends. Ranchers work all-nighters during calving season to help the cows give birth, because they are not always capable of doing it themselves. Cows have to be vaccinated to protect them from diseases. Ranchers work all summer to move cows from pasture to pasture

The problem with bison was that they were self-sufficient, limiting employment options.

to avoid over-grazing. They grow hay, cut it, dry it, bale it, move it, and work all winter to feed the herd. Ranchers often restrict cows to corrals then use heavy equipment to clean up piles of manure and return it to the fields, using other equipment to spread it evenly across the ground.

Cows left on the open range are unthreatened by predators and so spread out too much to properly trample organic matter and seeds into the soil. Instead, the animals graze the same tender young grasses again and again causing overgrazing and undertrampling at the same time. Lacking organic litter for protection, new seedlings struggle to survive in open ground and the land slowly turns to desert. Stocking rates fall because the land doesn't produce enough forage to support as many animals as before. Carbon that was once sequestered in the soil escapes through exposure and oxidation, exacerbating global warming. The solution to this problem is to build yet more fences, reducing pasture size enough to bunch the animals together and move them frequently, mimicking what nature accomplished with no fences and no work.

Instead of employing hunters and butchers to follow a natural herd, we employ countless farmers, ranchers, and veterinarians to mange domesticated stock, plus miners, loggers, and manufacturers to provide materials for fences, barns, and heavy equipment, plus the auto industry to manufacture pickup trucks, stock trailers, and semi-trucks, plus the petroleum industry to extract and process fossil fuels to power the mining, manufacturing, and ranching industries, plus ranch supply stores to provide seed and feed, gloves, water tanks, power tools, saddle tack, herbicides, and more. All these industries further require accountants, insurance agents, lawyers, policy makers, computers, printers, associations, conferences, and so on. It is all meaningless work, employing hundreds of thousands of people to do what nature did for free.

The end product is meat that is expensive and pumped full of growth hormones and antibiotics. Organically grown meat might be better, but the cost may be twice as high. In addition, meat is mostly packaged on Sytrofoam trays and wrapped with plastic, employing even more people to consume and dispose of natural resources.

In comparison, a nice roadkill deer on the side of the highway is free meat. For a couple hours effort one can secure a few hundred dollars worth of wild, uncaged, natural, hormone-free, antibiotic-free, organically grown meat to provide healthy, savory meals for weeks or months to come.

Like meat, almost anything that was originally free can be commodified and sold for profit. Physical fitness was once obtained for free by hiking, bicycling, chopping wood, or working on the farm. Now people pay money to work out in a gymnasium, employing 700,000 people in the process,[77] plus countless more in manufacturing jobs to produce all the exercise equipment and buildings. Suntans were once obtained free, but now tanning bed salons have become a $2.6 billion per year industry.

Water was once free and clean, and a person could safely drink from any spring or well and most rivers and streams. Now we filter, bottle, and transport water hundreds, often thousands of miles for sale in stores, exceeding $14 billion in annual wholesale value within the U.S. market.[78] The more we pollute the environment, the better excuse we have to employ people to extract fossil fuels for filtering, packaging, and transporting water, followed by recycling or disposing of the plastic trash. As if that weren't enough, there are already oxygen bars in some cities where people are employed selling breathable air.

Free Again

As demonstrated, employment provides the illusion of work, most of which is unnecessary. Any essential work is aided by technology, requiring progressively less labor to provide basic needs. The calorie

Cumulative Gigawatts of U.S. Installed Photovoltaic Capacity

100 GW projected by 2020

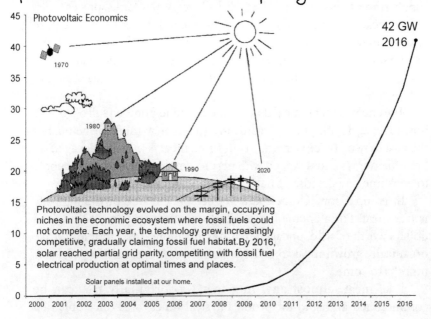

Photovoltaic Economics

42 GW
2016

1970

1980

1990

2020

Photovoltaic technology evolved on the margin, occupying niches in the economic ecosystem where fossil fuels could not compete. Each year, the technology grew increasingly competitive, gradually claiming fossil fuel habitat. By 2016, solar reached partial grid parity, competing with fossil fuel electrical production at optimal times and places.

Solar panels installed at our home.

ratio of human effort expended to food procured has shifted from 1:3 to 1:30 to 1:300 in the transition from hunter-gather societies to ox and plow agriculture to industrialization. Automation will likely shift that ratio to 1:3,000 and beyond, requiring less labor than ever to feed, house, clothe, and gadget every human being on the planet, or at least those with money.

Technological advances increase production efficiency, which ultimately lowers prices by swamping demand with ever-greater surplus. Solar panels, for example, were once astronomically expensive, literally. Early photovoltaic panels required expensive materials and manufacturing techniques and often consumed more energy than they could be expected to produce. The only reasonable application for solar panels was to power satellites in space; they provided a more economical solution than other fuel sources.

Gradual improvements in solar panel materials and manufacturing have led to steady increases in efficiency at progressively lower costs. Solar panels now produce far more energy than is consumed in construction. Solar became economical on remote cabins and communications towers beyond the reach of the electrical grid. Over the past few decades solar has crept slowly closer and closer to civilization and the grid. In some countries solar is currently more economical than fossil fuel energy, and soon that will be the case worldwide. Photovoltaic panels are already appearing on houses, businesses, gadgets, and in large-scale arrays that feed the electrical grid.

Solar technology is following a similar trend as computer processing, where capacity rises and prices fall, inexorably marching ever closer to free. The cost of solar modules drops about 20% for every doubling in cumulative volume; that works out to a 50% price reduction about every ten years.[79] Due to automation, the price of photovoltaics will effectively fall to zero, providing free electricity for all. The same is true for largely everything else that involves mining, refining, and manufacturing.

Information is also progressively free. As a young teenager eager to learn wilderness survival skills, there were only a few mediocre books available on the market. Now there are hundreds of wilderness survival books and instructional videos available for purchase, and thousands of articles and videos freely available online.

The problem of surplus abundance will become radically worse with increased automation. Amazon already employs robots to replace people in warehouses, and they have walk-in stores without checkout clerks. Driverless cars will replace trucking jobs and taxis. 3D printers will make it possible to print nearly anything that can be imagined or purchased from a catalog without the need for factories or stores or labor. 3D printers can even print whole houses, eliminating construction jobs.

Each increase in technological production creates more wealth with less work, requiring creative new ways to engage the general population in meaningless work to earn a living. Increased automation exacerbates the problem. It is unknown if the civilized world will redouble efforts to create meaningless work to redistribute wealth from producers to consumers, or if we might transcend the money economy altogether.

F or better or worse, even food will become progressively free. Many vegetables are already grown hydroponically in greenhouses, a process which is becoming increasingly automated. Researchers are also experimenting with lab-grown meat. Cells cultured in a lab can be grown into steaks without the inefficiency of producing bones, brains, or organs. As Winston Churchill predicted back in 1932, *"We shall escape the absurdity of growing a whole chicken in order to eat the breast or wing, by growing these parts separately under a suitable medium."*[80]

The primary challenge to producing lab grown meat is to exercise the tissue cultures to give the meat definition, so it isn't just mushy protein. At some point it is logical to expect that nutrients reclaimed from city sewers will be fed to tissue cultures to produce vegetables, grains, starches, and meat to return to the city. There may remain many specialty farms and ranches and self-sufficient homesteads, yet much of our crop and rangelands could ultimately return to wildlands.

The potential exists to create a futuristic, Star Trek-like world where hunger and poverty have been eliminated, money is no longer necessary, and people are free to better themselves and the rest of humanity. It is presently difficult to imagine how we might make the final transition or how that bright new world might function. Nevertheless, the transition to peace and prosperity is already underway, and for millions of people, getting there will be agonizing and costly. Increased automation will rain pink slips upon the working class, taking work away from people with mortgages to pay and families to feed.

Fortunately, anyone can avoid the pain by embracing green prosperity sooner rather than later. Make a plan and take action to eliminate rent or mortgage payments, high utility bills and other major expenses. Free yourself from the treadmill so that jobs and pink slips are irrelevant. If you don't have bills, then money doesn't matter. Invest, if you are inspired to, in thoughtful green enterprises to facilitate the transition to a sustainable world and the potential end of money.

"Human beings are the only animals who have to work, and I think that is the most ridiculous thing in the world. Other animals make their livings by living, but people work like crazy, thinking that they have to in order to stay alive. The bigger the job, the greater the challenge, the more wonderful they think it is. It would be good to give up that way of thinking and live an easy, comfortable life with plenty of free time. I think that the way animals live in the tropics, stepping outside in the morning and evening to see if there is something to eat, and taking a long nap in the afternoon, must be a wonderful life. For human beings, a life of such simplicity would be possible if one worked to produce directly his daily necessities. In such a life, work is not work as people generally think of it, but simply doing what needs to be done."

—Masanobu Fukuoka,
The One-Straw Revolution (1975)[81]

Green Prosperity for All
Rethinking Surplus Abundance

How do we dispose of surplus abundance? The answer to this question will define the twenty-first century and determine the fate of humanity, civilization, and the planet. Do we maintain meaningless resource consumption until we successfully collapse civilization? Or do we redirect surplus abundance towards enhanced infrastructure, ecological restoration, and colonization of the moon and Mars?

The popular vision of a sustainable economy is one of gentle austerity, living in harmony with the planet while accepting being less wealthy. I disagree. We have immense wealth. Scarcity and poverty are artificial conditions created by employing the masses to consume and dispose of surplus abundance. Rethinking the application of surplus is the single most important step required to create a sustainable economy, even if we don't do anything particularly green.

Mish Math

What percentage of the economy is dedicated to consuming surplus wealth? How many workers are employed doing meaningless work? What is the opportunity cost in trillions of dollars? A student of economics could form a doctoral thesis around these questions, calculating and referencing cumulative waste in the economy. For our purposes, however, specific numbers are irrelevant, and would quickly be outdated anyway. Instead, let's use a mishmash of readily available examples to approximate the amount of waste that could be reallocated towards more constructive purposes.

We've previously established that the United States and Soviet Union consumed enough wealth during the Cold War to rebuild the entire infrastructure of the world at that time. By itself, the U.S. has committed $5 trillion to Afghanistan and Iraq since 9/11, enough to install solar panels on every home in America, wiping out electric bills and greatly curtailing carbon emissions.

Annually, our income tax system wastes $400 billion/year in money and labor, enough to fund four missions to Mars every year. Our healthcare system wastes $1.4 trillion/year compared to Sweden's system of universal healthcare, which is far from the least cost example for comparison.

How about the economic cost of designing products to fail? What is the cost in trillions of dollars when nearly every product in every store is engineered to have an artificially short lifespan? What about the cost we pay for creating artificial necessities, such as embalming the dead and jacking funeral costs up to $8,000 per corpse?

By any measure, these are ridiculous numbers, adding up to trillions upon trillions of dollars of waste. The industrial economy has given us vast wealth, most of which we squander in systems designed to consume and dispose of surplus abundance. Public debate focuses on minor tweaks to tax and healthcare laws or defense spending without considering the bigger picture. With awareness and attention we can allocate resources more effectively in favor of a world of green prosperity for all.

Bicycle Highways

Like all nations, Sweden has elaborate systems to employ people disposing of surplus abundance. The difference between the U.S. and Sweden is that the Scandinavians gain more from it. For instance, America spends more on national defense than the next seven largest countries combined, while Sweden has invested heavily in public transportation. Although many countries offer good comparisons, I reference Sweden due to firsthand experience in the country.

Sweden is slightly larger than Montana with a population equivalent to Georgia, yet it has vastly more sophisticated infrastructure than either.

Touring Stockholm, for example, a single magnetic stripe card can be used to jump from bus to subway to commuter train or even boat to travel quickly to any part of the city. Stockholm Central station accesses layers upon layers of subways, and the newest platforms are futuristic and elegant. The system is efficient, and the subways, trains, and busses are clean and mostly new or in like-new condition.

In comparison, traveling from Sweden to Oakland, California felt like entering a third-world country. The BART commuter system was old, dirty, slow, and too loud to carry on a conversation. Some passengers plugged their ears to endure the journey. A one-way trip across the Bay cost almost as much as a 72-hour citywide pass in Stockholm, yet did not include bus fare beyond the limited BART routes. Outside the windows, views of the Bay Area were heavily covered in graffiti, litter, and old, decrepit cars. I couldn't help feeling that I had just arrived in an impoverished country.

In Sweden, train and bus service is available to towns big and small throughout the country, and local busses are prevalent in every town. Sparkling new busses continuously crawl the streets for passengers to transport across town or to local hubs to connect with larger cities.

Highways in Sweden seemed thoroughly adequate, yet Swedes also invested in a parallel system of bicycle trails and "bicycle highways" along most highways and main roads throughout urban and rural areas. Rather than sandwiching bicycle lanes between traffic lanes and parked cars, the Swedes largely built a separate system, providing safe trails and underpasses for cyclists and pedestrians. Consequently, bicycling is so popular in Sweden that parking racks for 500+ bicycles are common.

In comparison, the entire state of Montana has fewer bicycle trails than any moderate-sized town in Sweden. Only the largest cities in Montana offer local bus service, mostly underutilized with busses too few and far between to be of much use. Intercity bus travel to small towns is largely nonexistent. The nearest train station is a six-hour drive away, and since it is more expensive than flying, I have not yet been on a train in America. Being a rural state, we have no subways or commuter trains whatsoever. If you don't have a car in Montana, "public transportation" involves hitchhiking.

No state in America has infrastructure equivalent to Sweden's comprehensive, futuristic network covering all facets of transportation. Not only do we lack the budget to match Sweden's infrastructure, we lack the belief that such wealth is even attainable.

Granted, Swedes pay higher taxes, although not necessarily for the reasons we expect. As noted previously, healthcare costs are significantly less per person in Sweden at $4,900 per capita, compared to $9,267 per capita in America. The American cost includes a taxpayer subsidy of $5,960 per capita, meaning that the Swedes actually pay lower taxes for healthcare than we do.

The reason Swedes pay higher taxes overall is due to cumulative factors. Combine free healthcare with first-class public transportation and free higher education for all, and the costs start adding up. Moreover, Sweden had an open arms approach to immigration, accepting asylum seekers from all over the world. Immigration ultimately swamped the welfare system with 163,000 new applications in 2015, necessitating reduced annual immigration quotas. It is an immense tax burden to pay for housing, utilities, food, education, job training, and healthcare for tens of thousands of people who don't speak either Swedish or English and are therefore not readily employable.

Like any country, Sweden has established a system to consume surplus wealth by inventing work to keep people busy. Much of that surplus achieves measurable public benefit. Yet, so vast is the surplus that excess surplus wealth is expended upon unnecessary redundancies. For example, as a tourist, I thought the busses were arguably too new and too numerous, as if they replace the entire fleet every few years. Every town was crawling with busses, so many that they often ran largely empty.

In addition, Sweden employs surplus labor as legions of government workers who are paid to mind other people's business. For example, a Swedish friend expressed her frustrations at excessive nitpicking involved in building a home. Building inspectors would not approve the home for occupancy until the kitchen drawers were properly childproofed, even though she had no children.

In other words, the surplus abundance faced by industrial nations is so vast that even a country as progressive as Sweden fails to apply it all constructively. What would happen if we evaluated every job in terms of its net positive benefit to society and consciously strived to create an economy that eliminates meaningless work?

More Bang for the Buck

Past civilizations unconsciously consumed surplus wealth, primarily in the form of labor, by building great monuments or tearing them down. Countless civilizations crashed and vanished after consuming their natural resource base. Others unconsciously adapted, establishing long-term means to sustainably keep people busy, occasionally providing positive benefits in the process.

Societal change can happen consciously and incrementally or suddenly and unpredictably. The longer we delay consciously reinventing the economy, the more we risk unpredictably upending it through total collapse, chaos, loss of infrastructure, and potentially millions of fatalities. In collapse we risk losing all humanitarian and environmental protections, greatly exacerbating existing problems with no guarantee that any emergent civilization would provide better solutions.

Justification to consume surplus wealth has consistently been driven by the twin necessities of a) keeping people busy to maintain social order, and b) redistributing wealth among all members of society. Unless and until we reinvent the economy, those same necessities apply today. That's okay if we engage millions of people doing real and useful work.

Positive change requires awareness. If we are to survive and prosper in the twenty-first century we must take the bold step of consciously and collectively deciding how best to apply surplus wealth for the benefit of all.

For example, our state and national parks were developed for tourism by the Civilian Conservation Corps and similar programs during the Great Depression. Workers not only built roads, bridges, and buildings to enhance the parks, they did it with handcrafted quality that transcended mere utility. Stonemasons constructed buildings, bridges, and walls that have become historical features themselves. What if we revived public works programs and encouraged all young people to dedicate a year of service to the country after high school?

The Montana Conservation Corps currently offers a similar opportunity to a limited number of applicants who work on state and federal lands doing much needed trail maintenance and construction, fencing, tree planting, fuels reduction, weed management, campground improvements, and historical building renovation. Demand for labor greatly exceeds the size of the current program.

Similarly, we could re-evaluate the mission of the National Guard. Part-time citizen soldiers comprised much of the occupational force in Iraq and Afghanistan and bore significant casualties, even though their mission had little to do with guarding our nation. Through joint state and federal control, National Guard units are sometimes deployed to assist the public during and after natural disasters, a much needed and welcome service. What if the National Guard were employed exclusively to guard and assist the nation?

Due to onset of global warming, we can expect many more disasters, more hurricanes, tornadoes, floods, and wildfires, which are arguably the greatest threat to the U.S. mainland. The National Guard could be the primary response team to fight wildfires and manage natural disasters. If the Guard needed additional work between disasters, then how about installing solar panels on military bases and government buildings across America? Young people could join the National Guard and gain skills that could lead directly to job placement afterward.

China has already re-assigned 60,000 soldiers from the People's Liberation Army to take up shovels and plant trees to combat air pollution. Tree leaves collect particulate matter and absorb nitrous dioxide and carbon dioxide, gently filtering smoggy air. Doing meaningful work is popular among the soldiers provided they can retain their rank and entitlements.[82] Instead of a global arms race, we could initiate a global restoration race.

At all levels of society, we can make modest adjustments to employ people in much needed public works projects. For example, Congress has repeatedly inflated military appropriations to buy unwanted tanks for the Army merely to support manufacturing jobs in constituents' Congressional districts. Yet, tanks are arguably becoming obsolete on the modern battlefield anyway.[83] What if we maintained full employment in those Congressional districts by retooling factories to produce rockets for space travel instead of tanks for warfare? Let's employ the same people to produce equipment that carries us to Mars instead of the Middle East. These are adjustments, not radical changes, to gently shift the direction of society without upsetting the overall status quo.

These few examples illustrate a world of possibilities. The bottom line is that we have tremendous wealth at our disposal, more than enough to repair our infrastructure, pay off the national debt, convert the nation to clean, carbon-free energy sources, and provide universal healthcare. The cost is that we must abandon meaningless work and re-allocate our resources towards providing a prosperous and increasingly green economy for all.

A Manual for Changing the World

Changing the world is relatively easy for any planetary dictator vested with powers to impose whatever laws or taxes he or she determines are in the public interest. For the rest of us, our power to create change is limited to our sphere of influence and our ability to grow that sphere of influence. Like the Reinhold Niebuhr serenity prayer, *"God grant me the serenity to accept the things I cannot change, courage to change the things I can, and the wisdom to know the difference."*[84]

Individually or communally, anyone can truly make a significant positive difference in the world. For most people, however, the greatest obstacle blocking positive contributions is being stuck in the rat race engaged in meaningless work at an unnecessary job. That's reality, and everyone has to start somewhere.

If your sphere of influence is limited to daily survival, then start by developing an exit strategy. Formulate a plan to meet basic survival needs while eliminating expenses and reducing dependency on a job. Use the strategies outlined in this book to exit the economy in the shortest number of steps. Eliminate the need to pay rent or a mortgage and start investing in energy efficiency upgrades to reduce total throughput. Grow your own food or harvest surplus food from neglected fruit trees, roadkill game, and grocery store dumpsters. Reducing expenses reduces dependency on meaningless work, empowering you to be more selective in deciding which intermittent jobs you take. Succeeding at being one less worker on the corporate treadmill is a significant positive contribution to the planet in itself.

However, detaching from the economy to successfully become "less bad" can feel like a hollow victory. It's easy to achieve a measure of self-sufficiency and prosper off the waste stream of society. But being "less bad" isn't wholly more satisfying than being "bad." To make a truly positive difference in the world, it is necessary to expand one's sphere of inspiration and influence.

Being free from full-time work opens up opportunities to make more positive contributions, such as volunteer work, or potentially starting a green business. While other people have made far greater contributions to the world, my own contributions are not insignificant. As a father, three of my four kids were adopted, providing a home to siblings that needed a family. In addition, as a wilderness survival instructor, I've shared my love and knowledge of nature with hundreds of kids and adults. Working with the local public school, I've had each kid in every grade out for field trips every year from first through eighth grade, and I continue seeking ways to bring them back as high schoolers.

As an author, I've helped people discover a more intimate connection with the natural world through books such as *Participating in Nature*, *Foraging the Mountain West,* and *Botany in a Day.* This latter book has reached more than 100,000 people with an easier, more intuitive approach to plant identification.

As a builder, I've built three stone houses and numerous other structures, exploring and writing about alternative construction techniques to build better, energy-efficient, enduring homes.

In my volunteer work, I founded the Jefferson River Canoe Trail to encourage stewardship of our local river. I've led the acquisition of riverside properties for walk-in and float-in fishing access sites and campsites, saving these properties from development as home sites.

I've also established a fledgling Green University® LLC that offers positive alternatives to conventional college for our young people. None of these projects would have been practical if I were stuck in the rat race running a treadmill to nowhere. Taking the exit ramp early in life allowed freedom to pursue my dreams, including starting my own businesses. Being self-employed expanded my sphere of influence to make a greater contribution to the world.

A more impressive endeavor is the Urban Farming Guys who work in the blighted and crime-ridden Lykins neighborhood of Kansas City. With the bold mission "to help disadvantaged communities rebuild from within," Jason Fields and a few buddies moved in and started picking up trash, planting gardens, and renovating trashed houses. They invited neighbors to participate in community gardens and together they conducted original urban farming research through raised bed agriculture, greenhouses, hydroponics, mushroom farming, and aquaculture or fishing farming.[85]

Urban Farming Guys formed a 501(c)3 nonprofit in 2012 and kept growing. Using mostly recycled salvaged or secondhand materials, donations, and volunteer work, UFG has purchased dozens of city lots and renovated numerous buildings in the community, including a 20,000 square foot "maker space," much like a library full of tools for woodworking, welding, robotics, 3D printing, crafting, sewing, and food processing. They've built a team from the community that involves kids in afterschool art programs and adults in how-to classes and hands-on projects. UFG has given a positive direction to recovering drug addicts and felons to revitalize their own war-torn community.

Outside volunteers are welcome to participate and learn through month-long internships working alongside UFG and the Lykins community. Though UFG and many other programs, a novice can make a positive difference while gaining skills, confidence, and direction to formulate and tackle one's own projects.

It is truly possible to make a positive difference in the world, and the first big step is to establish an exit strategy from meaningless work and jobs. While the first half of this book has emphasized detaching from the economy to achieve a measure of self-sufficiency, the second half dives into the principals, theory, and strategy for re-engaging in the economy to make a greater positive impact. We begin with the principals of economic ecology then move into tools, goals, and guidelines to achieve your personal dreams and goals.

Part III
Principles of Economic Ecology

"Rather than domesticate animals for meat, Indians retooled ecosystems to encourage elk, deer, and bear. Constant burning of undergrowth increased numbers of herbivores, the predators that fed on them, and the people who ate them both. Rather than the thick, unbroken, monumental snarl of trees imagined by Thoreau, the great eastern forest was an ecological kaleidoscope of garden plots, blackberry rambles, pine barrens, and spacious groves of chestnut, hickory, and oak."

—Charles C. Mann
1491: New Revelations of the Americas Before Columbus (2005)[1]

The Economy as an Ecosystem
Spontaneous Organization

Our species has tinkered with nature for millennia, developing agriculture and forestry sciences, and experimenting with controls like fertilizers and pesticides. We ar1e so used to managing and manipulating the ecosystem that it often difficult to believe that nature can function without our help. As one European tourist asked a tour guide in Yellowstone National Park asked "Where do you put all the animals at night?" In the tourist's native country, farm animals were brought into barns every evening. It was an alien concept to think wild animals could survive on their own.

It can be challenging to accept that no one controls the ecosystem. How could anything so complex seemingly create itself from nothing, materializing and prospering on a wet rock hurtling through the cold vacuum of space? The fact that life started at all is induibitably a miracle, yet it is equally miraculous that life has continued to survive over the last 3.8 billion years. The sun has increased output by 25% in the natural course of its lifespan, yet temperatures on earth have remained comparatively stable. Without life, the oceans should have frozen, boiled, or the water molecules should have broken apart and the lightweight hydrogen atoms escaped into space, removing any possibility of water on this planet. Even without freezing or boiling, the oceans should have become too salty[2] to support life, given the amount of salt that washes off the continents each year.

How could living organisms, such as algae and bacteria, trees, grass, fungus, insects, birds and mammals, manage to keep the atmosphere intact and hospitable in such a hostile universe? How does the natural world function for even a season without some pest getting out of control, killing off most other plants or animals on the planet?

Life on earth seemingly cooperates to modify and maintain the biosphere in a condition favorable for life, as if the earth itself were alive. The biosphere is the emergent result of billions of individual plants and animals attending to individual needs, yet collectively creating something much greater.

In the late 1960s, British scientist James Lovelock proposed the Gaia theory suggesting that separate organisms could unconsciously modify the environment to be favorable for life. The principle is simple. Life has modified and been modified by the biosphere through a process called coevolution. Organisms that survive and thrive on the planet are those that help maintain a hospitable biosphere.

Consider a hypothetical planet that Lovelock called "daisy world," which is colonized by black and white daisies. Black daisies absorb light as heat and warm the planet, while the white daisies reflect light and cool the planet. Too many black daisies cause the planet to overheat, making the world inhospitable for them, yet better for white daisies. Too many white daisies cause the planet to chill, thus favoring black daisies that absorb heat. Black and white daisies spontaneously manage the biosphere at a comfortable compromise.

The real biosphere is vastly more complex, with billions of independent life forms functioning as a spontaneous system of checks-and-balances. For example, plants have extracted excess carbon dioxide from the atmosphere and sequestered the carbon as rich topsoil on the continents, calcium carbonate or limestone on the ocean floor, and highly concentrated fossil fuel deposits. Sequestering carbon has reduced the greenhouse effect and kept the planet cool, even while the sun has become warmer.

Life also controls the cloud cover and rain. Moisture evaporates from the oceans, forming water droplets around sulfur particles outgassed by marine algae. Marine algae thus affect planetary cloud cover and provide sulfur, an essential nutrient, to living organisms on land. Bacterial colonies along seashores coat salt crystals with a varnish that inhibits salt from dissolving back into the water, which helps prevent the oceans from becoming too salty. There is no detectable entity managing the globe, yet each independent life form seems to contribute to the stability and success of the whole.[3]

Like the natural ecosystem, our economy arose spontaneously, evolving from everyday actions of our ancestors struggling for survival, each collecting energy and modifying resources for the singular self-interest of staying alive. The economic ecosystem is diverse, highly complex, yet still spontaneously organized. It is highly efficient at generating products as complicated as cars and computers, which are manufactured from minerals mined around the globe, refined, shaped, transported, assembled, and shipped when and where they are needed.

Without any person or committee in charge, one might expect resource shortages every day, yet our stores are virtually always filled with items we want. We take this for granted in America, yet people from non-capitalist cultures are often amazed that our system works at all. Right up to the end of the Cold War, leaders of the Soviet Union were certain there was a secret agency in America, working behind the scenes to decide how much of everything to produce and where to send it.[4]

The economic ecosystem is an artificial entity we created, and yet it almost has a life of its own. Each of us affects and is affected by this ecosystem. Every purchase causes subtle changes in the economy. The economy likewise affects our decisions, bringing certain goods and services at certain prices, all of which vary according to the current "economic climate." We created the economy, yet no one knows precisely how to control it. The economic ecosystem is the result of millions of individuals making decisions they perceive will bring personal benefit.

Natural Harmony

Stepping into a meadow we are likely to perceive a scene of beauty. There are diverse plants and flowers, insects, birds, molehills, and sometimes deer, squirrels, or other wildlife. More likely than not, we see harmony. What we may not realize is that harmony is built upon both cooperation and competition as individual life forms seek to survive, store energy, and reproduce. Many species cooperate with each other, like bees and flowers, yet these are not acts of compassion. They help each other by obeying individual genetic needs for resources. Bees collect pollen for food. Flowers benefit as bees cross-pollinate other members of their species growing dozens of feet away.

There is also a great deal of competition within the meadow, mostly between the same or closely related species vying for similar ecological niches. In dense growth, pale plants underneath struggle to reach the light. Some seedlings live, yet the vast majority of never survive to maturity. Every living organism is in an eternal quest for energy and resources. Energy is used to transform raw resources into living products, with each species struggling to recreate itself to live on in future generations.

Plants and animals must hone their life cycles for efficiency to survive. Energy expended for something other than the ultimate goal of reproduction becomes a liability. Even a slight difference in efficiency between one species and another can mean the difference between success and extinction. Indeed, 99.9% of everything that ever lived is now extinct.

There is little actual waste in nature. Every living organism produces waste, yet those wastes are recycled as valuable resources for other species. For example, animal dung is full of nutrients utilized by everything from dung beetles to fungi to bacteria. Organisms grow and thrive on the so-called waste, enabling their survival and reproduction. Meanwhile, these species leave waste of their own, helping to recycle nutrients back into soil, worms, and plants.

Plants use these nutrients to grow and thrive, and they breathe in carbon dioxide and exhale oxygen as waste. Old, dead plants are composted back to fertilize the soil, and dead trees provide habitat and shelter for insects, birds, bats, and squirrels. Other species, such as ants, beetles, and fungi, eventually recycle dead trees back to soil, extracting their living in the process. Nature has developed closed-loop systems where wastes are recycled from one entity to another in a perpetual cycle.

The business world is theoretically similar, or could be. Energy and resources are converted into products and services that must find an ecological niche among consumers. Like nature, the economic ecosystem is built upon both cooperation and competition. Companies that survive and thrive in the economic ecosystem are those that produce useful products and services while minimizing wasted resources, energy, and labor. Businesses become extinct when they fail to produce a product or service with a niche, or fail to do so efficiently. As in nature, these ecological niches are continually changing. Newly evolved products out-compete old products for their consumer niche. Companies must evolve to find newer and better ways to keep their product territory or find new niches to inhabit.

In nature there are predators and prey, parasites, starvation, and genocide, but also cooperation and collaboration. Harmony and balance are sculpted through competition and killing. The predatory forces that make nature work so beautifully are the same forces that we often hate about economics. Perhaps it is because in nature we are at the top of the food chain, while in economics we are closer to the middle.

Survival in business is challenging when we are part of the process. When a competitor innovates and expends less effort to provide goods and services, it can drive a local business to extinction. People we care about may lose their jobs. We often react by protecting the businesses, such as by lobbying Congress to subsidize the business or to levy tariffs against the competition. Yet, without innovation, we would still be scrubbing laundry on washboards and riding horses for transportation. Economic extinction of a company may hurt us individually, yet often benefits us collectively.

Fortunately the death of a company is not the end of its employees. Extinction in business only means that people are free to make positive new contributions to society. Moreover, businesses can avoid extinction by modeling nature to utilize materials and energy more efficiently while recycling all wastes and valuable resources to generate new revenue streams.

Most businesses operate in single-mode survival, rather than seeking cooperative partnerships throughout the ecosystem, as emphasized by Gunter Pauli in *Upsizing: The Road to Zero Emissions*:

> *"When we harvest coconuts for their oil, we only use the oil; the rest is considered waste. When we fish in the oceans, some 30% of all fish caught are of no value to the fisherman and thrown back dead into the sea. When we ferment barley and hops into beer, we only extract 8% of the sugars; the fibers and the protein are considered waste, and given free of charge to cattle farmers. When we make a so-called 'green' detergent from the fatty acids from palm oil, we only use 5% of the biomass from the plantation; the rest is waste. When we log trees for their cellulose, we only extract a maximum of 30% of the hardwood's biomass; the rest is incinerated as black liquor, a cocktail of natural and synthetic chemicals. Humankind cannot claim it has designed an efficient system of manufacturing; on the contrary, it has a most inefficient system in place—to the level of absurdity."* [5]

In the economic ecosystem, wastes are problems that must be disposed of, often at great expense to a company or a community. However, where there is waste, there is opportunity. For example, sisal agave is grown for its fibers to produce strong natural ropes, yet only 2% of the biomass is extracted as useful fiber. The rest is considered waste. As noted by Pauli, the waste from sisal agave can be fermented to produce citric and lactic acid, which is more valuable than the fibers themselves. A business can survive and thrive by utilizing wastes as resources to generate new revenue streams.

Information Revolution

The science and study of economics was born at the dawn of the industrial revolution in England in the late 1700s and early 1800s. With fewer gains in food production and a burgeoning population base, Thomas Malthus and other early economists forecast a bleak future plagued by a class struggle for limited resources and mass die-offs of the human population to stay in balance with the carrying capacity of the land. It seemed apparent that people could only become wealthy at the expense of others, by taking a larger share of the resource pie. Capitalism was viewed as inherently predatory, because it allowed a few people to become rich at the expense of the masses. It is a stigma that justifiably lingers to this day. The pursuit of profit remains ethically questionable for much of the population. Communism and socialism were ideals created to divide limited resources more fairly.

A contributing factor to this one-pie view, according to Michael Rothschild,[6] author of *Bionomics: The Inevitability of Capitalism*, was that the world appeared static and unchanging to people of that era. It seemed that God had set the sun, moon, earth, and life in motion, and that all cycles would remain eternally the same.

Isaac Newton figured out the laws of motion describing planetary orbits around the sun, yet, he perceived it as a perpetual, unchanging system. Life also seemed virtually unchanged from one generation to the next. People did not know that life was continually evolving, or that technology and the economy could ever be different than it was. Only the population was growing.

The study of economics was logically patterned after Newton's physics. Economic philosophers searched for universal laws of economics. They developed models to describe phenomena of supply and demand and to predict product prices. However, these models were designed for a static, Newtonian-type economy. They were useless if factors changed. Remarkably, these original theories remain the foundation of economic thought today. Economists use essentially three-dimensional models to interpret a dynamic four-dimensional world. It is no wonder that every economic advisor seems to have a different forecast for the economy.

Today we expect change. We see cultural and economic evolution happening at accelerated speed. We know that even solar systems evolve or age. Stars are born from stellar gases that condense, fuse, and ultimately burn out or explode to seed new stars. We live in a culture of continuous evolution, where the only constant is change itself, as if evolution has been kicked into high gear. It has.

Culture and economy have followed a pattern of development strikingly similar to that of biological evolution. In each case, change is driven by the creation and exchange of information. It is a process that tends to accelerate with time.

Life started in the oceans approximately 3.8 billion years ago as single-celled organisms without a nucleus, including bacteria and blue-green algae, which are still with us today. These organisms reproduce asexually, each one splitting to form two exact replicas of the original. Blue-green algae used solar energy to convert resources into living tissue. They grew, copied themselves asexually and populated the surface of the oceans. Each alga divided into exact duplicates of itself and mutations were few and far between. That was the limited sum of life on earth until about 1.5 billion years ago, when cells developed specialized parts.

It was likely the result of several bacteria joining together that eventually led to specialization within a single cell. Cells developed separate organs or "organelles" for storing DNA, digesting nutrients, burning sugar to produce energy, and copying DNA into new proteins. These proteins were shipped wherever needed inside the cells for repairs. This new cell with specialized parts became the basis for all new life forms, including plants, fungi, and animals such as ourselves. The major difference between plant and animal cells is that plants have an extra set of organelles called chloroplasts that harness solar energy to combine water and carbon dioxide into sugar molecules. Sugar molecules are passed along to other organelles to fuel each step of the process of growth and reproduction. Our cells survive without chloroplasts because we eat plants, or we eat plant-eaters.

The rise of specialized cell parts allowed genetic information to be copied more readily and sped up the process of evolution, but just barely. Another 600 million years passed before the advent of another new idea: bisexual reproduction.

Bisexual reproduction allowed slightly different versions of genetic knowledge to be combined into new, living products. Sexual reproduction accelerated the evolutionary process and led to the development of multi-cellular organisms within 300 million years, the beginning of the Cambrian Explosion. These first creatures were essentially fluid-filled blobs with no bones, eyes, mouths, or brains.

The fluid-filled ocean blobs only lasted 70 million years before being wiped out by another new idea: the predator, also part of the Cambrian Explosion. In this context a "predator" is any organism eating either plants or other animals. Exactly how the first predators came about remains a mystery, yet they quickly wiped out the defenseless blobs. However, evolution favored nature's mistakes and mutants, particularly any organisms that mutated a defensive ability against predators. This, in turn, encouraged evolution of more advanced predators in a feedback cycle that quickly filled the oceans with diverse life forms from jellyfish, sponges, and worms to shelled animals and arthropods, the ancestors of insects, spiders, and crustaceans. The predator effect may have been the force that started the rapid colonization of land a mere 60 million years later, starting in the Ordovician Period.

To make the transition to land, plants had to evolve from floating in the nutrient stream to carrying the nutrient stream inside. This evolutionary jump was accomplished by plants forming a symbiotic relationship with fungus, according to paleontological researchers Mark and Dianna McMenamin.[7]

Fungus is neither plant nor animal. It is a third type of life that produces enzymes capable of breaking down dead organic matter, living tissue, and even rock. In theory, the presence of plant-eating animals made the open ocean a more hostile environment, thus favoring any plant life that could survive along the margin, such as a seashore, estuary, or stream. It is theorized that a defective proto-fungi attacked a proto-plant, yet failed to totally kill it. Instead, the fungus inadvertently began feeding the plant minerals from the soil while simultaneously extracting carbohydrates from photosynthesis. Today, 90% of all plants associate with fungus in the soil, and 80% could not survive without fungal partners. In many cases, fungi live in the core of the plant. Simple plants like clubmoss lack a complete vascular system for circulating water and nutrients, yet their fungal partners live inside their stems and provide that function.

The McMenamins examined high quality fossils from the beginning of life on land and found fungal hyphae inside the plant cells. This plant-fungus association internalized the nutrient stream and gave proto-plants independence to grow and evolve beyond water, setting the stage for explosion of new life forms. Within 100 million years, life on land was more diverse than within the oceans. In the remaining 350 million years since then, life on land seems to have evolved at ever-increasing speed. Today there are twice as many species on land as in the ocean, and although the surface of the planet is one-third land and two-thirds water, the land produces fifty times as much biomass or organic matter as the oceans.

We often say we are in the midst of the Information Age, yet according to Rothschild every age is an information age. Information is the heart of cultural and biological evolution.[8] DNA, for instance, is a biological means of encoding information consisting of a unique set of assembly and operations instructions for every life form on earth. In the economic ecosystem, our products are information. Every product is built of information.

Technological and cultural evolution mirrored the story of biological evolution. Change came very slowly at first. Our earliest ancestors began using crude stone, bone, and wooden tools. This body of knowledge was copied by example from one generation to the next for thousands of years. Each new idea eventually led to another. The advent of human knowledge was like a snowball in slow motion, gaining size and increasing speed over many thousands of years.

Homo sapiens first appeared about 200,000 years ago and spent most of the intervening time developing basic survival technologies. About 35,000 years ago our ancestors started engraving information onto bones. This developed into a full-fledged written language in Sumeria just 5,000 years ago.

Our species was already replicating its wisdom from one generation to the next, and the advent of writing made copying more efficient. It was still slow, because each piece of work had to be copied by hand. For example, a scribe might only be able to make one or two copies of the Bible per year. It was the invention of the printing press that put information and technological evolution into high gear.

As James Burke so eloquently demonstrated in the 1978 BBC television series *Connections*, the printing press allowed the cross-fertilization of ideas. For the first time in history, millions of books were printed and distributed. Like bisexual reproduction, cross-fertilization of ideas led to an explosion of new knowledge. The industrial revolution was the result.

Today the computer and Internet have led to a new cross-fertilization of technological ideas, as we communicate instantly all over the globe. The ability to collaborate with nearly anyone anywhere is continually leading to symbiosis of ideas into diverse new products, services, and ideologies, transforming the world we know.

Biological life forms mate to exchange and combine genetic information. This sharing of information leads to newer, more effective ideas for surviving into future generations. Knowledge is likewise exchanged in the economic ecosystem, leading to new and sometimes better products. Companies actively seek new genetic material to keep their products evolving ahead of everyone else. Any company that can put useful information on the market with the least expenditure of energy may survive the fiscal year to put forth a progeny of new ideas in future generations of products. Any company that converts wastes to profits will be even more successful.

The "genetic" information of culture and industry has a name of its own, called "memes." The term was coined in 1976 by Richard Dawkins for any idea or pattern of information which is introduced into culture and spreads like a virus from one person to another, usually undergoing further evolutionary change as it spreads.[9] Technologies are not memes, but they consist of memetic information, just as any species consists of genetic information. Any piece of information that is successfully replicated is considered a meme, although some memes survive and spread more than others. The word "meme" is a good example, because after Dawkins introduced it, the idea spread and influenced millions of minds around the world.

Spontaneous Stability

There are apparent weaknesses of the modern economic system, for example, that factories only have enough parts on hand for one day's work, and whole cities only have enough food to last about three days. Everything is connected and dependent on the power grid and information grid, such that any failure could immediately bring modern civilization to a grinding halt. It was this fear of imminent collapse that prompted hype over the Y2K computer bug at the turn of the millennium. Early computer clocks were not programmed to handle the date change from 1999 to 2000, inciting widespread fear that electronic networks might crash at midnight of the New Year. Fortunately, that didn't happen. Nevertheless, many people still live in fear that the whole complicated system will come crashing down at any time. They are as baffled by the principle of spontaneous organization as were leaders of the former Soviet Union.

While there is wisdom in having extra supplies on hand, it is also important to recognize the inherent stability of spontaneous systems. An ecosystem is like a matrix of self-repairing chains, where each link in the chain has the motive to stay connected and repair itself if damaged. If for any reason a link in the chain cannot repair itself, then the adjacent links merge to replace it.

For example, Mount St. Helens in Washington erupted in 1980, obliterating the surrounding ecosystem. Yet, within a year the devastated wasteland started to revegetate with seeds drifting in and filling wide-open ecological niches. If there is an ecological niche to exploit, something will exploit it. The web of life quickly repairs damage to the ecosystem and life goes on.

Similarly, disasters frequently strike the economic ecosystem, such as earthquakes that topple buildings, destroy roads, and interrupt power and water supplies, yet the damaged areas are quickly restored through the process of spontaneous organization. Businesses move in and take advantage of the situation to earn money by putting the built environment back in order, stimulating the local economy. Every link in the chain has something to gain by fixing the matrix in the shortest possible time.

In the natural ecosystem, re-colonization is random, as seeds are accidentally distributed into damaged areas. In the economic ecosystem, however, re-colonization is intentional and therefore faster. The economic ecosystem has a faster metabolic rate than its natural counterpart, as if seeds had their own propulsion systems to seek out ecological damage. Even if computer networks do crash, the flow of goods would quickly be restored because there are hundreds of millions of self-repairing links in the system.

Excessively Successful

Unfortunately, the strength and metabolic rate of the economic system is destroying its natural counterpart. The economy was born from the natural ecosystem, yet threatens to consume its parent with its fast and furious throughput of materials and energy. Our economy utilizes the strength and stability of ecosystem design to assimilate the living planet. The natural ecosystem has survived for billions of years through asteroid attacks, ice ages, a hotter sun, and mass extinctions. Can it survive the economic ecosystem?

We keep mucking up the natural world because we want to control nature to serve human needs. A meadow of wildflowers may be beautiful and harmonious, yet not necessarily edible. We tear into the fabric of nature, rip up what was there, and replace it with straight rows of single-species crops. We live off the accumulated wealth of nutrients until the land is depleted and desertified, then move on to other fertile fields. In our efforts to manage nature, we've only succeeded in denuding the landscape.

Today we appropriate roughly 40% of the world's biomatter to cover human needs,[10] far more than any other species on the planet. Yet billions of people still live in poverty, and everybody wants more material wealth. Biological systems are already stumbling through the initial stages of collapse. We have pumped the earth's atmosphere full of greenhouse gases and melted much of the polar ice cap. We have cleared tropical and old growth forests and destabilized watersheds, causing floods and droughts, while permanently wiping out thousands of plant and animal species. We have created deserts that are thousands of miles in size. Our vast oceans are being overfished and depleted, and yet human population is expected to grow by billions before potentially leveling off. If we try to give every person in the world the same lifestyle we know in the industrial world then there might not be a plant or animal left on the planet that isn't being raised for human use.

There are people who wish the societal matrix would collapse from a great catastrophe, believing that the natural world would be better off, yet it is a fruitless wish. Only a disaster on the scale of the meteorites that wiped out the dinosaurs could do that much damage to the economic ecosystem. However, a disaster of that scale would do greater damage to the natural ecosystem. Humans live in every corner of the globe, so hundreds of millions would survive even worst-case scenarios. As noted by Storm Cunningham in *The Restoration Economy,* "*Humans would likely be among the last of the larger life forms to go, because we share the adaptable super-survivor traits of cockroaches, starlings, and Norway rats.*"[11] Survivors would rebuild the economic ecosystem and recolonize the entire planet faster than the natural ecosystem could do the same.

Like it or not, the economic ecosystem is here to stay, and every minute spent wishing for its collapse is opportunity lost that could be applied towards constructively making it compatible with its natural counterpart. It is inevitable that we will ultimately create an ecologically sustainable economy. After all, there is relatively little left of the natural world left to exploit. Many people and corporations are discovering that it is more profitable to wisely steward our remaining resources. It is worthwhile to mimic nature and use resources as efficiently as possible, to "get more bang for the buck."

Any place there is waste there is opportunity, and right now the opportunities are seemingly unlimited. In our homes and in our businesses there is waste all around us—wasted time, wasted money, wasted resources, wasted energy, and wasted talent. No matter where we live or what we do, there are many ways we can learn to mimic the natural ecosystem to increase prosperity and make the world a better place for all. The faster we make this transition to a truly sustainable economy the more we will profit and the more of the natural world we can save.

Gardening the Ecosystem

Weeds appear to invade and take over farm fields and gardens. They seem to choke out the "good" plants. We often think weeds are "bad" and that we have to kill them to be able to maintain the landscape we want. The usual response to weeds is to fight them, pull them, or spray them. We deal with weeds as if they have malicious intent. Yet weeds do not grow unless there is suitable habitat.

For example, a suburban lawn is an artificial, yet basically stable environment, typically a monoculture of grass with a few weeds like dandelions. Rototill a section in the middle of the lawn and something new will happen. Within a season or two the exposed soil will be overtaken by weeds. The seeds were there all along, yet they had no space to grow in established sod.

Japanese farmer Masanobu Fukuoka (1913–2008) practiced what he called "do nothing farming," emphasizing no-plowing, no-fertilizing, no-weeding, and no-pesticides. According to Fukuoka, the idea that people grow crops is egocentric. Nature grows crops. He saw modern agriculture as doing-this and doing-that to grow crops, but it is meaningless work. With his do-nothing method he was able to obtain yields in his rice fields equal to the highest yields attained with chemical, do-something agriculture.[12][13] What he did do, in essence, was to gently manipulate habitat to favor desired crops. He worked with the laws of ecology to tilt the ecosystem in favor of his crops. The crops prospered and grew like weeds.

The economic ecosystem can be cultivated in a similar way. Individually we can influence local habitat to provide us with an abundant harvest. Collectively we can work together to tilt the economic ecosystem toward a crop of green prosperity for all.

In Zen it has been said that reverence is the elimination of all that is unnecessary. Fukuoka, sought a method of farming in harmony and reverence with nature as his goal. He then proceeded to eliminate all that stood in the way of the goal. Through careful observation of nature he eliminated the need for plowing, fertilizing, weeding, and pest control.

As a young man, I too envisioned a life in cooperation with nature. It was my dream to find a means by which we could live in sustainable balance with the environment.

Like many environmentally-minded people, I started with the perception that industry and money were inherently bad. I watched, listened, and studied the news, and it always seemed that ecology and economy were diametrically opposed to each other. The media portrayed a world where we had to make a choice between sacrificing the environment to save jobs or sacrificing jobs to save the environment. Given this narrow perspective, it was easy to perceive money as the root of the world's problems. The logical answer seemed to be to eliminate money by returning to a pre-industrial, hunter-gatherer or subsistence farming lifestyle. This ideology remains fairly common throughout the environmental community today. Of course, few people are actually willing to walk away from society to adopt a primitive lifestyle. And those who live primitively in less-developed countries have no intention of staying that way. The idea of un-evolving our culture is quaint but rather useless.

I realized as a teenager that if humanity is to live in balance with nature then people must desire that vision. Living green must be more appealing than the way people live now. In light of this, the logical solution was to create a lifestyle for myself in cooperation with nature that other people would desire to emulate for themselves. This insight nurtured my interest in sustainable living and self-sufficiency.

My desire to help save the earth was not the only motive. As a teenager approaching adulthood, I had needs of my own. Like anyone else, I wanted a nice house, a trustworthy car, a decent computer, and other cultural amenities. However, I had few marketable skills, and I didn't want a job. Getting a job and working my whole life was massively unappealing. I dreamed of being prosperous and helping the earth, yet also felt a strong need to avoid regular employment. Eliminating the obstacles of a mortgage, bills, and regular employment was the obvious initial track forward.

Like Fukuoka, the success I have known isn't just what I did, but what I eliminated having to do. I eliminated the need to spend thousands of dollars and several years on job training. I eliminated having a house payment and high-energy bills, and I eliminated many other expenses of daily living. I eliminated enough expenses to successfully eliminate needing a job, freeing me to pursue my own dreams in life.

I applied a similar ethic in business, seeking do-nothing methods to grow my publishing business, trusting successional processes over brute marketing. Where Fukuoka studied succession in the ecosystem, I studied succession in the economic ecosystem. My goal wasn't only to support my family, but also to seek means to influence and adjust economic metabolism, to hopefully nurture a more sustainable relationship between the economic world and the natural world.

"If a man walks in the woods for love of them half of each day, he is in danger of being regarded as a loafer; but if he spends his whole day as a speculator, shearing off those woods and making earth bald before her time, he is esteemed an industrious and enterprising citizen. As if a town had no interest in its forests but to cut them down!"

—Henry David Thoreau,
Life Without Principle (1863)[14]

Matter and Energy
Industrial Metabolism and Thermodynamics

All living organisms consume energy, modify resources from the environment, and produce waste. Those are inescapable facts of life at work in every cell of our bodies right now. Energy and material resources from food are consumed to build and maintain cells and to perform tasks like digestion, muscle contraction, and nerve conduction. Carbon dioxide and other metabolic wastes are eliminated via the lymph, vascular, and digestive systems, and by exhaling, each discharging wastes into the environment.

Although metabolism is defined at the cellular level, it informally applies to the whole organism, since plants and animals also consume energy, modify resources, and produce waste. Plants harvest solar energy to break down carbon dioxide and water molecules, recombining the parts to make sugars. Oxygen and eventually dead plant matter are waste products created and expelled in the process.

Animals, ourselves included, consume plants or plant-eating animals. We use oxygen to split sugars apart and release useful energy, discharging carbon dioxide, manure, and ultimately deceased bodies as waste products.

The natural ecosystem elegantly recycles wastes from one living being as useful resources to other living beings. Even dead plant and animal matter are useful resources, consumed by microbes and ultimately discarded as the waste that becomes fertilizer for a new generation of plants.

Matter is harvested, transformed, and discarded in a never-ending cycle. This is the Law of Conservation of Mass at work, which states that matter is neither created nor destroyed, yet can be converted in form. For instance, when adding a log to the fire, the wood is consumed, while matter is not. Energy is released when hydrocarbons are split apart in the presence of oxygen and recombined to form carbon dioxide and water vapor. The elements are still there, yet they've been converted from a solid to a gaseous state. Minerals are left behind as ash. Living trees continue the cycle, using sunlight to extract carbon from the atmosphere to build new wood, which brings us to the Law of Conservation of Energy, also known as the First Law of Thermodynamics.

According to the First Law Of Thermodynamics, energy can be converted in form, yet is neither created nor destroyed. The quantity of energy remains constant, while the quality can be altered. For example, plants harvest diffuse, low-grade energy in the form of sunlight and concentrate it into very dense or high-grade energy like wood, which may be further concentrated through sustained heat and pressure to make fossil fuels. Burning wood or oil transforms concentrated energy back to a diffuse form, dispersing it as heat. The quantity is the same, while the quality has changed.

However, while low-grade energy can be concentrated to make high-grade energy, it takes energy to make this transformation, which brings up the Second Law Of Thermodynamics, also known as entropy.

The second law states that energy is steadily degraded to less useful

Matter and Energy in Nature

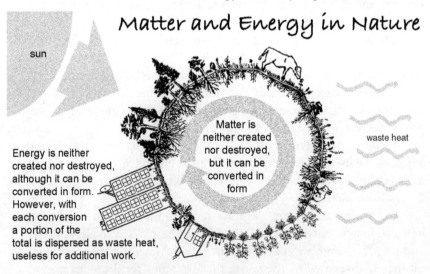

sun

Energy is neither created nor destroyed, although it can be converted in form. However, with each conversion a portion of the total is dispersed as waste heat, useless for additional work.

Matter is neither created nor destroyed, but it can be converted in form

waste heat

The natural ecosystem functions as a closed loop where all matter is recycled.

forms towards a state of equilibrium where no further work can be accomplished. As energy is converted from one form to another, a portion of the total is dispersed as useless heat. For example, coal can be burned to boil water to produce steam to generate a higher-quality energy in the form of electricity. However, two-thirds of the energy potential is lost as waste heat during the transformation. That is why it is expensive to heat a home with electricity. Three times as much coal must be burned to produce electric heat compared to burning coal directly at home.

Life seems to buck the second law of thermodynamics by concentrating energy to create complex organic bodies. Our living tissues are composed of molecules that should degrade into simpler forms, yet we utilize food energy to maintain and even strengthen our complex forms. It is only when we die and stop using energy that we lose form and degrade towards equilibrium with the environment.

The atmosphere similarly consists of highly reactive molecules that should break down into simpler forms. Without life to maintain the biosphere, the planet would become hot, waterless world without an oxygen atmosphere. Living organisms never escape the second law because they require a constant influx of new solar energy for self-maintenance. Diffuse waste heat is steadily radiated back into cold space to keep the planet from overheating.

Industrial Metabolism

Industrial metabolism acknowledges basic facts of existence, that all organisms, including human-made ones, consume energy, modify resources from the environment, and create waste.[15]

As illustrated, producing the final goods and services we want as consumers involves the production of many intermediate goods and services. Each step in the metabolic process requires inputs of material goods and energy and results in outputs of waste material and waste heat, plus the goods or services that were the purpose of production.

For example, pouring a concrete sidewalk begins with big machines that rip limestone or chalk and clay or shale from the earth. Inputs of energy and material goods in the form of fuel and equipment are used in the extraction process. Low-grade energy is discharged into the environment as waste heat radiating from equipment or discharged with the exhaust. Material wastes include unusable rocks and minerals, leftover oil jugs used to maintain machinery, worn-out equipment, and exhaust containing carbon dioxide and other gasses.

After extraction, the next step is to separate raw materials into pure calcium, alumina, silica and other materials, which requires new inputs of material goods and energy and results in new outputs of low-grade heat and material waste.

The pure materials are then mixed to make compound materials, especially tricalcium silicate, dicalcium silicate and tricalcium aluminate. Mixing requires additional inputs of material goods and energy and results in new outputs of low-grade heat and material waste.

The compound materials are formed into parts, in this case by mixing appropriate proportions to make cement powder, which requires

Industrial Metabolism

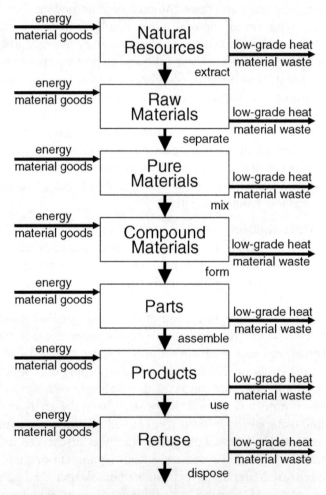

Every step in the production process requires inputs of energy and material resources and results in outputs of low-grade heat and material waste. Based on "The Relationship Between the Economy and the Environment" by Eileen van Ravenswaay, Ph.D.(2000).

more inputs and results in more waste.

At last the parts are assembled into products, in this case by mixing cement, lime, sand, gravel, and water to make concrete, which is poured in place and troweled smooth. New energy and material goods are used in the process, leading to the discharge of additional low-grade heat and material wastes, such as cement bags, exhaust from a cement truck, and lumber from framing the sidewalk.

The final product, the sidewalk, is now ready for use, at least until the elements degrade it beyond usefulness. At that time, further inputs will be required to jackhammer the old sidewalk to make space for a new one. This model of industrial metabolism applies to all products, from loaves of bread to automobiles, with varying degrees of throughputs.

The key difference between industrial metabolism and nature's version is that industry produces complex wastes that are not yet recyclable into new and useful products. Living organisms have had millions of years to adapt to each other, to occupy niches in the ecosystem, so that the waste of any one species becomes a valuable resource to another. The only true waste produced by the natural ecosystem is low-grade heat, too diffuse to use for any further work.

Businesses can mimic natural systems by utilizing wastes as valuable resources, especially when starting with organic resources. For example, as Gunter Pauli proposed in reference to breweries, *"When spent grain is used as a substrate for mushroom farming and earthworm cultivation, a cost of disposal is converted into a revenue stream. When the waste substrate from the mushroom farming is used as cattle feed or for further earthworm farming, it is once more generating revenues. When the waste from the earthworm farming is sold off as humus, it also makes additional cash. When the waste from the chickens and the cattle is used in a digester to generate biogas, it offers free energy. And when the sludge from the digester is further mineralized in algae ponds, and finally used as fish feed, the cycle of cascading wastes and generating revenues has resulted in a fascinating loop. It is making more money with little additional investments."*[16]

In this case, the original input was biological, starting with grain for brewing beer. Each step incorporates natural processes to create value from waste until all wastes have been fully recycled. A similar system can be created utilizing inorganic resources recycled through interconnected industries or hybrid systems with biological and industrial components.

A classic case of industry mimicking the natural ecosystem, called "industrial ecology" is Kalundborg Park in Denmark. It is considered an eco-industrial park because wastes from some businesses become inputs to other businesses. A series of materials and energy exchanges beneficially developed over a twenty-year period between neighboring industries, farms, and the local community. The exchanges were economically driven as each company sought ways to generate income from materials that were formerly considered wastes. Recognition of the environmental benefits of these exchanges came later.[17]

The industrial partnership includes a 1500-megawatt coal-fired power plant and an oil refinery, both of which are the largest in Denmark, plus a major plasterboard manufacturer, a biotechnology company, the city of Kalundborg, and many smaller businesses and homes.

The coal-fired power plant operates at about 40% efficiency with 60% of the energy potential lost as waste heat. This waste heat was formerly discharged through the smokestack, but today it is piped as steam to nearby businesses and 3,500 homes as a heat source, displacing dirty oil-fired burners that residents and businesses once depended on. The power plant uses saltwater for some of its cooling needs, sparing the fresh water lake nearby. Some of the hot salt water discharged from the plant is used in a series of fifty-seven fishponds in a commercial fish farm.

The power plant uses calcium carbonate in a reaction to pull sulfur dioxide out of the smokestacks, thereby producing two-thirds of the calcium sulfate (gypsum) used at the plasterboard plant. The remaining desulfurized fly ash from the power plant is used at a nearby cement plant.

The adjacent refinery burned a continuous flare of waste gases until the plasterboard company identified it as a potential source of low-cost fuel. Excess gas from the plant is now used at the plasterboard company, plus it serves as a substitute fuel to generate electricity at the power plant. Desulfurization of fuels at the refinery results in pure liquid sulfur, which is trucked to a sulfuric acid producer.

The biotechnology company produces industrial enzymes and more than 40% of the world's supply of insulin. Sludge from this biotech company and the fish farms is spread on local farm fields. Surplus yeast from insulin production goes to farmers as pig food.

Kalundborg Park demonstrates the economic and environmental benefits of closing the loop so that wastes from one enterprise become valuable inputs to another. While still dependent on fossil fuels, the system increases productivity while greatly decreasing dependency on new resource inputs. The web of exchanges conserves water, energy, and other resources while reducing pollution and generating new revenues, or at least reducing costs of waste management for those involved.

Competition and the growing costs of waste disposal will require other industries to form similar partnerships to stay competitive. Unfortunately, our economic ecosystem is far from matching the elegance of the natural ecosystem. Industry produces copious amounts of pollution, dumping all unrecycled waste into the environment. These are wasted opportunities that could create new revenue streams. The economic ecosystem will reach maturity only when we close the loop on waste production so that all wastes become useful to other enterprises or to the natural ecosystem, and the only actual waste produced is low-grade, useless heat.

For example, an aluminum can makes a complete lifecycle from grocery store to consumer through the recycling system and back to the store within a few months at most. A small amount of material is lost with contaminants each time around, yet newer technologies steadily improve the recovery rate. When nonpolluting energies like hydroelectric power are used in the process, then aluminum and scrap-metal recycling very nearly fits the model of a perfect cyclical economy.

Since matter can neither be created nor destroyed, we are limited to resources available on this planet, plus whatever might be imported from off world in the future, yet there is no limit to how many times we can reuse these resources, at least in principle. Therefore, the true limitation is not a lack of resources, but our failure to close the loop to effectively recycle them.

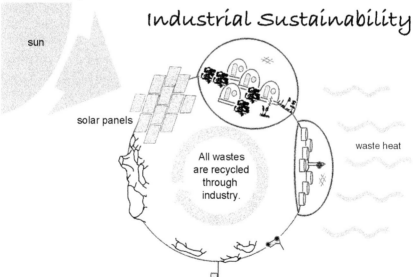

A colony on the moon or Mars would function as a closed loop system where all material wastes are recycled and the only true waste is diffuse heat. The "ecological footprint" is effectively zero.

In essence, a sustainable economy is defined as one that recycles all material wastes, either through the natural ecosystem or through industry, so that the only true waste produced is low-grade heat, too diffuse for any additional work. Presumably this economy would operate exclusively on renewable fuels, yet fossil fuels might also be used if the carbon and all other pollutants were removed or properly sequestered by the environment.

In other words, we can maintain consumption of organic resources at sustainable levels if we switch to inorganic resources for everything else. If we use nonpolluting fuels for production then we can recycle everything again and again without consuming the planet. This is the ultimate goal we must work towards.

Imagine a colony on the moon or Mars completely detached from the living ecosystem on earth. Without a natural ecosystem to recycle wastes, it must be done by industry. The economy necessarily becomes a closed-loop system where material wastes are recycled and the only waste produced is low-grade heat. Here on earth, the economy will probably remain a hybrid system, recycling some wastes through the natural ecosystem and all other wastes through industry.

Industrial Sustainability

The concept of a sustainable industrial economy is simple, yet the environmental movement hasn't distinguished between organic and inorganic resources. Organic resources are scarce, and we have exceeded the maximum sustainable load of resource extraction and waste production that the environment can handle. Fisheries are crashing, forests are disappearing, soils are eroding, and the climate is changing. Natural ecosystem processes are stressed to the point of failure, so the obvious response is to reduce consumption and live simpler lives, thereby reducing our ecological footprint.

An ecological footprint is an assessment of the arable land area required to sustain a group of people such as a family, city, or country.[18] How much arable land would be required to provide all food, paper, lumber, and other organic resources needed to sustain your lifestyle? How much land would be necessary to grow biofuels or sequester carbon from fossil fuels? The average American requires about 20 acres or 8.2 hectares of productive land to sustain their lifestyle.[19] Hectares are the standard unit of land measure outside the United States. Ecological footprint calculations are based on "global hectares," or gha meaning the average productive hectare of land.

My ecological footprint is presently estimated at 4.4 gha, much of that due to fossil fuel consumption for travel by car and airplane. Switching to an electric car will reduce my footprint to 3.2 gha. Check your footprint here: www.footprintcalculator.org.

Collectively, we already commandeer the resources of most productive land on the planet, about 12 billion hectares. That works out to less than 2 hectares per person now, steadily decreasing as world population increases. Industrialized nations presently maintain an affluent lifestyle only by expropriating resources from other parts of the globe, in effect stealing others' fair slice of the pie. It is estimated that we would need at least four planet earths to allow every human being the same consumptive standard of living as in America.[20] People in India survive on an ecological footprint of about 1.16 hectares per person,[21] yet most are seeking more and more amenities.

Statistics like these have spawned simple living movements with the noble purpose of proving that it is possible to live a modest lifestyle with a sustainable ecological footprint. For the most part, these movements emphasize returning to the past as homesteaders to produce one's own shelter, food, and fuel resources in harmony with the natural ecosystem. Although such projects are well intentioned, they are insufficient to convince the rest of civilization to drop everything and live as homesteaders, nor do they need to.

The ecological footprint model misses three critical issues. First, we can significantly reduce our footprint by optimizing use of organic wastes, as noted in the example for spent brewery grain. Producing more food and revenue from existing resources reduces the total ecological footprint, potentially reducing the arable land needed per person to survive.

Secondly, ecological footprint calculations do not adequately distinguish between organic and inorganic resources. Agreeably, organic resources are over-harvested, however, there

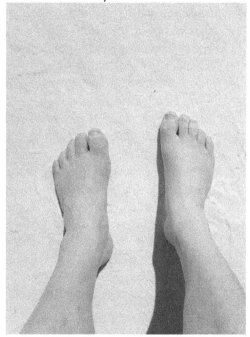

Switching from organic to inorganic resources leaves an ecological footprint that is deep instead of wide.

are always substitutes, such as e-mail in place of paper, steel or concrete in place of lumber, or superinsulation in place of combustion heating. The ecological footprint model acknowledges the living surface of the land but ignores inorganic resources, which can be used and re-used indefinitely.

Issues with organic resources became apparent with the push to promote biofuels as a green alternative to fossil fuels. Tropical forests were torched and bulldozed to make way for palm oil plantations, causing far more harm than good.[22] Corn and soybeans were also diverted to biofuel production, raising food prices beyond the means of the world's poorest people.[23] It is now widely recognized that food should be used as food, and only waste products should be converted to fuel. In the U.S., however, farmers have expanded corn and soybean crops and used their political clout to maintain ethanol production as a viable means to consume supplies and maintain artificially high crop prices. It isn't sustainable to build or power the world exclusively on organic resources, however, we can do it by including inorganic resources.

Third, ecological footprint calculations are based on fossil fuels, including the amount of land needed for plants to sequester carbon dioxide emissions. As we transition to alternative energy sources such as solar and wind, we effectively reduce the size of our ecological footprint without giving up our standard of living. The average American's ecological footprint has actually declined slightly since 2013 due to reduced reliance on coal.[24]

Counter-intuitively, we reduce the size of our ecological footprint by harvesting resources vertically instead of horizontally. In the past we expanded the resource pie by consuming the living surface of the earth, such as by logging forests for building materials and fuel. New technologies enable us to extract resources vertically instead, up towards the sun for energy and down into the ground for minerals and metals. In effect, we reduce our ecological footprint by going deep instead of wide.

By narrowing and deepening our ecological footprint it is possible and ultimately inevitable to create a sustainable industrial world economy that produces essentially no wastes except low-grade heat. To understand this more fully we must dive into the good and the bad of the Law of Substitutes in the next chapter.

"Europeans emerged from under the cloud of malnutrition and constant threat of starvation because their colonial empires produced lots of cheap food. Europeans outsourced food production as they built industrial economies. Between 1875 and 1885, a million acres of English wheat fields were converted to other uses. With a growing industrial economy and a shrinking agricultural land base, Britain increasingly ate imports. By 1900 Britain imported four-fifths of its grain, three-quarters of its dairy products, and almost half its meat. Imported food pouring into Europe mined soil fertility on distant continents to further the growth of industrializing economies. "

—David R. Montgomery,
Dirt: The Erosion of Civilizations (2007)[25]

Substitutes for Everything
Expanding the Resource Pie

In 1798 Thomas Malthus published *An Essay on the Principle of Population*. Malthus looked about his native England and saw an island of limited size inhabited by an exploding population of mostly destitute people attempting to produce more and more food from a non-expanding resource base. Although it was possible to make incremental improvements in agricultural production by working every scrap of land more intensely, there was no way to keep up with exponential population growth. Malthus perceived that the world was like a pie, and people competed against each other for slices of the pie. An individual could only become prosperous by taking another's share of the pie. Famine, disease, and war, he wrote, were the only means to keep population in balance with the food supply.[26] Upon reading Malthus' essay, writer Thomas Carlyle described economics as "the dismal science," an epithet that sticks to this day.

England was spared from Malthus' predictions through technological improvements that led to further increases in agricultural productivity, and by expanding the resource base through conquest, colonization, and importation of goods home to the motherland. Despite an even larger population today, England and the rest of the industrialized world prospers with material abundance, partly due to increasingly efficient extraction technologies, and also due to political and economic clout to expropriate resources from impoverished regions of the world.

In the twenty-first century it seems like we have expanded the resource pie for the last time. We have exposed every hidden corner of the world and maximized resource extraction to feed our insatiable appetites for material goods. Now we are faced with the questions: Did we ever truly expand the resource pie, or did we just find ways to consume it more quickly? Have we run out of resources to exploit, so that the ultimate fate is finally upon us? Will we soon experience the mass die-offs that seemed inevitable more than two hundred years ago?

The answer is both "yes" and "no." Yes we have exceeded the carrying capacity of the world, and biological systems are stumbling through the initial stages of collapse, but no, we have not run out of resources to exploit. As organic resources become increasingly scarce, we substitute more inorganic resources. The good and bad news is that like colonists on the moon or Mars, we will have little real dependence on what exists outside of the artificial world we create. The economic ecosystem can theoretically thrive even if the natural ecosystem is completely dysfunctional. Understanding how and why this future will materialize is critical to the goal of saving some residue of the natural world. Good or bad, the future revolves around the Law of Substitutes. In short, this law propositions that no product is absolutely irreplaceable; as the price of an item rises, people look for substitutes.

All Resources are Scarce

Economic and environmental theories are based on the idea that all resources are scarce. Material resources such as land, water, and food are scarce, as is human labor, which is a resource of time and effort. Because resources are scarce, they must be rationed.

In the developed world we usually ration scarce goods according to willingness to pay money. For example, crabmeat is scarce and more expensive than other meat options. Price effectively rations the limited resource, with some people willing or able to pay more than other people. There are other ways to ration scarce resources, such as group consensus, central planning, or alternative inducements. Athletic awards, for instance, are rationed according to physical abilities.

Supply and demand is the process of allocating scarce resources in a monetary society. Demand can be thought of as what we want, while quantity demanded is how much of a product or service we will purchase at any given price.

The Law of Demand states that there is a negative relationship between the amount of anything people will purchase and the price they must pay. Less will be purchased at higher prices. More will be purchased at lower prices. For instance, we may want to purchase dozens of different albums from our favorite musicians, but the actual quantity we demand is dependent on cost. How many albums would we buy at $100 a piece? How many would we purchase at $20? At 25 cents each?

Fortunately, for every scarce resource there are substitutes. Instead of buying and downloading a digital album, we could listen to the radio, find music videos online, sing to ourselves, listen to the sounds of nature, or seek a completely different type of entertainment like rock climbing. As the cost of an item rises, the substitutes become more appealing. If music albums cost $100 each to download, then most of us would favor alternatives.

Based on the law of substitutes, we can foresee that increasingly scarce organic resources lead to higher prices, making inorganic substitutes comparatively more economical. For example, wood houses are declining proportionally as metal framing, concrete, and composite materials are chosen as substitutes. Wood itself is being replaced, or altered and enhanced, by resins, to use less wood and more glue. Manufactured wood is an intermediate substitute that saves good lumber by reprocessing wood scraps into useable boards such as oriented strand board (OSB) or particle board. It is not practical for every person on the planet to have a wood frame house since resources are scarce. However, it is possible for everyone to have a nice house, because there are good substitutes for traditional lumber.

Today we manufacture cars and most goods with everything but living resources. A walk through any Walmart or Home Depot reveals surprisingly few biologically derived products, yet many composites of minerals, metals, and oil resins. We are becoming increasingly independent from the biological cycles of nature as we rely more on minerals to meet our living needs.

Extracting mineral resources still disrupts the natural ecosystem, yet potentially less than extracting organic resources. A tree-covered hill, for instance, may provide enough lumber to build a few hundred homes. However, if the hill is composed of limestone then it can provide enough cement for concrete to build thousands of homes. Excluding fossil fuel consumption, the ecological footprint of a concrete house is actually smaller than the ecological footprint of a wood frame house. By saving and re-applying topsoil, the quarry can afterwards be reclaimed and replanted to become biologically productive once again.

Regarding fossil fuels, cement is very energy intensive to produce, accounting for 5 to 7% of all carbon emissions. However, as covered later in the book, there are carbon-negative cement alternatives that absorb more carbon from the atmosphere than is discharged through the manufacturing process. Moreover, as the cost of solar and other clean energy sources continues to fall, the economy will inevitably shift away from fossil fuels.

Green Economy on a Dead Planet

The environmental movement was born in the 1960s and 70s when it seemed imminent that we would exhaust our non-renewable energy resources before the turn of the millennium. According to forecasts then, we should have largely exhausted oil and natural gas already. The obvious choice, and the rallying cry of the environmental movement was to return to the land and grow our own food and fuel in tune with the cycles of nature.

Ironically, use of biofuels in a vastly overpopulated world is not sustainable. Many developing countries are stripping the land for burnable fuels like firewood and animal dung, but this organic matter is needed

Dependency on biofuels is unsustainable in overpopulated regions.

to build the structure of the soil, enhancing its fertility and water-holding capabilities. Burning every available bit of firewood and dung reduces vital organic resources to inorganic ash. Excessive reliance on biofuels short-circuits the cycles of nature, leading to soil depletion and often desertification.

This environmental crisis is gradually being addressed by substituting direct solar technologies for organic fuel.[27] Solar cookers are typically simple, often made with cardboard, aluminum foil, and glass. More durable units are made with wood, insulation, and sheet metal. Nonprofit organizations, such as Solar Cookers International donate solar cookers to people in developing countries to improve their quality of life and economic prosperity. Solar cookers reduce reliance on biofuels, which is good for the environment, and also good for people. Solar cooking conserves labor otherwise needed to collect fuel and also reduces health problems associated with inhaling smoke from biofuels.

Solar technologies are typically categorized together with organic biofuels as "renewables," yet this combination is misleading. Solar harnesses the sun's energy independently from the organic ecosystem. Solar expands the resource pie beyond what living fuels can provide and allows organic resources to be recycled into the soil.

Photovoltaic technology enables developing countries to expand energy supplies beyond the limitations of the organic ecosystem. Due to falling costs, solar power is often the most economical source of electricity people can obtain. It is cheaper to put a solar panel on every roof than to construct a multi-million dollar power plant with transmission lines to every home.

Solar power would be cheaper for us too, if we did not already have utility infrastructure in place. In any case, the energy crisis is largely over. Alternative energy sources, such as solar and wind, are already cost-competitive with fossil fuels for many new installations. If need be, we could convert entirely to green energy in only a few decades. Given growing concern over global warming, we can expect, and we should demand, higher taxes on fossil fuels to expedite the transition to clean alternatives. Either way it is inevitable that we will wean ourselves off fossil fuels in favor of non-polluting alternatives. It is not a question of "if," but "when," and what might remain of the natural world when we finally make the switch.

Global warming coupled with other global environmental catastrophes could kill off most of the planet's biodiversity and flood coastal cities, yet the natural world would survive and the economy might still flourish. By the time we address global warming, it will be normal to live in a world where low-lying areas like New Orleans no longer exist above water. Sure, there will be chaos along the way, moving whole cities and millions of people to higher ground, but we have to build homes for hundreds of millions of new people anyway.

Despite falling birth rates, the U.S. Census bureau estimates that the U.S. population could potentially grow in excess of one billion people by the year 2100, mostly due to immigrants and their subsequent children.[28] Destabilizing the climate only exacerbates the problem, disrupting economies and displacing people. If a hundred million people are dying of hunger from climate change caused by industrial nations, how many do we let immigrate into the country, and how many do we condemn to die? Moving the entire coastal population inland will be a monumental task, yet it will happen over several decades, hardly a blip in a rapidly expanding economy.

The problem with the law of substitutes is just that, there are always substitutes. If sea levels rise, move to higher ground. If the weather is too hot due to global warming, then switch on the air conditioner and burn more fossil fuels staying cool!

Already we have polluted surface and groundwater supplies over vast regions of the planet, so people routinely use substitutes without realizing it. Cities build treatment facilities to clean the water supply, and homeowners install filters to remove pollutants missed by the city. Lacking a proper filter, people buy bottled water instead. Oxygen is sold in Tokyo as a substitute for polluted air. Tighter homes are being built, like miniature biospheres with sophisticated atmospheric controls and air filters. We have code orange Air Quality Index (AQI) days when the air quality outside is too polluted to exercise outdoors, and where school recess is held indoors. Air quality alerts are now part of national weather service reports.

No Compassionate Clause

Many people, especially younger generations, have awakened to the reality that we are consuming the living earth. Disenchanted youths want the civilized world to pay for crimes against nature for decimated habitats and species extinction. They wish that civilization would collapse from its own weight, disintegrate through rebellion, or suffer devastating natural disasters as retribution from Mother Earth.

However, any disaster, big or small, hurts the natural ecosystem more than our artificial one. The economic ecosystem is founded on the same principles of spontaneous order and stability as the natural ecosystem, yet it has a much faster metabolic rate, so it recovers faster than the natural world. In short, the economic ecosystem is arguably sustainable, while the real world is not. We can sustainably consume and destroy the natural world because there are theoretical substitutes.

In addition, like the law of gravity, the law of substitutes lacks a compassionate clause. Gravity doesn't make exceptions for people who fall out of airplanes without parachutes, and neither does the law of substitutes make exceptions for species without habitat or people who are not part of the economic ecosystem. Recall that a substitute for expensive music albums is to forgo listening to music. Likewise, a substitute for people or animals lacking food is to not eat.

Those of us plugged into the matrix of supply and demand have our needs taken care of. We have all the food and fun we want and we are somewhat insulated from the collapse of the natural ecosystem around us. However, much of the world's population is not plugged into the industrial matrix. They are stuck in the real world where pollution, climate change and starvation are genuine threats. We hardly notice now when a million people die of starvation. Will we notice when the numbers rise into the tens or hundreds of millions?

Worst-case scenario, the natural ecosystem will survive and recover with sufficient time, just as it did after the asteroid impact that wiped out the dinosaurs 60 million years ago, although it takes millions of years to re-establish optimal diversity. Meanwhile, surviving humans would no longer be dependent on the natural ecosystem for physical sustenance, being fully supported by the economic industrial system instead.

Fortunately, we can expect to do somewhat better than the worst-case scenario. The conversion to a green society is already underway. We will eventually transition to a virtually closed-loop, non-polluting advanced civilization.

Substitutes for Food

In a sustainable industrial economy based on inorganic resources, all wastes are recycled in a closed-loop system. However, food is an organic resource, and we depend on a healthy and stable ecosystem to grow our crops. We are organic beings who need to eat other organics.

Our journey apart from the natural ecosystem began thousands of years ago. Our earliest ancestors lived like other creatures of nature. Throughout most of each year they had plenty of food, yet there was always a season of relative scarcity. Population size was determined by the amount of food available at the bleakest point in the year.

Stone Age technologies enabled our ancestors to begin breaking free from natural cycles. Food storage allowed people to sustain a larger population through seasons of need. Fire, clothing, and shelter enabled people to band together and thrive in new habitats. Our Stone Age ancestors defied nature with tools and knowledge, greatly increasing the size of the resource pie.

Agriculture expanded the resource pie again. Our ancestors did not initially embrace agriculture as a way to work less. Planting, weeding, fertilizing, harvesting, and storing food was more work than wandering around eating whatever was in season. However, the land reached its carrying capacity 9,000 years ago in the Middle East.[29] Farming provided a stable food supply and increased the carrying capacity of the land a hundred times over. In the last nine millennia we have continued to improve our resource extraction and transportation technologies to support an ever-expanding population.

Still, people will need to eat in the future, and food is an organic resource. The threat of massive starvation and die-offs seems imminent, due to the rapidly expanding world population, climate change, and the ineptitudes of modern agriculture. Our farmers expend 5 to 10 calories of fossil fuel energy, depending on the source cited, for every 1 calorie of food produced. This is in addition to washing away thousands of tons of essential nutrients every year through human-caused erosion. These absurdities justify returning to sustainable farming based on the organic ecosystem's ability to produce and renew. We actually have the ability to grow most crops sustainably, at a net caloric gain, and at a profit, without sacrificing the soil. We can do it, and we need do it.

Instead, we are weaning ourselves from the need to grow crops outdoors, especially in densely populated regions. Commercial greenhouses cover nearly 175,000 hectares in Europe, 225,000 hectares in Asia, with 7,300 hectares in North America. Worldwide, there are 490,000 hectares or 1,900 square miles of greenhouses,[30] with more being built all the time. Destabilization of the climate only increases the demand for crops grown under plastic, and plastic is made from fossil fuels, ironically one resource we still have in abundance.

As we will see in the next chapter, there are many opportunities to greatly expand agricultural production, and we can even do so sustainably with or without the aid of technology.

We do not need to end our relationship with the living ecosystem. It is possible to grow and harvest organic resources sustainably. I personally enjoying gardening, growing fruit trees, and foraging for wild edibles. Nevertheless, to sustain the human masses we must increasingly substitute resources from outside the living ecosystem so life can continue its natural process of renewal. Sustainable use of organic resources can continue, yet only as a fraction of the new economy.

"Why would so many unrelated civilizations like the Greeks, Romans, and Mayans all last about a thousand years? Clearly the reasons behind the development and decline of any particular civilization are complex. While environmental degradation alone did not trigger the outright collapse of these civilizations, the history of their dirt set the stage upon which economics, climate extremes, and war influenced their fate. Rome didn't so much collapse as it crumbled, wearing away as erosion sapped the productivity of its homeland."

—David R. Montgomery,
Dirt: The Erosion of Civilizations (2007)[31]

Infinite Food Supply
Rethinking the Food Energy Pyramid

How many people can the earth sustain? There were 3.4 billion people in the world when I was born in 1967 and more than double that by my fiftieth birthday in 2017. Population numbers are surging, yet the rate of growth is slowing. The birthrate in industrialized nations tends to fall over time, and many industrial nations have achieved negative birth rates, actually declining in population. Nevertheless, the United Nations estimates that there will be 9.8 billion people by 2050 and 11.2 billion by 2100. Speculative long-term projections for 2300 A.D. include potential collapse to 2.3 billion people or a surge to 36 billion, with a median projection suggesting stabilization at around 9 billion.[32] There will be more people on earth before there are less.

Unfortunately, mainstream agriculture has largely plateaued in overall food production. Farmers have already claimed the most productive landscapes for crops, most of which are rapidly deteriorating or desertified due to soil loss, salt accumulation, urban development, and climate destabilization.

Mesopotamia, the cradle of civilization, arose through farming and later collapsed due to salt accumulation left behind by evaporating irrigation waters. Is collapse the ultimate fate for modern civilization? On our current path, yes. Globally, one-third of all cropland has been abandoned in the last forty years due to soil degradation and erosion.[33]

That number does not include crop and rangeland previously lost to desertification over the last few thousand years. Through poor crop and livestock management we created or vastly expanded the Sahara, Gobi, Arabian, and Syrian deserts, and are rapidly doing the same thing to the American West. Globally, we are still losing an estimated 24 billion metric tons of fertile soil per year to erosion.[34] Although less bad than before, American farmers still "export" more soil than corn from farm fields.[35]

The Green Revolution of the 1900s ballooned productivity worldwide through controlled irrigation, fertilizers, pesticides, and hybrid seed stock. Surplus food fueled a massive, global population boom. Yet by depleting our soils, we end up worse than before, with vastly more people and vastly lower productivity. Hundreds of great civilizations have risen and fallen in accordance with agriculture and soil lost. Can we avoid a similar fate?

The Food Energy Pyramid

Energy flow through the ecosystem is traditionally illustrated as a food energy pyramid. Land and sea plants convert solar energy into

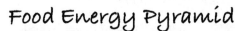

Food Energy Pyramid

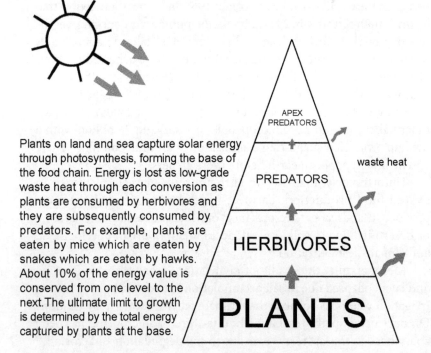

Plants on land and sea capture solar energy through photosynthesis, forming the base of the food chain. Energy is lost as low-grade waste heat through each conversion as plants are consumed by herbivores and they are subsequently consumed by predators. For example, plants are eaten by mice which are eaten by snakes which are eaten by hawks. About 10% of the energy value is conserved from one level to the next. The ultimate limit to growth is determined by the total energy captured by plants at the base.

APEX PREDATORS

waste heat

PREDATORS

HERBIVORES

PLANTS

living tissues and form the base to support all other life. Insects, fish, birds, and mammals consume plants and benefit from the stored energy. However, there is an inherent loss of energy with the conversion from plant matter to animal flesh. There are further losses of energy when predators kill and consume plant eaters, and again when predators eat predators.

As a rule of thumb, only about 10% of the energy value is converted from one level of the pyramid to the next. For example, 10,000 kilocalories of grass might produce 1,000 kcal of grasshoppers, which converts to 100 kcal of frogs, becoming 10 kcal of snakes, which converts to 1 kcal of energy value for a hawk. In this example, it takes 10,000 kcal of grass to ultimately support 1 kcal worth of hawk. The amount of activity throughout the pyramid is determined by how much energy is captured at the base by plant life. Technically, each level of the pyramid should be 10% the size of the preceding level, making a very short, squat pyramid, impractical for illustrative purposes.

World food supply is included in the energy pyramid, dictating the total carrying capacity of the planet. To optimally feed the most people, we can grow more plants at the base, and/or adopt more energy-efficient use of available production.

Starting with this later point, an estimated 36 percent of global crop calories are used as animal feed, and 9 percent are used for biofuels or other industrial uses, with the remainder consumed as people food. Conflicting statistics vary widely, with some sources claiming that 90% of all soybeans and 50% of all grains are consumed by livestock.[36] In the U.S., differing sources claim that 80% of all corn is fed to livestock,[37] and 40% is used for ethanol production,[38] which doesn't add up, such is the nature of statistics, but suffice it to say, very little is eaten by people. In other words, the tractors and combines that crawl across America's heartland are burning oil and losing soil to grow crops that are not actually needed for people. Farm subsidies offer profit incentives for farmers to flood the market with cheap food, which is allocated to unnecessary and unsustainable uses. It is part of our massive system to employ people disposing of surplus wealth.

Hunger experts point out that we could feed billions more people by transitioning to energy-efficient diets so that crops feed people instead of livestock. Cows have a poor conversion rate for feed into meat, with various sources claiming everything from 16:1 to 6:1 on grain. Other livestock is typically more efficient, including pork (6:1), turkey (4:1) or chicken (3:1).[39] Switching to meats with better conversion ratios, or eating grains directly, increases energy efficiency, so that the same food base can support a larger population. That's important when many developing countries export crop food to industrialized nations to feed livestock while people go hungry at home. By some accounts, we could support four billion additional people now just by diverting crops from livestock to people.[40]

Hunger activists recommend eating less beef, or better yet, going vegetarian to make better use of scarce resources. However, as is often the case, there is more to the story than meets the eye, and beef can be a highly efficient source of food energy. Fattening cows on grain is wasteful, and the fat is often trimmed off anyway. However, cattle can efficiently consume lower-quality food like grass, rather than grain, which is what they're adapted to eat anyway. Retaining or restoring grass cover helps hold soil in place, and herd animals, such as cows or bison, are essential for maintaining a healthy ecosystem, especially in brittle landscapes. As discussed later, properly managed grazing can trample carbon-rich plants into the soil, rapidly sequestering CO_2 from the atmosphere. In contrast, plowing and planting grain crops usually increases wind and water erosion and leads towards desertification. Similarly, deforestation in the Amazon is largely driven by agriculture to convert rainforests to soybean crops for livestock feed.

With proper management, livestock or bison can halt or reverse desertification, encourage soil building, and expand the food supply without consuming grain or soybean crops. Anyone concerned about the environmental and social impacts of eating beef need not quit, but merely switch to grass-fed meat.

In fact, we could significantly expand livestock and wildlife numbers if we start reclaiming deserts to their former health as grasslands, as outlined in the next chapter. Any croplands that are subject to desertification must necessarily also be returned to grasslands. In addition, the vast amount of cropland presently dedicated to raising animal feed and biofuels should be restored as rangelands and tropical forests.

While reclaiming deserts as grasslands, we can also increase plant productivity on croplands through stewardship and polycultures. Progressive farmers have successfully implemented crop rotations that halt and reverse soil loss and boost crop and livestock productivity. Small operations with diverse species are known to produce more food per acre than large, mechanized monoculture farms.[41] Converting lawns to gardens and developing permaculture plans can make each person's yard immensely productive. If needed, even roofs and walls can be planted. Bottom line, we could easily grow enough food to feed a global population of 11 billion people by 2100. We could expand food production even while restoring deserts, tropical forests, and wildlife habitat.

Decomposers: The Missing Link

The food energy pyramid illustrates a linear sequence consisting of plants → herbivores → carnivores → apex carnivores. It is a linear sequence because culturally we are linear thinkers as a result of industrialization and assembly line production, as discussed in *Roadmap to Reality*.

A core problem with the traditional food energy pyramid is that it doesn't include decomposers, such as fungi, worms, insects, and microbes that consume dead plants, manure, and dead animals. Many educators leave decomposers out of the food pyramid altogether. Some include them as the top level of the pyramid, since even apex predators die and decompose. Others place them below the pyramid as the recycling process that provides nutrients to the plants. Some place them off to the side in their own nethersphere. However, none of these solutions accurately depict reality. For example, fungi consume manure and dead plant matter to produce new food sources for herbivores. Worms and insects recycle organic matter and then become food for predators such as birds and fish.

Decomposers often work in moist, dark places, out of sight in the soil, so we don't fully appreciate the total biomass they contribute. As illustrated on the following page, one side of the pyramid should be dedicated to decomposers consuming wastes and producing food for plants and predators.

In his book *Upsizing*, author Gunter Pauli describes the "Brown Revolution," where we greatly expand fungi production on leftover crop residue to create new revenue streams and a significant food source for our growing population. This is especially important because fungi are high in protein like meat, and some mushrooms taste meaty. In addition, fungal mycelium leaves behind essential amino acids in the spent substrate, so the waste from mushroom farming can become highly nutritious feed for livestock. As noted by Pauli,

"Mushrooms derive their energy mainly from lignocellulose, a macromolecule available in abundance. About one-third of all the biomass on the planet is lignocellulose, commonly referred to as 'fibers'. This material is often considered waste in our industrial processing of agricultural and forestry products ... mushrooms are

the only species capable of separating lignin from cellulose and converting the components into carbohydrates. ... The small fungi and large mushrooms help the world by digesting these millions of tons of waste which would otherwise overwhelm the planet."[42]

Button mushrooms are most popular in the West, but relatively low in protein and they require pasteurized horse manure as a substrate. Other diverse species grow in many different mediums and climates. Coffee grounds are ideal for oyster and shiitake mushrooms. Utilizing all spent coffee grounds for mushroom farming would produce 25 million tons of new protein annually.[43] Imagine then, how much food we could produce by growing mushrooms in all the waste fibers from wheat, corn, rice, sugar cane, forestry, and farm manure!

Americans presently consume only 0.2 kilograms of mushrooms per person per year, compared to 65 kilograms per person in Hong Kong.[44]

Food Energy Pyramid with Decomposers

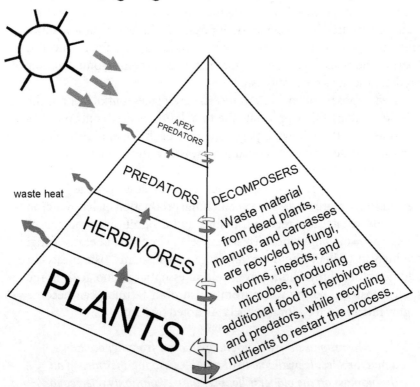

Decomposers not only recycle waste into nutrients, they also become food, greatly contributing to the total biomass of the food chain pyramid.

Since cultivated mushrooms are grown on agricultural waste, consuming mushrooms decreases demand for other crops and livestock. That means we can feed more people from the existing resource base, or better yet, rewild surplus agricultural lands to provide essential habitat for wildlife, of which many species are critically threatened or endangered.

Watering the Pyramid

Sunlight captured by plants at the base of the food energy pyramid ultimately dictates the total biomass produced at all levels of the ecosystem. By optimizing farming and ranching practices plus cultivating fungi on agricultural wastes, we could improve production to sustainably feed several billion more people before we reached the ultimate limits to growth.

However, sunlight is not the primary limiting factor. On land or in the oceans, plants need an optimal combination of sunlight, water, nutrients, and temperature. Most of the planet underutilizes sunlight due these other limiting factors, especially a lack of water, which is ironic given that two-thirds of the earth is covered with water. We can greatly increase food production by desalinizing seawater and irrigating crops in deserts, especially human-created deserts near oceans and seas.

Sundrop Farms practices "sustainable agriculture" by using solar power to desalinize seawater, which is used to grow vegetables hydroponically in greenhouses where the environment could not otherwise support farming. One 20-hectare "farm" near Spencer Bay, Australia, uses 23,000 mirrors to focus sunlight on a central tower, generating 39 megawatts of clean electricity for desalinization and winter heating. The facility produces 17,000 metric tons of tomatoes per year (15% of the Australian supply) without consuming soil, fresh water, or fossil fuels. That is a huge amount of food from a very small footprint. Additional farms have been built in Portugal and Tennessee.[45] This is only the beginning. Imagine similar farms lining the entire 3,000-mile northern coast of Africa, watering, farming, and reclaiming the desert we created. The production potential is immense, as is the total human population we could sustainably feed. As the cost of solar energy continues to fall, we can reasonably expect resurrection of the North African wheat fields that sustained the Roman Empire, only this time irrigated by desalinized seawater.

Arguably, the Sahara and similar habitats are ideal places for human habitation. Development of the most barren places on earth for civilization could free nature to reclaim otherwise fertile landscapes around the world.

Sundrop Farms does not indicate the source of nutrients consumed in the hydroponic system. However, since matter is neither created nor destroyed, we will one day close the loop on our food supply by piping treated sewage directly into such plant factories for recycling back into new food.

Food Factories

In developing countries people routinely recycle every scrap of human or animal manure. Manure is typically recycled through open fields and aquacultures. Algae cultures are also becoming popular. Raw wastes are composted or digested with microorganisms back to its basic nutrients, then used to fertilize ponds of single-celled blue-green algae. Algae use sunlight to photosynthesize sugars. An algae culture can produce fifty tons of protein per hectare per year, compared to only two tons from corn.[46] Algae cultures are efficient because the organisms are so simple. Algae expends no energy building extraneous leaves, stems, or roots like other plants, nor the bones, brains and guts of the animals. Alga is pure food.

The endless quest to reduce expenses and maximize profits will lead to many of our common foods being grown in vats, much as scientists now grow tissue cultures in petri dishes. The difference is in scale.

Researchers have learned to remove tiny tomatoes off the vine and grow them to maturity with nutrient injections.[47] Before long we will skip even that step to culture whole vats of tomato cells for use in ketchup and other products where the soup of cells is a sufficient substitute for whole tomatoes. We will pipe in nutrients from treated sewage to culture vats of wheat starch, milk, egg whites or yolks and meat.

It is technologically easy to synthesize simple sugars directly from air and water, however, it is extremely energy intensive. Living plants can produce sugars much more efficiently. We may never produce sugar as efficiently than plants, yet a net loss of energy conversion is not necessarily uneconomical.

When we convert low-grade coal or oil fuel into high-grade electricity, we burn three calories of fuel for each calorie of electric output. We accept this loss because electricity is more versatile; it can power our computers, lights, and robotics, while coal and oil cannot. Agriculture similarly converts calories of low-grade fuel energy into a higher-grade form at a net loss. Coal and oil are not directly edible, yet can be converted into food by powering farm equipment. As the next step in an evolving process, we may soon convert solar electricity directly into sugar at an even greater caloric loss.

The cost of producing energy is continuing to fall in real dollars as we find ways to harvest more power with less labor. When the cost of energy falls low enough it will be more cost effective to synthetically produce sugar in a factory than to drive into a field and harvest it. At that point the total labor consumed in both harnessing the power and manufacturing the sugar would be less than the labor involved in growing a crop. Along with nutrients recycled from sewage, this synthetic sugar could be fed to tissue cultures to grow whatever vegetables and meat we want. No longer constrained by the organic cycles of nature, our food supply would expand to meet all future food needs.

Forecast

To recap, we are rapidly eroding our most productive farmlands to the peril of future generations. On our present course, we are likely to see mass starvations, mass migrations, civil unrest, and potential regional wars fought over food, water, and climate issues. Sustainable global food production is theoretically achievable if we a) mimic natural grazing cycles to regenerate degraded rangelands, b) switch to grass-fed beef and cease cultivating crops like soybeans and corn for feedlot operations, c) reverse soil loss through more holistic, integrated agricultural systems and permaculture, and d) grow mushrooms on agricultural waste to feed more people from a smaller total footprint.

Adding technology to the task, we can sustainably desalinize seawater and reclaim thousands of square miles of human-created wastelands, vastly ramping up production to feed a growing population wild retiring and rewilding more productive landscapes. For better or worse, future technology promises indoor farming and the wholesale abandonment of farmlands back to nature.

With or without technology, we have the means to create a sustainable world, but will we implement it? Is the path ahead utterly bleak or fantastically abundant? Will we erode our last remaining soils or switch to sustainable agriculture? Will we feed the world or descend into the chaos of mass hunger, unrest, and warfare? Will hundreds of millions of people starve to death, or will we add billions more? Will we wipe out endangered species or release agricultural lands back to nature? The most probable answer is "all of the above."

"Our 'frontier-style' economic mode, in which we turn virgin land into farms, highways, and buildings—and irreplaceable virgin resources into products and waste—is reaching its natural terminus. Development has arrived at the ends of the Earth. Progress has nowhere to turn, except to revisit and restore what we've already wrought."

—Storm Cunningham,
The Restoration Economy (2002)[48]

Stimulating Succession
Birth of the Restoration Economy

European colonists relocating to America discovered vast open forests with wild fruits, nuts, and game in great abundance. However, eastern woodlands were not wholly natural. Through well-timed application of fire, Native Americans previously managed nature as a wild, do-nothing garden. Indians waited for cool spring or autumn weather to light fires that burned calmly through the understory, cleaning out underbrush without killing big trees or sterilizing the soil. The resulting open forests were optimized for edible and useful plants, berry production, wild game, and easy travel. With minimal effort, they manipulated successional levels of ecology to maintain a vast wilderness garden.[49]

The European method of gardening is and was vastly different. Whatever nature provides, we plow, pull, poison, or otherwise eradicate to make room for our preferred crops. We fight against succession, continuously killing anything that competes with or attacks our crops. We apply herbicides, insecticides, fungicides, and chemical fertilizer concoctions. Any species not desired is physically attacked and verbally vilified. A plant growing where it isn't wanted is a "weed," sometimes an "invasive weed," or worse, a "noxious weed." Similarly, wolves were systematically persecuted, trapped, shot, or poisoned with toxins infused into balls of fat and nails. Our European ancestors even brought dead wolves into court—sometimes dressed in human clothes—and conducted trials for their crimes.[50]

Our approach to issues within the economic ecosystem is similar. Too much crime? Attack the problem with more police, more prisons, and stiffer laws. Too much pollution? Attack the problem with more regulations and stiffer fines. Too much competition in the marketplace? Levy tariffs against the competition or offer subsidies to favor businesses.

Maintaining autocratic control over complex systems is unsustainable. We need to develop a holistic approach to managing both the natural ecosystem and the economic ecosystem. It is easier to manage people, nature, and the economy by nudging the ecosystem towards positive outcomes. Instead of trying to grow a crop yourself, adopt an ecosystem approach so that nature, or the economy, produces for you.

Individually, we may not have much power to influence broader choices of society. However, with foresight, anyone can garden the ecosystem to nurture a crop abundance and prosperity while also weathering deep changes coming to the economy. Collectively, we can engage each other in dialogue about the future and how best to nudge the economic ecosystem in favor of peace and prosperity for all.

Desertification

Eastern woodlands follow a typical sequence of ecological succession. If a major wildfire kills off a forest, grasses and herbs quickly grow over the barren ground. Shrubs and trees gradually fill in as fast-growing conifers bringing back forest cover. Slower growing hardwoods eventually overtake the conifers, resulting in a climax ecosystem with a dense understory. Like most of Europe, the eastern third of America benefits from adequate precipitation distributed throughout the year to maintain vegetative cover regardless of how the land is or is not managed. These moist landscapes are considered "nonbrittle."[51]

Western states typically receive less precipitation, and more critically, less reliable precipitation, retarding seedling establishment as well as biological decomposition. Succession in these "brittle" landscapes functions very differently from the nonbrittle landscapes of the East. Much of the West once supported deep, rich grass and massive herds of bison, antelope, and elk, as well as the wolves that hunted them. Unfortunately, settlement led to rapid desertification, transforming bountiful landscapes into harsh, barren, weedy tracts with little biological diversity.

Based on historical experience with nonbrittle environments, land managers assumed that all degraded landscapes needed rest to recover properly. Yet brittle ecosystems continue degrading without animal impact, leading to less and less vegetative cover over time. People didn't understand that herd animals and their predators are an essential part of the successional process. Predators keep big game animals bunched in tight herds. The herds graze and urinate in dense concentration, and most importantly, they trample everything in their path. Seeds are trampled into the soil, along with a healthy covering of old dead grass, weeds, and brush, all smeared with manure and bacteria to assist biological decay and fertilize new seedlings. And because herd animals leave devastation in their wake, they keep moving forward, leaving previously grazed lands to recover without further grazing pressure.

We disrupted this successional process when we built fences and introduced scattered livestock that graze lightly over the land again and again. Cows and sheep graze tender greens, yet they do not trample seeds or old dead matter into the soil. Green grasses are overgrazed as animals repeatedly cover the same ground. Dead grasses remain standing, choking out new growth. Instead of rotting into the soil, standing grasses slowly oxidize, returning carbon to the atmosphere. Bare ground between clumps of grass slowly spreads and crusts over, causing rainwater to drain off the land rather than soak in. Floods and droughts become problematic as rainfall washes away in quick bursts, rather than recharging the water table and re-emerging as natural springs. Invasive weeds colonize bare ground and get blamed as the problem, when they are merely a symptom, attempting to restart succession on barren soils. Stocking rates fall, and the land is unable to support much livestock or wildlife. Fire, natural or otherwise, only exacerbates the problem, burning up essential organic matter that should have been pounded into the soil.

Successional failure is most severe in southwestern states such as Arizona, New Mexico, and Texas. In many places, the original tall grass is completely absent, replaced by bare ground and creosote bushes. Lacking healthy examples for comparison, it is easy to believe that bare ground is normal.

Farther north, the land is just as dry, yet temperatures are cooler, and the land may lay dormant for half the year through winter. In the Great Basin Desert of Utah, Nevada, and Idaho, grass still grows two to three feet tall, yet with fifty feet or more of bare ground between one clump of grass and the next. Even here in western Montana, desertification is rampant, with progressively more bare ground showing between remaining grasses.

We are rapidly creating a desert to rival the Great Saharan Desert. The Sahara once supported rich grasslands and flowing springs. The fertile soils grew grains that supported the Roman Empire. A person could walk the entire northern coastline of Africa in the shade of trees.[52] Now it is a 3,000-mile strip of desert, sand, and rock. Likewise for much of the Middle East. We watch people battle over windblown sands from Libya to Syria, Iraq, and Afghanistan. At the root of this chronic civil unrest is desertification. These lands originally supported abundant, prosperous ecosystems. Wild pigs once rooted around in the rich cedar forests of Israel and Lebanon, but no more.

As mentioned, people naturally expect to remove livestock to allow degraded landscapes to rest and recover, yet the solution to these problems is to reinvigorate succession by mimicking the historical grazing sequence. Here in America, the ideal solution would be to allow free-roaming bison and wolves to roam the prairies again, yet that is not always practical in this day of private property and fences. It is more practical to focus on that which one can control.

As a landowner, for example, it is possible to mimic herd effect by dividing pastures into ultra small paddocks with portable electric fences to bunch livestock in a small area for a short period of time. Managing extra fences and moving livestock more frequently adds work, yet helps to stimulate new growth to cover bare ground. Mimicking natural cycles can enable ranchers to double, triple, or quadruple animal numbers, resulting in greater profit from the same land.

Similarly, livestock can be used in land reclamation to facilitate revegetation of old roads or mining work. Scatter seeds and hay over barren ground, and the animals will graze, trample, defecate, urinate, and leave behind a fertile seed bed where there was no topsoil.

A little knowledge of ecological succession is a powerful tool for transforming an impoverished landscape into an abundant, functioning ecosystem. As a landowner, it is possible to stimulate succession to increase productivity and abundance. As an investor, there is potential to buy degraded properties and reinvigorate them for profit. Better yet, start a bison ranch to help restore their numbers in hopes that one day the fences will come down and the natural grazing cycle will be fully restored.

The economic ecosystem is malleable in a similar way. By working with ecosystem processes and mechanisms of change, we can tilt succession in favor of a greener, more abundant world and nurture prosperity in impoverished communities.

Succession in Urban and Rural Communities

The American economy sprouted from a frontier mentality among the colonists. Beyond the narrow band of settlements along the eastern seaboard lay an uncharted wilderness of free land and resources stretching nearly three thousand miles to the Pacific Ocean. Colonists envisioned promise and prosperity beyond the edge of town and just over the next rise. Pioneers cut timber, dug mines, and built towns, roads, and railroads.

Development impact, resource depletion, and pollution seemed irrelevant in an apparently infinite landscape. Thomas Jefferson reportedly thought it would take a hundred generations to settle the West, yet we did it in five generations.[53] Economic growth shifted westward to the Pacific then bounced back, filling in missed niches along the way.

We filled the continent with so many houses, roads, and factories that each new development now comes at the expense of something sacred. New roads threaten critical habitat for endangered species. New mines and factories threaten drinking water supplies. New housing developments and parking lots chip away at our remaining green spaces and limit recreational access.

Any society that attempts to grow itself to infinity is inherently unsustainable. Developers push political and ecological boundaries, such as paving over wetlands until there is nowhere for floodwaters to go except into living rooms and bedrooms. Reckless resource extraction and development leads to toxic soils and polluted waters. The economy risks growing itself to death, bringing societal implosion, like many fallen civilizations before us. Alternatively, we can recognize limits to growth and shift succession towards a new economy based on restoration.

As Storm Cunningham emphasizes in *The Restoration Economy*, civilizations operate in three different modes of development:[54]

• <u>New development</u> is exploitive and depletes resources.

• <u>Maintenance and conservation</u> is reactionary, investing to extend the life of the built environment and conserve dwindling resources.

• <u>Restoration development</u> revitalizes what was there before. For example, if new development constructs houses in wetlands, restoration development might kick in later to move houses to higher ground and restore wetlands as green space.

Having exploited nearly all there is to exploit, the main driver of economic growth is now shifting from new development to restoration of decaying cities and farms and contaminated soils and waterways. Developments of the past century left ample opportunity for restoration in the present century. Opportunities abound in the swathes of old, decaying, and abandoned developments where real estate is cheap and opportunities abound to profit by stimulating succession.

At its peak in 1950, Detroit was home to 1.8 million people. The city was ideally located in the heart of the Great Lakes region, easily accessible by land or water and close to major centers for coal, iron, and copper production. Ford, General Motors, and Chrysler were all based in Detroit, and the city thrived. But what the auto industry gave, the auto industry took away. Factories relocated in search of cheaper labor. Detroit's population decreased in every subsequent census, dropping to 700,000 people by 2010, a loss of 61% of the population. A building analysis in 2014 revealed that 50,000 of the city's 261,000 structures were abandoned, of which 9,000 had fire damage, and 5,000 were recommended for demolition.[55]

Tens of thousands of homes were foreclosed upon as owners failed to keep up with monthly mortgage payments or property taxes. Thousands of homes sold for a pittance, some for as little as $1, many for $500 or $1,000, and some for $10,000 or more. The average home sale in Detroit was $7,500 in 2012, steadily rebounding ever since.[56]

Most such homes need extensive repairs. A $1,000 house may require $30,000 in restoration work to make it habitable, yet it is still a great deal to gain ownership of a home or the opportunity to flip and sell as an investor. For example, one person bought a house for $10,500 and invested $35,000 in renovation work, then sold the house for $86,499, making a profit of $41,000.[57]

Revitalizing an old house is good for the community. Fixing up a house inspires neighbors and raises neighboring property values. Money invested in the community for building supplies and labor helps stimulate the economy and tilt succession towards urban renewal and regrowth. In addition, vacant homes and whole city blocks have been bulldozed and turned into community gardens. Detroit has become a mecca for artists, writers, and urban homesteaders. These efforts revitalize the city to the benefit of all.[58]

Similar opportunities abound in most states throughout the country. For example, when we first moved to Pony, Montana in 1989, there were small, yet livable houses on the market for $15,000 to $20,000. My partner and I could have bought a house and moved in right away. Instead, we were interested in the more expensive and slower option of building our own home. Local real estate prices have risen substantially since then, so it would be more costly to buy a house or land now.

Many urban and rural communities across the country continue to struggle economically. Drive through rural America and you will see town after town with boarded up houses and storefronts. These are scenes of opportunity. Buy inexpensive real estate in a quaint country town, and avoid the need for a full-time job. Renovate a home, and help revitalize the local community. See property values grow over time.

Follow your dreams, which might include starting a business. With access to global markets through the World Wide Web, it is possible to operate a significant business from a small town. Where real estate is inexpensive, it is possible to attain the prestige of having a Main Street location at a bargain price. Where you lead, others will likely follow, stimulating successional change and prosperity throughout the community.

Incentivizing Succession

Every year there is a constant push-pull, tug-of-war between environmentalists and industry. Responding to concerns, government tries to regulate away problems like air and water pollution. Millions of dollars and incalculable human effort is wasted pushing and pulling each side of the issues. Environmentalists seek more control, while industries seek less. Through government bureaucracy, environmental organizations impose regulations that state how much any company can pollute and how to control that pollution. Industries respond to control by bucking the system. The longer a company can put off installation of pollution controls the better its bottom line. Industry has a financial incentive to lobby the government for less control, or to sue against regulation, or otherwise stall installation of pollution controls. There is no incentive to actually stop polluting.

Besides being largely ineffective, such laws are also unsustainable politically. Tighter environmental controls ultimately lead to elections favoring candidates who promise to roll back regulations in favor of business. If we hope to make real and sustainable progress towards helping the planet, then we need to play by ecosystem rules. We can apply lessons of ecological succession to nudge industry towards greener solutions.

For example, placing a value on pollution creates incentives businesses relate to. The EPA successfully implemented this approach in Los Angeles, where smog has been a chronic problem. Regulators placed a cap on the total amount of pollution that could be emitted locally. New industries coming into the area must purchase "allowance credits" to pollute from preexisting companies. If another company closes down or installs technology to reduce pollution emissions, then they can sell surplus allowance credits to the new company.

Allowance credits can quickly become very valuable. Companies that hold allowance credits can weigh the value of their credits as an asset against the cost of installing cleaner technologies. As credits become more valuable, there is increased incentive to clean up smokestacks so a company can sell its credits to someone else. New companies are incentivized to implement the most economical clean technologies available. Regardless how many new industries start up, there remains a cap on the total amount of pollution that can be emitted to the atmosphere. Moreover, the cap can be gradually lowered over time to progressively reduce emissions.

In 1990 the EPA expanded the concept of allowance credits to help control emissions of sulfur dioxide from utilities across the nation.[59] Government models predicted the cost of credits would be between $500 to $750 per ton of sulfur emitted. Above that price it would be more profitable to invest in technology to reduce emissions rather than purchase pollution credits. Industry models predicted costs in the range of $1,000 to $1,500 per ton, a cost they argued might be passed on to utility consumers. However, implementing allowance credits in a free-market system spurred innovators to find least-cost methods to reduce emissions. The sulfur credit market opened at $250 per ton and dropped to $66 per ton by 1996, before rising back up to $207 by the end of the decade. Sulfur emissions dropped by 37% nationwide in just one decade, at a fraction of the projected cost.[60] By 2016, sulfur emissions were 88% lower than 1990 levels.[61]

If a similar cap and trade system had been established for carbon emissions, it would have incentivized conservation, leading to more energy efficient homes, businesses, and automobiles. Fossil fuels would be used more conscientiously, stabilizing prices while leaving dwindling resources in the ground for future generations. Carbon trading could have stalled global warming and avoided trillions of dollars in economic harm.

For lack of federal initiative, California initiated its own cap and trade system for carbon credits in 2012. To soften the impact of implementing the new system, carbon credits were initially offered in abundance, with California's Air Resources Board slightly reducing the number of credits available each subsequent year. Emissions reductions were thus modest in the beginning, predicted to become more significant over time.[62] [63] Implementing a similar system nationwide or globally would facilitate the transition from fossil fuels to conservation and renewable energy. Carbon emissions could be steadily dialed back towards zero, reducing the degree of damage from global warming.

Replacement Succession

Until recently, it was popularly believed that only a few million people inhabited all of North and South America prior to European colonization, and that these Native Americans lived as savages in a vast, untamed wilderness. Nothing could be farther from the truth. Evidence indicates there were at least 100 million people in North and South America prior to European conquest. Many cities in central and South America were larger and more sophisticated than their European counterparts. However, early contact with explorers introduced new diseases that swept through the Americas, killing off 90 to 95% of all American Indians *before* colonists arrived. Some observers found countless skeletons strewn across the land, the survivors too few to bury the dead. Others found empty villages, decaying into the ground after signs of human remains largely disappeared. Europeans found their fertile forests ripe for colonization.[64]

Europeans experienced their own plagues throughout ten thousand years of agriculture. Close association with livestock enabled animal diseases to cross the species barrier from poultry, swine, cattle, and other livestock to infect humans with devastating effects.[65] Plagues were common throughout recorded history. The comparatively recent Black Death of the fourteenth century killed 30 to 60% of all Europeans,[66] followed by numerous recurring epidemics that killed millions more. Those of us alive today enjoy a degree of immunity acquired through millennia of costly natural selection.

Native Americans suffered the full breadth of natural selection in the span of a few generations as they were exposed to smallpox, measles, swine flu, whooping cough, tuberculosis, brucellosis, leptospirosis, anthrax, and malaria.[67] Any person lucky enough to survive one disease might fall to the next one. The Americas tragically experienced replacement succession, introducing new people, new culture, and hundreds of new plant and animal species that each became invasive across the western hemisphere.

Successional forces also sweep through our economic ecosystem, replacing traditional products, services, and business practices. Some people profit, while others lose their jobs or face bankruptcy. In the case of fossil fuels and other unsustainable industries, the sooner we transition the better. New "species," such as solar and wind power have become increasingly prevalent in economic niches once dominated by fossil fuels. The transition to a sustainable economy is underway, although not fast enough to forestall great damage from unsustainable practices.

Ambitious individuals can potentially facilitate the transition to a sustainable economy, strategizing to tilt succession across the broader economic ecosystem. Greener products and services can be introduced to out-compete inefficient old ones, creating a new standard or a new form of habitat that other businesses must adopt to remain competitive.

The economy in the coming decades will be led by businesses that provide valuable goods and services with the least throughput of materials and energy. Businesses that change the fastest will earn the most. Succession is already tilting in favor of a cleaner, greener world. It is inevitable that the economy will mature as a closed-loop system, yet there is much to be done to speed up the process.

Imagine a factory that reduces its material and energy costs by 75 to 90%, yet still maintains the same level of production. It would have a significant advantage over the competition. Eventually, all businesses will have to rise to a similar level of efficiency to stay competitive. The reason our economy remains inefficient is due to a lack of the information in the right places. People expect energy or resource efficiency to cost more money. They don't know or have not investigated the opportunities they are missing.

Rocky Mountain Institute (RMI), Amory Lovins' energy and resource think tank, works to connect people with information, showing corporations and governments that resource conservation is good for business. In the past, for example, power companies sought to meet increased demand through increased power production. RMI introduced least-cost planning, enabling utilities to compare the cost of expanding output versus the cost of utilizing, and in some cases providing, efficient technologies to stretch existing supplies. You may not have noticed the effects of RMI's work, yet they have changed the way virtually every power utility in the country does business.

One of RMI's major projects is to bring efficient cars to market. The organization originally advocated ultralight cars built of durable composite materials with small gas engines to generate electricity to power motors on each wheel. Ultralight cars offered the potential to achieve up to 200 miles per gallon. RMI encouraged a few start-up companies to begin designing ultralights then promoted the idea among mainstream automakers, prodding them to invest in research as well, or risk losing out in the coming auto industry revolution. At least two-dozen companies were inspired to start researching and prototyping electric and hybrid vehicles. [68] In 2000, Honda started mass-marketing its first gas-electric hybrid, the 70 mpg Insight. Soon after, the Toyota Prius was introduced, quickly becoming the most popular energy efficient car on the market. Tesla followed suit with all-electric vehicles, and the race was on.

Following RMI's lead, Elon Musk released patent rights to Tesla's automotive technology, encouraging others to compete in the race to make electric cars better and more affordable.[69] Thanks to RMI and Tesla Inc., most automotive companies are getting into the hybrid and all-electric vehicle markets, gradually pushing the technology towards greater efficiency for less cost. Major automakers are now phasing out the internal combustion engine in favor of greener transportation alternatives.

Rocky Mountain Institute has worked behind the scenes, tinkering with economic succession in simple but dramatic ways to make big changes in the world. You too can help nudge succession in favor of a better world, and there are an infinite number of ways to do so, especially by jumping into business and showing the competition how to make more profit with reduced throughput. As you lead, others will follow.

Change on the Margin

In the *Origin of Species* Charles Darwin proposed that the whole gene pool of each species was continuously undergoing gradual change. However, it would be difficult for any individual mutation to merge across a population. Mutant genes were more likely to be diluted away in the gene pool. For instance, the Huaorani tribe of Ecuador carries a recessive gene that gives many individuals twelve fingers and twelve toes. How does such a gene transition from recessive to dominant within a species? Naturalists were long bewildered by the absence of gradual change in the fossil record. There always seemed to be sudden, dramatic change from one fossil layer to the next.

Imagine a valley several hundred miles across, surrounded by mountains on all sides. Suppose that only one type of grass seed is deposited into this valley. The valley is ideal habitat for this particular type of grass. The valley fills up and evolution stalls. There are mutations, yet the grass is already optimized for the environment, and mutations fail to survive. On the margins of the valley, however, there are some diverse habitats. It may be wetter in the uplands on one side of the valley versus the other, or one area may be warmer or colder. There may be different soil chemistry. Valley grass may survive in these areas, yet would not prosper. Mutants constantly arise, and some variations would be more optimized to marginal environments, eventually creating whole new species. Thus, new species evolve on the margin.[70]

Then comes change. Perhaps the climate changes, causing the valley to become slightly warmer and wetter. The valley becomes more favorable to a grass species from the margin. The previously dominant species might survive in the new margins or be completely eliminated. The fossil record would show an apparent jump in evolution from one species to another. Thus, evolution proceeds gradually yet suddenly. The gene for twelve fingers and toes would not become dominant unless something catastrophic happened to the broader human population, leaving six-fingered humans to fill the void.

Environmental changes dislodge old species and create new opportunities. Optimized species from the margin rush to fill the void. In the absence of optimized species, evolution progresses at a rapid speed (relatively speaking), with many mutations surviving to fill ecological niches. The process stalls when habitats fill up. Therefore, favorable environments with fertile soils are often the least diverse. Evolution fills the ecological niches and stalls. More hostile environments require more creative strategies for survival, and more diverse species to economize sparsely available resources.

Like new species, new ideas and technologies evolve on the margin. As noted earlier, the first solar panels were extremely expensive to produce. They could not compete for habitat with cheap oil. However, oil was useless on the margin, that is in space, so solar panels were economical for powering satellites. In this manner, evolution proceeded gradually, and by 1980 solar panels were appearing on backwoods cabins, still on the margin, miles away from the power lines. It was more economical to install solar panels than to pay utilities thousands of dollars to extend power lines to remote cabins.[71]

As written in earlier incarnations of this book, *"Eventually—it really does not matter when—perhaps ten years, or fifty, but at some point in time, photovoltaics will become economically competitive right up to the utility grid. Solar cells will suddenly invade the economic niche of the fossil fuels, taking over the market habitat and dramatically altering the makeup of the economic ecosystem."*[72] In 2016, solar power achieved grid parity in twenty states,[73] signaling that we are on the cusp of a solar revolution.

At about this time, Elon Musk announced that SolarCity was introducing slate-like solar shingles, which are supposedly cost-competitive in new construction.[74] A solar roof can invisibly produce electricity to achieve greater self-sufficiency, run the meter backwards, or power an electric car.

Like photovoltaics, hundreds of other green technologies are evolving on the margin, from electric or solar-powered lawn mowers and ebikes to high-efficiency automobiles, better batteries, and workable fuel cells. Entrepreneurs recognize the demand for cleaner technologies to close the loop on pollution. Eco-pioneers are scrambling to develop and occupy new economic niches. Technological refinements will increasingly tilt market forces in favor of newer, greener products, dramatically changing our economy and its impact on the natural world in the decades ahead.

Some innovations, technological and otherwise, are so significant that they transform the entire economic-cultural landscape. Like introducing a carnivore onto an island that has evolved for millennia without predators, it changes everything. The microchip was one such idea. It altered the economic landscape, driving old industries out of business while creating niches for thousands of new innovations. We still feel the effects change reverberating back and forth through our economy, creating jobs for some while eliminating them for others.

Similarly, many New Age memes like healthy diets, herbs, and acupuncture originated on the fringe, yet transformed mainstream culture in relatively little time. We don't hear the term New Age much anymore, since New Age memes have become mainstream.

Memes that transform the way we look at the world are often called paradigms. Emerging paradigms and technologies that blend into mainstream living in the coming decades will rapidly transform the world we know.

With sufficient understanding of forthcoming ideas and innovations, we can help accelerate transformation of the economic ecosystem. We can make the world a better place while creating a life of abundance and prosperity along the way. Now that we have a broad view of the economic ecosystem and how it functions, let's consider potential tools for introducing substantive change.

Part IV
Tools To Work With

"[The scientist] pores over books night and day, straining his eyes and becoming nearsighted, and if you wonder what on earth he has been working on all that time it is to become the inventor of eyeglasses to correct nearsightedness."

—Masanobu Fukuoka,
The One Straw Revolution (1975)[1]

Materials to Work With
Open Niches in the Ecosystem

Living organisms extract resources from the environment and modify them into useful products. Material waste and low-grade heat are by-products of metabolism, yet material wastes become resource inputs to other organisms so the only true waste is low-grade heat. The natural ecosystem is a closed-loop system where all material wastes are recycled. To create a truly sustainable economic ecosystem, we must similarly form a closed-loop system so that all material wastes are recycled back into new and useful products, and the only waste discharged is low-grade heat. From this perspective the problem of sustainability seems as simple and as complex as figuring out what to do with garbage. The logical route forward is to examine waste and find ways to put it to use. Or maybe not.

I am constantly surprised to see underutilized and surplus resources when driving. I see piles of rocks carefully picked from farm fields and discarded in convenient piles. There are old vehicles and tires forgotten in backyards. I see piles of lumber and bricks and scrap metal. I see woodlots overgrown with dead wood, trees with unpicked fruit and worse, yards without trees. There are houses and buildings abandoned and falling apart. I see refineries burning off excess energy with flares that glow through the night and industrial smokestacks venting hot steam. Behind every business there is a dumpster full of resources to be hauled to the landfill.

There are many opportunities to profit by closing the loop on waste. Recycling is only one option. It is also possible to harvest virgin resources and eliminate waste through insightful design. Various strategies for effective resource use include: 1) scavenging, 2) recycling, 3) preventing waste, 4) choosing alternative resources, and 5) extending resource productivity.

Scavenging and Recycling

Hyenas, vultures, crows, dung beetles, and bacteria scavenge waste and consume corpses, helping out as recyclers in the natural ecosystem. Culturally, we often stigmatize scavengers. However, waste is so abundant and underutilized in the economic ecosystem that scavenging is an easy niche to prosper in. I've been a proud member of the scavenger class most of my life, salvaging secondhand materials to build our home, shopping for bargains at thrift stores, recycling scrap metals, and digging in dumpsters for anything useful. Anyone can live off the waste stream, reducing consumption of new products while diminishing the need for a steady income.

As I write this paragraph, I am sitting in the guest castle, a 10' x 10' outbuilding that serves as a nice getaway by my house. The project started with a large fiberglass satellite dish given to me long ago. The square castle was designed to fit the round dish roof, with turrets filling in the corners. I bought new windows, reinforcing bar, and about half the cement, plus the sand and gravel. Most of the structure was built with free recycled materials and the help of students from our Green University® LLC program.

Waste is abundant and underutilized in the economic ecosystem. This guest castle was built mostly with free and secondhand supplies.

The walls were constructed of cinderblocks salvaged from a scrap pile at a nearby block factory. Red, purple, and smooth cinderblocks were used underground where they wouldn't show. Natural-colored, cleaved cinderblocks of several colors were utilized above ground, giving the appearance of hewn stone. A neighbor gave me some twenty-five year-old bags of cement of varying quality, all of which were adequate for filling cores in the concrete blocks. I blended leftover latex and acrylic paints into the concrete both for extra strength and safe disposal. The satellite dish roof was insulated with scraps of rigid insulation and surplus foam camping pads prior to pouring the concrete dome, which is reinforced with old mesh wire fencing. The window and doorframes were built from plastic lumber salvaged from a dumpster. The door was purchased secondhand for $30. I improvised a thermopane skylight in the center of the satellite dish dome from a glass plate and salad bowl, sealed in place with silicone caulk. The woodstove was rusting in a friend's backyard, easily refurbished and installed. The log frame bed was found at the dumpster. The low-cost castle serves as guest housing and my own occasional get-away. Similar castles could be constructed for paying clients from mostly free materials, with the potential to earn a tidy profit.

My adjacent home included free rocks for the stone walls, some salvaged lumber, and secondhand windows for the greenhouse. As a builder, I started with relatively few recycled materials in my early projects, yet learned from experience to design subsequent projects utilizing available resources.

I built another stone house primarily with free, scavenged, and secondhand materials. To make room for the house, I dismantled an old mobile home with the help of students, recycling about 90% of the structure. Wall paneling was cut into strips and attached to recycled studs to make formwork to pour concrete footings. Fiberglass insulation was used in the attic of our bookstore. Aluminum siding went to the recycling center for cash, and the metal trailer frame was cut and rewelded to make a deck on the new house.

Most rocks came out of the hole we dug for the basement. We obtained free foam insulation panels from a SIP panel factory scrap pile, which was enough to superinsulate the walls and roof. There isn't much lumber in the stone house, and what there is came from a wood waste pile at the community dump. I bought truckloads of additional building materials secondhand from the local Habitat for Humanity Restore. Heavy-duty steel roofing was also purchased secondhand.

My publishing business also profits from scavenging, since we salvage shipping boxes and otherwise expensive packing materials from community dumpsters for wholesale orders. I don't make special trips to check dumpsters. Rather, I check dumpsters when passing by, and I am very selective about what I pick up. From building materials to garden hoses to food and furniture, I gain about $2,000 per year in savings from dumpsters. That's like free money I don't need to work for. I also collect valuable recyclables from dumpsters, including copper wire, aluminum, brass, and car batteries, trading them for actual cash at a recycling center.

Purchasing secondhand building supplies and clothing from thrift stores saves at least another $1,000 a year. Not having a mortgage or electric bill saves thousands more, making it possible to survive on very little and prosper on a modest income. The scavenger class can be one of the least-work, least stress ways to succeed in the present economic ecosystem. Due to thriftiness, I've always been able to afford decent computers, and I've had freedom to pursue my dreams.

I see recycling as a worthwhile effort to reduce the amount of garbage thrown away. Recycling also brings waste management issues and opportunities into consciousness. Recycling a couch, for example, is a very educational experience. Disassembling a couch produced small piles of scrap metal and clean firewood, plus foam cushions that make great utility sponges. The couch fabric was the only resource that was hauled to the dumpster, which I later learned could have been washed and handed off to Goodwill to be exported as rag material.[2] Recycling couches may not be a particularly lucrative business opportunity, yet this type of deep recycling awareness is helpful to facilitate seeing resources and opportunities anywhere.

Recycling Waste into Profit

While it is easy to live off the industrial waste stream, the lifestyle does little to close the loop on waste. There is only so much waste that can be utilized. I know from digging in dumpsters. Most of it is garbage.

Even good waste can be uneconomical as a business endeavor. To maintain consistent production it is necessary to have an uninterrupted supply of raw materials. Few enterprises could afford to continuously search the waste stream to find each additional batch of secondhand materials.

It is easier to close the loop on waste if there is a dependable source of relatively pure waste, such as glass, aluminum, or plastics from recycling centers, old tires from tire shops, or industrial wastes like sawdust or leftover cleaning solvents. With a large quantity of consistent waste it is easier to constructively put that waste to work.

In many cases, supplies may be obtained free or nearly so. For example, glass recycling is intermittently available in Montana. Glass is heavy and expensive to ship, so it is uneconomical to transport to facilities that can recycle glass into new products or downcycle it for use as aggregate. Therefore, anyone willing to start a glass-based business can obtain essentially free feedstock. A small-scale glass factory could produce custom jars or bottles for local food and beverage producers or one's own bottling operation.

Similarly, tires are massively abundant and greatly underutilized. Highway departments grind old tires as asphalt additive to make more flexible roads. Tires can be melted to produce oil that can be refined into gasoline or diesel. The leftover residue can be added to roads to extend the life of asphalt.[3]

Innovative builders stack tires like bricks and tamp them full of earth to make inexpensive, earth-insulated houses called earthships. At home, we have a sandbox made from a bulldozer-sized tire, a horse swing cut from a regular car tire, and doormats made from recycled tires. Several companies manufacture tire sandals. I posted my own tire sandal design online for anyone to use, although they require older bias-ply tires.

To close the loop, tires can be reduced to useful resources through

Foam insulation domes incorporating scraps of recycled insulation could be pre-cast in molds and assembled into houses where each dome forms a seprate room.

pyrolysis, applying heat without oxygen. One tire can produce the equivalent of 60 cubic feet of natural gas, plus petroleum coke equivalent to seven pounds of medium BTU coal, a pound of steel scrap, and waste heat useful for heating water, making steam, and generating electricity.[4] Upfront costs are relatively low, yet pyrolysis is not ideally efficient, since energy is required to drive the system. Concentrated solar heating may make these systems more economical to operate.

Look around and you will find many valuable wastes that can be obtained for little or no cost to start a manufacturing company. With my persistent interest in home building, I've wondered about recycling foam insulation scraps together in molds to cast structural insulation panels or even foam domes. Insulation scraps, broken into aggregate pieces, could be loaded into forms. Expanding foam insulation injected through small holes could fill the voids to create a solid product. I used a similar approach to successfully fill odd-shaped voids between insulation panels in the superinsulated stone house we built.

My favorite general-purpose recycler is an old fashioned wood-fired cookstove in my kitchen. Waste paper is in constant demand to start the fire. Unrecyclable waxed cardboard makes an effective fire starter in place of kindling. Tumbleweeds from the pasture are equally effective. The cookstove consumes random scraps of wood from building projects, old pallets, and salvaged boards, converting waste wood into cooking heat, free hot water, and household heat.

Americans discard enough paper and wood waste every year to heat a billion homes.[5] With the aid of ultra-clean fluidized-bed technology[6] there may be an opportunity to market a modern version of the household trash burner. Scrap wood, tree trimmings, and waste paper could be dropped in a hopper and chopped to bits, then injected into the fluidized-bed combustion chamber to fuel a water heater or household furnace. Hot temperatures, forced air, and thorough combustion eliminates most pollutants through fluidized-bed incineration.

Ideally, it is best to recycle waste into similar products, paper into paper, plastic into plastic, and glass into glass. However, direct recycling is not always practical due to cross-contamination, shipping expenses, or lack of market opportunities. As in nature, sometimes it is advantageous to downcycle wastes to other users and applications.

The waste stream from any single home or small business may not offer much profit potential, whereas communities or larger businesses have more potential. People in my small community still dispose of enough aluminum cans to purchase a new computer for the school every year. Enough wood waste is landfilled every year to meet most energy needs of the community. After an initial investment in a boiler and possible generator, the fuel supply is functionally free. These are opportunities that can be exploited to help close the loop on waste and improve profitability within a community. The first step is to watch for wastes and opportunities in the neighborhood. You may quickly discover more opportunities in the economic ecosystem than any one person can exploit in a lifetime.

Preventing Waste

There are many good opportunities to recycle wastes, yet recycling is not always the best route for creating a closed-loop economy. A better way maybe to start from scratch and rethink products to prevent waste. For example, collecting and re-using polystyrene packing peanuts is a good step towards reducing waste, but not as good as entirely replacing them with water-soluble starch-based packing peanuts. Polystyrene peanuts can be re-used many times, but ultimately end up in the garbage or as litter. Starch packing peanuts are re-useable and easily disposable in a compost pile or harmlessly washed down the drain. Any starch peanuts that are landfilled or escape as litter quickly dissolve into the soil, permanently eliminating waste.

Similarly, recycling plastics is essential, and a good step towards closing the loop on waste, but not necessarily the ideal endgame. Precious Plastic (www.preciousplastic.com) has developed open source plans for anyone to build tools to reprocess plastic waste into useful products, such as bowls, beams, or handholds for climbing walls. Anyone can download free plans and create their own recycling business, an essential step for dealing with an overwhelming waste problem. In the long-run, however, we must replace plastics with biodegradable, compostable, and/or water soluble substitutes.

Building on his studies in biological sciences, Kevin Kumala of Bali launched Avani Eco (www.avanieco.com) to tackle the plastic problem. The company produces single-use products that are 100% biodegradable, including straws made of paper and/or cornstarch, paper take-away boxes made from leftover sugarcane fiber, and cutlery made from wood. The company developed a cassava starch polymer used in products such as water-soluble grocery bags. The bags look like plastic, but readily dissolve in water, which Kumala demonstrated, then drank the water on video to emphasize the eco-friendly qualities of their products.[7]

In Japan, the electronics and office supply company Ricoh Company Ltd. adopted sustainability goals starting in 1992. Since then, the company has steadily sought to lower carbon emissions, incorporate sustainable and recycled components into their products, and redesign products to facilitate refurbishment, reuse, and recycling. The company applied a life-cycle approach, re-evaluating every product according to the source of parts and materials provided by other companies, the use of materials, energy, and water in manufacturing and operating their equipment, and the ultimate refurbishment or recycling of the equipment. Copiers and laser printers in Japan are mostly leased, rather than purchased. More than 200,000 used products are collected every year and fully recycled or refurbished and reused. More than 99.5% of Ricoh copiers are recycled in Japan,[8] greatly closing the loop on waste. Even the labels on individual parts are specially designed to dissolve during recycling without contaminating plastics during recycling. Imagine if all product manufacturers strived for similar goals!

In terms of housing, we are fully capable of designing buildings that do not need constant repairs and replacements. We can prevent thousands of tons of valuable resources from entering the waste stream by building lasting and sustainable homes in the first place. This is clearly a better option than merely trying to recycle all that waste into something else.

Imagine a well-designed house 3D printed with little or no waste, made from materials that require little or no maintenance over a lifetime of centuries. With proper design, it is possible to make houses as mostly closed-loop systems with little need for heating or cooling, no ties to the utility grid, no need for water or sewer hook-ups, and relatively little waste disposal. It is possible to build such structures, yet it requires starting from scratch in the design process, re-inventing the house in materials, form, and function.

In building cast-dome houses, for example, I would experiment with built-in permanent couches that follow the curve of the walls. Sculpted into the structure, built-in couches could have replaceable cushions. There would be no need to clean under the couch and no need to recycle, dispose of, or ever replace the couch. Building such houses may require some virgin resources from the earth, yet a long-lasting house would effectively close the loop by eliminating waste, now and in the future.

Alternative Resources

Starting a manufacturing business to consume waste or prevent it is one way to make positive change in the world, but may not be every person's passion. Retailing eco-friendly products can also help close the loop on waste.

For example, Americans consume 800 million gallons of gas each year just to mow grass. Unlike car exhaust systems, most lawnmowers lack emission control systems, spewing high levels of carbon monoxide, volatile organic compounds, and nitrogen oxides. According to the EPA, mowing a lawn for one hour emits as much pollution as driving eleven cars for one hour. Mowing grass contributes 5% of our nation's air pollution. In addition, people spill an estimated 17 million gallons of gas while fueling lawnmowers, more than the 1989 Exxon Valdez oil spill in Alaska.[9]

To expedite weaning ourselves off fossil fuels, getting rid of gas lawnmowers is a great place to start. One earth-friendly option is to forgo the lawn altogether, favoring instead a landscape of wildflowers, bushes, trees, and un-mowed grass. However, most people want at least a small area of neatly mowed lawn. It fits our cultural sense of order and makes a fun place to play. My yard requires considerable mowing to maintain a firebreak around the house during the summer wildfire season. Instead of giving up the lawn mower for hand tools, it is sensible to seek a reasonable alternative, such as an electric mower.

An electric mower still consumes energy, often generated from fossil fuels in distant power plants. However, as economy transitions to solar and other clean energy sources, electric mowers are the better long-term option. When allocating scarce dollars to create a more earth-friendly lifestyle, investing in an electric mower is arguably a better investment than spending the same amount of money on solar power. Start with the mower; invest in green energy later.

Purchasing an electric versus gas-powered mower makes a small, positive change in the economic ecosystem. It tells mower manufacturers to produce one more electric mower and one less gas mower. It also serves as a model to neighbors who might wonder about these newer and quieter machines. The net result in tilting the economic ecosystem is small, although cumulatively important as many others make similar choices.

Retailing electric mowers through a local store and extolling the benefits to customers is a bigger action. Manufacturing electric mowers and promoting them to retailers is a much bigger action, and being the inventor who makes the technology feasible is an even greater action. We cannot change the world in a day, yet there are plenty of opportunities for consumers and businesses to facilitate the transition to a sustainable economy.

Extending Resource Productivity

Extending resource productivity is about getting more mileage out of fewer resources. For example, aluminum cans are thinner now than in the past. More cans may be made from the same amount of resource.

Likewise, energy consuming devices such as incandescent light bulbs can be replaced with more efficient LED bulbs to produce the same amount of light with one-fourth as much energy, effectively extending the energy supply. Extending resource productivity reduces throughput of natural resources to provide the same level of prosperity with less impact on the natural world. Extending resource productivity is often very profitable, since a business can make more sales with less material.

On the flip side, products often decline in quality when manufacturers dematerialize overzealously. For example, hollow core interior doors consume fewer resources in the short run, yet they are also greatly inferior to traditional solid wood doors. Hollow core doors break, come unglued, or accumulate ugly scratches until disposal becomes necessary. Solid wood doors last decades longer and acquire a patina of wear. Products that are retained for lifetimes are more ecofriendly than those that end up in the landfill.

One way to extend resource productivity, even while manufacturing solid wood doors, is to monopolize additional steps in the chain of manufacturing processes.

In the Northern Rockies of Montana and Idaho, where seasons are short and trees grow slowly, large timber companies like Champion and Plum Creek mowed through nearly two million acres of virgin timber in twenty years. They left behind mountains of wasted sawdust and wood scraps, plus a wasteland of abused forests and eroding soils before moving operations to fast-growing tree plantations in warm and humid places like Georgia, Brazil, and New Zealand.

In the wake of the exodus, many local loggers and millers adopted a more sustainable approach. Entrepreneurs now use fewer raw materials while producing more salable, high-value products. Some mills consume trees at one end while producing finished window frames, doors, or furniture at the other end. Waste lumber is glue-laminated to make longer, more expensive beams, and scrap material is compressed to make chipboard.

Companies like RBM Lumber in Columbia Falls, Montana, work towards forest stewardship, removing select trees to allow the surrounding forest to prosper. RBM doesn't mill mass quantities of 2x4s or other structural lumber. Instead, every log brought to the mill is evaluated for its best use and milled accordingly to output high-quality products such as tongue-and-groove paneling, moldings, trim, and fir and larch flooring.[10] With word-of-mouth advertising and their reputation for quality, RBM lumber has grown to employ forty-eight people. According to their website, *"Our business has grown into a philosophy that greatly respects Creation and especially the Forest and the innate wisdom we find when we observe the forest. Our forest practices are unique and mindful of the balance and overall health of the forest."[11]*

Value-added industries employ more people and generate more income from fewer natural resources. In economic terminology this is also known as a vertical monopoly.[12] A business occupies multiple niches in the economic chain from raw resources to finished products.

I spent childhood summers with my grandmother in Virginia City, Montana, a historic mining town and tourist attraction. Gift shops were filled with plastic trinkets labeled "Virginia City, Montana" on one side and "Made in Taiwan" on the other. The products were hokey, from rubber tomahawks to poor-quality pocketknives and western-themed shot glasses. Gift shops were exporting a significant portion of their limited income dollars around the world to Taiwan, while much of the local population was unemployed when tourist traffic ceased from September to May.

Most businesses only deal with a single step along the chain of converting raw resources into salable products. Gift shops in Virginia City, for instance, usually sell products, rather than manufacture them. These businesses could make additional income by monopolizing other links in the chain with Made in Montana products. There is ample time and labor in the off-season to manufacture local products that would greatly increase incomes throughout town, instead of sending hard-earned money to Taiwan and China.

One of the finest examples of a vertical monopoly I know is Wheat Montana Farms & Bakery, located thirty miles from my home. Most wheat growers sell wheat straight off the field and barely make ends meet. However, Wheat Montana grows wheat, mills it, and bakes and distributes the final products. They grow varieties of wheat that are especially suited to the breads they bake, so their breads taste good and have a long shelf life with little or no preservatives. They filled economic niches from raw resources to salable products. Their unique approach made the company newsworthy, gaining free advertising through newspaper and magazine articles for their efforts.

Keep an eye out wherever you travel. Make it a game. Look for available resources that could be upcycled into opportunities. What resources do you see? How could those resources be utilized? Practice this skill wherever you go, and you may generate green business ideas you are passionate about bringing to fruition.

"If one farm household or co-op takes up a new process such as the waxing of mandarin oranges, because of the extra care and attention the profit is higher. The other agricultural co-ops take notice and soon they, too, adopt the new process... competition brings the prices down, and all that is left to the farmer is the burden of hard work and the added costs of supplies and equipment. Now he must apply the wax."

—Masanobu Fukuoka,
The One Straw Revolution (1975)[13]

Creativity
Eliminating Obstacles to Your Dreams

We have established that the economy an ecosystem in itself; it consumes energy and resources and produces waste. To create a sustainable economy, we must close the loop so that all material wastes are recycled through industry or nature. We can shift succession in the economic ecosystem while achieving personal Dreams and helping to make the world a better place. We can change the world through personal purchases, business choices, and through popular opinion and legislation. That's great in principle, yet where do we start in the real world? The answer is "creativity." Creativity is a key attribute that makes our species unique and different from most other creatures of nature. Our species can innovate completely new goods and services from available resources.

Innovation came slowly for our ancestors when there were limited resources to create with. Only so many new products can be made with sticks, rocks, and bones. Yet each innovation provided new ideas, new tools, and even new resources to work with, such as clay, glass, and metals. Now there are millions of resources to create with, and people continuously innovate new ways to use them.

If we are going to save the planet from ourselves, we must apply creativity towards creating smarter, more ecological goods, services, and systems.

Commodities versus Creativity

Wheat is wheat. One grain more or less equals another grain, and markets set the price according to supply and demand. If the world grows a bumper wheat crop, prices go down. If there is a wheat shortage, prices go up. That's the nature of commodities, and the wheat farmer has little say in the market price for his product. He does, however, have a guaranteed market and can profit by managing expenses to produce the most grain at the least cost.

In comparison, an artist earns a living through creativity, and a finished painting could sell for $10, $100, $1,000, $10,000... or not at all. An artist with an established reputation can demand a steep price. An unknown or mediocre artist might paint hundreds of paintings with little or no value beyond gifting them to friends. Creativity offers potential for great reward, yet can also be a challenging path to earn a living.

Many products and services lay midway between the extremes of commodities versus creativity. For example, a burger establishment serves hamburgers like commodities, competing against similar restaurants to provide a decent burger at a competitive rate. However, a restaurant can also incorporate a creative element, serving gourmet or niche burgers in an upscale or offbeat environment in order to charge a higher rate for a premium product and dining experience. Thus, all products and services can be placed along a continuum between commodities and creativity, often melding aspects of both.

Products and services that can be measured in caloric terms tend to have market prices that reflect invested calories. Whether a person grows wheat or cleans hotel rooms, long-term prices tend to correlate with the caloric effort expended. A hotel maid can find better wages temporarily in a boomtown, such as might be found near oil fields, but only until the higher wages attract enough workers to drive prices down again. Similarly, the wheat farmer may temporarily prosper if drought hits other wheat farmers and reduces the global wheat supply. Otherwise, the price of wheat tends to follow the calorie cost to produce it. If demand remained high for any length of time, then more farmers would plant wheat until the burgeoning supply caused prices to drop again. Farmers do not determine the price of wheat, the market does. In economic lingo farmers are called *price takers*.[14]

The price of gold also reflects the cost of mining it. We often think gold is expensive because supply is rare in comparison to demand. However, there is plenty of gold in the world, yet few companies mining it. Gold is expensive because it requires many food and fuel calories to extract it from the ecosystem. Whole mountains must be torn down, ground into powder, and washed with cyanide to extract very small amounts of the precious metal. When purchasing gold we trade money representing many calories of energy, which the mining industry uses to replace those expended for machinery, fuel, and employees.

Gold prices may surge when the economy falters, as investors buy precious metals in the attempt to guard against losses to inflation or falling stock prices. However, the long-term price of gold reflects the average number of calories required to mine it. An increase in gold prices inspires more people to start mining, which increases supply and brings gold prices back down. Conversely, falling demand and lower gold prices puts mining companies out of business when they fail to regain expended calories. Demand does not dictate the long-term price; it only dictates the number of people employed producing the supply.

Similarly, farmers switch to other crops when wheat prices fall below their break-even point and return to wheat farming when prices rise again. Over the long haul, the price of wheat remains pretty consistent with the average farmer's cost of producing it.

Prices become more variable as commodities are refined into products. A farmer cannot set the price per bushel of wheat, yet the cereal company can, within reason, adjust the price of a box of cereal. The farmer earns only a few cents for the wheat in a box of cereal, while a cereal company adjusts the price of its product up or down searching for a price that maximizes profit.

The farther a product or service is removed from nature, the less its price is tied to the expended calories. The miner has no say over the price of gold, yet the jeweler can, within reason, adjust the price of a gold ring.

Products and services that are less tangible and farther removed from the natural ecosystem have increasingly variable prices. A carpet cleaning business is reasonably tangible because a certain amount of calories must be expended to clean a carpet. Thus there is only a limited variability between the costs of hiring one carpet cleaner versus another. However, the services of a lawyer or a football player are less tangible. Neither produces, modifies, or services any kind of product. Both expend calories of effort, yet neither converts those calories into products or services that can be physically measured. Therefore, the costs of their services tend to be much more variable. A lawyer might charge $100+ per hour, depending on demand for their services. A good football player can negotiate for millions. Their jobs are based on unique personal skills so there is no direct correlation between the calories expended and income.

Opportunity Knocks

On the surface it might seem most profitable to pursue creative products and services that allow the entrepreneur to set the price, rather than producing basic goods and services as a price taker. Who would want to produce commodities if their value follows the cost of production? But take another look:

While lacking control over the price of basic goods and services, at least there is a virtually guaranteed market. Wheat or gold will sell, and carpets must be cleaned. Profit isn't made by controlling the market, but by creatively controlling production expenses. Profit comes by expending fewer calories than other people in the same business. When dealing with basic services and commodities you directly control whether or not you make a profit. That is not the case with products and services that are further removed from the natural ecosystem.

Enterprises detached from nature may have great profit potential, yet also a greater risk factor. A writer can produce a book, yet there is no guarantee anyone will buy it. A few authors have made a fortune with the pen, while many writers have poverty-level incomes. Similarly, there are many rich football players, yet far more earning little to nothing. Success with creative or skill-based products and services requires making them desirable and/or marketing them effectively so that people want your offerings.

Many products and services have commodity-like qualities with creative improvements. For example, cereal is like a commodity since

Some people achieve great financial success through creative endeavors, such as books and movies, while most people earn little or nothing.

239

it is made from basic ingredients and there are many different brands of cereal to choose from. However, a creative element applied to produce and market "Nutritional Sugar-Blast Cereal" may command a higher price. Profitability becomes a combination of providing goods and services people want, while keeping expenses, and therefore prices, down to reasonable levels.

Synergism

Lichens are symbiotic organisms consisting of fungi and algae. They can exist as separate species, yet together they form composite organisms with expanded capabilities. The fungus provides a protective structure encasing a colony of single-celled algae. Lichens insert thread-like anchors into tiny cracks to colonize barren rocks and tree trunks. Lacking actual roots, lichens are nourished by water and mineral nutrients that land on their surface. Algae capture energy through photosynthesis, feeding carbohydrates to the fungi in exchange for living quarters. The symbiotic relationship enables the fungi and algae to thrive together in harsh environments where neither could grow independently.

Efficiency and elegance in natural systems stems from deep integration between component parts. Resources are used and recycled between widely different species of plants, animals, and fungus. Each organism produces waste, but not pollution, because the waste of one species is a resource for another.

Industrial civilization produces harmful wastes and pollution because businesses have operated in single resource mode, focusing on narrow lines of production while discarding leftover wastes into the environment. The emerging trend is towards synergistic resource management optimizing productivity from waste.

For example, cement is one of the world's most vital products used in construction of houses, buildings, roads, and bridges. As a stonemason, I've used a great deal of cement in my house-building projects. However, cement is also very energy intensive to produce, exhausting waste heat and carbon dioxide into the atmosphere.

The principal raw material in cement is limestone or calcium carbonate ($CaCO_3$). Marine microorganisms extract carbon from the atmosphere, sequestering it in their carbonaceous exoskeleton until death deposits them on the seafloor, accumulating to immense depths over millions of years. Cement production reverses the biological reaction, by heating limestone to 750°C to separate the material into highly reactive calcium oxide or lime while off-gassing carbon dioxide.

Of the total carbon dioxide emissions, 40% comes from burning fossil fuels, while 60% is chemically released from the limestone.[15]

Lime is then combined with siliceous sand and heated to 1,500°F to produce tricalcium silicate, the cement that reacts with water to produce artificial stone. Globally, we produce 5 billion tons of cement every year, accounting for up to 7 percent of all carbon emissions.[16] However, cement also absorbs carbon dioxide from the atmosphere after construction, recapturing an estimated 43% of the carbon lost from the original limestone.[17]

According to the traditional business model, a cement plant focuses solely on manufacturing cement while discharging immense quantities of carbon dioxide and waste heat into the atmosphere. The need to reduce emissions is viewed as a cost, rather than an opportunity. Carbon can be captured from the exhaust and sequestered by injecting it deep underground making the cement carbon neutral, but at great expense.

More synergistically, carbon capture can be viewed as an opportunity for new revenue streams. For example, carbon dioxide can be bubbled into algae ponds to produce food or fuel, converting waste gases into revenue.[18] As fuel, algae could then be used at the cement plant itself, partially offsetting energy consumption.

Alkaline materials such as calcium hydroxide or a combination of caustic soda and calcium chloride are sometimes available as waste products from other factories, and they can be combined with carbon dioxide exhaust to form calcium carbonate powder ($CaCo3$), essentially remaking limestone. The process also works with pH-adjusted seawater or alkaline brine water.[19] The powder has cement-like properties, currently used to replace a portion of cement in concrete mixes, with the potential for 100% replacement, producing carbon-negative cement. This product is already being used to manufacture cement board, and the technology is available for licensing from the Calera Corporation (www.calera.com).

Carbon dioxide can also be captured and spun into carbon nanotubes, useful to create lightweight, high-strength products such as car bodies.[20] Oxygen stripped out from this process as a waste product and pumped back into the cement furnaces to obtain a hotter, cleaner burn with less energy input.[21]

Carbon dioxide in captured and purified forms has hundreds of different applications, far too numerous to list here. In addition, waste heat from a cement plant can easily be captured and utilized to heat local homes, businesses, or greenhouses at a profit while reducing overall energy consumption of the surrounding community. Any factory with a smokestack has the potential to covert waste into revenue with a little creative imagination and research.

Look around and notice opportunities for synergistic resource use. Our local hot springs, for example, has enough extra hot water to run a significant greenhouse operation. I can imagine a beautiful jungle atmosphere of ripening vegetables served in an onsite restaurant. A business like that could capture income from swimmers, vegetables, meals, and lodging Certain types of fast-growing fish do well in warm water that is otherwise discharged into the creek, and food scraps and greenhouse compost could feed hogs.

Warm springs in Idaho have been converted into farms for catfish, tilapia, trout, sturgeon, and even alligators.[22] Warm springs are relatively rare, yet similar facilities can be created by harnessing waste heat off any factory.

Synergism is about imagining creative ways to achieve multiple goals with a single effort, like hitting two home runs with a single swing of the bat.

Noncompetition

The fiercest competition in the natural ecosystem is often amongst the closest kin.[23] [24] When same or similar plants or animals compete

I considered launching a business to manufacture custom-built stone hot tubs. This one had a waterfall built into the adjoining wall.

for an ecological niche then minor gains in resource efficiency can make the difference between success and extinction. To avoid extreme competition, species diversify and specialize. For example, cows and sheep share a similar niche as grazing animals, yet they have different dietary preferences. Cows prefer grasses, while sheep favor leafy forbs. This minimizes competition so they can share habitat with little overlap.

Businesses also specialize to avoid competition. No single market can cater to the needs of everyone so there are many specialized economic niches, each with its own clientele. For instance, there are many types of grocery stores from mini-marts to co-ops to supermarkets and warehouse markets. All sell groceries, yet they occupy different niches in the economic ecosystem. The real competition is not between the big guy and the little guy, but between similar stores, such as one mini-mart across the street from another. The best way to beat the competition is not at all.

Sadly, too many entrepreneurs jump into business without an ounce of creativity, such as opening a McDonalds franchise in close proximity a Wendy's or Burger King. Why not try something original and different, freeing yourself from price wars between franchises?

When I was young and brainstorming potential businesses, I considered building custom stone hot tubs, especially after constructing one for my in-laws. It was built of concrete and stone, well insulated, and even featured a stone waterfall, bringing a touch of nature to the home. In contrast, fiberglass hot tubs from different manufacturers are similar to each other and all steadily degrade until they become eyesores. I saw one dropped whole into the community dumpster recently, somebody's backyard dream destined for the landfill. My stone hot tubs would have been vastly more permanent and highly unique, establishing a non-competitive niche in the hot tub market.

My partner and I built a stone house on speculation, selling it after completion. Passersby were very interested in the project. Most houses are so alike that people crave something unique. People stopped by the construction site nearly every day to ask about it. They looked at other new houses and said those houses "lacked substance." We did not need to advertise our work because the product advertised itself. Furthermore, its uniqueness appraised at a higher price than similar-sized houses, so we were not competing with mainstream contractors. We found our own niche.

Selling Savings

In business, most get-rich schemes involve taking someone else's money. Whether you are selling a widget or providing a service such

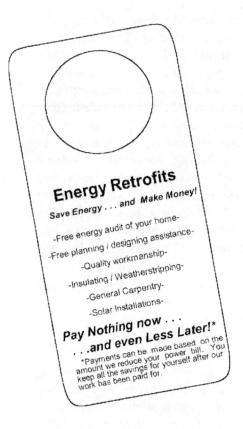

Energy Retrofits

Save Energy . . . and Make Money!

-Free energy audit of your home-
-Free planning / designing assistance-
-Quality workmanship-
-Insulating / Weatherstripping-
-General Carpentry-
-Solar Installations-

Pay Nothing now . . .
. . .and even Less Later!*

*Payments can be made based on the amount we reduce your power bill. You keep all the savings for yourself after our work has been paid for.

as tree trimming, the consumer has a finite number of dollars to spend. Imagine instead a business that actually enriches people.

The history of free enterprise is often a story of exploitation of consumers and the environment, yet it doesn't have to be that way. One can help make the world a better place through entrepreneurship, such as by selling savings. Earn money by helping others save money. Help make customers wealthier by taking their money. There are billions in potential profits and opportunities that need to be exploited for everyone's benefit.

For example, Allied Energy in New Jersey works with homeowners to create custom energy conservation plans that may include insulating, weather-stripping, and upgrading to more efficient heaters. Most upgrades are completed in a day and reduce energy consumption by 25%. Completing four house projects conserves as much energy as removing one house from the grid. The company did 5,000 such projects in its first six years of business, proving that selling conservation is a profitable business model.[25]

Given that energy efficiency upgrades save money, the work could potentially be offered at "zero cost," eliminating the need for customers to raise cash upfront. Efficiency work could be financed and repaid through monthly energy savings. Customers would pay the same amount as their original average energy bill, sending less to the utility and more to the efficiency contractor. When the bill is paid off, the customer then gains the full benefit of the savings.

There are fortunes to be made by helping other people reduce expenses. It can be a "win-win-win" deal. It is good for the contractor, the customer, and the environment, a winning combination that makes first class word-of-mouth advertising material. A business that earns money for its customers will have no shortage of clients.

As noted in earlier versions of this book, *"I would be delighted to make someone rich if they would sell me secondhand and recycled building materials at a savings over what we would pay for new materials. This customer is ready to spend money. All I need is for someone to exploit the opportunity and say they are open for business."* Fortunately, the nonprofits Habitat for Humanity and Home Resource have since filled that niche here in Montana. I've spent thousands of dollars buying secondhand building materials. I'm thrilled to support their programs while saving money on my own projects.

The Art of Nothing

Masanobu Fukuoka became disillusioned with conventional industrial farming. He recognized that agricultural scientists were always inventing something new for farming. First there was the plow, then fertilizer, then specialized seed, then herbicides, then pesticides, always something new that would purportedly boost yields and increase profits. Fukuoka understood that each new advance led the farmer to expend more money and labor, or in our vocabulary, more food and fuel calories. He saw it as a snowballing effect; agricultural science marched forward always creating something this or something that or something new for agriculture. Fukuoka took the opposite approach.

Instead of finding ways to add complexity, Fukuoka researched ways to eliminate work. He studied diligently in his fields for years to invent something less. Through trial and error in rice and barley fields he learned how not to plow, how not to fertilize, how not to weed or use herbicides and pesticides. Instead, he manipulated succession in the ecosystem to favor semi-wild crops. He eliminated most steps of farming beyond broadcasting seed and harvesting grain. With his "do-nothing" approach Fukuoka succeeded in raising some of the highest yielding crops in Japan with little effort expended in food or fuel calories.

True laziness is a virtue. Seek success by creatively avoiding the need for extraneous work. A lazy person possessed with a Dream is a force to be reckoned with.

Some of the most productive days in my own life are spent wandering aimlessly in the mountains. I take time to reflect on my dreams and to brainstorm the best routes towards achieving them.

People in our culture often feel too guilty to spend a day walking. There is a strong work ethic in Western culture and people feel they should be doing something, regardless of whether or not the effort helps achieve any goals. Yet, I know from experience that wandering aimlessly can be immensely productive. A day spent walking alone, creatively brainstorming ways to eliminate work, can easily save a week of effort towards achieving a goal. Before undertaking any action towards achieving a goals, try asking:

1) Is this action truly necessary to my Dream?
2) How can I simplify this project to eliminate extra work?

Among all tools for making a positive impact in the world, creatively eliminating work is often the most difficult to grasp. Achieving a dream or goal implies action, a do-something approach. This is especially true in business, where the basis of success is production. Doing nothing to achieve a goal seems counterintuitive. We are programmed to work hard and achieve more. However, the do-nothing approach explores laziness, "What happens if we do not do this or that?"

Gas stations used to pay servicemen to pump fuel, check oil, and wash windows. Then someone asked "What if we provide a discount for customers to pump their own gas?" Once the question was asked, self-service quickly became industry standard. Gas stations later installed self-service payment systems so people could pay at the pump. Self-service saves time for customers who no longer need to stand in line at the counter. Self-service eliminates work, allowing gas stations to reduce employee numbers and cut fuel prices for customers. They do not have to serve customers at all, a true do-nothing approach!

My publishing company operates very similarly. The business has only one telephone line, which averages about four phone calls per week, mostly received as voicemail messages when we are elsewhere. Otherwise, customers place orders via the Internet, and we need only pack and ship the books, some of which is outsourced to a fulfillment service.

In establishing the business, I initially implemented similar discount rates and terms as other publishers. However, college bookstores frequently ordered *Botany in a Day* in quantity then returned overstock books for a refund after each class, even if that necessitated re-ordering the same book six months later. The books were seldom returned in mint condition and could no longer be sold as new books. Moreover, I didn't have a sophisticated accounting system to track back and forth payments, nor the time or staff to process the paperwork. Being out of the office most of the summer, processing returns often didn't happen until mid-winter.

Out of frustration, I finally wondered, "What would happen if we eliminated the returns policy for wholesale orders?" Much to my surprise, nobody protested. Bookstores have secondary markets for overstock books, or they can hold the books until the next class. By eliminating this one chore, I simplified the business, reduced my labor, negated a minor but persistent stress, and no longer have to pay refunds. Aside from writing books, I average about half an hour per day running the business.

Our Most Powerful Tool

Creativity is our most powerful tool. However, we have a knack for making things unnecessarily complicated. We have access to so much knowledge and so many resources, yet we apply it so ineptly. For example, we have the resources to economically build highly efficient houses that require neither heaters nor air conditioners for comfort. Instead we tack together poorly designed structures and spend hard-earned dollars to heat them through winter and cool them in summer. We scrape and repaint every few years. We replace carpet, linoleum, and the water heater every fifteen to twenty years and the roof every thirty to fifty. It is no wonder that sustainability seems so implausible when we have to practically rebuild the entire infrastructure of our country several times each century! Through force of will we have managed to conquer nature and accumulate material wealth, yet with unfathomable waste. Rather than creatively designing the whole package, architects typically draw up house plans then pass them along to a mechanicals specialist to determine what kind of heating and cooling equipment is needed to maintain the internal environment.

Imagine an automobile company trying to design a car this way, where one department creates a body, the next creates a frame, and the next has to find space to install the engine and attach the wheels. A good car could not be built without intensive collaboration between all departments, and the same is true in architecture. An integrated approach leads to a higher quality structure, and usually lower cost. We spent four years designing our house before we started construction. We strived to integrate many diverse parts into one efficient whole, gaining a higher quality end product with less cost upfront and fewer maintenance costs overall.

In nature, resource efficiency is everything. Species that use energy and resources economically survive to put forth a new generation of progeny. In our homes and businesses we can be the most successful if we creatively mimic nature to use resources as economically as possible to achieve our dreams. Applying a do-nothing approach to creatively eliminate unnecessary work from the beginning can lead to more success with less effort!

"Flood a field with water and stir it up with a plow and the ground will set becoming as hard as plaster. If the soil dries and hardens, then it must be plowed each year to soften it. All we are doing is creating the conditions that make a plow useful, then rejoicing at the utility of our tool."
— Masanobu Fukuoka,
The Natural Way of Farming (1985)[26]

Technology
Putting Calories to Work

We have many tools at our disposal, from human creativity to labor and money, but usually, when we think of "tools" we think of technology. Technology includes everything from pen and paper to cars and computers. It is technology that has enabled our species to escape the cycles of nature, to harvest bigger crops, to thrive in cold climates, even to leave the biosphere for space. Technology enables us to express our creativity and accomplish great dreams. A mere lever enables us to move objects far bigger than we could by brute force. Technology gives us power. Yet it is a dangerous power. Technology can free us from mindless labor or it can enslave us.

In junior high I listened to other boys brag about how they blew away a coyote or deer with a gun. Guns gave them a false sense of power, and that abused that power. It is easy to do.

As a species, we like technology so much that we often go to work before we've defined our goals. As author Allan Savory points out in *Holistic Management*, people reach for technological fixes without evaluating cause and effect in the ecosystem.[27] We get a sense of power driving a bulldozer or applying chemical fertilizers and pesticides. We treat symptoms more than causes, such as building check dams to control erosion, instead of re-introducing beavers to build check dams for free or rebuilding the health of the soil to better absorb precipitation where it lands. Savory describes technological "fixes" as non-goals.

Everyone is prone to misusing tools. We create work for ourselves merely because we are enraptured with our tools, as if "technologically feasible" is sufficient cause to undertake a project. As noted previously for home construction, our society constantly builds and rebuilds inferior houses. We use technology to mass-produce building materials, yet we mass-produce more work. People reach too quickly for tools without thinking or planning. Heaters, air-conditioners, inefficient windows, short-lived siding, and other maintenance expenses are technological fixes that do not address the real issues. They are non-goals.

Wise use of technology lies in planning and organization. Choose appropriate technologies to create essential goods and services with the least possible waste.

Mass-produced Goods and Services

One of my first significant experiences with power tools was building railings for stairs on apartment buildings with my brother near Seattle. He bid the job and had enough work for both of us. We made a prototype railing to ensure that it looked good, and then he set up a template. I had to measure the length of each railing, but otherwise I simply cut pieces to fit the template and nailed them together on the pattern. I hauled each completed railing to the stairs and installed it. With the template I was able to work very quickly, and I was paid per foot of railing. It was a great job considering I was young and had no real carpentry experience. I earned more per hour than many seasoned carpenters on the project, and I did better work than the previous carpenter who attempted the same job. More than anything, I learned the importance of organizing work into repetitive, simple tasks. I learned how to achieve consistent quality and relative speed, the essence of mass-production.

Mass-production lowers the cost of goods. A new car would cost hundreds of thousands of dollars if the manufacturer assembled it in your driveway. A completely customized car might cost millions. Interchangeable parts and streamlined assembly save calories of effort. Mass-production dramatically brings down the cost per vehicle so that cars are reasonably affordable.

Housing costs could fall by a similar amount if houses were mass-produced like automobiles. Visionary architect and inventor Buckminster Fuller (1895–1983) saw the advantages of mass-production in the 1920s and developed innovative house models that could be factory-made. Fuller advocated mass-production as a means to maintain quality control and reduce cost. His ideas were remarkably advanced for the time. He designed houses with windmills for electricity, moveable interior partitions, vacuum-sealed double pane windows, gray water systems, and automatic doors. Fuller utilized engineering concepts to design the most house with the greatest strength from the least materials. The parts were so compact and lightweight that they could be transported in a container and assembled on site by hand. Fuller's ideas were perhaps too revolutionary. The dome-shaped houses were radically different from conventional home styles. Beech Aircraft offered an initial bid to produce his kit homes in the 1940s, but neither the company nor its bankers would ante up the capital to tool up for production, even though 37,000 people submitted unsolicited orders.[28] Tooling up the factory would have cost billions in today's dollars, but would have produced very affordable, long-lasting houses.

Mobile homes are the closest facsimile to Fuller's idea, although he would likely be insulted by the comparison. Mobile homes are mass-produced and portable, built with lightweight materials like Fuller's domes, yet they lack his thoughtful, integrated planning for efficiency and durability.

The housing market remains an open niche in the economic ecosystem. Most houses are still assembled the old fashioned way. Every house plan is different and every piece must be individually measured, cut, and hammered in place. Prefabricated homes are making a dent in the housing market by building and shipping houses in sections with standardized materials and designs. Otherwise, these new houses are no better than traditional homes.

A house is typically our biggest investment in life, as well as the most environmentally harmful, because there is such a large throughput of resources to build and maintain the structure. To achieve true sustainability, we need to close the loop on wastes. Mass-production offers the potential to produce houses that are far more efficient, less costly, and very profitable.

With the aid of mass-production it is possible to make low-cost virtually self-sufficient closed loop houses that require no inputs of energy for heating or cooling, no ties to the utility grid, and no need for water or sewer hookups. To achieve that level of efficiency there must be as few parts as possible, because the junction of every part offers potential loss in materials, time, and energy. By casting these structures in large molds from lightweight insulating materials, it would be possible to transport the modules to a site and assemble an entire home in a matter of a few days.

Closing the loop on housing wastes can transform the world we live in, yet it is only one segment of our economy that needs attention. There are other opportunities that desperately need attention to make the world a better place.

Handcrafted Goods and Services

While mass-production can help reduce wastes of time, energy and materials, it is not the answer for everything. There are some goods and services, such as handicrafts or haircuts, which are not readily mass-producible.

It may be undesirable to streamline haircut efficiency to the point that a hair stylist could accelerate from one haircut every twenty minutes to one every half minute. Yet, increases in efficiency are possible by sharing workspace and advertising costs among several stylists. The cost of a haircut may remain high compared to other goods and services that become increasingly automated.

The same is true for handicrafts like natural wood furniture. In the age of mass-production there is considerable demand for unique, hand-built furniture like rustic frame bed or reclaimed wood tables. Ironically, mass-production is what makes handcrafted goods affordable. Streamlining production throughout the economy reduces the price of most goods and services, giving people surplus wealth to spend on otherwise uneconomical choices like handcrafted furniture. In other words, there are still opportunities to make a living without mass-producing anything. However, the income potential may be smaller too.

There is a limit to how many haircuts or rustic bed frames or tables one can complete per unit of time, so it is difficult to increase income once capacity is reached. A salon owner can employ multiple stylists or open multiple salons. Similarly, a furniture-maker can increase production by employing additional craftsman. Expanding the business and hiring help can generate greater income, but also increases risk and stress.

Economy of Scale vs. Diseconomy of Scale

The phrase "economy of scale" relates to mass-production. A large, specialized factory can mass-produce a product to dramatically reduce the cost per item. As the size of the factory goes up, the cost to produce each unit goes down. The automobile industry is a good example, with multibillion-dollar factories turning out thousands of cars at a fraction of the cost compared to custom-building each one. Similarly, in order to bring down the cost of lithium ion batteries for electric vehicles and surplus grid storage, Elon Musk constructed a $5 billion "Gigafactory" near Reno, Nevada, one of the biggest buildings on the planet. It is also the first factory designed to manufacture batteries from raw minerals to finished product, with a product output rate reportedly "faster than bullets from a machine gun," according to Musk. The project is insanely expensive, yet brings down the cost per battery enough to greatly expand automotive and solar energy applications.[29]

On the other hand, the larger the factory or farm, the more units that must be produced to break even. That is one of several "diseconomies of scale." Farm foreclosures are driven by diseconomies of scale. Investments in materials and equipment allow farmers to produce more food, but also require farmers to produce far more just to break even. But the bigger the harvest, the lower its value as surplus swamps demand. For example, the inflation-adjusted price for wheat in 2016 was at an all-time low since the U.S. Civil War. On average, the industrial wheat farmer spends $315 per acre to produce 50.5 bushels of wheat with a sale value of only $174.[30] Farm subsidies help offset these losses to a degree, but high yields and low prices ultimately overwhelm the small or medium-sized farms where expenses per bushel tend to be higher. These farmers are forced to get bigger or sell out.

Some farmers have sidestepped the problem of scale by switching to small-scale specialty crops, seeking alternative niches in the economic ecosystem. Some farmers continue growing basic commodities such as wheat, yet they switch to organic markets to fetch a higher return, or they plant chic alternatives to conventional grains, like quinoa, buckwheat, teff, or amaranth. Wheat Montana Farms has prospered by baking and marketing breads from their own specialized varieties of wheat.

Others farmers are switching to herbal crops for spices and health supplements. Some farmers utilize greenhouses to produce seedlings or to grow vegetables all year long. Community Supported Agriculture is another alternative, where families pay for a share of a diverse crop of local vegetables from a farm. There are even farms where customers pay to pick their own fruits or vegetables. Any family farm with a flair for innovation can find a way to dodge diseconomies of scale and remain profitable.

Centralized mass-production technology decreases the cost of many goods and services from cars and airplanes to travel services (i.e.: internet ticket reservations), yet there are many situations where mass-production is less practical or efficient. One issue is that a single, specialized factory must be custom built for its task, greatly inflating costs. Instead of building one big factory, it can be more economical to mass-produce many small factories.

For example, coal, oil, gas, or nuclear power plants are big facilities designed to mass-produce electricity. However, each power plant is typically unique in design, making it expensive to build and maintain, one of the diseconomies of scale. In comparison, mass-producing smaller power plants could cost at least ten times less per kilowatt of generating capacity, observed Amory Lovins in *Soft Energy Paths*.[31] Rather than constructing a single centralized 1,000-megawatt coal-fired power plant to serve 900,000 homes, we could build twenty 50-megawatt natural gas power plants and distribute them more equally across the service area. The more units constructed, the lower the cost per megawatt of capacity.

Continuing this line of reasoning, solar power is becoming vastly less expensive than big energy facilities as mass-production reduces the cost of manufacturing millions of solar panels. Diseconomies of scale inherent in operating and maintaining the national power grid have left wide-open niches for small, localized alternatives like solar, wind, and local hydroelectric projects.

Falling costs make it increasingly economical to install solar cells on rooftops to replace or supplement power from the grid. Buildings equipped with photovoltaics can store surplus power in batteries for nighttime, or use the electric current to split water to make hydrogen gas. Fuel cells then convert the hydrogen gas into electricity as needed for homes or electric vehicles. Fuel cells are already used in some civic bus systems.

Fuel cell technology also enables any building or automobile to produce its own electricity from natural gas, a good transitional fuel as renewable energy gradually replaces fossil fuels. Fuel cell cars can even generate electricity to feed the utility grid when parked. A typical car is parked 96% of the time, so every fuel cell car is a power plant on wheels, generating electricity and income for its driver while at home or at work. If all U.S. automobiles were converted to fuel cell technology, the total electric generating output would be at least six times that of the national power grid. [32] However, hydrogen technology remains less developed and more expensive than solar power, thus limiting its potential market share.[33]

Whether fuel cell technology becomes economical or not, small-scale electricity production and storage may ultimately bankrupt utilities[34] and bring an end to the national power grid and the power lines that blight our skylines.

Other highly centralized industries can be out-competed by smaller, more decentralized facilities, including reuse of recyclables such as scrap iron, aluminum, glass, paper, or plastic. For example, it is inherently inefficient to produce a glass bottle in a centralized location and ship it hundreds of miles to be filled at a bottling plant. The bottled product must then be shipped to stores. Afterwards, scrap glass must be shipped hundreds of miles back to be recycled into new bottles.

The cost of returning glass, or any other recyclables, is so high that it is often cheaper to dispose of it or downcycle it to lesser uses. Recycled glass can be used as a hydroponic rooting medium or for filtration in swimming pools. It can be melted and spun into fiberglass insulation, or even better, expanded glass foam blocks, which are both insulating and structural. Recycled glass is also ground up and added to asphalt. It is useful as an abrasive for sandblasting, as silica in cement production, as a flux/binder in ceramics and bricks, as friction in matches in ammunition, an additive and flux in metal foundry work, and as filler in paint and plastics.[35]

Fortunately, wherever there is waste there is also opportunity to close a loop and make a profit. Most recyclables are essentially free for the cost of extracting them from the waste stream. A small, mostly automated glass bottle factory could be placed in every town to convert glass waste into new bottles for local food producers. Even better, build an appropriately scaled mini-mill right next to a bottling plant, and glass can go from recycling bin to bottle factory on a conveyer belt to the bottling facility without human labor, packaging, or transportation. Closing these kinds of loops in the economic ecosystem improves the profitability of recycling and greatly reduce damage to the natural ecosystem. There is a tremendous opportunity to be had in mass-producing mini-mills for glass, aluminum, metals, paper, plastic, or any other recycled commodity. In the interim, any enterprising individual can design and build their

Used glass is expensive to ship to centralized factories for recycling, a major diseconomy of scale.

own mini-mill from off-the-shelf components to make high value goods from waste products.

Automated Production

Assembly lines of workers have been the hallmark of industrialization, with thousands of people employed to do monotonous, repetitive tasks. Methods developed by Henry Ford for manufacturing low cost automobiles in Detroit have largely been exported to cheaper labor markets around the world. Technology giants have developed the ability to tool up for a new product and mass-produce tens of millions of units per year, thanks in part to warehouses of underpaid workers committed to near slavery conditions in China and other developing countries. Now, in the twenty-first century, we are rapidly transitioning from an industrial economy where people operate machines to an automated economy where computers operate machines. Robotics are expensive up front, but work 24/7 without bathroom breaks, complaints, liability issues, or wages. Least-cost labor markets cannot compete with workers that require no compensation. In the coming decades we will see increased automation in every sector of the economy and more worker displacement than ever before.

Mass-Production of One

Mass-production reduces the labor required to produce goods and services by making thousands or millions of identical copies. A business invests vast sums of money to build tools to mass-produce a product, then manufactures and sells enough copies to pay for the initial investment and make a profit. The next step in mass-production is "mass-production of one."

Improved computers and robotics are increasingly flexible in production, so that mass-produced goods can be individually customized. Levi was one of the first businesses to provide customized production, by opening a shop where people could have their measurements taken and fed into a computer. The computer makes a customized pattern and sends the specifications to the factory where material is automatically cut. The tools of mass-production are utilized to create a single, individualized item.[36]

Similarly, customized book printing enables microprint runs of a title, even a single printed copy if necessary. As a publisher, I have had to decide in advance how many copies to print of each book, such as 1,000, 2,500, 5,000, or 10,000 copies. Book printers must customize printing for each print job, so small print runs cost more per book. Placing a large order reduces cost per unit, yet increases risk as the total job cost quickly soars into tens of thousands of dollars.

Print-on-demand technology makes it feasible to print small numbers of books for prototyping a new title or testing markets. The author or publisher formats the book and uploads it to a print-on-demand service. Computers automatically process the files for printing and provide a digital proof. Once the book is finalized, the author/publisher can order a print run of a single book or as many as desired. The profit margin is not as high, but neither is the risk.

Similarly, 3D printing technology makes it possible to produce a single, customized item by merely uploading plans into a computer. 3D printing was started in 1984 by inventor Charles Hull using ultraviolet lights and light-sensitive plastics similar to those used by dentists to seal and protect teeth. Hull attached a light to a computer-guided arm then pointed the light beam into a vat of polymer, hardening a thin layer of plastic wherever the light moved. A platform under the hardened plastic then dropped a millimeter, submerging the item under more polymer, allowing subsequent passes of the ultraviolet light to build 3D objects. Hull's first test product was a teacup.[37]

Newer 3D technology uses diverse materials and methods to make everything from automotive parts to dentures, heart valves, and houses. Automotive companies previously had to laboriously sculpt clay, carve wood, or machine steel to make prototype parts for new cars. Now they design parts on a computer and print them in 3-dimensional form. The technology also enables 3D faxing because an idea originated on one computer can be sent electronically to another computer connected to a 3D printer.

With 3D printing technology there is little need to tool up big factories to mass-produce millions of identical copies. A factory can consist of a 3D printer able to print anything that it is instructed to. These kinds of technologies may radically change or eliminate the need for big box retail stores like Walmart, since individuals can print their own customized goods. Larger items can be ordered and delivered from 3D factories via the Internet. Entrepreneurs will find ample opportunity for profit by building and selling 3D printers and related supplies and services. Moreover, anyone can innovate useful products and sell the plans. Most promising, 3D printing may break the mass-production paradox where goods must be manufactured to fail to justify keeping factories running. A 3D printer can print other products without retooling.

Even houses can be printed, either by 3D printing modular components, or by moving a printer to the jobsite. Early 3D houses have been printed from concrete, foam, and various polymers. German designer Markus Kayser did a "solar sinter" demonstration project in the Sahara, using a Fresnel lens to melt desert sand with sunlight, effectively printing test objects in glass.[38] With an abundance of sand and sunlight, whole houses could potentially be printed at zero cost for materials or energy for the basic shell.

Self-Replicating Production

The future of mass-production is to create products that build themselves. For example, imagine automated solar cell production, where solar powered robots mine desert soils, or the surface of the moon, and use the minerals to self-replicate, producing more solar panels and more robots, exponentially spreading across the landscape until switched off. All the technological hurdles have been achieved to produce such a system. It might cost up to $100 billion dollars to integrate the technologies into one coherent system, yet when activated in a place like the Sahara desert, it would cost nothing more to maintain. A colony of self-replicating solar powered robots covering just a little over 10% of the Sahara desert could provide three times the world's current energy supply. Any future expansions of the energy supply on this planet or elsewhere would be as free as taking a few robots from one colony and transporting them to start a new colony.[39]

Self-replicating technology is inevitable, and it will radically change the world. After all, as energy becomes progressively free, it will be increasingly economical to desalinize vast quantities of seawater for urban consumption and mass-irrigation projects. Likewise, we can expect self-sustaining tunneling machines that bore through mountain ranges, melting waste material into glass or metal walls lining the tunnels. Such tunnels might be used for high-speed transportation, or simply as pipes for irrigation projects.

Instead of reclaiming places like the Sahara or the Middle East through stewardship, developers will likely turn to technology to pump hundreds of millions of gallons of desalinized sea water inland for irrigation. Saudi Arabia already irrigates the desert this way, except that their desalinization plants are initially powered by petroleum. Self-replicating solar power plants will provide the necessary energy to sustainably reclaim man-made deserts.

Self-replicating solar technology isn't new, since that's how plants function. Researchers are working to understand photosynthesis in plants at the molecular level. Already they've reproduced several steps in the process using artificially-made molecules.[40] We may have microscopic self-replicating solar "plant" panels before scientists find funding to build a larger robotic version.

Either way, self-replicating solar technology will eliminate pollution from fossil fuels, helping close the energy loop of the economic ecosystem. It will greatly increase the throughput of material resources and energy, but in a potentially sustainable manner. We are good at building thing; what we really need is more technology to recycle our garbage.

Self-Replicating Molecular Machines

It is often easier to make products than to unmake them. A typical couch, for example, consists of a wood and metal frame plus polyurethane foam pads and a fabric of natural or synthetic materials. It is impractical to separate the raw ingredients to recycle them into something new. Worn out couches are hauled to the landfill and buried for future generations to deal with. Imagine, however, if you had the ability to disassemble an old couch atom-by-atom, sorting each element into its own pile.

Nanotechnology is the stuff of science fiction. Molecular machines are so small that thousands of robots could fit on the head of a pin. If we can manipulate matter on the atomic level then theoretically we can build or unbuild anything we dream up, from a silk spider web to a glittering diamond, as long as it doesn't violate the laws of physics.[41]

Molecular technology already exists in living organisms. Plant cells manipulate matter on the atomic level, transforming water, gases, and elements from the earth into living tissue. The cells in our bodies perform similar molecular transformations, utilizing plant and animal matter as raw material.

Scientists are years away from building molecular machines, yet they are finding innovative ways to harness existing nanotechnology imbedded in living organisms. Insulin for diabetics is produced by genetically engineered *E. coli* bacteria. The necessary mechanism was already there. Scientists merely switched the programming that tells the bacteria what to produce. Research will eventually eliminate the need for bacteria so that insulin will be produced by non-living molecular machines.

The exciting part about living nanotechnology, similar to systems found in plants and animals, is the potential to manufacture complex materials at normal temperatures from simple resources with no toxic wastes. As Janine Benyus pointed out in *Biomimicry*, spiders take flies and crickets in one end and produce superstrong silk out the other end, five times stronger than steel per ounce of material. Spider silk is also much stronger and more elastic than Kevlar, found in bulletproof vests, a material manufactured from petroleum products boiled in a vat of sulfuric acid at a temperature of several hundred degrees.[42]

Spider silk has to be strong and stretchy to withstand the impact of flying insects. If spider silk were reproduced at human scale and used to make a fishing net, it would be strong enough to catch an airplane in mid-flight. This is just one of many materials produced in nature that is being copied for human use. Since spiders are difficult to manage, researchers transplanted spider silk genes into microorganisms to produce spider silk proteins. The proteins are purified and forced through microscopic pores to form fibers. Researchers anticipate using spider silk for everything from textiles to car bodies and as a general replacement for ecologically harmful plastics.

Similarly, scientists are researching ways to use living molecular machines to disassemble past messes. Toxic wastes that have leached into the ground are a particularly challenging problem. Traditional treatment options include excavating contaminated soil and hauling it to a containment site, or drilling wells and installing pumps to circulate neutralizing chemicals through the poisoned ground. A simpler method for decontamination is to employ specialized bacteria that break down substances like polychlorinated biphenyls (PCBs) into simple, nontoxic components.

Producing toxic-eating bacteria doesn't necessarily require genetic engineering, as there are already many highly specialized microorganisms in nature, billions of them in a single teaspoon of soil. Scientists search contaminated sites for signs of useful bacteria, then mass-reproduce them in vats for release on a larger scale.

Commandeering micro-machines inside living organisms is an intermediate step towards being able to create similar technology. Scientists are already building simple gears atom-by-atom. As with the industrial revolution, each new piece of machinery becomes a tool to build other more complicated machines. According to Eric Drexler in his book the *Engines of Creation*, the "holy grail" of nanotechnology is to build a "general assembler."[43]

A general assembler would be a programmable molecular machine capable of following instructions to build anything, including an exact duplicate of itself. An army of assemblers could produce sugar from air or diamonds from carbon. An assembler could also be programmed to build something much more complex, like a rocket.

Programming an assembler requires instructional code much like our own DNA, yet with many more redundancies to prevent mutations. The DNA in a single fertilized egg contains all the necessary information to build an entire human being. Micro-machinery within a cell grabs necessary building blocks as they float in fluid. The egg builds itself into a complex living, breathing human.

If you were to load a tank full of car parts and shake it to eternity, it is sometimes said, it would never assemble itself into a car. Yet, that is more-or-less how some of our future products will be built. A single assembler, planted as a seed in the bottom of a large fluid-filled tube, would grab ingredients as they float by and build itself into whatever it was programmed to make. With this kind of technology it is possible to manufacture products as radical as a spaceship of pure diamond, designed for superior strength with minimal weight.

Equally important is the ability to disassemble or recycle anything. General disassemblers would do just that, separating garbage into its constituent atoms. Scientists have already discovered bacteria that produce plastic-eating enzymes, which is crucial to help solve one of our most vexing waste problems.[44] [45]

Other wastes will cease to exist when nanotechnology comes of age. Granted, there is also risk in working with machines so small that it would be virtually impossible to find one if you dropped it. What would happen if disassemblers got loose and started disassembling the planet? In the *Engines of Creation* Drexler outlines a plausible safeguard against these kind of disasters, which is worth reading for more details.

It is difficult to predict how soon the first molecular assembler will be built, although it could happen before 2050. It will only take a year or two after the first one is built to be able to construct anything else that does not violate the laws of physics.

While it is important to know what is coming, it is perhaps more important to effectively utilize what we already have. We have the necessary technology to close the loop on waste in the economic ecosystem, to create a world of abundance without pollution. You can profit now and make the world a better place by applying technologies to appropriate tasks to produce real goods and services with the least possible waste.

"The reality is gas prices should be much more expensive than they are because we're not incorporating the true damage to the environment and the hidden costs of mining oil and transporting it to the U.S. Whenever you have an unpriced externality, you have a bit of a market failure, to the degree that eternality remains unpriced."

—Elon Musk (2011)[46]

Energy
Squeezing Useful Work from Every Calorie

Energy is the tool that runs all other tools. Every action we make, from smelting ore to flexing muscles, uses energy. Wealth is also based on energy, and fuel calories are like cheap labor. Americans are wealthy partly because we harness the energy equivalent of 100 to 300 people working 24/7 to produce our goods and services.[47] Future prosperity is partly contingent on continued use of cheap energy.

If energy were scarce then our lifestyles would necessarily change. However, if energy is abundant then we will continue supplementing our lifestyle with fuel calories. Since matter itself is energy, the future seems promising.

Industrial Energy Pyramid

Similar to the food energy pyramid discussed earlier in the book, there is also an industrial energy pyramid, depicted here as a step pyramid. All available energy sources form the base of the industrial energy pyramid, including fossil fuels, biofuels, solar, wind, and nuclear power. Each energy source has immense, sometimes mind-boggling potential, as detailed throughout this chapter.

Fossil fuels have historically been the most economical energy source, although that is changing rapidly. As the price of photovoltaics continues to fall, demand for solar is growing exponentially.

Solar is less expensive than ever but still costly up front. Investing in conservation to reduce energy consumption still yields a faster payback than investing in solar power. There are many opportunities at home and work to increase energy efficiency and save money while reducing carbon emissions. Conserving energy reduces the number of solar panels ultimately required to provide electricity, once again saving money.

Energy typically accounts for only a few percent of the cost of running most businesses. However, energy efficiency benefits from a whole-systems approach, often leading to complimentary cost savings. For example, engineers typically design industrial pumping systems by placing tanks where convenient, then adding pumps and pipes as needed after-the-fact. But Eng Lock Lee, an engineer from Singapore, develops plans in reverse. He lays out the pipes using the shortest possible lengths with the greatest practical diameters to minimize friction. Shorter, fatter pipes reduce friction enabling smaller, less-costly pumps. His factory designs cost less in materials and labor to build and are three to ten times more energy efficient.[48] In an increasingly competitive global marketplace these savings on materials, labor, and energy make the difference between survival and bankruptcy.

The same principal is true at home. Americans consume immense quantities of energy, the fuel calorie equivalent of employing 300 laborers, yet most of that energy potential is lost as waste heat without producing anything of lasting value.

An individual can conserve resources and save money through smart planning at home or in business. In a home, for example, the water heater, kitchen, bath, and laundry should be placed near each other to centralize plumbing and reduce water loss while waiting for

Industrial Energy Pyramid

As with nature's energy pyramid, there are losses from the initial energy input with every conversion in the system. Most energy is lost generating electricity, but other losses occur through power lines, in motors, gears, pumps, and pipes Losses compound, so that each step loses a percentage of the remaining total (30% is recovered from the power plant, and 9% of that is lost in transmission). In a typical industrial pump, only 9.5 units of work is performed out of an initial input of 100 units of fossil fuels.

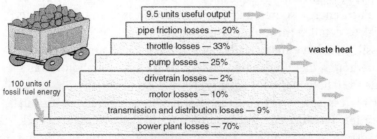

Based on 'A Typical Industrial Pumping System.' Natural Capitalism (1999).

hot water to reach the tap. Similarly, optimizing a home for passive solar gain requires creative planning to develop an appealing floor plan with south-facing windows. Significant energy savings can be achieved with inexpensive materials and innovative planning and design work. Retrofitting after the fact is beneficial, although seldom as good as doing it right the first time.

Principles of Energy Efficiency

Whether you are an enterprising homeowner or businessperson, there are several keys for smart energy use. Whole systems thinking, as described with industrial pumping systems, may be the most important key. Systems thinking should consider: 1) demand-side management, 2) life-cycle costs, 3) energy type, and 4) complimentary functions.

1) Demand-side management. Converting the typical American home to solar power can cost tens of thousands of dollars due to inefficient house design. Unfortunately, builders are not typically rewarded for resource conservation. Consequently, a typical new home is riddled with leaks, which is much like buying a sinking ship.

A few innovative and conscientious contractors build highly efficient homes and market them as niche products. Some promise to pay homeowners if their utility bills run higher than advertised. These builders set new standards that help educate homebuyers to demand energy efficiency. People who experience living in an energy-efficient home may find it unsatisfying and appalling to return to an energy waster.

Installing solar panels without first investing in energy efficiency is like installing bilge pumps on a sinking ship without repairing holes. Whether building, buying, or already occupying a structure, the key to saving energy dollars is to evaluate end-use or "demand-side management." Focus on the service you want, such as "a warm, dry place," then choose the least expensive means, either plugs or pumps, to achieve your goals. Plugs are usually more economical than pumps.

2) Life-cycle costs. Would you rather have $100 to spend today or $110 a year from now? Most of us want the money now, foregoing the opportunity to gain 10% interest. Money can be spent immediately for entertainment or invested to increase future wealth. People typically perceive money as worth more in the present, instinctively discounting its future value, choosing short-term cash over long-term growth. Yet, energy efficiency often provides a good return for the investment if you are willing to pay upfront to reap long-term savings.

The return can be even better than the stock market. For example, Rocky Mountain Institute demonstrated that a $20 investment in a low-flow showerhead can pay for itself in savings in one year. Low-flow showerheads conserve water, so less energy is employed to heat water. The savings comes in lower power bills. RMI documented that a $20 low-flow showerhead can yield $17 to $25 in energy savings every year with a gas water heater or a $47 to $71 in savings with an electric water heater. RMI compared this investment to a certificate of deposit and a savings or negotiable order of withdrawal (NOW) account. A $20 investment in a CD would yield only $1.60 in a year, and the same investment in a savings or NOW account would yield only $1.20.[49]

I'm always amazed when traveling to see how many hotels and campgrounds use water-wasters, creating high energy bills multiplied by every user. In addition to being profitable, energy conservation is good for the environment since fewer fossil fuels are consumed. Conservation is also be beneficial to utilities. Power plants are expensive to build, and it is often cheaper for utilities to help customers conserve energy rather than pay for new electric generating capacity. A utility can serve additional customers without building another power plant. Thus, utilities often have programs to help customers conserve energy, such as free energy audits, extra insulation for water heaters, and coupons or reduced rates on LED light bulbs.

3) Energy type. In order to create a small temperature difference, such as raising the temperature of a home tens of degrees, Amory Lovins in *Soft Energy Paths* suggests that the need should be met by a source that provides heat in tens or hundreds of degrees, rather than in thousands of degrees with a coal-fired plant or trillions of degrees with a nuclear reactor, which is "like cutting butter with a chainsaw." The "soft approach," according to Lovins, is to use high-grade energy, such as electricity and gasoline, only for tasks that require it. Lower grade energy can be used for other tasks.[50]

When a utility generates electricity it must burn three units of lower-grade energy, like coal or oil, to produce one unit of high-grade electricity. Two-thirds of the energy potential is lost as waste heat in the conversion. Electric space heating is expensive, because three times as much fuel must be burned to generate electricity compared to burning coal or oil directly. Due to backwards energy use through conversion losses, we burn up 27 years worth of stored, fossilized sunshine in this country every day.[51]

Granted, coal and oil are dirty, so it is helpful to burn it hundreds of miles from home. Switching to relatively clean natural gas or propane are reasonable choices for efficient use of energy. Even better, invest in weather-stripping, super-efficient windows, and more insulation. With the aid of a simple passive solar hot air collector attached to the house, it is possible to slash energy consumption, even while keeping inefficient electric backup heat.

Likewise, an electric clothes drier relies on high-grade electricity when only low-temperature heat is needed. A gas clothes drier is therefore more appropriate to the task. It is all too easy to plug in electric gadgets and appliances, so we use electricity to do many tasks where it is not required. Switching to alternative fuel sources wherever possible immediately saves two-thirds of the energy that is otherwise lost generating electricity from fossil fuels. By matching energy types to end uses and installing efficient appliances, it is possible to meet the electric demand of the ordinary American home for only a few thousand dollars worth of photovoltaics, giving a pay-back rate that is increasingly competitive with grid-delivered power.

4) <u>Complimentary functions.</u> Another key to effective energy management is to match complimentary energy uses. For example, refrigerators consume energy to pump heat out of a box. Heat removed from the refrigerator, plus extra heat given off by the compressor, is radiated into the room. Meanwhile, the water heater burns fuel to heat water, and the air-conditioner works to remove all this extra heat from the house. An appliance that pumps heat from a refrigerator into a water heater would effectively accomplish two jobs with less energy.[52] New houses should be designed to accommodate water heater-refrigerators; the energy savings may be well worth the extra design work.

Complimentary energy use is essential to keeping costs down in businesses that have high energy bills. Just about every business in this country, from restaurants to laundromats to major industrial plants, utilize energy to serve customers while discarding waste heat back to the environment. This waste heat can be harnessed in many ways for simple tasks like heating greenhouses, homes, and water. For example, imagine a laundromat that utilizes vented dryer heat to pre-warm washing water or warm a neighboring greenhouse.

By adopting energy efficient technologies and strategies, Rocky Mountain Institute long ago documented that we could reduce our electric consumption by 75% across the country at a cost less than we pay to produce it! We can reduce our oil consumption by 80% for less cost than we can drill for more, and we can cut our greenhouse gas emissions in half at a profit.[53]

Powering the Future

Future prosperity depends on abundant energy. World energy consumption is growing rapidly as developing countries seek to increase productivity and improve their standard of living. Global power use is often measured in terawatts. One terawatt (TW) can power approximately 10 billion 100-watt light bulbs, or 70 billion 100-watt equivalent LED bulbs. Operating that many bulbs for one hour consumes 1 terawatt hour (TWh) of electricity. Global energy demand equals 158,000 TWh, equivalent to a continuous output of 18 TW.[54] That's like every person on earth using 24 100-watt bulbs all the time (or 165 equivalent LEDs). The aggregate figure includes all energy sources, including fuels burned in cars and other fuel expenditures that do not produce electricity.

We often hear news of impending energy shortages, so it is helpful to evaluate the scope of potential energy sources. As detailed below, energy is vastly abundant.

Fossil Fuel Future?: Fossil fuels, including oil, natural gas, oil shale and coal, are organically derived, principally from the Carboniferous Period from 300 to 360 million years ago. Coal, for example, primarily formed from primitive trees that grew and died, but didn't decompose because cellulose and lignin adapted microbes had not yet evolved to recycle fibrous material. Shallow-rooted trees absorbed carbon from the atmosphere, grew to great heights, fell over, and accumulated to tremendous depths. The cumulative weight of the dead trees compressed the wood waste to peat, eventually forming 90% of the coal we burn today.[55]

Fossil fuels are dirty and primitive compared to other fuel sources, yet were easy to use and sufficiently abundant to incubate the industrial economy. At the dawn of the twenty-first century there are still enough fossil fuels to power the economy for hundreds of years ahead, yet we must transition to cleaner fuels to halt global warming, acid rain, and city smog.

Natural gas, a byproduct of oil drilling, is cleaner than other fossil fuels and has become a transitory energy source, reducing reliance on electricity from coal until solar, wind, and other green technologies take over.

Fossil fuels could remain potential sources of energy if carbon and other pollutants were vastly reduced or completely stripped. For example, carbon can be captured and sequestered into products such as gypsum for plasterboard. If industry extracted and sequestered gasses and particulates from all emissions then it would be possible to burn fossil fuels without endangering the climate. Nevertheless, there are higher end-uses for fossil fuels than converting them to ash, and we would be better off to conserve fossil fuels as ingredients for other products.

Burning Biofuels: Biofuels from living matter can potentially provide much of our energy supply, since total annual wood waste is estimated to be the equivalent of 50,000 TWh, roughly equal to world energy consumption in 1970.[56]

Not far from my home, the University of Montana-Western in Dillon installed a 13 million BTU/hour biomass boiler to burn wood chips from local sawmills, saving an estimated $60,000 to $75,000 on energy costs per year.[57] In my community there is enough wood waste (branches, stumps, and lumber) burned in slash piles or hauled to the landfill at taxpayer expense to potentially heat and power every local home and business. The fuel is free for any small power plant to burn it. Look around your community for wood wastes. Any waste is a potential opportunity to close a loop and make a profit.

The problem with wood burning is that the resource may have higher potential uses. For example, every time we burn a tree we lose the

Energy Glossary

Barrel—A volume of crude oil measuring 42 gallons, the equivalent of 5.8 million BTU's.

BTU—British thermal unit. The amount of heat required to raise the temperature of one pound of water one degree Fahrenheit, or 251.996 calories.

Calorie—The amount of heat required to raise the temperature of one gram of water one degree Celsius, the equivalent of 4.184 joules.

Joule—A joule is the same as a watt-second. It is the work done when a force of 1 newton acts through a distance of 1 meter.

Watt—1 watt is equal to 1 joule per second or 0.239 calories per second or 3.4192 BTU's per hour. A 100-watt light bulb uses 100 watts of electricity per hour.

Kilowatt—One thousand watts. Utility bills are measured in kilowatt hours. A typical small, portable heater uses 1.5 kilowatts (1,500 watts) per hour.

Megawatt—One million watts. A typical coal-fired power plant generates 1,500 megawatts of electricity.

Terawatt—One trillion watts. Used to describe the total potential of energy sources.

Quad—One quadrillion watts. Used to describe the total potential of energy sources.

opportunity to produce lumber from it. Even wood chips have potential use for chipboard or paper. Equally important, organic matter is essential for soil health, which we lose by turning it to ash. Most importantly, we lose the tree itself, potentially diminishing the health and well being of the ecosystem.

Methane, also known as biogas or renewable natural gas, is produced from anaerobic digestion of organic wastes, especially manure, sewage, and food waste. Many sewage plants flare off methane gas, torching it for disposal. However, Grand Junction, Colorado, population 59,0000, captures methane and uses it to run the city's fleet of forty natural gas vehicles, including garbage trucks, dump trucks, street sweepers, and city busses. The city saves $400,000 per year in fuel costs with its free methane.[58] [59]

Heartland Biogas, also in Colorado, is the largest anaerobic digester project in the world, producing methane from food scraps and dairy manure. Heartland's partner, A1 Organics, collects food waste from area restaurants, grocery stores, and distribution companies, providing the biogas plant with 140,00 gallons of food waste slurry per day.[60]

Methane is a greenhouse gas like carbon dioxide, but 21 times as effective per molecule at trapping heat if it escapes unburned into the atmosphere.[61] Methane is considered responsible for 18% of global warming.[62] Feedlot animals fattened on grain significantly increase production of methane gas. Gas can be captured and used profitably from feedlot manure, although it is ecologically better to raise grass-fed beef.

Burning methane destroys its greenhouse gas properties. Manure slurry leftover from gas production serves as fertilizer that may be applied back to the land. Watch for large manure piles at ranches and feedlots along roads. Every manure pile is an opportunity to close a loop and make a profit. I've been shocked to see numerous ranches that allow valuable manure to accumulate unused in immense piles or illegally bulldoze it into a river. Manure is fertilizer and fertilizer is money. Manure can easily be redistributed to fertilize farm fields.

In the U.S., methane gas is principally used where captured from landfills. Organic trash buried underground turns anaerobic, slowly decomposing and releasing methane. Pipes strategically place in a landfill harvest methane for decades after a landfill is capped.

Overall, methane is best used in small-scale onsite applications. For this reason, home-scale methane plants, similar to septic tanks, are becoming popular in developing countries such as China and India. HomeBiogas (www.homebiogas) has developed a small-scale inflatable biogas plant for the yard that digests food scraps to produce gas. Daily food wastes generate enough methane to cook for two or three hours a day.

Ethanol, a type of grain alcohol usually made from corn, is often blended with gasoline and heavily supported by government mandates and subsidies. Ethanol production is more political than practical. Ethanol production requires 1 unit of invested energy, primarily fossil fuels, to produce 1.3 units of ethanol equivalent energy, the lowest energy return on investment (EROI) of any major energy source.[63] Ethanol burns cleaner and reduces ozone pollution, but is less energy dense, requiring more fuel. Ethanol is not economically viable on its own, thus requiring tens of billions of dollars in federal taxpayer subsidies. In addition, consumers pay more for fuel and more for food, since corn ethanol production competes with corn as a food source.[64] Ethanol production effectively creates many jobs, but at the cost of permanently eroding precious topsoil. Ethanol production derived from fibrous farm waste has potential as a noncompetitive fuel source, but the technology hasn't yet matured to market.

Hydroelectric Potential: Hydroelectric power is a form of solar energy, since the sun creates weather that delivers water from oceans to mountaintops. Water flowing downhill to the oceans is one of the cheapest and most reliable sources of power. Electric-intensive industries like aluminum smelting often locate factories near hydroelectric power plants to take advantage of this low-cost energy.

Most of the largest and best sites for generating hydroelectric power have already been exploited with dams and turbines. Unfortunately, these dams interfere with natural stream processes and have decimated fisheries in many locations, leaving once abundant species teetering on the brink of extinction. Part of the problem is that dams usually release water through turbines as needed to meet power demand, disrupting natural flows. Some dams are now being removed to restore ecosystem health, while others are adjusting output volume to better maintain fisheries.

Streams offer great potential for small-scale hydroelectric developments. Rather than building a big dam, a portion of the stream water is diverted through a long pipe to a turbine before being returned to the stream. The pipe descends in elevation and size prior to maximize water pressure before reaching the turbine. Two local systems have mile-long pipes buried under the roads. They generate enough electricity on average to power our three local communities, about four hundred people total. These hydroelectric systems only divert a fraction of the water, so it is difficult to notice the missing volume. Many other small hydroelectric opportunities abound, especially for home-sized power sources in rural areas. Hydroelectric turbines have also been developed to generate electricity from low-head sources such as water flowing in irrigation ditches.

Blowing in the Wind: Wind power is also a form of solar energy, since the sun creates temperature turbulence that generates wind across the globe. Wind power was historically used to mechanically lift water from rural wells. Electric wind turbines were developed in the late 1800s and commercialized in the 1920s, bringing electricity to rural farms and ranches.

Wind-generated electricity grew rapidly until the Rural Electric Administration (REA) subsidized distribution of centralized power to rural areas. The positive intention of supplying low-cost power to rural farms had the unfortunate consequence of killing additional investment in wind power, killing the industry by the 1950s.[65]

The federal government began supporting wind power in the 1970s by funding research into utility-scale wind turbines. With the aid of tax breaks and other incentives, the technology has improved and increased in capacity since that time, now providing 6.3% of America's electricity.[66]

Any frequently breezy site has potential for wind power development, keeping in mind that over-development can alter the natural viewshed, kill birds and bats, and riddle the landscape with maintenance access roads. Historic metal windmills were fully recyclable, which is not the case for today's composite materials when components wear out.

Global surface wind power potential is estimated at 400 terawatts. Lofting turbines on kites into atmospheric winds could garner another 1,800 terawatts.[67]

Solar Superpower: Solar radiation striking the surface of the earth is equal to about 350,000 terawatts of power.[68] Additional solar energy strikes the outer atmosphere and bounces back into space. At 24% efficiency, 3,800 square miles of solar panels (a square 62 miles per side) in a sunny desert could generate as much electricity as our nation consumes.[69] That's the good news.

Add in roads and workspace around the solar panels, and the actual acres grows exponentially larger. Besides, solar panels must be geographically distributed to feed the grid evenly and to compensate for localized cloudy weather. Unfortunately, utility-scale solar projects are typically built by bulldozing and sterilizing desert landscapes and productive croplands, bringing us one step closer to creating a green economy on a dead planet.

Ideally, solar panels should be installed on rooftops, which could supply approximately 40% of our nation's electrical needs using current technology.[70] Solar panels can also be installed over parking lots, on military bases, and on toxic industrial sites where little else can presently grow. Photovoltaic technology can also be incorporated into siding, windows, paint,[71] and the entire body of a car.[72] We urgently need to stop bulldozing living systems for solar power production.

Solar panels can also be placed in space to collect solar energy continuously without interference from atmosphere or nightfall. The energy would be transferred down through focused microwave beams,[73] which is theoretically safer than it sounds.

Solar energy also includes solar hydrogen gas. Hydrogen gas is produced with solar electricity or high heat by splitting water apart into hydrogen and oxygen. Hydrogen gas is useful as a substitute for inadequate battery technology. Solar electricity can be stored as hydrogen gas then converted back to electricity through fuel cells to power homes or automobiles.

Solar power is considered competitive with fossil fuels for many new energy installations. Unfortunately, the upfront cost is still considerable. Investing in energy conservation first provides immediate economic and environmental savings. When a building is as efficient as possible then consider installing photovoltaics.

It is also possible to build solar-powered rockets. A "solar sail" on a starship can be unfurled close to the sun, such that the sun's light will push it to a fantastic speed, allowing it to coast to another star system. Such a device would still take a few centuries to get to the nearest star, but this ranks among the best proposals for interstellar travel.[74]

Awash in an Ocean of Energy: Oceans are immense reservoirs of potential energy that may be harnessed via tidal power, wave power, ocean currents, and temperature differences. Each method has pros and cons, better applicable to some areas than others. Given that half the population lives within 50 miles of a coast, oceans can be a viable local source of energy.

Tidal Power: Ocean tides are created by gravitational pull from the moon and sun drawing water towards their mass, creating two bulges or high tides in the ocean, and two opposite low tides. Rotation of the earth moves the bulges around the planet, resulting in two high tides and two low tides every day. Being closer, the moon has greater pull than the sun. Aligned together, the moon and sun cause larger tides, whereas positioned on opposite sides of the planet, they partially cancel each other out, resulting in lower tides.

The range between high and low tides varies from a few inches up to fifty feet due to differences in the shape of the ocean floor. The narrow shape of Canada's Bay of Fundy funnels tidewater into a small space, causing fifty-foot tides. That is an enormous amount of power that could be captured by trapping water behind a dam at high tide and releasing it through a turbine at low tide. Unfortunately, tidal projects such as this endanger wildlife and negatively impact estuary habitat. Less damaging systems generate electricity in the tidal current as water moves higher or lower. A test turbine operating in the Bay of Fundy produces enough electricity for five hundred homes.[75] Worldwide potential for technically feasible tidal power is estimated at 1 to 2 terawatts.[76] However, tidal projects should be limited to areas where other alternatives are impractical to minimize ecological harm.

Wave Power: Listen to crashing waves on the beach. Every wave is a potential source of energy. Waves are caused by wind dragging across the surface of the open ocean, blowing towards shore. Unlike a stream, which provides a constant source of energy, waves cycle in pulses, making energy capture more challenging. Fortunately, there are now numerous approaches to convert wave power to electricity. Technologically feasible wave power could produce up to 2 terawatts of power[77] with the potential to produce up to 10% of global electricity by 2050.[78] However, there are concerns regarding impacts to marine wildlife due to potential entanglement with mooring systems, underwater acoustics, electromagnetic fields from electricity production, and potential changes in shoreline habitat due to changes in wave intensity.

Ocean Currents: Ocean currents are like rivers moving within the water, caused by wind, temperature, and salinity differences, tidal forces, and the earth's rotation. Sailors rely on ocean currents to carry ships across the seas. Ocean currents also carry weather. For example, water from the Gulf Stream cycles northward past Europe, moderating continental weather.

Ocean currents are about 800 times denser than wind currents, so a 12-mph ocean current has the equivalent force of a 110-mph gust of wind. Harnessing just $1/1000^{th}$ of the energy of the Gulf Stream passing by Florida would supply 35% of the state's electrical needs. One environmental concern is that ocean currents attract denser concentrations of marine organisms that would likely be impacted by power-generating facilities. Also, it is unknown how much power could be harnessed without noticeably slowing ocean currents. Plus, there is concern that global warming could change or stall ocean currents.[79]

Temperature Differences: Oceans absorb about 75% of solar energy that strikes the planet. The +/- 40°F temperature difference between the warm surface and the cold depths makes sea thermal power possible, also known as ocean thermal energy conversion (OTEC) with a total potential output of roughly 100 TW.[80]

Warm water vaporizes a fluid with a low boiling point, such as ammonia (78°F), and this vapor drives a turbine to generate electricity. Cold water pumped up from ocean depths condenses vapor back to liquid to restart the process. The pumps bring nutrients up from the seafloor and invigorate sea life in the vicinity. Sea thermal power requires large facilities to be efficient, so it will be most useful to industry and cities located along coastlines. One advantage to sea thermal is that the process can desalinate water, a resource more valuable than energy. A 105-kilowatt prototype OTEC plant is producing electricity for the Big Island of Hawaii. The technology works and just needs financing to achieve full-scale production.[81]

Ships or floating islands can also be equipped for OTEC, and the electricity used to split seawater to make hydrogen gas. For safety, hydrogen can be combined with nitrogen extracted from air to make ammonia, an alternative fuel for modified gasoline-powered engines. About 2,000 OTEC ships could provide enough fuel for all U.S. cars.[82]

Geothermal Planet: Our planet is a slowly cooling ball of molten matter covered by a thin, floating crust. Heat escaping from the molten planet gives us hot springs, volcanoes, and geothermal energy potential. The energy potential of the earth's core is off the charts, since it has and will be cooling for billions of years to come. Readily harvestable heat from existing vents, however, totals only about 10 terawatts of power annually.[83]

Geothermal power is cheap and easy to develop. Most large sites have already been harnessed, yet many untapped smaller hot springs exist. One issue with geothermal power is that it competes with scenic or recreational uses of thermal water. However, many hot springs have excess hot water that can be developed for small power systems while maintaining existing pools. Even better, warm water left over from power generation or bathing can be piped through houses, businesses, or greenhouses for radiant heat. Geothermal greenhouses grow large vegetable crops in northern climates without the cost or impact of fossil fuels. Although the income potential seems obvious, many small hot spring owners have yet to take advantage of the opportunity.

Fission and Fusion Facts: The Big Bang created a universe of hydrogen and helium. These original materials were squeezed into heavier elements under massive gravitational pressure in the cores of stars. Our solar system is built from other stars that long since collapsed under their own weight and blew debris across the vast emptiness of space.

Radioactive materials are among the heaviest elements, which slowly decay into more stable forms. Their radioactive half-life is the amount of time it takes to decay half of any given amount of material. They've been decaying for billions of years since being blown from previous stars. Our planet was initially much more radioactive at the dawn of life, and there were likely many spontaneous nuclear explosions.

Nuclear power plants control the decay of radioactive elements, especially uranium-235 and uranium-thorium, releasing vast amounts of energy from small amounts of material. Although non-renewable, the energy potential for nuclear fission is very high—at about 100,000,000 terawatt hours.[84]

Nuclear fission began with atomic bombs in the 1940s. Either thorium or uranium can be harnessed in nuclear reactors. Of the two, thorium is more abundant, safer, generates more energy per ton, and produces less dangerous waste products. Governments funded research into more risky uranium reactors because a by-product of refining and using uranium is weapons-grade plutonium, essential for nuclear warheads. Consequently, we use the most expensive, least-safe nuclear reactors, giving us Three Mile Island, Chernobyl, and Fukishima. We also have enough nuclear weapons sitting idly around to kill everyone on the planet several times over, plus extremely hazardous nuclear waste that must be secured for the next 10,000 years without leaking into the environment.[85] We also have to worry about terrorists obtaining nuclear waste and contaminating cities with "dirty bombs." In addition, operational nuclear power plants must be managed at all times to cool the fuel rods to prevent a nuclear meltdown. Unattended nuclear reactors may not shut down properly to avert nuclear disaster.

Nuclear power was once touted as being the energy of the future that would be "too cheap to meter." Today nuclear electricity is our most expensive form of conventional electricity because it takes many calories of food and fuel energy to safely build and operate the facilities. Energy is consumed mining, transporting, and refining the uranium. Additional energy is lost as waste heat, and energy must be expended to store the spent fuel for eternity. Many nuclear power plants have been mothballed early because it is more economical to terminate them unpaid than to continue generating expensive electricity.[86]

In comparison, molten-salt thorium reactors are theoretically fail-safe. When the temperature reaches a certain threshold, the liquid expands, separating fissionable material and slowing nuclear reactions to let the core cool. Reactors are designed like a bathtub, with a drain in the bottom. Too hot, and the plug melts and drains fuel into a shielded unground tank.[87] Thorium reactors could theoretically tap more energy from the fuel, greatly reducing nuclear waste. Thorium is three times as abundant as uranium and does not require enrichment. The reactors are more compact and do not require massive containment structures, such that smaller reactors could be mass-produced and linked in series. These molten-salt reactors could also potentially run on spent uranium from existing reactors, effectively using up the most hazardous waste on the planet.[88]

Had we invested in thorium reactors decades ago instead of uranium, it likely would be one of our least-cost power sources, and we may have averted warming the globe with fossil fuel emissions. Today, China is leading the effort to jumpstart research into thorium reactors with the intent of being the global leader and supplier of thorium technology.[89]

It could be argued that solar power should become our primary source of electricity instead of nuclear. However, large-scale volcanic eruptions are periodically common, filling the atmosphere with dust and plunging the globe into winter for years at a time. Under such conditions, a thorium reactor would provide insurance that solar power cannot.

In addition to ground-based applications, fission may be necessary for space travel. Chemical rockets are limited in speed. Travel time to Mars is about six months. Travel to the nearest neighboring star system would take thousands of years. More fuel enables more speed, yet fuel adds mass, which requires more fuel, a no-win situation. Nuclear fission can lighten the load, enabling rockets to travel farther faster by creating nuclear explosions beneath the ship for propulsion.[90]

Nuclear <u>fusion</u> is the reverse of fission, like the sun, where lighter elements are fused to make heavier elements. Fusion experiments involve isotopes of hydrogen known as deuterium and tritium. Regular hydrogen has one proton, while deuterium adds a neutron and tritium has two neutrons. A molecule of water (H_2O) includes two hydrogen atoms and one of oxygen. In the oceans, approximately 1 in every 6,700 hydrogen atoms is deuterium, which can be readily extracted. Tritium is a short-lived radioactive form of hydrogen usually produced from lithium. Waste from a fusion reactor is nontoxic helium.[91]

Like fission, fusion depends on non-renewable resources, yet the earthly supply dwarfs imagination, with a total potential of 300,000,000,000 terawatts of power.[92] Given the energy potential and fact that it runs on seawater, fusion is often touted as the fuel the will be "too cheap to meter" as was once believed about fission.

Taxpayer subsidized researchers have spent billions of dollars and sixty-plus years of work attempting to achieve sustainable fusion. Most work has focused on large-scale fusion power. However, NASA researchers are now developing small reactors for expedited space travel within the solar system, which would seem to be equally useful as small, localized power plants on earth.[93]

Free Everything

Although the reader is unlikely to build a fusion or fission power plant, it is helpful to consider the range of presently available energy options to power the future. We often talk of scarcity, yet energy seems likely to become increasingly abundant and inexpensive in the future. As the cost of energy rapidly approaches free, so too will the cost of everything else. If energy is effectively free, then so too is desalinization, tunneling, pumping, building, and space travel. For better or worse, free everything will enable great projects, such as refilling the Dead Sea and the Salton Sea, or desalinizing seawater to irrigate and restore the entire 3,000-mile-long Sahara Desert.

On the other hand, people tend to use abundant resources very poorly. Every time fuel prices go down, Americans revert to buying bigger gas-guzzling vehicles. What will we do when energy is too cheap to bother closing the front door? As Amory Lovins quipped back in 1977, *"If you ask me, it'd be little short of disastrous for us to discover a source of clean, cheap, abundant energy because of what we would do with it."*[94] The future is fraught with great potential and great peril.

"It is astonishing as well as sad, how many trivial affairs even the wisest man thinks he must attend to in a day; how singular an affair he thinks he must omit. When the mathematician would solve a difficult problem, he first frees the equation of all encumbrances, and reduces it to its simplest terms. So simplify the problem of life, distinguish the necessary and the real."

—Henry David Thoreau,
Letters to Harrison Blake (1848)[95]

Labor
Adding Caloric Value

The worldly goods of an individual hunter-gatherer could be transported from camp to camp in a backpack or travois. Their material wealth was like a grain of sand on the beach compared to the natural world around them. Today, most people live in a fabricated environment. Many people go to the grave without ever leaving the matrix of human society to experience the real world. Human society is rapidly blanketing the planet with a built environment. Every city, road, dam, farm, garden and greenhouse is constructed directly or indirectly by the labor of human hands. Labor is the force that built the world. Even in the emerging age of automation, technology still requires a degree of human labor to design, build, and install it.

As a homeowner or businessperson, one makes daily decisions about allocating labor to efficiently achieve goals. Sometimes it is more cost-effective to outsource jobs, and other times it is economical to buckle down with a do-it-yourself attitude. Unfortunately, many people enter adult life ill equipped to do anything themselves.

In past cultures, kids started adult life young, and they started with essential skills and material wealth needed to survive. In many Stone Age and primitive farming cultures it was customary for a community to build a new home for a newly married couple. Young people started their adult lives with no house payment, no land payment, no power bill, no water bill, few taxes, and certainly no phone bill. They paid for water by bucketing it from the creek, and they paid for fuel by gathering firewood. Neither is a horrible price to pay. Young people also entered adulthood with a viable trade.

Customs are different now. Kids formerly married off at twelve to sixteen years old now remain dependent children until age eighteen, and are often supported through college and more. Many still live at home until their late twenties or thirties. Directly or indirectly, young adults often receive thousands of dollars of parental subsidies before fully supporting themselves. Even so, young people do not necessarily enter adult life as prepared as past generations.

Survival Skills

Work and family are largely separate realities in the modern world, unlike 99% of human history. Our ancestors grew up immersed in family trades, absorbing life skills much as we absorb language. Hunter-gatherers transitioned to adulthood with all the tools and skills they needed to survive. From shooting a bow and arrow to tanning hides to cooking, they had experience. In other cultures, people grew up with trades like carpentry, farming, weaving, or blacksmithing. They knew a viable trade when they left home. In comparison, children in our culture remain children longer, and often seek employment knowing little more than how to flip a burger.

That doesn't mean the past was better. Surviving with little more than one's bare hands isn't easy. The world was a rough, tough place, and people worked hard. Young people today have infinitely greater opportunities throughout their lives. Yet they also face enormous challenges. Children often leave the nest with minimum wage skills to survive in a world with $70/hour expenses.

It is difficult to find a decent job when employers only accept experienced applicants. Employers want experience, yet experience requires employment. College does not necessarily make this transition to adulthood easier. Students might work minimum wage jobs to cover living expenses and obtain loans to cover tuition. By graduation, a high-paying job is necessary to pay off tens of thousands of dollars of student debt.

For me, transitioning to adulthood seemed ominous. I didn't want a job, and I despised the idea of working up the ladder one-dollar-per-hour at a time. It could take years to progress from minimum wage to a living wage, and I wasn't sure I could survive employment that long. It seemed like a lot of sweat and tears just to break even.

While some employment was necessary, I was determined to avoid employment as much as possible. Judicious spending helped minimize employment. Equally important, I hired myself as a stonemason, carpenter, plumber, and electrician to stretch the value of scarce dollars.

Our income didn't represent many calories, but we traded those calories for materials. Then we invested additional calories as labor to transform those materials into a valuable product, our home. We started with little, yet invested ourselves to multiply the value of our income.

As a custom, passive solar stone and log home, the house would have been enormously expensive if professional contractors did the work. Instead, we hired ourselves. There were no job applications, no taxes, and we "earned" almost as much as professionals, although we worked slower because we were learning on the job. Our W-2 forms indicated that we earned only about $10,000 per year, yet we earned much more through the investment in our home. Hiring ourselves was the easiest way to earn top wages with no previous skills.

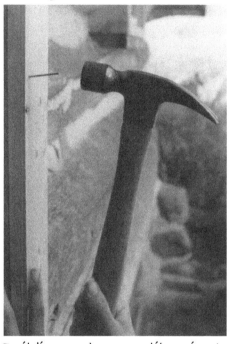

We gained experience, developing a semi-professional skillset on the job. Working for ourselves was like going to college, only better, and it cost less to build our house than to pay college tuition and rent. We graduated with a degree in experience. Our diploma was the house, built and

Building our home was like going to college, only better. Our diploma was the house, bought and paid for.

paid for. I've since applied that experience to other building projects, and to writing my book *Living Homes: Stone Masonry, Log, and Strawbale Construction*, which continues to generate an income decades later.

Costs and Benefits

Each of us is a producer and consumer. We produce goods and services through work. We consume goods and services during and after work. As producers we must choose between employment for ourselves and employment through others. As consumers we choose between hiring others to help us with tasks like cleaning carpets, cooking meals, painting the house, vehicle maintenance, and fixing the plumbing, versus doing the work ourselves.

Each choice is an exercise in weighing costs and benefits. If a high-paying job is available then it may be advantageous to outsource projects, such as building a house. If low-paying jobs are the only option then a healthy do-it-yourself attitude may be highly profitable.

Similarly, starting a business may produce significant income or perhaps only enough to survive. Profit margin helps dictate whether to hire jobs out or tackle them head-on. Any choice offers potential benefits, but also a cost in forgone opportunities. Choosing one solution requires giving up alternative possibilities. This cost/benefit analysis must be revisited and re-evaluated moment-by-moment as relative costs and benefits change.

As with all economic decisions, money is only one factor, personal goals are another. For example, I greatly dislike working on cars. Out of necessity, I've learned my way around an engine and completed essential repairs. I've also slipped with the wrench too many times, whacking my knuckles against steel. I gladly pay triple my hourly income to hire a mechanic to do automotive work. Writing is good for my career, so working more as a writer and less as a mechanic fits my goals. On the other hand, if the repair bill were so high that I would feel compelled to seek outside employment to pay for it, then I might tackle the work myself as the best option to remain unemployed.

Consider your own Dreams and choose the most direct route to success. Some people dream of becoming doctors or scientists, requiring conventional college education. That path works, as does becoming an aid worker in underdeveloped countries. It is okay to not get rich, provided you are following your Dreams.

Many people dream of having a fulfilling career and a comfortable degree of material wealth. It is necessary to continually weigh the relative importance between opportunities available at any moment. As a writer, for instance, I must choose between spending income on consumer goods, such as groceries or furniture, or on supplies for production, such as a computer upgrade.

There is no secret to the process of weighing costs and benefits. We operate this way instinctively when making choices we hope will yield the greatest advantage towards achieving our individual wants and needs. That's what we do in the candy isle choosing between M&Ms and Butterfingers. Which opportunity yields the greatest satisfaction, and what opportunities do we forgo to get it? The purpose of discussing costs and benefits is to consciously consider other potential choices. For example, what if the need for a candy bar stems from excessive work at a dissatisfying job? Not buying the candy bar may be the first step towards not needing the job.

Dollars and Sense

Many high-paying jobs pay surprisingly low wages when factoring for extracurricular time and monetary expenses. In their book, *Your Money or Your Life*, authors Joe Dominguez and Vicki Robin describe an employee earning $440 for a standard 40-hour week. That works out to $11 per hour. Outside factors associated with work also costs time and money. Commuting costs time and money, as does buying and dressing up with clothing, jewelry, and cosmetics. A job may necessitate expensive restaurant meals, coffee breaks, and other decompression time and escape entertainment. These activities add time to the 40-hour week and reduce net income. The authors show a 40-hour, $440 week becoming a 70-hour, $280 week. A wage of $11/hour wage is worth only $4/hour after properly accounting for all time and expenses. [96]

When weighing adjusted income against the cost of hiring professionals for home or car maintenance, it may be highly profitable to learn handyman skills. Do-it-yourself work may pay a better wage than working for anyone else. Furthermore, there are no taxes on money saved.

Suppose someone offers to paint your home for $2,000 labor, plus the cost of paint. No problem. You can earn $2,000 at work. Unfortunately, taxes eat up about one-third of a typical income, so it is necessary to earn $3,000 to raise $2,000 to pay the painter. Doing the work yourself saves $3,000 which is tax-free income.

Economists often consider do-it-yourself work as part of the barter economy, like trading with one's self. Calories of effort are expended and a reward is attained, yet the gains are not traceable as income.

Consider an example given by Jude Wanniski in *The Way the World Works*. A man hires a housekeeper to clean his house. He pays income taxes then pays the housekeeper. They fall in love and get married. He continues employment at a job, and she continues cleaning as part of the relationship, yet it is no longer a formal job. Government records indicate that a job was lost and the IRS can no longer levy a tax on the housekeeper's income. The newlyweds gain a tax savings as a result. [97]

We gained in a similar way by building our home, changing the oil in the car and truck, and cooking simple meals. Hiring other people would have necessitated high paying jobs, which would have necessitated paying tens of thousands of dollars in taxes.

It isn't practical to do everything from scratch, such as making rubber and tanning leather to make shoes. Yet many do-it-yourself tasks are highly worthwhile and rewarding, from painting a room to changing spark plugs in a car.

Most importantly, lowering expenses through do-it-yourself labor can reduce the need for a job. Plus, anyone who doesn't need full-time work is available to choose temporary higher paying or higher quality jobs. For example, some people take summer jobs working on fishing or crabbing boats in Alaska. In this case, the hours are long, the work is hard, and the living conditions challenging, yet experienced deckhands can earn up to $20,000 during a three month season. Fishing boat captains typically award deckhands a percentage of the total take, paid in one lump sum at the end of the fishing season. Actual pay varies widely according to the size of the haul, market prices, and the experience of the crew.[98]

As with everything in life, it is essential to consider core Dreams and goals. It isn't practical to do everything, and it isn't healthy to work all the time. I maintain a satisfying quality of life by not being employed. Therefore, I chose to do automotive work to the degree necessary to remain unemployed. Nowadays, with an established writing and publishing business, I gladly pay others to change the oil or replace the starter. It is all a matter of choices, and we all have choices in everything we do.

Closing the Loop on Wasted Labor

Even successful businesses typically waste more than 85% of their time delivering goods and services to customers. Better time management isn't about working faster and harder; it is simply about closing the loop on wasted effort. For example, United Electrical Controls, Co. (U.E.C.) in Watertown, Massachusetts, studied process flow in the factory where they manufacture temperature and pressure sensors and controls. From start to finish, one product traveled twelve miles within the confines of the 50,000-square-foot facility, adding significant time and labor to the manufacturing process. The factory was organized according to workstations, so that each item had to be transported from station to station.

U.E.C. corrected the problem by rearranging workstations around products. For example, instead of bringing products to a centralized welding station, the company spread welders around the factory as mini-stations along assembly lines. Streamlining the process greatly reduced the distance products traveled and reduced lead-time on customer orders from 10 to 12 weeks to about 2 days. A product that once traveled twelve miles could now be completed in forty feet.[99]

Effective time management requires mentally separating actions into two categories: actions that create wealth and those that don't.

Assembling a part or writing a contract helps generate wealth, while transporting goods within the company or filing sales reports do not. Effective time management entails minimizing calories of labor expended for chores that do not contribute to the final goods and services.

Time management also applies at home. Consider how much time is spent looking for things each day like keys, shoes, or socks. Any repetitive, nonproductive chore is an opportunity to close the loop on wasted time, resulting in freedom to do more meaningful activities. Putting shoes and socks and keys in the same place every day is a simple way to become a more effective time manager.

Another form of time management is to double-up on transportation, to avoid coming or going empty-handed from point A to point B. For example, when walking thirty-some feet from the kitchen to the cellar for canned goods, I always check the counter for recyclables that need transporting to the cellar. Such efficiency may seem trivial, yet thinking this way at home leads to similar thinking in business, leading to greater efficiency in transportation.

More importantly, it is possible to eliminate some trips entirely or delay them until a more pressing need requires a journey. Time management is especially important in rural areas. My home is sixty miles away from the city. I initially made the trip once or twice a week, typically consuming an entire day in the process. I eventually trimmed necessity down to once or twice a month, effectively gaining an extra month of free time each year, while also saving money and reducing pollution. The downside is that many projects that might be completed in a day must be set aside until I finally make the drive to town, but eventually, it all gets done.

Urban residents have easy access to stores, but consequently waste more time and resources making quick dashes downtown for errands that could easily be combined. One or two half-hour trips each day adds up to hundreds of hours and many miles over the course of a year.

"After years of consulting in many countries for clients who managed many different enterprises, and whose sophistication varied greatly, I came to the conclusion that the majority of farmers and ranchers actually plan nonprofitability, and then complain loudly when they achieve it!"

—Allan Savory,
Holistic Resource Management (1988) [100]

Money
The Biggest Bang for the Buck

Money is the tool that runs the world. Money can move mountains, or conserve them. Money offers freedom or can enslave us. Money becomes symbolic of our goals as we pursue it to trade for goods and services. Paradoxically, money is the tool we use to facilitate a strategic exit from money dependency. Even if we succeed in eliminating monthly rent or mortgage costs and other major monthly bills, it is difficult to entirely escape the need for money. At some point we need a job or self-employment to gain more dollars.

Money must be invested to gain money, even if only to commute to a job or buy new work clothes. Whether our goal is to play the guitar or start a guitar factory, judicious application of money can facilitate our hopes and dreams. Can we harness the tool of money without becoming harnessed to it?

Direct Pointing to Real Wealth

Money can be a powerful tool to achieve your personal and professional goals. Unfortunately, many people get caught up in the illusion of money and lose sight of real wealth.

For example, state governments often embrace lotteries as free money, like enacting a voluntary tax. Only people who want to play will pay. It's logical in monetary terms, as long as one ignores the bigger picture. In terms of real wealth, many people are employed to run a lottery. People work to create scratch-and-win games, attempting to dress the same game a dozen different ways, pumping out continuous updates to make the lottery seem new and different. People are employed cutting down trees, making paper, doing graphic design, printing, shipping, distributing, selling, accounting, and disposing of the waste. Then there is the big pot, the actual lottery, potentially worth millions if your number is drawn. The lottery employs a small army of people to create, administer, and monitor. They are employed to consume wealth, rather than produce it, taking a portion of lottery sales to pay for their houses, cars, food, utilities, and fun.

People who buy lottery tickets are often motivated by the persistent desperation of running in a rat race with no end in sight. Why not? It just costs a dollar or two now and then. With so many other bills to pay, sloughing off a buck here and there seems like a worthwhile gamble for the remote chance to pay off all bills and attain true financial freedom. Yet, it is exactly that kind of thinking that traps people in the rat race, working a job to nowhere. Studies have shown that poor people spend more income on lotteries than wealthy people, and sales are highest in the poorest areas. The lottery exploits the poor and further exacerbates their situation.[101] While the revenue seems good on paper, the real-world effect of consuming resources without producing anything actually reduces wealth in the long-term. States initiate lotteries to help fund education, yet studies have shown that non-lottery states ultimately spend 10% more on education.[102]

Fundraisers that sell products to benefit a cause are similarly questionable. Girl Scouts sell cookies. School groups often sell boxes of oranges. Everyone sells t-shirts, and some organizations raffle off new cars or vacation cruises. Yet, any item purchased for resale necessarily increases the amount that must be raised by the nonprofit.

For example, selling boxes of fruit is a respectable means to pay for a school field trip to Washington, D.C. Students pre-sell oranges and grapefruit such that all fruit is sold before it arrives. Upon delivery, the customer receives quality fresh fruit, students earn a cut without the risk of owning inventory, and the vendor takes a cut for making it all possible. That's okay, except it greatly increases the fundraising target. If students sell a 20 lb. box of oranges for $25, they keep $10, and the supplier takes $15. If the goal is to raise $3,000, then students must make $7,500 in sales, sending $4,500 out of the community. The fundraiser must take in 2-1/2 times as much money compared to asking for straight-up contributions.

As president of the Jefferson River Canoe Trail, our group raised $270,000 to purchase a walk-in fishing access site and public paddler campsite. We were fortunate to obtain a $195,000 grant towards the project, and we had $9,000 in savings, leaving a gap of $66,000. We could have poured all our time and effort into managing bake sales, banquets, auctions, t-shirts, marathons, canoe races, etc., but instead we simply told people about our project and asked for cash donations. I thought it might take three years to raise the necessary funds. Yet, we raised all of it within a few months. That included nearly $20,000 in additional small grants and more than $46,000 in cash donations from local Montanans and Lewis & Clark trail enthusiasts.

That doesn't mean fruit sales, t-shirts, and special events are not viable fundraising methods, especially for general funding drives. The important issue is to evaluate each proposed action in terms of real wealth.

The same fundamental rule applies to a homeowner, business owner, nonprofit, or government entity. Does a lottery produce wealth or consume it? Does a nonprofit fundraiser have a specific, worthwhile goal that people will support even without a reward? Does a business proposal genuinely benefit consumers or fleece them? Does purchasing a plastic picnic table make a net-positive contribution to the yard, or will it end up in the dumpster two years later? Keep real wealth in mind to effectively apply the tool of money.

Risk or Security?

Anyone earning a 7% return on stock market investments while paying 5% interest on a home mortgage would logically leave the money in stocks and make monthly payments on the loan. What happens,

We raised $270,000 in grants and cash donations to buy a new campsite for the public on the Jefferson River Canoe Trail.

however, if the stock market crashes and the original investment in the stock market plummets? If the economy goes into a recession then it may be difficult, if not impossible to maintain sufficient employment to continue paying the mortgage. Given enough time, the market will probably recover, yet by then, the homeowner risks defaulting on the loan and losing the house, or being forced to sell stocks at a loss. In a good economy or a bad one, paying down debts and reducing risks gives piece of mind and financial security to weather whatever comes.

Having few expenses can also benefit a new business enterprise. Fledgling businesses often experience lean times in the beginning, so it is arguably easier to start a business if you can survive without money. A lifestyle that requires a $30,000/year income immediately plunges a new enterprise $30,000 into the red. On the other hand, launching a business is more manageable and less stressful with living expenses of $10,000/year.

Minimizing expenses at home and in business provides a measure of insurance through the ups and downs of the local, national, and global economy. Recessions are comparatively unimportant when cash flow isn't critical and expenses are few. Assets cannot be repossessed if you have no debts. If need be, go on vacation until the economy picks up again. Having few expenses gives you control to avoid being a puppet of the economy.

In a good economy or a bad one, having few expenses allows one to drop prices as necessary to be competitive. Lower prices are helpful to the consumer, which means more customers and more potential profits for the businessperson. A lower break-even point provides flexibility and security to deal with whatever situation comes along.

The freedom of not needing an income also facilitates running a business that may be only marginally viable. For example, it may be difficult or stressful to turn a hobby into a business when dependent on it for income. Not needing much money allows more time and flexibility to grow the business, reducing the risk that job stress might extinguish the original passion for the hobby.

Starting a survival and sustainable living skills school has been a lifelong dream for me, one that evolved slowly as a hobby business over nearly thirty years. In that time, I've experimented with many different classes and marketing strategies, figuring out what works and what doesn't. My original business, Hollowtop Outdoor Primitive School, LLC (HOPS) eventually evolved into Green University® LLC for adult programs and Outdoor Wilderness Living School, LLC (OWLS) for youth programs.

Other yearlong adult programs cost more and provide less, typically requiring students to rent housing and buy their own food while enrolled. Green University® LLC tuition is significantly lower and includes food and lodging, because students camp in wickiups, tents, or an earthlodge, and primarily eat readily available free food. In addition, student mentors learn by teaching through OWLS programs for public schools, enabling OWLS to offer affordable rates for cash-strapped public schools.

Operating these programs gives me freedom to practice Stone Age skills without turning it into drudgery and work. In addition, students often have limited resources and could not afford to attend if prices were high. Because my lifestyle does not require a big income, I can keep prices low and market to people with modest incomes. More people can pay for classes, and I can continue sharing skills without feeling pressured to turn a substantial profit.

Effective use of limited calories, incoming and outgoing, has allowed me to pursue meaningful business choices. Effective use of calories will similarly enable your own success. Eliminating personal and business expenses results in a stable economic foundation necessary for launching a prosperous enterprise. If a project makes sense in terms of real wealth, then evaluate it against other promising options to determine which action yields the greatest marginal reaction.

Marginal Reaction

It is a chilly winter day to walk over the hills and through the woods a mile to Grandma's house. A light coat initially seemed warm enough, but now the shivers set in a quarter mile down the trail. Do we return to the house for more clothing or shiver all the way to Grandma's house, dreaming of hot coffee and apple pie at the end of the trail?

Choices made in the past are considered sunk costs. We cannot pick up our footprints and undo past decisions. We live in the present moment on a narrow margin between the past and future. A step just taken is immediately sunk in the past, while the next step forward remains a future variable. Counter-intuitively, sunk costs are often said to be irrelevant to future planning.

The sunk cost in the walk to grandma's house is the quarter mile already traveled. From a purely economic perspective, it doesn't matter where we've been. All that matters is where we are. Consider anticipated costs and benefits from the present position. Pushing on towards Grandma's house, we arrive there sooner, but at the risk of becoming dangerously cold for the remaining 3/4 of a mile. On the other hand, we would benefit by returning 1/4 mile for warm clothes, but at the cost of having to walk 1 1/4 miles from the present position to reach our final destination.

Where we have been has little bearing on where we go in the future. It does not matter if we have been a student, a beggar, a criminal, or a hundred thousand dollars in debt. Past actions are sunk costs that merely determine where we are at the present time. What matters most are the choices available now, on the margin. We can compare options and weigh the expected additional cost of each potential action, seeking the greatest marginal reaction for the investment.

In matters major and minor, we deal with sunk costs and marginal decisions every day. For example, fifteen dollars spent at the theater becomes a sunk cost at the moment of purchase. What happens if it is a lousy movie? Do we endure the movie to get our money's worth? Does the initial bad investment justify making another investment of time in the attempt to salvage the original investment? From an economic perspective, sitting through a lousy movie only raises the sunk cost to $15 + two hours of time. Making decisions based on sunk costs is the tail wagging the dog, or steering from behind. Sound decision-making requires a degree of detachment from the past to consider all the options from one's present position.

Suppose a grocery store buys fifty crates of bananas at 50¢ per pound just before the price drops. Store managers expected to sell bananas for profit at 75¢ per pound, but must lower the price to stay competitive and move inventory. Unloading bananas at 50¢ per pound would help avoid a loss, but only if customers buy them. What happens if competitors sell bananas for 25¢ per pound? The store may be forced to match the lower price. In terms of marginal reaction, it is better to sell inventory at 25¢ per pound than to try and recover the sunk cost and not sell them at all.

On a personal level, sunk costs and marginal decisions can be gut-wrenching. When we pay $5,000 for a used car we expect it to run. If the car breaks down two months later, we have to make a new decision. Do we pay $1,500 to repair the car? Or do we sell the car and invest $1,500 toward a replacement? The original cost is theoretically irrelevant to any decisions now. We must weigh the expected costs and benefits of all known options given the current situation. What do we expect from the car in the future? Should we fix the car and keep it? Should we sell it as is? Should we fix it and sell it?

Marginal decisions can be difficult to make when sunk costs are high. For example, many college students go through two or three years of schooling before realizing they would rather switch majors or possibly quit school altogether. Like walking to Grandma's house in the cold, the student is already part way there. Does the student keep going and finish, or chuck it all and start over?

Decision-making would be easier if sunk costs had no value, yet that is seldom the case. For instance, if a $10 million ship hits a reef and sinks, the value is a sunk cost, literally. Nevertheless, the ship may have value if it is recovered and restored. Standing on the margin between the past and future, we dismiss the original $10 million investment and compare present options. Do we abandon the wreck and spend $10 million on a new ship or invest $7 million to recover and refurbish the remains of the old ship? Sunk costs are irrelevant, yet sunken assets often retain value that shape future decisions.

Similarly, is it better to demolish an old house and start over or keep the house and restore it to satisfactory condition? Starting from scratch may cost more for materials, yet require less labor than fixing up an old house. Keeping and restoring the structure may make a nice house, but what if the floor plan or building design doesn't match the dream? These are not easy choices to make.

In corporate America, it is a numbers-only game, often leading to obscene waste. For example, it is not unusual for a company to purchase a perfectly good five-year-old storefront and demolish it. The commercial lot and business has value, yet the acquiring company perceives greater value in razing the structure and building something completely different. In many cases, buildings are demolished without reselling salvageable materials because such efforts, even when profitable, would delay building and opening the new store. Sales from the future store are calculated as more valuable than profits from reclaimed building materials.

Economic principles function the same for individuals and small businesses, yet the results are often dramatically different. For example, I once helped a friend remodel a shack into a cozy little home. Any reasonable person would have demolished the house and built from scratch. The building started as a tiny 8 x 12 tarp shed, a wood frame structure on a concrete slab covered by a blue tarp. Someone later added plywood and steel roofing, plus a slightly larger addition set on pier blocks. The walls and roof were insulated with fiberglass bats and sealed off with clear plastic. The building had doors and windows, a woodstove, partial wiring, and an unused water supply pipe from the well hidden under the floor. The walls were neither square nor plumb, sometimes off by inches. The house was riddled with mice that could be seen and heard overhead through the plastic barrier that covered the insulation.

The reasonable, logical choice was to bulldoze the structure and build a new house. On the other hand, this was home, and there was nowhere else to live or surplus money to build a new house.

Instead of investing tens of thousands in a new structure, renovating the shack necessitated spending a few hundred dollars at a time to improve the shack over several years. The plywood walls of the original tarp shed were covered by ugly plastic house wrap, so we tacked up old chicken wire and troweled on cement stucco to beautify the exterior. Then we poured a shallow foundation under the addition, bonding the pier blocks together to prevent mice and cold drafts from coming under the wooden floor. We racked our brains to figure out how best to add a bathroom, and eventually removed an adjacent tarp shed and connected that concrete slab with new footings to the existing house. We salvaged free lumber for most of the framing work and roughed in the plumbing and wiring. Eventually, the mouse-ridden fiberglass insulation was removed and replaced with sprayed-in foam. The plasterboard and fixtures soon followed.

Intermittent investments of time and money resulted in a surprisingly cozy little home. It wasn't a dream house, but well within the financial and experiential ability of the owner. The house later became a charming rental property. Sunk costs may be irrelevant, yet the asset had sufficient value to sink more time and money into the project. Short-term economics often drive marginal decisions into long-term commitments.

We make decisions on the margin every day, collapsing future variables into choices sunk in the past. By acknowledging sunk costs and consciously considering our choices on the margin, we can more easily detach from the past and focus directly on present opportunities.

Beyond Money

In economics, marginal reaction is exclusively a numbers game. For example, an automobile factory tooled to produce an outdated car must decide whether to partially retool to update the car, or to completely retool and produce a whole new car. Optionally, the factory could produce something other than cars. Investments already made in the factory are sunk costs. It may be cheaper to retool a little bit than a lot, but the critical factor is the expected additional costs and benefits of each enterprise from the current position. The company would crunch numbers and pursue whichever option seems to offer the best marginal reaction for the additional investment.

The real world is more complicated, since we must include non-monetary assets, income, and expenses into the equation. For example, having good business connections may lower initial costs of entering a particular enterprise. And some occupations, such as spraying pesticides, have health and environmental costs that should be factored in, even if the numbers look good on paper. Other options might offer a poor return financially, yet be very fulfilling at heart. The best choices maximize momentum towards our overall dreams and goals with the least total expense.

A high-paying job may be a quick fix for financial woes, but it not always the best choice. I walked away from nice job offers when I was broke and had bills to pay. I would have gained money while neglecting equally important goals, like raising a family and developing my writing. I have been successful because I stick to my goals, even when my choices seem to defy common sense to others.

Marginal reaction is helpful for comparing multiple potential courses of action, as illustrated in the Comparing Options figure. Note that the illustration does not include a time dimension. The time required to break even and turn a profit is vitally important to decision making. Sometimes an option with a short payback period, yet less income potential, is better than an option with a long payback period and greater income. Achieving a small, but quick return on an investment allows for reinvestment in other new opportunities.

And while some enterprises have high start-up costs to provide a steady income later, other options may have lower startup costs, yet more long-term costs. Determining the optimal marginal reaction for the effort is often an intuitive process.

As my own publisher, I choose how many books to print at one time. Large print runs cost more upfront, yet reduce the cost per book. If I pay out-of-pocket, I pay the cost of forgone opportunities while cash is tied up in inventory. What return could I get on alternative investments? If I use credit to print books, then I have to pay interest on the borrowed money. How long will it take to sell the books, and what could I do with my credit line if it were not tied up in inventory?

All possible choices lay on the margin until the moment of decision. Which choice or combination of choices will yield the greatest reaction for the investment? Keeping the whole goal in mind, including tangible and intangible factors, may be the most difficult part of decision-making process.

Positive Reaction

Marginal reaction helps guide incremental decisions where there is a point of diminishing returns and where the best solution is a combination of investments. However, it is easy to get caught up in numbers and miss the bigger picture.

For example, consider insulating an attic to make a home more energy efficient. The first layer of insulation conserves the most energy, and the savings on utilities helps recover the cost of installation. Each additional layer of insulation costs the same amount, yet contributes incrementally less toward energy efficiency. Marginal reaction reminds us to add only as much insulation as will recoup the investment within a reasonable amount of time. Adding more insulation does not bring a good return on the investment. Marginal reaction requires analyzing all available options to find the best action, or best combination of actions to help achieve one's combined goals.

If the goal is to make the house warmer with optimal profit in terms of a lower power bill, then we must consider each available technology to achieve the goal. Weather stripping doors and windows may bring a greater profit on the investment than insulating the attic. More likely, a combination of both weather-stripping and insulating will provide the greatest overall savings for the investment.

But following the math too closely leads a person astray from the broader vision. Back before it was economical to do so, I installed photovoltaic panels to run the meter backwards and zero out my utility bill. A green energy rebate helped offset much of the initial cost, yet my system still didn't pencil out as a sensible financial investment. However, producing my own power and running the meter backwards was immediately satisfying, and I've greatly enjoyed opening my utility bill ever since. Most of the time I pay only a $5/month meter fee, and I am always thrilled to pay it. Instead of marginal reaction, I invested in positive reaction. Installing solar panels met core goals for sustainability and was also richly educational. Moreover, investing early helped stimulate demand that has progressively lowered the cost of solar panels for everyone. All things considered, I received a great return on the investment, even if the numbers didn't add up.

Marginal reaction is helpful for detaching from sunk costs while evaluating the pros and cons of possible choices from the present situation. Just be careful to avoid getting caught up in the numbers game, and keep the bigger picture in mind. Sometimes a positive reaction is more valuable than a marginal reaction.

"It is difficult to begin without borrowing, but perhaps it is the most generous course thus to permit your fellow-men to have an interest in your enterprise."

—Henry David Thoreau,
Walden (1854)[103]

Credit
Calories to Start On

Every person's garden is unique. A small corner plot and some hand tools may suffice to raise calories to trade for essential goods and services. More acreage requires a higher level of commitment and possibly intermittent use of a small tractor, yet yields a bigger harvest. Five hundred acres is serious business that may require big machines to reap the harvest. Some people neither have nor want a garden plot of their own, preferring other work in exchange for calories. Everyone's situation is unique, as are each person's dreams and goals. Success entails divining the most optimal path from vision to reality.

A corner plot may be adequate if calories are invested towards paying off debts and reducing monthly bills. A big dream may require expanding the garden to grow more calories. The safe route for expansion is to reinvest some calories from each harvest, slowly expanding production capability without going into debt. A faster and riskier path to expansion is to borrow calories to invest in a bigger farm and plant a bigger crop while strategizing to pay back borrowed calories plus interest. Expanding the farm may require more work, at least initially, yet also brings greater potential rewards.

Stepping Up

Living in an industrialized country, it is easy to fritter away $50 or $100 without much thought. Yet, that can be a life-changing fortune to millions of people who scrape by from meal to meal. Without goods or services to trade there is no way to enter the economic ecosystem and break the cycle of poverty. Every day is a new challenge to survive.

In 1976 an economics professor in Bangladesh initiated a bold experiment. Muhammad Yunus offered small loans averaging just $67 to those in need, especially women with children who were strongly motivated to improve their lives. The average annual income in Bangladesh was $150 at the time, and over half of the population qualified as poor, owning no more than a half-acre of land. A loan of $67 wasn't much money, even when adjusted for inflation, yet it enabled poor people to enter the economy and reliably keep the family fed and sheltered. It was enough to start over 500 different small businesses, including growing crops, agricultural processing, sewing, weaving, garbage collecting, vending, shoemaking, blacksmithing, carpentry, fishing, crafts, leatherwork, food preparation, and vehicle repair. A basic hammer, saw, and tape measure is enough to empower impoverished individuals to enter the local economy and earn a living.

Muhammad Yunus' loan experiment was so successful that he expanded the program to form Grameen Bank. Through the bank, people apply for loans at interest rates of 1 to 4% per month versus 10 to 20% typical of high-risk loans. The bank was so successful that by 1987 it grew to more than 400 branches throughout Bangladesh, serving 8,000 villages.[104] By 2017, the bank had 2,600 branches and nine million borrowers, 97% of them women, with an astounding 99.6% repayment rate.[105]

Loan applicants are not required to read or write, and there is no collateral lien requirement. To apply for a loan, fifty people of the same sex must form a support network in groups of five. With the aid of bank personnel, they cooperatively evaluate the strength of each loan request. When an agreement is reached, loan money is given to two of the five members of each support group. After six weeks, if repayments have been made on schedule, the next two members of each support group will be provided loans. Six weeks later the fifth person in each group gets their loan. Those who borrow are required to save a few cents per week into a special bank account, which is then used to make new loans. As a result, the borrowers own 95% of the bank.

Grameen Bank has been so successful that similar programs have started in many other impoverished regions of the world, including America's inner cities. As of 2017, Grameen America has 20 branches in the U.S., providing loans to 95,000 low-income customers.[106]

Leaping Forward

Growing a business entails a degree of gambling. When we plant a crop we gamble that the weather will be favorable and our crops will mature. The economy, like Mother Nature, is not very forgiving. Americans start about 400,000 new businesses every year, and 350,000 of them succumb before the first year is out. Few of the remaining businesses ever become truly successful.[107] Many achieve minimal sustainability and still require years to turn a profit. Your first business may fail too, and that is okay, because that is often a part of the process of moving forward.

Try, try, and try again. It is a familiar theme among motivational speakers. Many millionaires started with multiple business failures before achieving success. Often, they bounced back and forth multiple times between success and failure, making millions, then losing everything and filing bankruptcy before trying again. You may not desire to be rich, but it is still important for business management to understand how individuals jump from rags to riches.

A business may grow slowly and steadily to success without ever becoming a big business. A farmer with a small plot of land could plow incremental profits back into land acquisitions to slowly grow the business. Or the farmer might obtain a large loan to invest in a big farm, big equipment, and big production.

Big debt comes with big risk. The farm must produce at maximum capacity to pay bills and fend off the debt collector. Outside factors, such as flood or drought or low commodity prices, can sink an indebted farm at any time. If successful, however, bountiful harvests could pay off all debts and provide a sizeable income for years to come.

The main problem with the yo-yo route to success, making millions and losing it again, is that the borrowed money belongs to somebody. People loan or invest money because they believe and hope to share in the profits of success. But what happens to them if the business fails?

Sadly, many enterprises are little more than investment scams created to bilk people out of life savings. Promoting gold mines is a classic example. Gold is abundant in the Tobacco Root Mountains near my home, yet scattered in small pockets that seem promising, but don't amount to much. Our local history includes 150 years of gold scams, investment schemes that spent people's money, contaminated the environment, and went bankrupt.

When I moved to Pony in 1989, the Chicago Mining Company was buying up old mining claims. They built a cyanide vat-leach mill site on the hill above town to process gold ore, plus a plastic-lined tailings impoundment to contain toxic mining waste "forever." Looking at the scheme on paper, they had a promising operation with scores of mining claims to feed the mill and produce a wealth of gold to benefit their investors. In actuality, the gold didn't matter, so long as they could sell the operation to gullible investors and walk away with a wad of paper dollars.

The community was split between proponents who worked for the company and opponents who were concerned about contaminating the groundwater. The project moved forward through state approval and construction despite obvious flaws. The tailings impoundment leaked cyanide into the groundwater the first time it was used. The company went bankrupt due to its own ineptitude, and taxpayers paid $700,000 to minimally clean up the site. Investors lost their money, and thirty years later, the town is still plagued by invasive weed problems emanating from unreclaimed ground. And since the mill building was never torn down, bits of fiberglass insulation are blown all over town every time the wind blows.

Business ventures and personal endeavors should aim high and profit by making the world better, not worse.

One way to help insure success is to start small. Every great idea entails a learning curve to work out the bugs and refine the vision. Growing peaches in Montana might seem like a great idea, but try a test plot first with a number of varieties. Plant an acre of peaches. That way you can absorb the loss if and when the trees freeze and die. That is preferable to planting and losing a thousand acres of peaches and defaulting on a loan.

I had a big dream to start a house construction company and build hundreds of stone houses. Stone houses are real, solid, and long-lasting, unlike conventional frame construction. We built our own home mortgage-free, then borrowed money and built another stone house on speculation. Most of the work we did ourselves, so there was little financial risk, just a lot of labor. I planned to build one house that year, two houses the next year, doubling the enterprise every year. However, it quickly became evident that stone masonry was too labor intensive to mass-produce houses.

I continued researching and experimenting with alternative building methods towards the dream of eventually mass-producing quality, high-efficiency homes. I helped my brother build a tilt-up stone house, in which stone walls were poured flat on the ground, then lifted into place with a crane. It is a great method and readily applicable to mass-production, although more suitable for high-end homes, while I would prefer to market affordable family homes.

I still explore construction techniques for building efficient homes with stone masonry or other materials. Prototyping is slow, because each time requires rethinking house construction from the ground up. My current thoughts include using a re-useable form to cast foam domes that can be connected together to form each room of the house. Fortunately, other people are leaping forward with plans to mass-produce affordable 3D printed houses, which is probably a better process than casting the parts in moulds.

I encourage thoughtfulness and experimentation in launching your own business. Take time to build a solid foundation. A good foundation will support a sizable enterprise later on, while a hastily built foundation might bring your dream to the ground just when you were finishing the roof.

Caution with Credit

A hunter-gatherer must expend calories to walk to and harvest a food supply. A farmer must also expend calories to harvest calories. He must till the field, purchase seed, and plant it. Your harvest will similarly require a start-up investment, and like the farmer, probably a substantial calorie input to get the ball rolling.

Some entrepreneurs are fortunate to have surplus calories from savings or inheritance to invest. Being your own banker makes everything easier. For most people, however, calories are scarce, which may be a primary motivation for launching a business. Lacking a surplus, outside financing becomes a necessity.

Credit can be a powerful tool, yet dangerous when used poorly. Lacking experience, young people can get into serious trouble when they discover credit. They spend money without first earning it, and before long they are committed to monthly payments on a car, television, and credit cards to boot. Credit is beneficial when invested in production and problematic when spent on consumption.

As noted by Paul Hawken in his book *The Next Economy*, oil is more valuable to a poor person than a rich person. A poor person buys gas for a tractor to increase his income. A rich person consumes gas running to the grocery store, decreasing income.[108]

Gas consists of calories of energy, and money is a token that represents calories. When borrowing money to buy gas, the gas should be applied to increase production. Consumer debt is counter-productive, while producer or business debt is often a good investment. A home equity loan is a poor method of financing a vacation, but a good way to finance a sound business plan.

Paying cash to build our home took much longer than building on credit, but probably cost much less. Working on a lean budget and buying materials one paycheck at a time incentivized a conservative approach. We calculated lumber orders down to inches with little waste, and we salvaged old lumber and make do with the resources at hand.

Keep your Dreams clearly in mind, and you will successfully manage credit and other resources to transform those dreams into reality.

Sources of Credit Capital

<u>Family</u>: Families are great sources of financial and moral support as well as a minefield of potential problems. Parents, children, siblings, cousins, or aunts and uncles are possible sources of start-up loans or investment dollars. On the other hand, there may be spoken or unspoken strings attached to family dollars, leading to a sense of entitlement in decision making and profit sharing. Also consider what happens if the business goes belly-up.

Borrowing from family members adds substantial risk, because there is potential to lose much more than money. Family relationships must come first, so be certain of your business venture and equally sure the loan can be repaid, even if the business fails.

As a young man without a reliable income, I needed my mother's signature to obtain a bank loan to purchase land and build a stone house for sale. In the truest sense of the word, we built on speculation, because my partner and I had little credibility to launch a construction business. However, I was confident about the venture because we were not contracting anything out, and we borrowed double the amount we spent on our own home. In the worst-case scenario, the project might have strung along for several years, eating up profits with interest payments on the loan. Fortunately we completed the house and sold it within a year, which wasn't too bad for stone house construction.

<u>Partnerships</u>: Partnerships entail pooling resources with one or more other people. Ideally, everyone shares the vision, rewards, work, and risk. Working as a team on multiple fronts can enable rapid advancement towards a common goal. Conversely, partnerships become a liability if hampered by poor communication, incompatible work ethics, or conflicting goals. A team working together towards a common vision is a powerful force, while a team working towards slightly different visions can be a disaster.

<u>Credit Cards</u>: Credit cards are shockingly easy to obtain. Obtaining one credit card helps build one's credit rating to obtain another. Credit companies accessing credit records and send "pre-approved" credit

applications, so within a few years it is possible to accumulate a dozen different credit cards with $100,000 credit to apply at your discretion. Banks are astonishingly loose about issuing credit cards. They evidently rake in enough profit to cover losses from the few individuals who default on payments.

Paying short-term interest on credit card debt may be justifiable for a business investment, if the business expands rapidly enough to produce a sufficient return to pay off the debt plus interest and still make a worthwhile profit. Unfortunately, accumulating +/- 20% interest on the debt can rapidly erode potential profits.

Credit cards are notorious for usurious interest rates, which are best avoided. Fortunately, many credit cards offer promotional low interest rates for six to eighteen months. I used to bounced debt from card to card for book printing projects, frequently paying 0% interest for the loans. Nowadays, credit cards typically offer a choice between a low interest rate, such as 0% for twelve months or 2.99% for eighteen months. It seems like a good deal, except for the +/- 4% transaction fee, which is basically the same as charging 4% interest for a year. A missed payment allows the bank to revoke the low interest offer and charge normal rates, typically 17 to 21% interest. And it's important to pay the debt or transfer it to another card before the offer expires.

Consumer debt is best avoided except in special circumstances. Credit cards are convenient for consumer purchases if paid off each month without incurring interest fees. Credit cards are useful to buy time, too. We lived on credit cards for a few months while waiting to sell the house we built on speculation. Holding title to the completed house was like having money in the bank, just not as liquid. When the spec house sold we immediately paid off all debts.

Banks: Banks are surprisingly difficult sources for loans. The vetting system is counter-intuitive, considering that credit card companies (banks) give substantive credit to nearly everyone, while brick and mortar institutions typically won't lend money unless the applicant already has sufficient income to pay it off.

Applicants must complete a thorough financial statement and provide tax returns to show proof of income. It is a chicken-and-the-egg problem for an entrepreneur wanting to borrow money to launch or expand a business. The bank wants proof of income before loaning funds to generate an income. If that income doesn't exist, this it may be necessary to find a willing co-signer who has sufficient income to guarantee the loan.

All banks play by similar rules. However, there are exceptions, and it can be productive to try multiple banks in the quest for a loan. A former neighbor graduated from college with a masters degree in business administration (MBA). Jim was a ski bum, owning little more than his truck and ski equipment. On one outing he visited a local hot springs and fell in love with the place. The property was for sale, so Jim spent six months writing up a comprehensive business plan. Bank after bank laughed him out the door when he tried to apply for a $1 million loan with no assets and no income. However, one small town banker was impressed by his gumption, commitment, and detailed planning. The banker approved the loan and Jim bought the hot springs. He operated the business for seven years, often struggling to pay bills and keep the enterprise afloat, but never defaulted. He eventually sold the property for twice what he bought it for.

Loan requirements became more stringent after the Great Recession of 2008. Nevertheless, it is still helpful to shop around if one bank denies a loan. I've had an account at the same bank my entire adult life, and it is nice to be recognized when I walk in the door. Unfortunately, I was denied a loan to buy a twenty-one acre parcel for my Green University® LLC program while in the midst of divorce. However, the seller's bank allowed me to assume the existing mortgage because the seller was struggling to make monthly payments. If there is a will, there is a way. Keep trying until you find a workable solution.

SBA Loans and Grants: The Small Business Administration does not accept, process, or administer loans. Instead, the SBA provides guidelines to authorized banks to issue low-fee commercial loans that are partially guaranteed by the federal government. SBA lenders review, approve, and administer loans on behalf of the agency. The government is at risk if a business defaults on a loan, but so is the bank. The government covers only a portion of the loss if a loan is defaulted, while the bank absorbs the remaining loss.

Also, the SBA does not offer business start-up or expansion grants. However, there are grant opportunities coordinated through the SBA for research, innovation, and development costs for specific goals identified by federal agencies. These Small Business Innovation Research (SBIR) and Small Business Technology Transfer (STTR) programs, also known as America's Seed Fund, are one of the largest sources of early-stage capital for technology commercialization in the U.S. See the SBA website for additional details on grants and loans: www.sba.gov.

Grants: Grants funding is available from many private foundations and a few government programs. Most grant funding is oriented towards schools, local governments, and registered 501(c)3 nonprofit organizations to benefit people or the environment. If your business plan benefits social or environmental causes, then consider establishing a nonprofit. For example, a recycling business could organize as a nonprofit, becoming eligible to apply for grant funds. Instead of pocketing profits directly, the director and other employees can be paid a salary, which is essentially the same thing.

In my experience, there is a substantial bureaucracy cost involved in setting up and maintaining nonprofit organizations. We originally established the Jefferson River Canoe Trail as a 501(c)3 nonprofit, which required a great deal of work that could have been applied more directly to the Canoe Trail vision. The IRS later ruled that we were a private foundation instead of a publicly supported charity because I was the primary donor in the early days of the organization. To reduce red tape, we abandoned the filing and re-organized as a chapter of the Lewis and Clark Trail Heritage Foundation, riding on the 501(c)3 of the parent organization. That reduced our paperwork substantially and still gave us legitimate nonprofit status.

The Jefferson River Canoe Trail could do large fundraisers and apply for operating grants to pay board members who do most of the work. Thus far, we have preferred to run it as an all-volunteer organization. We've applied for and received a number of separate grants including $1,200 + $1,300 + $800 + $2,500 + $5,000 for printing maps and brochures, plus $45,000 to facilitate acquisition of a 4.7-acre property for a public float-in campsite and walk-in fishing access along the Jefferson River. Most recently, we raised $270,000 in grants and donations to acquire an additional 30-acre riverside campsite and fishing access site for the public.

Some grants are available to for-profit businesses as well, especially for business development projects in impoverished regions. In addition, a for-profit business can assist customers in applying for grants to purchase their services.

For example, I teach ancestral wilderness survival and nature skills to public school kids through Outdoor Wilderness Living School, LLC (OWLS). I could have established OWLS as a nonprofit organization to qualify for grant funding and fundraisers. However, going the nonprofit route would require a board of directors, meetings, elections, membership drives, and fundraisers, plus substantial paperwork with the IRS to establish and maintain 501(c)3 status.

For simplicity, I chose the for-profit route. However, we often work with public schools, and they are eligible for grant funding. Therefore, I link schools with the grant sources, so they apply for funds for students to attend OWLS field trips. Last year, the business was supported in part by $3,500 in grant funds secured by the schools.

I have also received small grants for fencing materials related to weed projects in my community. In addition, I received an $11,000 grant through the power company to subsidize solar panel installation on my home back in 2002 as part of a residential solar energy demonstration program. The demonstration program was a means of introducing solar in the community through early adopters. Artificially stimulating demand helps bring down the cost for others.

Some grant sources are easier to work with than others. Large grants typically require more paperwork than small grants. Some applications require days or weeks of work to complete all the steps, while other grants can be completed within an hour or two. Government grants often require substantial paperwork, while private foundations are more casual.

If your nonprofit or for-profit enterprise has been founded to make the world a better place, then there are probably grant funds to support the effort. Finding suitable grant sources requires a bit of internet sleuthing and likely requires phone calls to people with similar interests to get pointed in the right direction. I've developed a list of grant sources applicable to my various endeavors, adding and subtracting from the list over time.

Grant funding isn't free, because it requires calories of effort to submit a quality grant application. Winning a grant generally entails significant additional work that must be completed to ensure proper use of the funds. However, it is a win-win situation if the grant award pays for a project you are passionate about.

Creative Financing: There is no limit to unique and creative financing strategies. Real Goods, a company selling environmental and energy products, borrowed money from customers. They included a blurb in their mail order catalog seeking to borrow funds for two and three years at 10% interest. They borrowed twice from customers, once for $150,000 and again for $100,000. They were flooded with money from established clientele. The company had to return excess checks.[109]

The Earthwise store in Virginia raised start-up capital by soliciting money from friends, relatives, and acquaintances. They asked for $100 from each person to stock the business. For each $100 received, they issued a certificate for $120 worth of merchandise, redeemable 90 days after the store opened. That is a good deal both ways, since stores purchase goods wholesale at a 40 to 50% discount off the retail price. A $100 loan would buy up to $150 in wholesale merchandise. The consumer gained $20 in savings as lender, while the store pocketed up to $30 profit as the borrower.[110]

Crowdfunding: The Internet and social media enabled the rise of crowdfunding, which people have successfully used to raise cash for everything from product development to paying off medical bills or personal educational travel. Crowdfunding can be an excellent means to finance upfront costs for bringing a new product to market. For example, a publisher might spend $20,000 to $40,0000 printing a new book, then begin a marketing campaign to find customers. Crowdfunding seeks customers first, often raising enough cash to pay the print cost ahead of printing. For example, Paul Wheaton of Wheaton Labs crowdfunded a permaculture deck of cards, seeking $18,500 to finance the print cost. Enthusiastic supporters pledged $70,000 to the project, greatly increasing the initial print run beyond expectations.[111]

That doesn't make crowdfunding a slam-dunk for easy money. A good crowdfunding campaign requires a good product and great marketing. Wheaton runs the permies.com permaculture forum and has other email contacts adding up to tens of thousands of people. He is widely connected throughout the permaculture community, making it easy to reach thousands of potential customers.

A successful crowdfunding campaign can require hundreds of hours to fine tune the sales pitch, produce professional photographs and videos, gather contacts, and strategize to get people excited enough to pledge real dollars. A $50,000 fundraising campaign can pencil out to minimum wage for all the hours invested. Nevertheless, a marketing campaign is a necessary part of any new endeavor. The big difference is that crowdfunding sells the product before the bill comes due.

Part V
Turning Dreams into Reality

"Do what you love. Know your own bone; gnaw at it, bury it, unearth it, and gnaw it still. Do not be too moral. You may cheat yourself out of much life so. Aim above morality. Be not simply good—be good for something."

—Henry David Thoreau,
Letters to Harrison Blake (1848)[1]

Freedom to Bloom
Transcending Invisible Walls

What do you want to be when you grow up? A fireman? Policeman? Teacher? Veterinarian? Doctor? Lawyer? President? This was the standard menu of options when I was a child. Younger generations have a longer, more diverse list, but either way, it is still a list. What seems like free choice is merely multiple choice. Moreover, the choices are slowly whittled away by parents, teachers, peers, and culture. Be practical. Do this. Don't do that. You should go to school. Jump through these hoops and good opportunities await you. Get this degree and take that job to earn a good salary. Now sit and shake your paw, and you'll get a treat.

Whatever dreams people had as children are filtered away through shoulds and should-nots until they lose a grasp inherent interests and vision. We condition our children to choose something from the menu. The infinity of human potential is reduced to a single word or title. "I am a plumber." Our title becomes our purpose, existence, and identity. "I am a public relations specialist." What do you want to be? Why can't we just be ourselves?

Each of us owns freedom to create our own path in life, yet few people actually do. Cultural conditioning becomes an invisible prison. Many young people who attend Green University® LLC complain about "the system," blaming society for limiting their freedoms while bound by invisible walls within themselves.

I grew up in Montana before the era of No Trespassing signs. A person could climb over fences and roam the open countryside largely oblivious to differences between private and public lands. At the age of twenty, my partner and I walked 500 miles across Montana as if there were no boundaries. In comparison, I've had out-of-state students who acted confined to my property while living within walking distance of 100,000 acres of public land. They were free to wander and explore yet didn't leave the property. Spend enough time in an imaginary prison and it becomes one's permanent cage.

Whatever the situation, we need not be limited by what lay behind. The narrow margin between the past and future is full of possibilities and potential. From this moment, we are free to dream, free to choose, free to bloom, free to shatter all imaginary walls and shackles, and free to pursue our own path in life. If that path has become confused and vague, let's create anew, constructing a course forward from the current vantage point.

Beyond Money

People often dream of making millions. Yet, money itself is neither a dream nor a goal. Money is only a token that represents calories of energy. It doesn't have value until traded away for real goods and services. If we dream of being rich, it isn't the money we want, it is the goods and services that money can potentially buy. For example, many people dream of being rich enough to travel the world. Yet, rich people often lack time, unable to travel more than a few weeks per year. On the other hand, young people often travel for months or years with little cash. Some work along the way, immersing in communities in a deeply experiential way. If travel is the dream, then focus directly on the dream, and you will succeed.

Many people dream of being rich enough to travel the world, yet rich people often lack time, unable to travel more than a few weeks per year.

Money drives decision-making and life choices for most people. Consider, is the decision to become a mechanic or electrician a dream or a financial choice? Does an entrepreneur sell water softeners because it is the fruition of a childhood dream?

Few people actually follow their hopes and dreams. Instead, people pursue money, conditioned to believe money is the path to achieving dreams. In business, entrepreneurs are coached to ask, "What does the customer want?" In writing, authors are coached to ask, "What does the reader want?" Millions of people are employed providing products and services they think other people might want, rather than asking, "What do I want? What is meaningful to me?"

I believe people are most successful when pouring energy into endeavors that really matter at a deeply personal level. The more personal the investment, the greater the potential for success. For example, I wrote *Botany in a Day: The Patterns Method of Plant Identification* to answer my own questions about plant identification and herbal properties. I rejected publisher recommendations to "improve" the book and decided to publish it myself according to my own vision. Customer needs were considered, yet only secondary to my vision. I wrote the book I wanted to read, which coincidentally proved useful to other people. Through gradual improvements, multiple editions, and multiple print runs, I have sold 100,000 copies of the book.

I've seen other authors crank out plant books on contract to minimally satisfy publisher demands and cash a paycheck. A publisher with a nationwide nature series might contract with a writer to produce a field guide to Mississippi plants, even if the author has never set foot in the state. The final product might sell by the cover photo and title, while the content lacks quality or authenticity. The author may be qualified to produce excellent material in their area of expertise. Instead, they consume precious natural resources for a product that doesn't provide the customer full value for the purchase. That doesn't help anyone, and it doesn't make a best-selling book. Similarly, the World Wide Web is cluttered with poorly written or copy-and-paste blogs and articles whose primary purpose is to serve as click-bait for advertising and affiliate marketing without providing any substantive content.

Money potential is an important factor in decision-making as a secondary consideration, not a primary driver. Anyone passionate about restoring and maintaining old buildings might buy and renovate fixer-uppers to flip for profit or to retain as rental units, establishing a steady, passive income. Renovation work is the passion, while money is the secondary consideration that makes the work financially sustainable.

The endeavor is less likely to succeed if passive monthly income is the goal, and fixer-up rentals are perceived as the solution. However, a spare bedroom or spare house can reasonably be evaluated for supplementary rental income potential. The additional income could contribute towards realizing one's true hopes and dreams without becoming entrenched in an all-out detour in the opposite direction.

We are so culturally conditioned to follow any path but our own that it becomes challenging to imagine or believe it is possible to live one's own hopes and dreams. If that sounds familiar, try planning yearly vacations first.

Throughout my adult life, that has been a consistent policy in my annual planning. Vacation adventures went on the calendar first, scheduling work in afterwards. These were not high-dollar vacations since I've always lived within my means. A vacation might entail an extended canoe trip in Montana or backpacking in the canyons of southern Utah. Adventures are plotted on the calendar at optimal times of year, leaving plenty of months and weeks left for work.

My vacations have become increasingly elaborate, including five weeks in New Zealand, four weeks in Italy, and three weeks in Sweden over three subsequent years. I avoid traveling during holidays when airline tickets are expensive and sites are crowded. By being flexible in terms of dates and duration, it isn't difficult to find round-trip tickets to Europe for less than $500. Travel from Montana is still expensive, so I often drive 800 miles to Las Vegas for international flights. February is my favorite travel month, frigid at home, yet moderate and rarely busy elsewhere. I pepper the calendar with a mix of travel and adventure plans: canoeing, camping, and wild food harvesting outings, leaving more or less time for work, depending on my work objectives for the year. Prioritizing vacations is a giant step towards staying focused on living your own hopes, dreams, and goals.

That Four-Letter Word

What is your goal? Is that an intimidating question? Is your mind drawing a blank? Defining a goal or goals is an uncomfortable subject for many people. Some people think they don't have goals or don't want to commit to them. But more often than not, people lack a mental file labeled "goals." Defining goals is rarely taught at home or in school. However, we all have hopes and dreams, even if they are not fully defined as goals. Our hopes and dreams embody all that is meaningful to us, engendering a warm, fuzzy feeling about the potential for a better tomorrow. Hopes and dreams include our personal aspirations and best wishes to friends and family members. Hopes and dreams represent life in the ideal world.

Instead of retrieving the entire file in detail, our brain shortens the sequence. We access a file labeled "hopes and dreams." If it is a pleasing file, which it should be, then our brains give us a minute dose of elation. Goals, on the other hand, tend to be more complicated, implying a left-brained, logic-driven, step-by-step plan for success. Hopes and dreams are uplifting and motivating, while goals are daunting and stressful, implying commitment, accountability, and potential failure. To ensure success, let's de-emphasize goals and focus on hopes and dreams.

One of the greatest challenges to achieving hopes and dreams is to bring them into focus. Hopes and dreams are often vaguely defined. Success requires crystalizing them into a well-defined vision. A clear vision can then be divided into specific project goals to tackle one step at a time.

Defining a vision can be more challenging than actually achieving it. For me, inspiration comes with dreams that seem visionary, yet may require years of refinement before coming to fruition. For instance, I launched a nonprofit organization called 3Rivers Park to focus on conservation and recreation on the local Gallatin, Madison, and Jefferson rivers that make up the Missouri River Headwaters. A couple years later, our working group dropped the Gallatin and Madison rivers to focus on the Jefferson River, which is part of the Lewis and Clark National Historic Trail. We renamed the organization the Jefferson River Canoe Trail Association, using the Lewis and Clark theme to focus on purchasing suitable campsites for river paddlers. We later dropped our independent 501(c)3 status to become a Chapter of the Lewis and Clark Trail Heritage Foundation. Years later, we are discussing simplifying our name to the Jefferson River Chapter of LCTHF. Meanwhile, I foresee possibly expanding the canoe trail vision beyond the Jefferson, upstream along the Beaverhead River and downstream along the Missouri, with the potential to create a national water trail from here to St. Louis. The evolving vision is related yet distinctly different from the original idea to create a regional park.

Similarly, my initial vision to create a school took fifteen years to evolve from Hollowtop Outdoor Primitive School LLC into Green University® LLC and Outdoor Wilderness Living School LLC (OWLS). Through years of additional refinement, Green University® LLC coalesced seemingly disparate ideas about wilderness survival and sustainable living into a four-level program. Instead of freshman, sophomore, junior, and senior grades, we have hunter-gatherer, homesteader, caretaker, and ecopreneur. I've invested nearly three decades in envisioning and launching this school as a secondary project to my writing and publishing career. I've spent most of my life crystalizing the dream. When the vision is right, the school will bloom.

Other people may be more skilled at crystalizing dreams into vision at the beginning of the process, either individually or in focus groups. Certainly, the more time spent reflecting on and evaluating a dream, the more readily it will coalesce into reality. Define the dream and broadcast it to the universe with all your heart and soul. From there, a good vision will take on a life of its own.

Tortoise vs. Hare

Our culture is very action-oriented to make things happen. Call it bulldozer mentality. Sometimes it is necessary to plow into a job to get results. I recall working on my house and feeling so overwhelmed by the totality of the vision that I sat down and looked up at the roofless sky for hours. At last, I would berate myself for not getting anything done, then fly into a working frenzy. Attacking the problem can be an effective way to energize the effort and get the ball rolling.

Conversely, the bulldozer approach can lay waste to the world, consuming resources, time, and energy on a poorly defined vision. This is one reason so many businesses fail so quickly. Entrepreneurs invest everything all at once to launch a business, rent office space, buy furniture and computers, advertise, and hire employees. But, without a fully crystalized vision, a business doesn't quite take off or loses

Green University® LLC operates on a twenty-acre riverfront campus for now, with the potential to become a significant accredited college.

direction, and the entrepreneur soon burns through investment money and personal energy. The business folds, and the investment is wasted. Through experience I have learned that most powerful tool is the vision. When the vision coalesces, the rest will fall into place.

I envision eventually scaling Green University® LLC up to become a significant accredited alternative college. I've imagined buying a nearby abandoned orphanage as a college campus. At least $2 million is necessary to purchase the property, and its buildings would need renovation, work that could be contracted out or performed by students as educational experience. The college would need to hire full-time staff, develop classes, a curriculum and standards, and conduct a marketing campaign for student enrollment to make the enterprise fiscally sustainable. Cumulatively, it is a large, even daunting project, although totally reasonable and achievable. In other words, I can see the end goal. I just need to plot a course to get there.

As of this writing, Green University® LLC operates on a twenty-acre riverfront field camp with wickiups and an earthlodge for student housing. We do not have a full-time staff, although experienced students mentor incoming students, making the program sustainable on a shoestring budget. We have gradually improved the infrastructure so that the camp is progressively more comfortable through our long Montana winters. Each year we expand the number of classes and events, and soon we will explore the feasibility of offering credit for some classes in conjunction with local universities. These are good half steps towards becoming accredited. Once accredited, prospective students could apply for student financing or attend with funding from the G.I. Bill for veterans.

I could plow into the dream of Green University® LLC like a bulldozer and make it happen. However, I still have books to write and trips to take. I plan to spend six months canoeing 2,500 miles down the Missouri River from its origin at Three Forks, Montana to its confluence with the Mississippi at St. Louis. So, I'm content to nudge Green University® LLC forward a little at a time for now, until the time is ripe for the final push. Call it a Tortoise and Hare philosophy. Rather than burn up personal energy running full tilt, I'll methodically refine the vision, taking many small steps towards the end goal. I expect to be near the finish line by the time I begin the final sprint.

Whatever your ambitions, the most essential step is to define the vision to crystallize your hopes and dreams into reality.

"If one advances confidently in the direction of his dreams, and endeavors to live the life which he has imagined, he will meet with a success unexpected in common hours. He will put some things behind, will pass an invisible boundary; new, universal, and more liberal laws will begin to establish themselves around and within him; or the old laws be expanded, and interpreted in his favor in a more liberal sense, and he will live with the license of a higher order of beings. In proportion as he simplifies his life, the laws of the universe will appear less complex, and solitude will not be solitude, nor poverty poverty, nor weakness weakness. If you have built castles in the air, your work need not be lost; that is where they should be. Now put the foundations under them."

—Henry David Thoreau,
Walden (1854)[2]

Crystalizing the Dream
Creating Your Personal Vision

Launching a green business is a laudable dream. Earn a profit while making the world a better place. Looking for ideas? Try bulldozing virgin elk habitat to build eco-friendly houses. Consider an ecotourism enterprise to bring hotels, roads, and sustainable revenue to the last uncontacted tribes in the Amazon. Obliterate critical habitat for Mohave desert turtles to install ten square miles of solar panels. Many so-called green businesses do more harm than good.

Great dreams require a system of checks-and-balances to ensure that endeavors are not conflicted and self-defeating. In shorthand, this means that any dream or action must simultaneously achieve three interconnected criteria:

a) desirable quality of life,
b) economic prosperity
c) ecological sustainability

I developed this three-part "litmus test" as a means of testing ideas for "saving the world." Swamp filters, for example, provide a good green alternative to chemical sewage treatment facilities for cleansing wastewater. Swamp filters include cattails, hyacinths, and other swamp plants, along with microbes on their roots to extract nutrients and contaminants from effluent. Swamp filters look like natural swamps and provide wildlife habitat and even parklands for people while cleaning water more effectively at less cost than conventional chemical treatment systems. Swamp filters pass the three-part litmus test as a win-win-win solution, except where real estate is expensive, since swamp filters require more acreage than other sewage facilities.

The litmus test provides a quick and easy means to screen out whacky ideas proposed by myself, friends, colleagues, business people, and politicians. An idea might initially seem attractive for one reason, yet fail to pass all three criteria. People are easily led astray chasing dollars by unsustainable means that ultimately diminish quality of life individually or collectively. Manufacturing and selling fidget toys like spinners, for instance, makes money for some individuals by consuming and disposing of precious natural resources, which is unsustainable and ultimately threatens the viability of civilization for all.

In 1988, Allan Savory published his book *Holistic Resource Management*, which demonstrated how land managers could heal desertified rangelands while doubling, tripling, or quadrupling livestock numbers. In terms of range management, the methodology met all three criteria of the litmus test. Moreover, the book included a comprehensive three-part holistic goals-setting process that included statements about quality of life, economic productivity, and long-term sustainability. Subsequent editions of the book were retitled *Holistic Management* to reflect broader applications beyond land management. The book not only passed the three-part litmus test; it offered an expanded version of my test. *Holistic Management* is a must-read for anyone working directly with the land or managing natural resources.[3]

The envisioning process outlined below is similar to that of *Holistic Management*, except that Savory's book focuses on the natural ecosystem, whereas *Green Prosperity* is oriented towards the economic ecosystem. Credit also goes to Charles Hobbs, author of *Time Power*, for defining self-unifying principles.

<u>Self-Unifying Principles:</u> What kind of person do you strive to be? How do you act towards yourself and others? Self-unifying principles are a personal code of behavior. It's pretty simple. Consider how you would like to be treated by other people. If you treat all other people as you like to be treated, then you already have a well-developed code of behavior.[4]

For example, my personal code of behavior is to *treat all people as equals and with respect. I aim to be a caring, compassionate, and honest person. I want to give loving support to my family, allowing my children to create and achieve their own unique personal visions. I want to strive for excellence and make a positive contribution to our local community and the world as a whole. I want to be responsible, while also retaining a high-level of personal freedom to do whatever I want. I seek to live with a feeling of peace in my heart. Yet, I will stand up when necessary to defend myself, my family, community, country, and the planet that sustains us all.*

I cannot claim to be consistently successful at implementing my idealized self-unifying principles. The dissolution of my marriage and family threw my life into a multiple-year tailspin. I realized that my overwhelming desire to avoid conflict had led me to compromise core beliefs in order to maintain peace within the family. Through loss and grief I learned how to stand up for myself, resulting in healthier relationships with friends and family, and I amended my code accordingly.

Even well disciplined people struggle to act with grace and dignity all the time. A written code of self-unifying principles provides a benchmark from which to measure progress. Define your own unifying principles and then refer to them frequently. Are you living as the person you strive to be? Which behaviors are consistent with your ideals? Which behaviors require monitoring and reflection to steer in a more positive direction? Clarifying and prioritizing values enables one to focus on specific issues and helps nurture behaviors that are congruent with beliefs.

If this package of reflection, writing, and monitoring does not suit your personality, try a more intuitive approach: Whom do you admire as a behavioral role model? It doesn't have to be a real person. Think of someone who handles life situations most admirably. As a young adult, my principal role model was Captain Jean Luc Picard from *Star Trek: The Next Generation*. I admired his diplomacy, dedication, fairness, and nobility. Picard was my principal role model, the persona I strived to emulate. Role modeling his character helped make me more successful overall. Consider your own idealized role models. Study them well, and strive to match their best qualities.

<u>Quality of Life:</u> What are your hopes and dreams? What matters most in life? Do you dream of being alone, sleeping in dirty blankets under an overpass? Probably not. Quality of life is the ultimate goal, the warm and fuzzy dream we all want to be healthy and happy, surrounded by loving friends and family, living in a caring community in a healthy

world. Defining quality of life seems like stating the obvious, yet it is too often neglected as people chase the almighty dollar in the hopes that money can buy happiness.

People often disregard quality of life when making life choices. Individuals take high paying jobs merely for money, such as working with toxic chemicals in oil fields, disregarding basic quality of life issues. Corporations similarly chase profit at the expense of life, leaving a depleted, polluted planet for future generations. Corporations consist of people, and it seems strange and unfathomable that they or anyone would purposely degrade the planet for profit. How do such people face themselves in the mirror each day?

Quality of life gives purpose and meaning to all other actions. It is the goal behind all other goals, the vision we strive to live for. For example, *I desire a happy, healthy, and fun quality of life for myself and loved ones. I value a clean and beautiful home and landscape, with abundant wildlife habitat and nutritious homegrown food. I want to maintain a close relationship with nature. I value my freedom to set my own schedule and do whatever inspires me. I seek to have sufficient income to live comfortably and without worry. I value travel and adventure, and I seek to explore our amazing world. I value my community, both locally and globally, and wish for peace and prosperity for all people. I value the natural world and believe all species own the right to existence and quality of life.*

When doing an exercise like this, it is important to have a vision that extends beyond yourself to the broader community. Many personal values, such as peace and security, can only be achieved through collective effort. If you seek peace and security only for yourself, then you may decide to install bars on the windows, buy an arsenal of weaponry, move into a gated community, or hire a security guard. But, is that really peace or security? If your vision includes community, then work with neighbors to create a peaceful and secure environment for all, thus eliminating the need to fortify each home.

Similarly, many people move to Montana and buy small ranchettes because they value wide-open spaces. Unfortunately, each person wants the best piece. As a result, much of western Montana has been chopped up into twenty-acre tracts, degrading the open space everyone values. If each person instead valued space for the whole community, then they would locate within existing communities. People could continue migrating here, and there would still be open space for everyone to enjoy.

Action Statement: What do you want to do in life? Ski? Ride horses? Paint? Cook? Innovate? An Action Statement is a description of activities you would enjoy doing personally and professionally.

In terms of a career, an Action Statement is a description of what you might enjoy doing to produce the necessary income to support your Quality of Life. Actions should be fairly broad, such as "skiing," rather than a specific job such as "ski instructor." Ski instructor narrows the field of opportunities too much, and the income may be inadequate to meet your Quality of Life goal. "Skiing" on the other hand, is broad enough to encompass many possibilities, such as opening a ski shop, a ski-related manufacturing business, a ski touring company, or a thousand other options.

Write down any actions that come to mind, allowing for opportunities to blend interests and come up with something new. Make a word list and/or write a paragraph. For example, *I seek to produce a profit while making the world a better place for all through media, such as books and videos, as well as classes and other products. Specific interests and activities I enjoy include: primitive living, reading and writing, speaking, learning and teaching, photography and art, alternative technologies, traveling, quantum physics and spirituality, construction, politics, gardening and farming, space exploration, raising animals, and entrepreneurship.*

The Action Statement doesn't need to specify what you will do for a living. Start with broad categories of interests. The details will come later.

Description: When you have defined Self-Unifying Principles, a desirable Quality of Life, and Actions that excite you then start formulating a combined Description. The Description is the sum of the criteria from the first three statements.

For instance, consider a sampling of my own criteria. My Self-Unifying Principles includes values such as respect for others and inner peace. My desired Quality of Life includes personal freedom and a close relationship with the natural world. Actions that excite me include: Stone Age skills, writing, teaching, speaking, helping the earth, resourceful construction, doing art, and involvement in space.

Formulating a Description is a matter of meditating on possible avenues to meet most or all criteria. Having extensive criteria may seem excessively complicated, yet it actually helps clarify likely possibilities. For example, Stone Age skills is one interest, and teaching is a separate interest. Either is general, yet together they become specific. Adding other criteria only makes the description more specific. An interest in Stone Age living may seem entirely unrelated from sustainable building and construction, yet there was a measure of continuity in teaching *"primitive and contemporary living skills"* back when I founded my first survival school. Since then, the vision gradually evolved into

an increasingly cohesive message in which the *"Green University®
LLC Immersion program connects the dots from wilderness survival to
sustainable living in the modern world."*

How might you combine criteria to create a possible means
live personal hopes and dreams? Toss around some ideas. Don't be
shy. Wacky ideas are fine; anything counts at this point in the game.
Impractical ideas can be weeded out later. Starting an international
corporation may seem impossibly complex, yet many such corporations
exist so it is definitely possible. Flapping your arms and flying also sounds
impossible, but now there are wingsuits, jet packs, and hoverboards that
enable people to fly without an airplane.

In 1968, NASA contracted with Dr. George Land and Beth Jarman
to develop a creativity test to facilitate hiring the most creative engineers
and scientists. The test worked well for NASA, and since it was geared
towards creativity rather than knowledge or experience, they decided to
test it with children. Of the 1,600 five-year-old children initially tested,
98% were creative geniuses. Shocked by their findings, they followed
up on the test as the children matured. At ten years old only 30% of
the children still tested as geniuses, and by fifteen years old only 12%.
Applying the same test to 280,000 adults revealed that only 2% qualified
as creative geniuses. [5]

Researchers describe creativity as divergent thinking as opposed
to critical, convergent thinking. Divergent thinking goes outside the
bounds of normal solutions, while convergent thinking judges the
practicality of those ideas, narrowing options down to legitimate
possibilities.

As we mature, we encounter criticisms like, "That's not realistic.
That's impractical. What a dumb idea. That's impossible." When creative
ideas are immediately dismissed, our creativity is diminished, especially
when we internalize those criticisms and learn to censor ourselves.
Divergent and convergent thinking are both important, yet when fired
together, brain activity effectively slows down, and we become less
creative.[6] Therefore, it is important to allow yourself and your team
ample time for free-flowing creativity, holding off on critical evaluations
during the creative phase. Float along with your imagination and dream
freely. Each person must feel free to express ideas without being shot
down. Instead, try giving honorary rewards for the most outrageous
ideas to simulate out-of-the-box thinking. Every idea, no matter how
far-fetched, should be added to the list for consideration. The creative
process should facilitate the free flow of ideas. Later, re-assess as a realist
and rework your dreams to make them feasible.

The values and action criteria we listed for designing and building our home included low cost, low maintenance, durability, energy efficiency, water efficiency, fire resistance, earthquake resistance, natural feeling, and openness, to name a few. Writing a description to match all criteria required research. For example, we had to research energy-efficient construction, emphasizing low cost, low maintenance techniques. Subsequent research provided more specific criteria, suggesting that the house should be bermed with dirt on the north side, with most windows on the south side and a heat source in the middle.

As more criteria comes together, the sum of all criteria becomes a well-defined description. Criteria for our home may have exceeded a hundred specific points, many of them very precise, such as installing most windows on the south side, while positioning the kitchen sink with a window view, yet next to the wood cookstove, which had to be near the center of the house since it is also a heat source, which necessitated an open loft overhead to distribute heat throughout the house. We spent four years drawing house plans partly because we had specific criteria that required various versions years to meet all the criteria. We tried many combinations before arriving at an optimal floor plan.

The description goal is a summary of how to meet most or all the criteria. It may seem like extensive criteria could be cumbersome, since it took four years to draw our house plans but I disagree. Many owner builders don't consider their criteria adequately. Their project may be more expensive or more work than imagined, or they may not be satisfied with the final results. The same could be said of other businesses and projects that are started without considering all criteria. Taking time to meet essential criteria leads to greater satisfaction with the end product.

Again, try not to be critical of ideas that bubble to the surface, no matter how zany they might seem. Adults often skip the dreaming stage and start out as realists. Most houses, for example, are square and sterile, designed by adults who've been conditioned to see a house as a box. A child, on the other hand, might design a fantasy house of indoor forests and ponds, slides and swings, which is exciting, yet not wholly practical. Combining fantasy and reality, my house includes a large greenhouse as the entryway, with a stone tub-shower on one end and a path of steppingstones to the cellar on the other end. I grow orange trees and hibiscus in Montana and have a constant source of greens throughout the winter. There is even a rope swing in my house, hanging nineteen feet down from the ridgepole.

Hopefully, your own description goal will reflect both the imagination of a child and the realism of an adult. Whatever your project, be sure to check it against your holistic vision as well as the Testing Guidelines of the next chapter before swinging into action.

Potential Pitfalls

Be mindful of potential pitfalls to the envisioning process. Building a common vision with a team sounds like a great idea, and it works for some situations. Yet people often have wildly divergent dreams and goals of their own, and attempting to give people ownership of a dream that isn't theirs is inappropriate and will ultimately backfire. A more holistic approach is to acknowledge that people can share the same road to different destinations. One person has wheels; another offers the gas. A third person knows the terrain. The fourth brings lunch for all. People hop on and off at different points along the way, each contributing to the whole while gaining momentum towards their own unique personal destiny. Rather than trying to corral people into a single vision, try acknowledging that each person's path is unique and special. We each benefit for the time we are together.

The process outlined above is one approach to crystalizing hopes and dreams into a vision. There are other approaches to a similar outcome. Use whatever process feels right or consider hiring a life coach. If you already know what you want to do just make sure your vision includes a strong sense of values upon which to base future actions.

If you don't have a grand, encompassing vision yet, that's okay too. Keep your options open and continue to explore all life has to offer without committing to a specific life goal. Freedom is a value in itself and can be expressed as part of your Self-Unifying Principles and Quality of Life Statements. Define your values as clearly as possible, and the rest can wait.

Project Goals

By itself, a holistic goal is too broad to guide daily actions. It is therefore necessary to determine actionable project goals that contribute towards achieving the overall holistic goal. Every task undertaken, whether learning an instrument, starting a company, or baking bread, must be chunked down into individual steps. Playing "Mary had a Little Lamb" on the piano is an essential step before attempting Bach. Following through with exercises in this chapter establishes an outline for your personal symphony. Now learn each instrument and play each note. Small chunks facilitate success every step of the way.

It isn't necessary to immediately reduce an entire vision to chunks, and parts of the vision may remain amorphous or nebulous in the beginning. I find it helpful to work backwards from the grand vision, outlining steps that need to happen until I connect with my present situation.

In the case of Green University° LLC, I mentioned potentially buying the old orphanage for a college campus. I'd need to raise at least $2 million for the property acquisition, and considerably more for renovations. It is a considerable sum, yet less daunting after the experience of raising $270,000 in one year for a campsite on the Jefferson River Canoe Trail. Now I know it can be done.

Working backwards, possible avenues for fundraising include a) reform Green University° LLC as a nonprofit organization and seek funding through grants, donations, low-interest loans, and crowdfunding b) significantly expand marketing for my books to increase sales enough to buy the property with my personal income, c) explore a potential partnership with the current owner or seller, d) create a cooperative partnership with individuals who want to be personally involved, or e) seek other benefactors, partners, or venture capitalists to invest in the enterprise.

These are all valid routes, and I'm open to any possibility that may seem most opportune along the way. However, I am also well aware that forming a nonprofit organization, establishing a board of directors, and applying for grant funding would require hundreds of hours of meetings, planning, assessments, business proposals, sales pitches, and computer screen time. What would happen if I applied the same amount of effort towards marketing books to raise the necessary cash? As an author, it makes sense to continue my primary profession as a path forward, rather than to set aside my writing to initiate some other approach to fundraising. In terms of my holistic goal, I am making progress as long as I continue writing and publishing. In other words, my project goal is to finish this book and several other writing projects.

I'll continue incremental improvements to Green University° LLC classes and our field camp facilities as time allows. All options for scaling up the university remain on the table for assessing and re-assessing along the way.

Too summarize, a holistic goal provides an essential reference point to check project proposals for consistency with the overall values and vision, yet it can be too broad to guide daily actions. Defining specific project goals helps provide tangible, manageable chunks to work on. The following Testing Guidelines will ensure that your project matches the overall goal. If a project passes all the tests, then you effectively have both a destination and a map to get there. Then it is time to run with it.

"The cost of a thing is the amount of what I would call life which is required to be exchanged for it, immediately or in the long run."

—Henry David Thoreau,
Walden (1854)[7]

Testing Guidelines
Weeding out Non-Solutions

From cradle to grave, hunter-gatherers rarely left a lasting trail of their passing. We may find a few arrowheads in the dirt or a pictograph beneath a protected overhang, providing a momentary connection to our ancestors. In contrast, *Homo sapiens var. industrialis* leaves behind a trail of wasted plastic, glass, metals, and toxins that will endure for centuries or millennia to come. Long after we individually turn to dust, our diapers will still fester in landfills, along with pretty much everything we've ever purchased. Every lamp, chair, couch, mattress, cup, bowl, television, basketball, coat, hat, shoes, and toothpaste tube will outlive us, and almost none of it is recycled. The same for all our creations. Great ideas quickly turn to action, often too quickly, as we follow one path for a while then abandon it for another. A brilliant idea one day turns into a mass of broken PVC pipes and plastic sheathing flapping in the wind another day, ultimately carted off to the landfill, adding to our growing legacy of environmental waste.

How can we avoid wasting time, energy, and natural resources on dead-end, short-term projects? Double-checking every proposed action against our holistic goal as well as a series of Testing Guidelines will help identify potential oversights. Only when we have worked out potential bugaboos do we spring into action.

Test of Time
"Time," it is sometimes said, "is what keeps everything from happening all at once." Some people contend that everything does happen at once, and time is merely a perception that enables us to sort it all out. Perhaps I've watched too many science fiction shows, but from

my perspective, everything does happen all at once, as if there are only 'todays.' There are todays where we were active, todays we are active, and todays we will be active. What happens if we plan ahead as if we only have todays?

It is easy to imagine doing a project tomorrow. In an instant we create a mental movie sequence of anything from driving across town to driving across the country, from building a birdhouse to building a home. In a matter of minutes we can imagine enough projects to keep busy for a lifetime.

Any new project becomes a commitment that may require attention down the road. For example, many prospective owner-builders jump into a house construction project with great excitement, yet struggle to reach the finish line months or years later. They are overwhelmed by the sustained effort required, or build too big and run out of money, thus abandoning the project to go back to work. Partially completed homes are surprisingly common on the market.

The future always comes around. We face the consequences of past choices today. Investing, or not investing, in a retirement account affects us 'today,' the day we retire and tap into the account. Retirement may seem decades away now, but that day will become today sooner than we expect. What that retirement account looks like depends on prior decisions made about the so-called future. When setting events in motion try imagining the future as if it were happening now. Eventually it will be.

I have occasionally helped others with remodeling projects for business ventures. Sometimes, when building new walls or tearing them down, I sense that there is no difference between one action and the other. For example, I once helped remodel a rented office, installing soundproofing, one-way glass, and new carpeting. Being a rented space, I reasoned that the work would eventually be undone. Sure enough, today came along a couple years later, and I helped undo the remodel and reframe the walls. In retrospect, we remodeled today, and we unremodeled today. They were different todays, but they were still todays.

Seeing the world this way can make it difficult to get anything done, and that is the critical point. Think about future impacts of each action. Why do something today if it requires undoing it another today? A homeowner might be excited to install new wall-t0-wall carpeting, yet surprisingly soon after, that carpet is doomed to be ripped out and hauled to the landfill. Wouldn't it be better to install tile or hardwood flooring that will last vastly longer?

It is tragic to see a twenty, thirty, or fifty-year-old building falling apart from the weather or being torn down for replacement. The original builder's work is nullified, their efforts and energy expended without substantial meaning or purpose. Granted, everything eventually returns to dust, yet we do not advance as a species if every generation must build all new houses and every twenty years those structures need major repairs. Time and resources are squandered that could have been dedicated towards higher purposes. Projects that serve multiple generations effectively reduce redundant work, freeing others to make their own positive contributions.

As an author, I've enjoyed writing occasional newspaper and magazine articles in exchange for small payments, and more importantly, an author byline advertising my books. I recycle some articles afterwards, publishing them on my website or as content in books. It's a win-win deal for me. Magazine articles are effective marketing tools, so it is logical to contemplate starting a periodical.

However, producing a newspaper or magazine is like writing a disposable book, and periodicals often favor content that quickly falls out of date. Every issue requires new content, editing, advertising, printing, distribution, and billing. As soon as one issue is out the door, it is time to start working on the next one. The work is never done and vacation never comes. People inflict superfluous work on themselves, all destined for the recycling bin.

People do not advance doing disposable work or paying the same monthly bills over and over again. Doing a task today is fine. Repeating the same task every today is much like Thoreau's example of throwing stones over a wall and throwing them back. It is more sensible to keep all todays in mind and search for permanent solutions to close the loop on wasted time and resources.

I encourage people to Dream big, to reach for their highest potential. It is equally important

Writing newspaper and magazine articles brought free publicity.

to recognize the implicit cost of achieving a dream as well as the cost of not achieving it. Any dream, great or small, requires an input of time, energy, and resources. It is necessary to choose between many different possibilities to decide which life path to walk. Whatever your Dream, whether raising a family or starting an international widget corporation, you must give up life to bring those Dreams to life. Be certain that your choices are truly worth your life. Only then will you experience a new level of self-unification and find abundant energy to achieve your greatest Dreams.

Weakest Link

My first car was a hand-me-down 1979 Datsun 310 in high school. It wasn't fancy, but it was fuel efficient and easy to maintain. As a young adult, life was simple, and I had few responsibilities other than maintaining the car. Then I married, bought land and a heavy duty 1973 Jeep pickup, and started building a house. Owning two vehicles, I quickly discovered, doubled maintenance requirements, splitting my attention between two competing needs. Instead of giving full TLC to one vehicle, it became necessary to compare issues and decide which repair on which vehicle was the weakest link in need of attention.

The Weakest Link test originates from the fact that a chain is only as strong as its weakest link. That link will fail when the chain is stretched to its breaking point. The Weakest Link guideline emphasizes identifying and strengthening that weak link before working on other tasks. Focus on the most important task towards achieving your Dream before moving to the next task.

As adults, most people quickly acquire many responsibilities, necessitating chronically split attention to address competing weakest links. In addition to vehicle maintenance needs, there may be a marriage and family to nurture, a house that needs cleaning, repairs and yard work, employer demands, bills to pay, and taxes to file. Anyone self-employed must also prioritize between dozens of weakest links in running a business, such as deciding whether to apply time and money to advertising, product development, employee training, paying down debts, building maintenance, or interior design. There is also a needs to self-indulge in personal time and space to unwind and recover. If there are twenty chains, each with a weakest link, how do you determine the weakest weak link? Do you go to your son's baseball game or develop a new advertising campaign? Do you deal with an oil leak in the Chevy or mow the lawn? Do you give your store a fresh coat of paint or go on a date with your special someone? Allocating time and money towards any weakest link requires giving up an opportunity to allocate those resources toward another weak link.

The correct answer in terms of values is that family comes first. Invest in loved ones. Take that special person on a date. Spend time with the kids. However, the real world is messier than that. Do you go to your son's baseball game at the cost of not going to your daughter's music concert? Any activity done with one child takes away the opportunity to do something with another. Being all together takes away the opportunity for quality one-on-one time. Date night takes time away from both children. Over-investing in family could come at the cost of losing a business contract and with it, the means to support the family.

Unfortunately, while strengthening any one weak link, other links tend to atrophy. As any adult knows from experience, life can become a marathon of weak link repairs, rushing from emergency to emergency in the hopes of preventing a big snap where everything flies apart. In a fast-paced, often overwhelming world, the ability to focus and complete one task at a time is vital to success and sanity. It is easy to be torn in different directions, accomplishing nothing at all. So how do you identify the weakest link when all links seem near the breaking point? How do you allocate scarce resources towards addressing weakest links in multiple competing chains? The answer lies with keeping your eye on the Dream and testing possible actions against your holistic vision.

A Dream consists of many integrated goals. The weakest link may be personal, organizational, or informational. It may relate to quality of life or business, like product development or marketing. Determine the weakest link in each area and compare results to determine the weakest link overall. The weak link may require working late at the office to finalize a contract, or it might require taking the day off to picnic with the family.

Personal Needs: Sometimes when faced with overwhelming demands and no clear order of priorities, the weakest weak link may call for a personal reboot. Take time to go for a walk in the forest, on the beach, or to the park and back. Research shows that time spent in nature reduces stress and blood pressure, boosts the immune system, accelerates recovery from illness or surgery, increases energy levels, and improves sleep.[8] Many people go and go and go, then compensate by getting sick or breaking a leg, necessitating a time out.

Take a break before succumbing to stress. Connecting with nature facilitates greater clarity of focus, deepens intuition, and boosts overall happiness. The more off balance or agitated, the greater the need for a mental and emotional reboot. A casual walk can be meditative, while a grueling hike can help burn off steam before doing anything rash. Take time to reflect upon your Self-Unifying Principles. What kind of person do you strive to be? How do you act towards yourself and others? Attending to personal needs can help prevent regrettable actions and unnecessary stress on other weak links.

Quality of Life: In the mayhem of daily life and an urgent to-do list, it is easy to lose sight of the basics. Quality of life is the goal behind all goals. For most people, quality of life is about family and friendships, health and happiness. What good is success in business if the cost is losing it all? Strengthening quality of life does not usually require much money. However, it may demand taking time from work to spend quality time with loved ones. Attending to quality of life ensures that there remains a heartfelt reason behind work goals and duties.

Organizational: Technical and operational aspects of most projects are usually simple compared to negotiating human interactions. In any venture from marriage to business to government, the weakest link is often a lack of effective communication and subsequently a lack of cohesive vision, consensus, and cooperation.

The business world, which theoretically optimizes efficient allocation of people, energy, and materials, is fraught with inefficiencies due to organizational weak links. Innovators in big companies are often discouraged rather than encouraged, told to follow orders rather than suggest novel solutions to vexing problems.

Businesses that become engulfed in bureaucracy are doomed to be out-niched by companies that address organizational weak links. For instance, one East Asian factory consumed $7.00 worth of electricity to manufacture each hard drive. They were out-niched by a streamlined start-up company that used only 13.5¢ worth of electricity to manufacture an equivalent product. The inefficient factory went broke two months after the new one opened.[9] Staying competitive in the marketplace requires consistently good current communication and vision throughout an organization.

Informational: Organizational and informational weak links are often related, as impaired communication leads to failure to seek out or implement best practices. Rather than doing meaningful research, people, businesses, and governments continue operating in traditional fashion without reflection or review.

Basic research is often the most profitable part of work. On a personal level, a consumer may study prices and quality of every item they select at the grocery store, yet buy a house without researching quality and energy efficiency. Businesses often make similar choices, spending more time researching the price of office supplies than evaluating efficiency in a new office building or factory. Thoughtful building design could save thousands or millions of dollars per year in energy costs, yet this necessary information may not reach decision makers.

<u>Production:</u> In terms of production, there are potential weak links at home or in business. For example, growing sprouts in jars is an economical alternative to buying greens in winter. Cooking larger stews and freezing the surplus for future meals can save money versus buying instant foods. In business, the weak link may be product quality or marketing. As an independent entrepreneur, it is easy to be so busy writing, building, or consulting that very little time is allotted for marketing. Weak links in production are often organizational and informational in nature. Address those issues first, and weak links in production may be strengthened comparatively quickly.

Growing sprouts in jars can save money versus buying greens.

<u>Crisis Management:</u> The Weakest Link guideline is helpful to achieve any goal, and it essential during times of crisis. When feeling overwhelmed, turn to your Dream. What is the single weakest link towards achieving your core objectives? There may be times when it seems necessary to put a dream on hold while working another job, or stabilizing an emergency situation. Stop to assess your vision and the best route forward. A minor course correction may suffice, rather than plowing a whole new route. It is easy to get lost in the middle of a

crisis situation. Remember the Dream and assess the shortest route to achieving it. Upon review you may find that the weakest links are not so weak after all.

Root Cause

One behavior that greatly threatens our collective survival is our tendency to address symptoms of problems while ignoring underlying causes. The purpose of the Root Cause test is a) to ensure that we search for the roots of a problem, and b) ensure that we evaluate potential effects of our solutions.

If crime increases we react by building more jails and enacting tougher laws, without asking what caused the uptick in crime. When we find unwanted weeds, we react with poison, without asking what ecosystem factors enabled them to spread. In medicine we fight illness as a problem, instead of seeing it as a potential symptom of an unhealthy lifestyle, environmental factors, poor diet, or emotional stress. We focus on what makes people sick while ignoring what keeps them healthy.

When floods damage homes and farms, we react by building dams and dikes for flood control, when most floods are at least partially human-caused due to poor land management that causes precipitation to run off rather than soak into the soil. If a city lacks sufficient water then we react by drilling more wells or building dams to increase water supply, without realizing that it is cheaper and more effective to simply replace inefficient, water-wasting appliances in the community.

If it is cold in the house then we treat the symptoms by turning up the thermostat, ignoring the real problem of insufficient insulation. If there is not enough energy to serve everyone, then we react by building more and more power plants, without realizing that it is once again cheaper to merely replace inefficient appliances, so the existing supply will serve more users. If we run short of money then we think we must raise our income, while billions of other people prosper on far less.

As a rule, cause and effect in mechanical systems, like a washing machine or a house, is relatively simple and linear, compared to cause and effect in an ecosystem. If a washing machine breaks down you can replace the broken part. Even in a house with high energy bills, it is relatively easy to move beyond the symptoms to the true problem of not enough insulation.

Organic processes, like the natural or economic ecosystems, are inherently nonlinear, so cause and effect can be more difficult to predict. For example, plagues of locusts can eat the leaves off nearly every living plant. I've experienced it on my own homestead, where hoards of hungry grasshoppers consumed every green plant, then ate the tips off of spruce tree needles. Grasshoppers ate black plastic off the garden, whole zucchinis off the vine, and even chewed on my students' notebooks in the middle of a class.

Farmers may watch with horror as their fields, their very hopes and dreams, are stripped by hoards of locusts. People often react to the "problem" by pouring money into pesticides to stop the invaders. Unfortunately, by the time grasshoppers are mature enough to cause visible damage, it is too late to make substantive difference with pesticides. Watching grasshoppers die may provide satisfactory vengeance, but at enormous expense with little economic return.

Grasshoppers can also be controlled with parasitic bacteria called semisphore that consumes grasshoppers from the inside out, turning them to mush. The bacteria is broadcast over the pasture, infecting grasshoppers that consume it on plants. Other grasshoppers get infected by cannibalizing those that have died from the bacterial parasite. Introducing this predatory bacteria seems like a sensible ecosystem approach, and it does work, yet it is expensive for large areas and must be applied early in the season to kill grasshoppers before they mature, with some carryover to the next season.

Some farmers see the fallacy of attacking a problem plague after it has erupted, having the supposed foresight to save next year's crop by torching this year's, thereby toasting the hoppers before they reproduce. Unfortunately, burning off organic matter compromises the soil's ability to capture and hold water in the soil, which is essential to rot grasshopper eggs before they hatch. Grasshopper plagues are naturally greatest after dry spring weather, so it is essential to retain soil moisture. Torching a field only aggravates the root problem.

In ecosystem processes it is difficult to see solutions when preoccupied with problems. In this case, grasshoppers are the problem, yet healthy soil is the solution. It is important to adjust farming practices to enhance organic matter in the soil to trap moisture and rot future grasshopper eggs. Working with the natural ecosystem to support predators that kill and eat grasshoppers that hatch is also helpful. In the meantime, consider utilizing an oversized bug vacuum to capture and dry locusts as high-protein food for chickens or other livestock.

Cause and effect in the economic ecosystem can be similarly convoluted. A family restaurant, for example, might do great business until a competing restaurant opens up down the street, siphoning off sales. Is the competitor the root cause of our problem? Do we treat the problem like a grasshopper plague and attack the newcomers in the effort to eradicate the competition? Will badmouthing their food or reputation be any more effective than attacking a grasshopper invasion? Probably not.

Here again, we need to set aside the superficial problem to focus on the deeper solution. What is our positive vision for the restaurant? What kind of clientele do we seek, and how do we attract them here? How can we make the food tastier, the service better, and the atmosphere more inviting? Do we make the outside more appealing with fresh paint, new architecture, more organic or solar features, or new trees in the parking lot? Refocus on the positive vision, reconsider the Weakest Links, and then determine which issue needs to be tackled first to solve the root cause of losing business.

Addressing the root cause can be more convoluted in some businesses. For online retail stores, daily sales regularly rise and fall, often inexplicably. If sales falter considerably or completely cease, the issue may require priority attention. What is the root cause of the slowdown? Is the website no longer loading properly? Is there a problem with the website or a problem with the web hosting service? These root cause issues are relatively easy to solve and restore service. But other factors that impact sales are less obvious. Internet outages or widespread computer viruses can impact whole regions, affecting sales. Major national or international news events tend to influence online sales. Changes in search engine algorithms can send customers away or bring them back. Even major weather events alter sales up or down.

As long as the website is functioning properly and customers can find it, then none of those issues really matter in the long term. The critical issue is to provide quality products, a pleasing website, and a convenient customer experience, along with a marketing plan to help bring people in the digital door.

Whatever the problem, sometimes it is more effective to focus on positive solutions. When the kids are fighting with one another and we join the fight by yelling at them for yelling at each other, we only escalate the problem. In order to achieve positive results, sometimes it is helpful to leave the problem behind and focus on the solution, in this case by finding a common vision for how each person wants to be treated by each other. If all parties contribute to creating a vision and brainstorming ways to achieve it, then the fighting may be resolved without addressing the problem issue. The Root Cause test reminds us to take a solutions-oriented approach. Once we have defined what we want in positive terms, can we plot a course to achieve it.

Ecosystem Impact

We live in a world of abundance. We have ample resources to sustainably allow everyone on earth a life of prosperity and comfort if we steward natural resources wisely. As consumers we have power to vote with our money. Products and services exist on the market only as long as consumers buy them. We control whether or not we invest our collective resources in real goods or real waste through the purchases we make. We can always make sensible choices as long as we ask these simple questions:

1) Does this choice help achieve my Dream?

2) Does this choice represent a worthwhile application of resources and energy?

3) What happens to the waste when this product is no longer useful?

Everything we purchase is ultimately destined for decomposition, recycling, or the landfill, mostly the latter. This is not something we usually think about at the time of purchase. But, I've seen entire hot tubs and motorboats dropped into the community dumpster. These items are not recyclable, so the dumpster is the final destination from the moment of purchase. For that reason, I avoid buying new products, such as new clothes, mattresses, cars, or computers, favoring secondhand and reconditioned items instead. I try to find a means to recycle old goods before upgrading to newer models.

Everything we purchase is ultimately destined for decomposition, recycling, or the landfill, mostly the latter.

As entrepreneurs, we have additional power to choose how material resources and human labor are utilized. We can use resources wisely if our goal includes a vision extending beyond ourselves to the broader community. Businesses only waste resources when they chase the partial goal of money.

For example, as if plastic packaging wasn't bad enough, candy producers have created disposable plastic toys, even battery powered toys, filled with small candy compartments. Whole factories are dedicated to consuming resources to manufacture toys for candies that intended for disposal, squandering the resources of the planet.

While we are not likely to wean the global population off of candy any time soon, we can offer more sustainable choices. Some companies are selling chocolates and candies with ingredients from organic and fair-trade sources. Some offer fully compostable packaging. Why not go all the way, and produce sweets and treats that are sweetened with sugar alternatives such as stevia? It is possible to produce products that combat obesity, diabetes, cavities, pesticide use, poverty, and litter that still make tasty Halloween treats.

Whatever your project, whether it is a new personal purchase, an innovative new product, or a new marketing campaign, ask yourself, "Does this proposal make wise use of precious resources? What is the impact of this project on the natural ecosystem?"

Community

Americans value our personal freedoms, freedom to dress as we choose, to speak what we believe, to seek our own religion, to choose our own work, and to manage our property as we please. We like doing what we want when we want, and we don't like other people telling us how to live. Of course, freedom comes with responsibility to respect the rights of others. As the saying goes, "One man's right to swing his fist ends where another man's nose begins." We own the burden of being reasonable and prudent in our actions toward others.

Property rights are a good issue. We can buy land and do whatever we please with it, at least within reason. Problems develop if we act without considering our community. Regulations start with extreme cases, such as individuals who turn their land into a toxic waste dump. On the surface, it seems like an "environmental problem," yet we are by nature an anthropocentric species, so the real issue at stake is property rights. The problem with toxic waste is that it doesn't stay confined to a property. Toxins migrate through air and water to violate other's freedoms.[10] Therefore, we implement laws prohibiting toxic waste dumps.

As people live ever closer together, we logically continue to lose freedom, while gaining more control over what our neighbors can and cannot do. We cannot operate an unsightly junkyard on any piece of property we choose, nor could we open a noisy nightclub in the middle of a subdivision. Freedoms are shortest where people live closest together. In many places it is illegal to build a tree house in the yard or leave a lawn uncut.

As citizens, we typically appreciate laws limiting other people's freedoms, yet hate when those laws apply to ourselves. Like children tattling on each other, we call the law to control neighbors when they fail to use their land in a reasonable and prudent manner. The law may seem like a citizen's ally, something we the people created. Yet when others call upon the law to limit our own freedoms, we suddenly perceive the law as bureaucracy out of control. No law can compensate for the duality between these perceptions. The obvious solution is to be reasonable and prudent in our own actions. The Community test reminds us to consider how our actions might affect other people.

Having good neighbors starts with being a good neighbor. Before acting, stop and consider how others will react. If we give consideration to each other and strive to be reasonable and prudent in our own actions, then we can obviate the need for more laws that ultimately limit our own freedoms.

Granted, you and I are reasonable and prudent, and the real source of the problem is everybody else! It is therefore unrealistic to think that our thoughtfulness will stop the plethora of new laws that continue to control our lives. Consensus building is desperately needed as a proactive solution rather than a reactive law.

Consensus building is the process of getting together with neighbors to discuss common concerns and to create a common vision for the community. By talking and planning with neighbors, we can better understand what each other expects and needs, fostering respect for each other, even as we work towards our unique and individual dreams.

The main value in consensus building is flexibility. Written laws are inflexible, and we all suffer for that. I recall one family that had to dismantle a playhouse built for their children because it was on stilts, a foot or two above the height allowed by the zoning code. I saw the playhouse, and there was nothing unreasonable about it. It simply didn't fit the strict rule of law. Most people are reasonable and flexible, especially when their own needs and concerns are heard. A group of people who listen to each other can find reasonable and prudent ways to meet the needs and concerns of each individual without the need to call for more government regulations.

The Community test is not just about property rights, but should influence every decision, from pet ownership to hairstyle. How would the neighbors react if you sported a green Mohawk? How would they react if you kept skunks for pets? The Community guideline is a reminder to respect the local community. Granted, there are proper times to challenge the status quo, to try a new fashion, or voice a new ideology. In each case we must weigh the potential costs and benefits against overall holistic goals.

Only when we have established a well-defined goal and a plan for achieving it, can we test potential costs and benefits before considering shaking up the neighborhood. Charles Darwin understood the impact his Theory of Evolution might have on society because the discovery deeply impacted his own faith. He knew evolution would shake the foundation of Western culture, yet he also understood that he had to publish. After formulating his theory, he spent an additional twenty years collecting evidence to counter every reasonable argument before publishing *The Origin of Species*. Darwin ultimately published the work when he learned that another biologist had independently arrived at the same conclusion. Darwin published first to be rightly credited for the discovery.

Before taking any action, consider the effects towards neighbors and community. Consider potential means to achieve goals without compromising the rights or happiness of other people.

Some causes are important enough that it is necessary to shake up the neighborhood. Plan carefully to achieve the objective without it backfiring. Establish a positive goal and a realistic plan for achieving it. Consider potential costs and benefits behind every possible approach, and know in advance what challenges to expect and how to circumvent obstacles. If you have adequately considered community, then it is time to take appropriate action, whether that involves planting a tree or igniting a revolution.

Intuition and Instinct

The holistic goals process and testing guidelines are primarily left-brained activities. This logic-driven analysis is helpful to reduce impulsive decisions that might backfire and compromise one goal for another. For example, Elon Musk has demonstrated remarkable ability to radically increase accessibility and affordability of everything from solar roofs to electric cars and space launches. However, his decision to sell flamethrowers to raise quick cash[11] could create legal and political problems if a customer torches another human being, an animal, or starts a wildfire that consumes thousands of homes. Thoughtful checks and balances can help avert poor choices.

Most good plans will test positively through logical checks and balances and instincts. On the other hand, logic doesn't own the market on wisdom. Intuition can trump rational decisions, voiding proposals that seem reasonable or validating ones that seem unlikely. Question your instincts, but don't dismiss them. Some courses of action are guided in faith, their reason for being revealed later.

When I first looked at the property that became our Green University® LLC River Camp, the seller was asking $340,000. That was far above my means, yet I felt a deep connection to the twenty-one acre parcel, as if it were meant to be. The lot stayed on the market for a long time, slowly dropping in price to $300,000 then $260,000. A couple years later, in the midst of my divorce, I negotiated a buy-sell agreement to purchase the land for $200,000, yet the bank wouldn't approve financing due to my personal situation, and the deal fell through. Quixotically, I

Sometimes intution is more important than logic.

still felt a connection, like it was meant to be, even while it seemed impossible to obtain. I finally acquired the property in the depths of the Great Recession, paying $165,000, or less than half the original asking price. Intuitively, I understood it was ours all along, even though I couldn't logically deduce the path to get there.

Whatever issues you face, and whatever solutions come to mind, give a quick check through each of the testing guidelines outlined above before swinging into action. Also review the chapter *Money: The Biggest Bang for the Buck* to test Marginal Reaction and the financial logic behind your plan. If everything checks out, then you are ready to rock and roll.

A traveler met a wise man on the road just outside of town. The traveler said, "I am new in these parts, and I am looking for work. How is the economy here?" The wise man returned, "How was the economy in the town you came from?"

"The economy was in a shambles," the traveler said. "There was no work anywhere, and I had to leave because of it." The wise man said, "Unfortunately, the economy here is in much the same condition." And the traveler passed on his way.

Soon another traveler came along and met the wise man at the edge of town. The traveler said, "I am new in these parts, and I am looking for work. How is the economy here?" The wise man again returned, "How was the economy in the town you came from?"

The traveler replied, "It was in very good shape; there was much work to be found and many opportunities." The wise man then said, "You are fortunate. Our economy is in fine shape and this is certainly the land of golden opportunity."

—Thomas J. Elpel
Direct Pointing to Real Wealth (2000)

Management Cycle
Monitoring and Flexibility

Whether we discover a world of prosperity and abundance or a world of poverty and hardship depends on what we choose to make of our situation.

Success begins with understanding ecosystem basics and tools for making change. Form a holistic goal then generate proposals to accomplish that goal. Ideas are then tested for compatibility with the goal and for sustainability with the ecosystem. Finally, implement an action plan and monitor progress. What seems like the final step in the process is actually just the beginning.

Every action changes the situation, and even with thorough research it can be challenging to accurately predict the outcome. Monitor results of your actions and compare against expectations. Be flexible to adapt to the unexpected. Each action results in a new situation, and the cycle begins again.

Some goals have clear end points, such as saving money to buy a car. Other goals are long-term projects, such as building and maintaining a home. The management cycle continues as long as the goal remains in process.

The Holistic Management-Soft Systems Cycle illustration summarizes the cycle in four steps. The four management steps are 1) define the situation, 2) generate possible solutions, 3) test proposals against the holistic goal to choose the preferred options, and 4) implement solutions. We instinctively use a similar process for minor and major decisions throughout our lives. Being conscious of the process facilitates more thorough decision making.

The Holistic Management-Soft Systems Cycle was developed by Cliff Montagne, a retired associate professor of soil science at MSU-Bozeman. He was inspired by the circular process first identified in the Myers-Briggs personality inventory for testing how people solve problems. Their model metamorphosed into the "soft systems" process in the

Holistic Management-Soft Systems Cycle

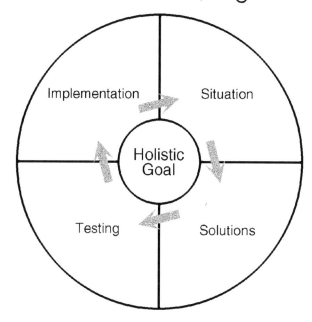

The management cycle revolves around a holistic goal. The existing situation is defined and compared to the goal. Solutions are proposed and check against the goal and Testing Guidelines. Ideas that pass the tests are implemented, creating a new situation to continue the cycle.

Based on *'Holistic Thought & Management'* by Cliff Montagne.

book *Systems Approaches for Improvements in Agriculture and Resource Management* by Wilson and Morren prior to Montagne incorporating the holistic goal at the center.[12]

The *situation* is the who and what under management. It is a description of the people and resources being managed, plus the community and ecosystem that supports the endeavor. The situation should also include a problem statement indicating obstacles to be overcome to achieve the goal.

The next step involves brainstorming possible *solutions* to resolve the problem by more clearly defining goals along with potential tools, actions, and even paradigms or new ways of thinking. Then we move to *testing* solutions for compatibility and sustainability with the goals using testing guidelines outlined earlier. Ideas that pass these tests are implemented in a holistic way, encouraging learning and growth, time management, monitoring and flexibility. The situation is re-evaluated as actions are implemented, and the cycle continues. This decision-making process works for managing a household or a business, as well as government agencies and international problems.

Dave's World

This real life scenario was submitted by my friend Dave, who is nearing retirement. His situation may be familiar to many readers. Dave isn't satisfied with his present employment, yet has substantive reasons to keep the job:

Holistic Goal: My core values include being close to nature and nurturing myself, family and friends, my community, and nation. I desire a simple life with quality possessions. I own and appreciate a nice efficient home, reliable transportation, running water and electricity. I value good food and reasonable pleasures like a decent music collection and occasional travel. I seek ample free time to pursue my interests, plus quality time with friends and family, and time to simply relax. I enjoy outdoor recreation, and I like living in a rural setting with wilderness nearby. I prefer to avoid shopping malls, traffic jams, and mass media. I want to spend more time with the local dance community and regional primitive skills groups and with friends. I want to spend more time with my wife and pets. I have no interest in consuming for the sake of consuming or pursuing a false version of the American Dream. I would like to be a good temporary resident on Earth by treating it with respect and helping the planet recover from human mistakes including my own past wasteful consumption.

I seek to make a positive contribution to the world with a meaningful livelihood while earning a living. I do not want to join the 'rat race,' work for a large bureaucracy, or contribute to the madness that is destroying the planet. I would like to support my local land base and help others live more sustainably. Whatever I do for a living, I would like it to include outdoor activity, something that stimulates my interests, and something that is not damaging to my mental and physical health. I want to work on solving the roots of our problems rather than symptoms. I'd like to vary my schedule with different types of activities every few days. My interests include the outdoors, primitive skills, photography, dancing, yoga, meditation, consciousness, ecological economics, special thinking, and big picture issues.

Situation: My present job isn't satisfying, yet I need to support myself and my wife, who requires expensive healthcare. We have no children.

Define the Whole Under Management: The whole under management includes my life and my livelihood in Montana. As a government employee, I earn a relatively high salary by local standards. My wife earns limited supplementary income working part time with social services, and also contributes a lot to our household. Our house and cars are fully paid off and we have no debt, although we have recurring annual expenses (such as taxes, car maintenance, food, etc.). My skills include excellent big picture thinking, an economics background, creativity, a wide and diverse social network, and diverse interests. I am willing to leave my comfort zone with regularity.

I can take early retirement in six years time. That will guarantee half my current salary, but without benefits. Retirement income will provide a measure of security, and I will gain freedom to follow my own dreams. I will still need supplemental income to cover healthcare expenses.

I value my community, including the people, resources, plants, and animals that live here. My state is a relatively income-poor state, yet the state is abundant with natural resources, wilderness, and environmental quality. As the state capital, my town has a lot of state workers and many services to support those workers. It also has a fairly large artistic and spiritual community, and the cost of living is reasonable. Open space and trails for recreation are within walking distance.

Solutions

The "problem" is an unsatisfying job, but what is the solution? It is important to set aside the problem and consider the bigger picture by stating or restating a goal in positive terms. Then brainstorm ideas to achieve the holistic goal.

Hypothetical Goal Stated In Positive Terms: I seek to establish a way of life and livelihood that meets my core values and helps the betterment of all species on Earth. My aim in life is to raise human consciousness, including my own, on many different levels in concert with my diverse interests.

Brainstorm Possible Solutions for the Stated Problem:

1) Quit my job and create a green business. This business might involve "consciousness retreats" or provide a quality product or service.

2) Reduce my hours at work and seek part-time work in a more satisfying job while conserving money and hopefully allowing more free time for personal interests.

3) Keep my current job until retirement in six years, while preparing post-retirement plans.

4) Keep my current job until the retirement cutoff and continue working the same job halftime to retain benefits.

5) Save money and then quit my job, living unemployed with few expenses.

Testing

Now we turn to the testing guidelines to crosscheck each of the above proposals.

Test of Time: If I consider all of my "todays" together, which proposals provide the most benefit for the most todays? Quitting my job today would feel great today, but what about tomorrow's today? How about today a year from now or ten years from now?

Weakest Link: Quitting my job to start a green business (option 1) would resolve the immediate problem of disliking my job. However, I do not presently have a clear vision for launching a green business, how to fund the start-up, or how to survive without my present income. Emotional blocks from past conditioning are also significant issues. For example, I cannot imagine giving up the security of my income, and I've been taught that I should have a job. Should I quit and force myself beyond my comfort zone?

Keeping my job (options 3 and 4) does not immediately address the problem of disliking my job, and simply quitting my job (option 5) does not address the desire to make a positive difference in the world. Reducing my hours at work and taking a second job through an existing business in holistic health (option 2) may facilitate the work transition with less risk and stress and is somewhere between option 1 and option 3.

On the other hand, keeping my job for six more years (option 3) would allow retirement at age 52, providing freedom to pursue my true dreams more actively. I could take a few months vacation post-retirement then have financial freedom to pursue a more satisfying job or volunteer work. If retirement were farther away, then sticking with the job would definitely not pass the weakest link test. In the meantime, I can start researching and planning post-retirement plans.

Root Cause: Which proposals address the root cause of the problem? Transitioning out of my present employment gets to the root of the problem, provided I have something to transition into.

Just quitting (option 5) does not address the desire to help other people, at least not in the short term. Other proposals address that desire to varying degrees. Quitting my job may not be possible without much greater savings. On top of that, my wife's medical bills are high at the moment, necessitating supplementary income. Option 3 will address the root cause within six years and allows for good income and freedom.

Ecosystem Impact: How might these proposals impact the ecosystem? Which proposals make optimal use of the earth's natural resources and energy? I consume limited resources commuting to work and maintaining my job, such as purchasing clothes for work and going out for lunch sometimes.

Quitting my job and starting a new green business might use the most resources initially, although these things could be designed in a sustainable way and might lead those who attend my retreats to use resources more wisely. In the long run, this could be the best use of resources and the most likely option to save resources. Options 3 and 4, continuing with my job full time, might use the most resources in the long run because I would likely continue consuming conveniences. The other options are somewhere in between. Option 5 uses the least resources for my household, but does not initially help others save on resource use.

Community: How will this proposal be accepted by my neighbors and culture? There could be pressure from peers and parents to keep my job. Option 5, living with few expenses, may have some positive feedback from others in terms of living a simple and more sustainable life. Less consumption under Option 5 is nice as well. Options 3 and 4 would not provide as quick of a positive change as options 1, 2, and 5, unless I can figure out how to make my current job more useful.

Marginal Reaction: Which proposal generates or maintains the most additional income from the least additional investment? My sunk costs are high in terms of past work dedicated to this job. Sunk costs are "irrelevant," except that in this case they are not. I am six years from early retirement, at which time I can collect a modest retirement income for the rest of my life. From my present position, working a few more years will give me a guaranteed retirement income, which is far less risky than trying to suddenly reinvent my life and start a business in the private sector.

<u>Summary</u>: There is no obvious winner here, so maybe some combination of these options is the best route, or perhaps there is something I have not yet considered. Option 3 doesn't immediately address the problem, but in the long run, sticking it out at work appears to give the greatest marginal reaction to carry me towards my holistic goal. At this point, option 3 is what I am pursuing.

Implementation

Once a plan has been selected then the process of implementation begins, including prioritizing an action list, learning and growth for all who are involved, financial planning, careful monitoring to see what happens, plus flexibility to change if needed. In this case, implementation involves showing up for a job Dave dislikes for another six years, which seems entirely reasonable, yet also feels disheartening.

On the other hand, implementation brings us around the Soft Systems Cycle to a "new" situation: Dave now plans to take early retirement at age 52. That gives him six years to brainstorm post-retirement solutions, save money, and take solid steps to prepare for a new and different life and livelihood. Moreover, whatever his future brings, he will have the security and safety net of retirement income to

Develop a clear picture of the goal, and the subconscious mind organizes behaviors towards achieving it.

support his path forward. Thus, his new situation includes a) solidifying post-retirement plans, and b) creatively coping with the same job for six more years. Dave can explore ways to make a positive impact with his time at work. He will brainstorm possible solutions and proceed through the cycle again. He may consider other solutions, including transferring within his department or changing government agencies.

Your Turn

The near-retirement example provided in this chapter is a fairly common scenario, and Dave's situation is actually pretty good. He and his wife own a nice, energy-efficient home mortgage-free in a town they like. They each own a car. They have no debts. Six years from now Dave will have freedom from his job, plus guaranteed income for life.

Compare this example to the scenario of an 18-year-old who could potentially achieve virtual retirement in about five years, by working, saving, and paying cash for a decent car and a good house in a region where real estate prices are undervalued. Being free from rent or a mortgage by age 23, he is thus free to spend the rest of his life pursuing his dreams, including possibly starting a green business.

In either example, the path is roughly the same, although Dave will be 52 instead of 23. In addition, he will have actual retirement income, unlike our 23-year-old, who has few expenses but also no established long-term income.

How is your situation similar or different? Can you create a five-year retirement plan (or partial retirement plan) from your present position? Do you even want to? Does your debt or family situation require a longer plan, perhaps dropping out of the rat race in ten years instead of five? What would you do with your life if your home and car were paid off, and you were free to do anything you wanted? Everyone's situation is unique, and your solutions may be entirely different from those outlined here. Give it a whirl, and see what new opportunities arise as you reawaken your dreams and imagine the road ahead.

Follow-Through

It is said that you can identify your priorities by noticing whatever thought first comes to mind upon waking in the morning. I know this to be true. When considering Dreams and establishing priorities, those priorities come to mind with the rising sun. If the priority is to listen to the birds, then you will hear them. If the priority is to give a better speech, then you will awake to an audience in your own mind.

The human brain is remarkable in its ability to solve problems without consciously thinking. Develop a clear picture of the goal, and the subconscious mind organizes behaviors towards achieving it.[13] Granted, a few moments of mental imagery won't make one's dreams materialize. But keep those dreams in mind from morning to night, and you will soon find the resources needed to realize them. Focus on the dream with sustained willpower, and the keys to success soon fall into place.

Be careful about creating deadlines. Reality isn't very structured or scheduled. Goals with deadlines seldom work and often cause unnecessary stress. Counterproductive deadlines can ultimately delay progress towards a goal. For example, if the goal is to play a song well on the piano then we can concentrate on achieving that end. However, attempting to perfect the song by a particular date can shift focus from the musical experience to the clock on the wall. The more time spent stressing about the passage of time, the less focus there is on the music. I've tried many times to set deadlines for goals and often found that life didn't work according to plan. The more I focused on deadlines, the less I accomplished. If I stressed too much, I just got sick.

On the other hand, many people have amazing dreams and ambitions, yet fall into a rut of complacency and day-to-day routines. Our culture encourages people to procrastinate in high school and college, staying up all night before deadlines to finish assignments on time. Stressing over a due date can be a good way to shift out of a routine and build momentum to get the ball rolling. Get on track with the dream, then let go of the clock and focus on the task at hand. Eventually you may find less and less need for deadlines as you create a positive daily routine of pursuing your greatest dreams. Spring is my primary annual deadline. I write in winter and play in summer, so I try to wrap up projects before the weather becomes irresistibly warm outside.

Be mindful that there will always be setbacks, even with the best of plans. At those times it is essential to reflect and reconsider every aspect of the Dream to get a fresh start. A long walk will often clear struggles with self-doubt and quickly solidify renewed belief in the Dream, invigorating a whirlwind of ideas to get back on the path to success. Physical movement stimulates mental and emotional flow. With long-range and intermediate goals in mind, I often define an action list every day. Sometimes I plan out my day before I rise from bed. Often I envision the day before falling asleep the night before. Then I know exactly what to do in the morning.

Whatever your dreams in life, now is the time to seize the moment, make a plan, and swing into action.

"The history of the woodlot is often, if not commonly, here a history of cross-purposes, of steady and consistent endeavor on the part of Nature, of interference and blundering with a glimmering of intelligence at the eleventh hour on the part of the proprietor. The latter often treats his woodlot as a certain Irishman I heard of drove a horse—that is, by standing before him and beating him in the face all the way across a field."

—Henry David Thoreau,
Faith in a Seed (1862)[1]

Afterword
Global Warming
Can We Save Ourselves?

Dig into the earth, and pick up a handful of soil. What color is it? Healthy soil is often rich brown to almost black. Minerals can influence color, but the main colorant in soil is organic carbon. Without the hand of man, Mother Nature extracted carbon from the atmosphere and enriched the world with plants and trees, animals that feed upon them, and the rich soil that supports it all. Accumulations of organic carbon were so vast as to become a geologic phenomenon, forming mountains of coal and rich oil deposits. Limestone, also a form of carbon, was formed through the accumulation of microorganisms in the sea, deposited in immense layers, later pushed up to form mountain ranges and continents. Removing all of that carbon from the atmosphere helped maintain livable global temperatures even as the great heat lamp in the sky has significantly increased its intensity.

Our species was born into a Garden of Eden, a world of great riches and abundance. Like the deer or lion, we were originally part of the garden, foraging and hunting to sustain ourselves without attempting to rule the domain. But then we ate from the Tree of Knowledge, becoming like gods ourselves with the power to manage the garden. We replaced natural order with straight rows. We replaced wild herds with domestic stock. We built roads, dams, cities, empires, and war. And we began to reverse the flow of carbon that Mother Nature had so diligently sequestered away.

The Carbon Cycle

About 225 billion tons of carbon dioxide naturally enters the atmosphere each year from processes like respiration, decay, and fires. That carbon is removed from the atmosphere by plants, forests, and marine microorganisms. Human activity has tipped the balance by adding 5.5 billion tons of carbon dioxide to the air each year from fossil fuels, plus 2.2 billion tons from deforestation,[2] and 2 billion tons from loss of soil carbon. More critically, deforestation and soil loss handicapped nature's ability to extract carbon from the atmosphere.

Excluding water vapor, the atmosphere consists of 78% nitrogen, 21% oxygen and 0.9% argon. Other traces gases, mostly carbon dioxide, make up an additional .039% of the atmosphere, up from 0.028% prior to industrialization. Two-atom molecules like nitrogen and oxygen vibrate at high frequencies, reflecting heat back into space. However, 3-atom molecules like carbon dioxide, water vapor, nitrous oxide, and sulfur dioxide all absorb heat, trapping heat in like a window, hence the term "greenhouse effect." Carbon dioxide and other trace gases comprise a very small part of the atmosphere, yet keep the earth's surface about 59°F warmer than it would be without them, so even a small total increase in greenhouse gases can have a significant impact on climate.

Although our contribution of carbon dioxide is relatively small in comparison to the amount recycled by nature, we have greatly increased the proportion of carbon dioxide in the atmosphere and continue to do so.

Loss of soil carbon is one of the least-recognized factors in global warming. Plowing soil increases contact between organic carbon and atmospheric oxygen. Carbon oxidizes, reacting with oxygen to form carbon dioxide. Soil was built from atmospheric carbon, and plowing returns it to the air, depleting our soils while exacerbating global warming.

Global temperatures began to rise soon after the dawn of agriculture and the start of desertification from poor agricultural and grazing practices. Not so long ago, northern Africa grew the grain that supported the Roman Empire. Now the Sahara Desert is a wasteland the size of the United States, and it's soil carbon is back in the atmosphere. Scientists calculated that agriculture and deforestation contributed 340 billion tons of carbon to the atmosphere between 7,000 years ago and the start of the industrial era. Much of this carbon was re-sequestered by the environment, with the remainder contributing 0.7°C to 1.2°C to global temperatures prior to industrialization.[3]

Our species spread around the globe, dramatically reversing carbon sequestration on every pasture and farm. The faster we've consumed the planet, the faster temperatures have risen. Since the industrial revolution began, an additional 78 - 133 billion tons of carbon have been oxidized from soils into the atmosphere due to mechanized agriculture,[4] along with 140 billion tons of carbon lost due to deforestation.[5]

Poor livestock management compounds the problem. Mother Nature once utilized vast herds of bison, elk, antelope, wildebeest, zebras, springbok, and elephants to trample organic carbon into the ground, literally building soil from air and sunlight, as lions and wolves shepherded the animals across the prairies. We reversed this cycle by killing off predators, fencing prairies, and raising stock that spread out too much to trample anything, while staying too long to allow regrowth. Lacking herd effect to trample seeds, manure, and vegetation into the soil, plants fail to re-establish, leading to progressively more bare ground exposed to the ravages of wind, rain, and oxidation. One-third of all carbon dioxide added to the atmosphere came from soil.[6]

Add carbon emissions together from soil loss, mechanized agriculture, deforestation, and our fossil fuel orgy, and we have a planet-killing recipe for global warming.

Sphere of Influence

World population has more than doubled since 1970, bringing with it a massive expansion of poor land management and exploding use of fossil fuels. Global warming is happening so fast that anyone who wasn't born yesterday has witnessed the changing climate. Like a bus hurtling towards a cliff, we've seen the problem coming for decades, yet failed to do anything better than insert the ear buds, close our eyes, and distract ourselves with cheap entertainment. The day of reckoning is here, and we are now in crises mode. So what can we do about it?

Immediate concerns aside, the long-term prognosis actually looks pretty good. Innovators around the world are tackling the carbon problem from many different angles. Electric cars are coming of age, and automakers are announcing plans to phase out the gasoline engine in the coming decades. New energy technologies are beginning to out-compete fossil fuels in the marketplace. New cement and paints have been developed that absorb carbon dioxide from the atmosphere, offering the potential for carbon-negative infrastructure. Progressive ranchers have switched to holistic practices that mimic nature's process for trampling carbon into the ground to build soil. Farmers have developed no-till agriculture to avoid plowing, and are using crop rotations to increase soil carbon, rather than deplete it. The problem of global warming has been solved; we just need to implement those solutions. It's too bad we didn't start a few decades earlier when we had more time to react.

The greatest challenge to global problems is that our individual ability to make a difference is limited to our sphere of influence and seemingly insignificant contributions. We can start by reducing, eliminating, or reversing our personal carbon footprint. Obvious steps include improving household insulation and weather-stripping or installing better windows, and a solar water heater or solar air heater, as well as switching to a more fuel-efficient vehicle or buying an electric car or ebike, maybe even generating our own electricity from solar or wind. Less obvious steps include "hardening" a home to reduce long-term material throughput. For example, instead of replacing worn carpet with new carpet that will also be thrown away someday, try switching to durable wood or tile flooring. Systematically upgrade a house to reduce the materials and energy needed to maintain it. Plant fruit trees to absorb carbon, provide shade in summer, and produce free food. Above all, take steps to reduce expenses and eliminate dependency on employment that directly or indirectly contributes to global warming.

Anyone in business has a greater sphere of influence. Many of the same techniques applied by an individual household can be applied at work as well to reduce the carbon footprint. In addition, a business can re-examine each product and service to reduce or eliminate its impact, much as Japan's Ricoh Company has done with its life-cycle approach to laser printers. Optionally, a business can actively market products and services to help others reduce their impacts, such as producing or selling electric lawnmowers, insulating houses, or bringing carbon-absorbing cement and paint to market. Or choose farming or ranching processes that rehabilitate the land and actively sequester carbon in the soil, sharing the know-how with neighbors. The greater the size of the business, the greater the potential for positive impact to shift the economy away from fossil fuels towards a more sustainable future.

Every step taken is an essential contribution to solving our carbon problem and reversing global warming. Unfortunately, our individual contributions often seem insignificant against the global scale of the problem. Collective efforts are desperately needed to stimulate global results. Collective action is possible, and it has been done, as previously noted for the global ban on ozone-depleting CFCs.

Similarly, the nationwide cap-and-trade systems for sulfur dioxide and nitrogen oxides have fantastically reduced emissions since 1990. A similar program for carbon emissions could have easily averted global warming at a net profit. And though we are slow to react, a cap-and-trade system is still desperately needed. In fact, there are many potential approaches to discourage carbon emissions and encourage carbon sequestration with a net positive benefit on the economy.

For example, no-till farming forgoes the plow and uses a drill to plant seeds in the soil. Conserving organic matter on the surface reduces erosion and increases soil carbon. By using no-till farming combined with cover crops between harvests, American farmers could sequester 300 million tons of carbon per year into the soil.[7] Global adoption of similar practices could potentially offset present annual carbon emissions. Unfortunately, rather than address root causes of global warming, we are presented with distracting debates about speculative geo-engineering proposals for treating the symptoms. Engaged in theoretical discussion, we delay applying known and readily deployable solutions.

Treatments versus Cures

Hundreds of creative ideas have been proposed to combat the effects of global warming while largely ignoring root causes. These ideas include:

• Erect a 100-kilometer shade of lightweight material between the sun and earth to reduce incoming solar radiation.[8]
• Seed the stratosphere with sulfur particles to better reflect incoming sunlight.[9]
• Use naval guns to blast dust into the upper atmosphere for the same purpose.[10]
• Adjust the fuel mix in airplanes to burn rich, leaving ribbons of sun-reflecting vapor.[11]
• Add iron dust to oceans to stimulate microorganisms to sequester carbon dioxide.[12]
• Build hundreds of millions of mechanical CO2 scrubbers to remove excess carbon from the air.[13]
• Use airplanes to bomb deforested regions with fast growing tree seedlings in protective biodegradable cones. The trees will absorb carbon as they grow.[14]
• Dump powdered limestone in the ocean to rebalance skewed pH levels and increase capacity for carbon dioxide absorption.[15]

These are not wholly unrealistic proposals. The 1883 eruption of Indonesia's Krakatoa volcano ejected enough sulfur dioxide and other particulates into the atmosphere to lower summer temperatures in the northern hemisphere by about 2.2°F for five years. Weather remained chaotic through 1888. Los Angeles, normally receiving an average of 15 inches of precipitation, was deluged with 38 inches in one year, the surplus rain attributed to the eruption. [16]

Similarly, the earlier 1815 eruption of Indonesia's Mount Tambora, preceded by other volcanic activity, triggered the "Year without a Summer" in 1816. Crops failed due to a shorter growing season and mid-summer frost and snow. Coupled with resource scarcity due to the Napoleonic wars, the volcano directly or indirectly killed 200,000 Europeans and countless others around the world.[17]

Although major volcanic eruptions offer short-term cooling effects, they also inject massive quantities of carbon dioxide and water vapor into the atmosphere, exacerbating the longer-term greenhouse effect.

Volcanic evidence suggests we can unquestionably cool the planet with large-scale geoengineering projects. However, tinkering with the atmosphere could trigger unanticipated consequences for unanticipated participants. If the U.S. were to experiment with geoengineering we might accidentally trigger a famine in India or Africa and floods in China or the Amazon.

Given the unknowns about geoengineering, a healthy dose of skepticism is warranted. From a holistic standpoint, we shouldn't dismiss geoengineering proposals out of hand; instead, we can apply the Holistic Management-Soft Systems Cycle to consider all potential actions to solve the global warming situation.

Situation

Problem Statement: Global climate is threatened by greenhouse gas emissions, especially carbon dioxide released from soil carbon, mechanized agriculture, deforestation, and fossil fuels.

Define the Whole Under Management: The whole under management includes the global ecosystem and the global economic system, including all businesses, people, and cultures. The management team includes policy makers, scientists, and citizens groups.

Solutions

Hypothetical Goal Stated In Positive Terms: The goal of the management team, briefly stated, is to help all people attain a satisfying quality of life and provide an equal opportunity to produce an income and attain economic prosperity. Long-term healthy functioning of the natural and economic ecosystems is required to sustain quality of life and production activities.

Brainstorm Possible Solutions for the Stated Problem: In addition to creative geoengineering proposals mentioned earlier, let's add:

- Enact carbon taxes to favor green alternatives to fossil fuels.[18]
- Apply fees to sales of gasoline-powered cars to fund rebates towards electric car purchases (known as a "feebate" system).
- Establish a cap-and-trade system for carbon credits that a) reduces carbon emissions over time or b) includes provisions to gain credits through carbon sequestration projects.
- Create incentives to sequester carbon in soil using best practices for farms and ranches.

Testing

How can we stimulate succession in the natural and economic ecosystems in favor of our stated goal? In evaluating and comparing proposals we must test them against our goal, against the testing guidelines, and against each other.

Test of Time: Would we have a global warming problem today if we had considered all of our todays decades ago when scientists raised concern about greenhouse gases? Probably not. The problem was easily avoided then. Looking back at each of these proposals from the perspective of "today" fifty years from now, which proposals seem to offer the most long-term potential?

Weakest Link: Is climate change the weakest link in the overall goal to help all people in the world attain a satisfying quality of life and economic prosperity? Possibly, since climate change threatens worldwide agriculture, coastal cities, and increases the probability of natural disasters.

Which proposal best addresses the weakest link in attaining the goal? Proposals from the first list primarily treat symptoms of global warming by consuming additional natural resources, thereby increasing expenses without producing new wealth or reversing problems at the source.

Proposals from the second list are incentive-based, encouraging individuals and businesses to make economic choices that reduce carbon emissions or increase carbon sequestration. *Carbon taxes* are initially painful, yet incentivize energy-efficiency and alternative energies for homes and businesses to conserve fossil fuels and therefore conserve money. *Feebates* would penalize buyers of gasoline-powered cars while rewarding buyers of electric cars, boosting market incentives to make the next car a zero emissions vehicle. *Cap-and-trade* systems initially raise costs, yet also incentivize innovations to reduce emissions to save money, leading to rapid emissions reductions. Rewarding farmers and ranchers for measurably *sequestering carbon in the soil* (possibly funded through auctions for carbon credits) could stimulate significant discussion and investment in actually removing carbon from the atmosphere and putting it back in the soil where it belongs.

Each proposal from the second list addresses core problems and provides economic incentives to either reduce emissions or begin reversing them, so any or all, or a combination of approaches, could be identified as the weakest link.

Root Cause: Does the proposal resolve the source of the problem or merely treat symptoms? Proposals from the first list deal largely with symptoms of global warming. Several proposals invite continued carbon emissions and hope to compensate for it by reflecting excess heat or attempting to remove carbon after it is produced. Proposals from the second list address root causes of the problem.

Community: How will a proposal be accepted within the human community? Some potential solutions would visibly alter the sky, possibly offending many people. Other ideas might be technically sound, yet defy common sense, such as burning additional jet fuel to offset the impacts of fossil fuels, or purposely adding sulfur to the upper atmosphere when we've worked so hard to reduce emissions in the lower atmosphere. It could be difficult to build public support for these ideas. Carbon taxes, feebates, and cap-and-trade systems can face political opposition from impacted industries, creating an added challenge. Rewarding farmers and ranchers to sequester carbon could be politically popular, depending on the source of reward funds.

Ecosystem Impact: Does the proposal make optimal use of the earth's natural resources and energy? What other effects might a proposal have throughout the natural and economic ecosystems? Proposals from the first list increase resource use and fossil fuel consumption in the effort to mitigate impacts of fossil fuel dependency. The true effects on the natural ecosystem for several of the proposals are unknown, while we can reasonably guess the impacts from other proposals. Proposals from the second list incentivize smart resource use or directly improve ecosystem health.

Marginal Reaction: Which proposal generates the most additional income from the least additional expense? Some proposals from the first list would cost relatively little, yet do not bring a measurable return on the investment. Other ideas, like solar satellites, would be very expensive now, but could eventually provide some revenue in return. Proposals from the second list, such as a carbon tax, carbon credits, feebates, or rewards for carbon sequestration would actually increase wealth by encouraging more efficient resource use and healthier, more abundant soils.

Implementation

Implementation begins once a plan has been selected. Implementation entails prioritizing an action list, fostering learning and growth for all who are involved, plus financial planning, careful monitoring to see what happens, and flexibility to change as needed. Several proposals show significant promise, yet only one proposal, or a combination of proposals, addresses the weakest link and commands the primary focus for implementation. Additional proposals may be implemented as time and resources allow.

For example, assuming an agreement was reached on carbon credits, the effectiveness of the program would need to be monitored from day one. Unforeseen incentives that harm people or the environment need to be remedied as discovered. If carbon trading doesn't seem effective at reducing carbon emissions over time then the program may need to be modified, replaced, or supplemented by other available proposals. Making a change in the ecosystem leads to a new situation, and the process starts over.

We are fully capable of creating a prosperous and sustainable civilization for all. The question is, "Will we?"

We may also find through monitoring that the results do not come fast enough because we have waited too long to begin. If unprecedented heat waves make major cities like Phoenix, Arizona uninhabitable, then it may be necessary to re-evaluate geoengineering proposals for economical means to stabilize a crisis situation.

The holistic management cycle continues as long as the goal remains in process. Implementing this process facilitates better decision making in everything we do, from managing a household to running a business or resolving global warming.

We are fully capable of halting and reversing global warming and other global-scale catastrophes. We are capable of creating a prosperous and truly sustainable civilization for all. We can save ourselves and provide a world of abundance to our children. The question is, "Will we?"

Regardless of what happens on the national or international level, every person is free to make a positive difference today. We can transition beyond mindlessly consuming disposable products to invest instead in our individual hopes and dreams. We can take steps now to exit the rat race and reduce or eliminate dependency on jobs that consume resources without purpose. We can permanently resolve monthly expenses and gain newfound freedom to pursue individual passions, whether that is to walk across the country, volunteer for a nonprofit organization, or start a green business and market world-changing products. Every step taken towards our personal destinies is an opportunity to expand our sphere of influence and inspire others.

Detaching from the old economy imparts newfound freedom to shift the economic ecosystem from unsustainable to sustainable, from struggling to prosperous. Anyone choosing to launch a green enterprise can make a positive difference in the world at a net profit. Together we can bring an end to meaningless work and waste, nurturing in its place a world of prosperity and abundance. For most people, the critical first step to green prosperity is simply to quit your job and live your dreams.

Notes & Bibliography

To conserve paper, all end notes are posted online at:
http://www.hopspress.com/Green_Prosperity_Notes.htm

Book Bibliography

Applebaum, Herbert. Work in Non-Market and Transitional Societies. State University of New York Press: Albany. 1984.

Benyus, Janine M. Biomimcry: Innovation Inspired by Nature. William Morrow and Co.: New York. 1997.

Cunningham, Storm. The Restoration Economy. Berrett-Kohler Publishers, Inc.: San Francisco. 2002.

Dasmann, Raymond F. Environmental Conservation. John Wiley & Sons, Inc.: New York, London, Sydney, Toronto. 1976.

Dey, Hendrik W. The Aurelian Wall and the Refashioning of Imperial Rome, AD 271-855. Cambridge University Press: Cambridge, UK. 2011.

Diamond, Jared. Guns, Germs, and Steel. WW Norton & Company: New York. 1997.

Dilts, Robert, Tim Halborn, Suzi Smith. Beliefs: Pathways to Health and Well-Being. Metamorphous Press: Portland, Oregon. 1990.

Dominguez, Joe & Vicki Robin. Your Money or Your Life. Viking Penguin: New York, NY. 1992.

Drexler, Eric. Engines of Creation: The Coming Era of Nanotechnology. Anchor Library of Science. 1987.

Elpel, Thomas J. Direct Pointing to Real Wealth. HOPS Press, LLC: Pony, Montana. 2000.

Elpel, Thomas J. Roadmap to Reality. HOPS Press, LLC: Pony, Montana. 2008.

Evans, E.P. The Criminal Prosecution and Capital Punishment of Animals. Faber and Faber: London, Boston. 1987.

Farb, Peter. Man's Rise to Civilization. Discus Books/Avon Books: New York, NY. 1968,1969, 1971.

Fukuoka, Masanobu. The Natural Way of Farming. Japan Publications, Inc.: Tokyo & New York. 1985.

Fukuoka, Masanobu. The One Straw Revolution. Rodale Press: Emmaus, Pennsylvania. 1975.

Graeber, David. Debt: The First 5,000 Years. Melville House: Brooklyn & London. 2011, 2012, 2014.

Harris, Marvin. Cows, Pigs, Wars, and Witches. Vintage Books/Random House: New York, NY. 1974, 1989.

Harris, Marvin. The Sacred Cow and the Abominable Pig. Touch Stone Books/Simon & Schuster, Inc.: New York, NY. 1985, 1987.

Hawken, Paul with Amory & Hunter Lovins. Natural Capitalism: Creating the Next Industrial Revolution. Little, Brown & Co.: Boston, New York. 1999.

Hawken, Paul. The Ecology of Commerce. Harper Business/Harper Collins Publishers: New York. 1993.

Hawken, Paul. The Next Economy. Holt, Rinehart and Winston: New York, NY. 1983.

Heyne, Paul. The Economic Way of Thinking, 4th Edition. Science Research Associates, Inc.: Chicago, Palo Alto. 1973, 1983.

Hobbs, Dr. Charles R. Time Power. Harper & Row Publishers: New York. 1987.

Hollender, Jeffrey. How to Make the World a Better Place. Quill/William Morrow: New York. 1990.

Lappe, Francis Moore. Diet for a Small Planet. Ballantine Books: New York. 1971, 1982.

Layton, Bradley Edward. Zero Waste in the Last Best Place. iUniverse: Bloomington, Indiana. 2017.

Lee, Richard B. The Dobe !Kung. Holt-Rinehart-Winston Inc.: New York, NY. 1984.

Lerner, Steve. Eco-Pioneers: Practical Visionaries Solving Today's Environmental Problems. The MIT Press: Cambridge, MA. 1997, 1998.

Lovelock, James. Healing Gaia: Practical Medicine for the Planet. Harmony Books: New York, NY. 1991.

Lovins, Amory B. Soft Energy Paths. Harper & Row, Publishers, Inc.: New York, NY. 1977.

Mann, Charles C. 1491: New Revelations of the Americas Before Columbus. Vintage Books/Random House, Inc: New York. 2005, 2006.

McMenamin, Mark A. and Dianna L.S. Hypersea: Life on Land. Columbia University Press: New York. 1994.

Montagne, Cliff. Holistic Thought and Management. 1997 Study Guide PSES 421. MSU-Bozeman.

Montgomery, David R. Dirt: The Erosion of Civilizations. University of California Press: Berkeley, Los Angeles, London. 2007, 2008, 2012.

Olson, Miles. Unlearn, Rewild. New Society Publishers: Gabriola Island, BC. 2012.

Packard, Vance. The Waste Makers. David McKay Company, Inc.: New York. 1960.

Pauli, Gunter. The Blue Economy, 3.0. Xlibris. 2017.

Pauli, Gunter. Upsizing: The Road to Zero Emissions. Greenleaf Publishing: Sheffield, UK. 1998.

Rothschild, Michael. Bionomics. A John Macrae Book, Henry Holt & Co.: New York, NY. 1990.

Savory, Allan. Holistic Resource Management. Island Press: Covelo, CA. 1988.

Stansberry, Porter. The American Jubilee. Stansberry Research. 2017.

Thoreau, Henry David. Faith in a Seed. Island Press: Covelo, CA. 1996.

Thoreau, Henry David. Life Without Principle. 1863.

Thoreau, Henry David. Walden. Holt-Rinehart-Winston Inc.: New York. Twentieth Printing. 1966.

Wanniski Jude. The Way The World Works. Basic Books, Inc., Publishers: New York, NY. 1978.

Index